世纪高教

上海世纪出版股份有限公司高等教育图书公司　出品

北京天则经济研究所编

中国经济学

2004

执行主编

张维迎

世纪出版集团 上海人民出版社

Foreword

Zhang Weiying

It happened that I was honoured by UIE with the assignment of being executive editor in chief for the project of *Economics in China, 2004*. Like all my predecessors in previous editions, the task is to pick out, amongst the papers recommended by the members of Compiling Committee, what I think is rather representative in terms of both focus and level of domestic research that year. Of 41 papers stacked up high on the table, 17 came to pass, making their lucky way to the final print. A tricky business, I have to say. But what matters is how the Jesus I juggled them all out.

The sticks at hand are in three. One is the focus that is expected in line with some eye-popping issues bubbling up in the on-going reform. Two is the rigor as well as the norm (or standardisation) looked for in either academic or practical travails. And the last is the value inherent that would go a long way towards the build-up of knowledge and experience in the field. Little doubt, there are very much more than these 17 of the winning pack that live up to the par, only dropped in the last minute's consideration for the mere sake of space available. Tough luck, as they are unwittingly rendered to team up with the group of also-rans. My apology all the same. It might yet be more comforting to know that the judgement exercised purely stays with me, not further beyond.

And that leaves us to those last ones standing, whose footholds, admittedly, scatter all over the place. In general, they spread over as wide the areas as that of regional disparity in both income and growth, the process of market integration, governmental behaviour and laws, rural economy and its labour markets, restructuring in both state-owned factories and banks, reform in the land ownership regime, and others. From here on out, I will make use of the remaining space to sketch out the story about each of our lucky survivors.

The one that heads the crowd in this edition is Dong Xian-an's paper, *Regional Income Disparity 1952—2002: Some Explanations*. Indeed, there is no secret that in recent years regional income disparity has been one of sizzling issues that gobble up bulk of the resources available to those sparkling brain-trusts in the country. No surprise, then, there are a slew of studies devoted to it, covering half century's development. What makes Dong's work superlative is that not only does it round them all up in one exquisite shot, but with anecdotal evidence and statistical justification retools the analyses in two of the popular hypotheses. One of them holds that the gradual shift in the scale as well as tightness of state control over both goods and factors markets would seriously impact on growth of regional economies. The other states that growth in different provinces could possibly diverge if labour mobility is restricted under the circumstances of relatively free flow of goods and capital.

With elastic and restricted statistical devices, the author tested his growth model that takes in such explanatory variables as human and physical capital, composition of agricultural sector, income disparity between urban and rural households, industrial make-up, ownership structure, scale of local government, size of firms, household formation and so on. To no one's surprise, the model confirms that there exists significant positive-correlation between the growth of human capital and that of economy. As with the relationship between ownership structure and growth, the model predicts that for each percentage point of increase in public ownership, the growth would shrink by around 1.69%—1.9%. Similar result is also projected as to the scale of government, which says, for every 1% expansion in government size, the growth would suffer in a range of 0.04%—0.27%. The policy implication, then, for tackling income disparity could not be clearer: investment in human capital, smaller government, and lower proportion of state-owned economy.

Still on the subject is the paper written by Wang Xiaolu and Fan Gang, entitled *Changing Pattern of Growth Disparity in Different Areas and Factors at Work*. As the header goes, their work provides some explanation about the changing pattern of the disparity over the period of the 80's and the 90's of last century, taking into account the flow of labour, capital, and other resources, the role it plays, and the impact exerted as result of the shift in both market institutions and structure. The authors find that in both relative and absolute terms the hiatus between the eastern seaboard and the central-west inland has been broadening over the past two decades. The fundamental cause, however, is the difference in productivity, which has seen the profit-chasing capital of both home and abroad pouring into the east, fanning up market activities and tearing open growth rift.

Nonetheless, as Messrs Wang and Fan observed, over time the productivity of capital per se has been dwindling as the flux to the east continues. This trend, plus the heavy public work sustained in the west, would in the long run be conducive to the back-flow of the capital. Yet, that would again depend on some discernible uplifting of the regional total-factor productivity that has so far shown no sign of turnaround. One imperative suggested, however, is to improve regional investment environment that includes such measures as bettering the price system, raising the stake in the private sector, upping the level of governance in both firms and governments, revamping the R&D regime, quickening the pace of urbanisation, and so forth.

All of that seem just fine until one looks at the domestic market that, either by laws, regulations, or simply local xenophobic jitters (or, nicely put it "protectionism") has long been a collection of separate, self-contained pieces. These scattered entities not only in their capacity stem the free-flow of almost every moving objects in and out of the provincial fiefdoms, but to that effect, block any optimal allocation of resources and the realisation of regional comparative advantage. Indeed, much ado could come to little without an adequate level of market integration — one of essential attributes of a modern economy that entails unrestricted movement of labour, capital, and other resources as well as goods and services.

Fan Jianyong's empirical effort, *Trend of Market Integration, Regional Specialisation and Industrial Concentration — As well as Their Impact to Regional Disparity*, is one of those in the edition that dig into this buzz-raiser of economic chat-rooms in the country. Probing into the data covering the period of 1980—2001, What the author saw was that the level of regional specialisation and market integration had somehow lifted a notch or two (by and large concentrating on the coastal areas), though still hovering at a low level comparing to the international norm. To put it another way, the formation of regional advantage or specialisation was still in the early stage. And that may help explain the merry-go-east scurry of the manufacturing heavyweights, which in the wake of their haste split up the chasm lying in between.

That said, one of the ID-bearing symbols of the integration is the convergence of the factor productivity in different regions. *Flow of Production Factors between Provinces and Differences in Their Marginal Productivities*, the presentation of Gong Liutang and Xie Danyang, offers the first-ever empirical study on the subject. What they did is first to come up with some individual production function for each of 28 provinces, and with them they worked out the changing pattern of productivity differentials in both labour and capital. Much to their surprise, the authors were struck by the fact that, while the differential in marginal revenue of capital was trending down over the period of 1970—1989 and levelling off thereafter, the labour's were moving in the opposite direction after 1993, even back as high the level as the 70's by the time of 1999.

That kind of finding on labour's is certainly running against ex-ante expectation as well as relevant international experience that says the differential in marginal labour productivities of different regions ought to be narrowing, or at least stabilising, along with expansion of an economy. One reasoning for that twist, as the authors suspected, is that it could be due to the upsurge of the flow in both labour and capital, especially the latter, as different provinces drawing up various kinds of preferential policies to entice inward investments got their ways.

While Messrs Fan, Gong and Xie come up with their anecdotal proofs to the woes of the market, others spare no time doing their duties as to root out the guilty parties involved. It doesn't have to take a sage to figure out which one would be first out and take the mother of all beatings — "local protectionism", broadly deemed as the biggest drag on the stride of free trade and local specialisation. Though much blamed, notorious, and with all nasty stuff slapped on, to nail it down will one need proofs. And that is where Bai Zhongen et al fit in with their piece of evidence, *Regional Protectionism and Degree of Industrial Concentration: Determinants and Trend*.

With the toil and moil, the authors have pulled off a huge database that contains both time series and cross-section information in 32 sectors of 29 provinces over the period of 13 year (i. e. 1985—1997). Moving across the time in the mist of the dripping figures, these number crunchers then pinned down what they think are the main culprits in stunting the growth of industrial clustering, which take the ordering of local protectionism, historical legacy, scale economies and external shock. As with the felonry of all convicted — the protectionism, the verdict pronounces: the bigger share of state-owned economy does a sector have or the larger fiscal revenue does it contribute, the lower is it in industrial concentration, as local bosses have every incentive to keep it out of potential rivalries.

While there is no jarring opinion on the overall conviction, some writers would like to dispute on the pecking order of factors at play, particularly the external impact on the integration of domestic market. Li Jie and Sun Qunyan are two amongst them, who present their case with the argument, entitled *Impact of WTO Membership on Lessening Regional Protectionism: Reshaping the Beer Industry*, which exploits the notion of regional price disparity — one of the symptoms of segmented economy.

The authors make use of the monthly price index in beer market of 40 major cities in detecting the trend of price divergence for the tenuous leads. Three conclusions bear out from their work. One is that over the time-span between Jan. 1997 to Mar. 2003, the overall picture was less encouraging, though improving. Two is that, if separating the trend at the cut-off point where the measures of reducing domestic trade barrier came into effect, the price-spread of the latter half had been narrowing, mostly around dual centres of Beijing and Qingdao. And the last one that tees up the point is that the WTO entry was noticeably the driving force behind those free-trade measures adopted by the central and local governments.

So much for the integration, before getting dizzy, it seems a good idea to take a bit of shift, turning to some agricultural matters. Now that the economic activities are undergoing a major changeover from the ancestral paddy-land practice to the modern-day urban mass-production, the drudges that are left behind on the land of yore will more than ever deserve public interests. This book also takes in 4 papers that have gone all the way to meet their unremitting grievances head on.

Since the mid 80's of last century, the state has here and there fashioned a swathe of measures purporting to alleviate widespread poverty in rural areas. One of them is the project trained on those penny-strapped counties in the hope of affording some much-craved relief to the low-income rural households. The success of it will inevitably be hinged on the targets so chosen that the finite resources could possibly produce the maximum outcome. *Project Targeting in Rural Poverty Alleviation*, a study carried out by Yue Ximing and Li Shi, is one of the efforts that see to the process with gripping intensity.

With the data available from State Bureau of Statistics, the authors took stock of the following two facets of the matter: one is the target accuracy as to those counties chosen by the state; the other is the distribution pattern that links up the provinces, the counties and the households concerned. The upshot that their observation has come to is that there was some discernable improvement nationwide in the process of selection in 2001 compared to that in 1993, as there exhibited significant negative correlation between counties selected and the average net earning of the households concerned. Yet, up an echelon or two at the provincial level, such a correlation started blurring out. Worse still, there was no clear statistical evidence indicating that the poor had received more support financially than other groups.

In another study, *Rural Industrialisation and the Role of Human Capital*, the authors, Chen Yuyu and Xing Chunbing, look at the role of education in the play-out of alleviating game with the effort made in detecting the relationship between the levels of wages, labour employability and the length of education. They noticed that, while the average level of wages was rather independent of the length of education, the labour employability was nonetheless positively related to it. Specifically, the likelihood of being employed increases by a range of 2.3%—3.2% with every one additional year of education. And that may translate into the increase in the average level of household incomes by 1.2%. Better yet, the level of education is also related to the kind of compensation received: higher the level of education, higher the chance to obtain it at risk-free time rate as oppose to piece related one.

While the level of education affects the employment and the average household income in the rural markets, what about the state of heath? Wei Zhong with his study, *The Role of Health in Non-farm Employment and Wage Determination*, gives it a go with the similar working technique, but using the data from 1993 *China Nutritional Survey*. As much expected, the parallel conclusion has been generated: while the state of health does not affect much of the average wage level, it does lift up the probability of employment, and thus translate into an increase in the average level of household earnings.

Staying on with the topic of rural health is the presentation of Gao Mengtao and Yao Yang, *Sex, Life Cycle and Investment in Health within a Family — An Empirical Evidence of Examining of Farmers in China*. Admittedly, there is no shortage of similar studies abroad concerning the investment in family health. Yet, most of them fall short of the comparative advantage enjoyed by different members of a family, especially by difference sexes, in the non-market activities. Plug it in together with the factor of life cycle, the model that draws on the health data of rural households obtained from 8 provinces, has patched up the hole left by their overseas colleagues. As a bonus, the study stumbles upon something new that says female members in the period of childbearing and infant caring should reign supreme in the scheme of family health investment.

Now, turning to those ever-lasting stories of the state-owned something. For all their eternal quality, the fervency received has somehow started tailing off, as those countless nagging talk-shops have at length guzzled up all the words that domestic economists care to produce. Little it seems needed except politician's stomach. Yet, amongst the precious few, the glumness has a glossy sheen to it. *Welfare Burdens, Moral Hazard and Sofe Budget Constraint*, the paper co-authored by Lin Yifu and Li Zhibin, is one of the few that remain as the rare beholders of the state-owned beauties.

The paper represents Prof. Lin's long-held view that the low efficiency in the state-owned firms has nothing to do with their ownership structures, but is by and large the result of policy-induced welfare burdens that inevitably leaves a bend in the budgetary discipline. Under the circumstances of asymmetric information, goes the argument, managers of firms, be it public or private, would have every incentive to slack off their budget constraints as market pressure mounts. Yet, the obligation of public welfare is just there to provide a much-hankered lifeline for those head-scratching execs plotting their escape with the desperation of Showshank lifers — the "hidden action" broadly known in the trade. Little doubt, asserts the professor, reliance on the markets for the end of redistribution is always the second-best arrangement as it unavoidably alters the behaviour of firms.

Taking a slight turn to the banking sector, there we have

two field studies handy. The first one is Zhang Jie's *Re-capitalising and Reform in State-own Banks — A Perspective of Political Economics*, which tries to read into the intention and the fallout of fiscal re-capitalisation in the sector's reform. The study has produced quite an observation of some time-honoured practice repeatedly tried out by those bureau-geeks in charge of the reform. In a nutshell, it is no more than a glossing-over makeshift that invariably shines up to the external pressures. The authors argues that mere fiddling with a few technical parameters that may appear to have measured up to the international standards won't make a dent in the chronic ill of the system. Specifically, the shake-up in the fashion of reducing the share of public ownership in the sector alone would not go anywhere in the absence of economy-wide restructuring. The process of the reform, insists the author, should lie over the long haul in an evolving manner.

Indeed, there is no secret that the domestic banking system is creaky under the heavy loads of bad loans and bedevilled by the trouble of low efficiency. The consensus on the gloomy nature of the sector boils down to the ownership structure and the state of soft budget. Yao Shujie, Feng Genfu and Jiang Chunxia, then, decided to have a dig at the issue, resulting in their field report, *The Issue of Efficiency in China's Banking*, which sampled 22 domestic banks over the period of 5 years between 1995—2001. Not surprisingly, their finding has chimed with the conventional wisdom. In particular, as the reading reveals, the banks without the sloppiness in their budgets more often than not outperforms those that are grossly coddled with cash-feed by the powers that be. As well, the efficiency level of the non-state-owned is on average higher than that of the state-owned by a range of 11%—18%.

And that at length brings to an end the long-running stories of the state-owned affairs. Time to move on to some legal matters as well as that concerning governmental behaviour. Admittedly, recent years have seen the academic economics be all the sign of overgrown species, not just being exuberant on its own turf, but crawling out onto once deemed arid patches, and in time with the fruits of all colours decking out the landscape. Sauntering down a trail, your editor cannot but stretch out, making it three for the book's collection.

The first one, *Enforcement of Third Party Rights in the Formal Contract and Optimal Arrangement*, is a co-work done by Yang Ruilong and Lu Zhoulai, where the authors try to figure out the likely sources of wide-spread wage dispute in the domestic bricks and mortar trade. The study put much of its stock in the ideas of contract theoreticians as it wrestled with the reality of unpaid services that long piques our rural folks. In the eyes of the authors, the perpetual wrangling over the pay does not rest with much-rapped tatty deals made in words between the toilers and their bosses. It does, in truth, have much to do with the formal agreements drawn up between project owners and the developers as well as that between the developers and their subcontractors.

All the same, the failure to honour such a verbal deal,

however shabby, would be more than enough to persuade those folks into some plan B solution, to wit, law of jungle in the streetwise manner as they take the matter into their own hands. What then? Instability ensues. That said, the knot of tangling up comes in two. One is the unenforceable nature of formal contracts, thanks to the fact that those bureaus in charge outwit the system by making a smart, but otherwise devious use of their third part rights in the rent-seeking pursuit. Two is that the judicial power gets tampered as vested interests start to throw in their weights. There, it becomes all too obvious, reckoned by Messrs Yang and Lu, that in a practical world of conflict interests, the knack of shoring up the third party rights lies in the need of striking a balance. And that gives rise to some optimal arrangement in the contract regime.

Next comes our story of governmental behaviour. For some years now, the nation has been revelling in much of the hoopla of political melodrama that has seen the ruling sort have at last brought in an alien species, called "democracy", in some unlikely areas of countryside. The news carried by the state-express of media bandwagon travelled wide and far. Yet, for those in of touch, it is little more than a morphing type — a laughingstock at best. On one hand, we have those much-touted ballot boxes fixated by law in the rural habitats, purporting presumably to bring about some balances and checks to the local fiefdoms where the lords would be expectedly more sympathetic to their subjects, not least in those open-ended taxes, levies and fees. On the other, our folks just above the nether regions have watched their pockets becoming even thinner each year as they bother to exercise the right to fill up those boxes.

So enigmatic was the phenomenon that it prompted Messrs Zhang Qi, Liu Mingxing and Shan Wei to take all the pains of burying their heads into the tossed papers groping for the clue. As they at length emerged, so did the story that takes a topping of *Regulations, Soft legal-constraints and Rural Grass-roots Democracy*. The fact, as it reads, that the local officials are time and again loaded with honourable public duties without a single penny in sight would coax them into the village foray. Worse, they constantly get the better of their superiors in search of the spoils as they slyly exploit the subtlety in the world of hidden information. Surely, there is a certain level of calculated risk from the ballot box. Yet, it won't go awry so long as to tag along in the back of political wisdom that says, "always err on the side of the powerful". And so, enjoy the free ride.

On the other side of the flip, the guys at the top are facing their own set of choices in some ancient dilemma of cake eating. In other words, they cannot have their hips tightened and keep the dignity of strengthening the electoral rules they have made. Alas, the picking has found them nestling up to their own piggy bank while winking back a few lingering tears that welled up at the pangs of conscience. In any case, it should not have come as a surprise. The guys at the helm would go bananas, after all, just to see the back of the alien in this land of "implausible". That aside, the symptom has since been dubbed with some nicety as "soft legal-constraints". That is to say, the rules are simply not binding now that no reinforcement is forthcoming.

Speaking of reinforcement — a legal baloney for the punishment dished out, probably the first thing that might flash by is that long end of the rope dangling in the air, too ghastly to have anyone dream of dancing on it. Yet, in the eyes of those pedants in the economic profession, it is merely a fashion of incentive. Rules, they may insist, will be heeded if people set store heavy enough by it, be that balm or bane. That idea, however, has begun gaining much of the oomph these days in the area of public services where academic boffins have churned out heaps of papers seeking for the nuances of the beauty.

Still, it is way off the impeccable as almost all dwell on the monetary stimulus brought about by the measure of administrative independence and financial accountability while turning a blind eye to the most obvious and critical part of the incentive structure — career promotion. It is here that Zhou Li-an, with the story — *Incentives and Co-operation: Promotion in the Public Services* — As well as the Reason of Long-term Existence of Local Xenophobic Jitters and Rebuilding Problems, has made an important contribution. In fact, it is the first-ever study that takes into account the impetus of promotion in the public services, in which a simple model of payoff game is built to project the possible effects on the likelihood of competition and co-operation amongst regions.

Hard luck, the upshot of the model has given a thumbs-down to such a stimulus. The play-out of the game reads that the chance of moving up the ladder would take the wind out of the sails of local chiefs in any of their joint efforts, the moment they sit back relishing that entertaining idea of scraping pass each other in a pulsating race.

Politics, as broadly recognised, is some unforgiving zero-sum-business where the uprise for one would spell the downfall for another, and probably for good. And that may render a clue to those scandalous exercises where the local equals were found busy in pulling each other's rug rather than shoring one other up in a supposed regional co-operation. Non-too-pleasant story, though. Yet, the study does at least provide us with a new perspective in viewing the persistent local protectionism and other infamous activities going on in local development.

And that brings us to the last leg in the tour of the book. We shall wind it up by taking a trip to the site of the crumbling land-ownership edifice. From the past decade on, the switch to urban-based existence has been put on its top gear. The neck-breaking pace of changeover has unavoidably pitted the powers that be against its closest allies — peasants, over the pesky issue of land transfer and expropriation. On one hand, bulking up of urban-based activities entails a speedy handling of land-transfer. On the other, there has been no such a law available that would provide the guidance. As it is, turning its back on the fizzing, yet illicit activities would see the state flirt with a tantalising uncertainty at its peril. Yet, trying to live up to the existing rules would likely to smother the market gaiety with a consequence of checking the tempo of urban expansion.

What makes our rubbernecking economists steady their bobbling heads and ultimately wade in with zealotry this round is not the way that the parties at loggerheads are squaring up to each other, but the nature of the squabble. Not only is it likely for the state to skim on its obligations once again and short-change the light-headed rustic folks with the dim-sum, but it could possibly poison the entire haggling regime in the trade. *Property Rights and the Regime of Expropriation in Farmland — Great Choice of China's Urbanization*, a paper from Zhou Qiren, is one of the efforts made that would like to see off the poisonous stand-off by offering some possible way-outs for the antagonists. One of solutions, contends the author, is to scrap the clause in the Constitution that says, "all urban lands belong to the state", making it the last straw for the cracking regime of farmland expropriation, while encouraging the development of land transfer market.

Now, we have at length reached the crossing line in the run of our stories. A whit of pity, admittedly, as it falls short of that sort of happy ending normally tagging along in American motion pictures. Yet, we do hope readers to enjoy the stories that might help enliven some of the idle moments of your daily life. Before we go, some appreciation I feel constrained to accord. All of our 17 papers selected for the book, *Economics in China, 2004*, come from *Economic Research*, *World*

Economy, *Economics Quarterly*, *China's Social Sciences*, and *China' Social Science Review*. Also my acknowledgement for the rest of 24 members who took part in the compiling process. And then, so long!

目　录

CONTENTS

前　言

张维迎

《中国经济学——2004》由我担任执行主编，如同过去几届执行主编的职责一样，我的任务是从各位编委推荐的论文中选择我认为最能代表中国经济学界这一年里研究成果和学术水平的论文。编委们共推荐了41篇论文，我从中选择了17篇。我选择的标准是：第一，论文所研究的问题是中国经济改革和发展中重要的问题；第二，论文具有严谨、规范的理论分析或实证数据检验，或二者兼而有之；第三，在论文所研究的问题上取得有价值的进步，能形成重要的知识积累。当然符合上述标准的论文不止这17篇，由于本书的篇幅所限，个别符合上述标准的论文也未能入选，在此，我对作者表示抱歉。此外，需要声明的是，我的判断肯定不能代表所有编委的判断，更不能代表所有读者的判断，故请读者原谅。

收入本书的17篇论文的内容涉及地区差距、市场一体化的形成、政府行为和法律、农村经济和农村劳动力市场、国有企业和国有银行改革、土地制度改革等方面。下面，我对这17篇论文的主要内容做些简要的介绍。

中国经济发展中的地区收入差距一直是国内外经济学界普遍关注的问题，有关这方面的研究成果可以说层出不穷。收集在本书的董先安的《浅释中国地区收入差距：1952—2002》一文对近年来学术界解释中国半个世纪以来地区收入差距演变的各种假说进行了归纳、分析和检验,同时提出并检验了 2 个主要假说和 4 个推论。这两个假说是:一,中国经济制度过去 50 年的演变,特别是政府对产品市场和要素市场的控制范围与控制力度的演变,对各省级经济体的经济增长绩效和收敛特征可能产生重要影响;二,在产品市场与资本要素市场具备相对更加自由的流动性的条件下,劳动力要素市场的流动性一旦受到压抑,集聚效应就有可能使得经济发生两极分化。作者使用弹性分析和条件收敛分析,检验了人力资本、物质资本、农业生产结构、城乡差距、产业结构、产权结构、政府规模、企业规模、户口结构等多组解释变量对地区经济增长与收敛的影响,并估计了其影响力的大小。特别地,作者发现,人力资本的增长与经济增长之间存在显著的正相关;就产权结构对地区经济增长的效应而言,国有经济的比重每增加 1%,经济增长率就显著地降低 1.69%—1.9%;而政府规模每扩大 1%,经济增长率降低 0.04%—0.27%。这些结论表明,提高人力资本投资,降低国有经济的比例,精简政府机构,将对缩小地区差距有重要的积极影响。

王小鲁和樊纲的《中国地区差距的变动趋势和影响因素》一文考察了 20 世纪 80 年代和 90 年代中国地区经济差距的变动趋势,分析了资本、劳动力、人力资本等生产要素在各地区间的配置与流动状况及其原因,这些因素对地区差距变化的作用,同时也分析了制度变革和结构变化等因素对地区经济差距变化的影响。作者发现,我国东部沿海地区和中西部内陆地区之间,在经济发展水平方面,无论是绝对差距还是相对差距都还在继续扩大。其原因主要是由于地区间生产率的差别以及由此引起的资本流动所致,在过去 20 年间,市场导向的外商直接投资以及民间资本流动使资金大量流向东部,加速了东部地区的经济增长，同时也扩大了地区差距。但资本的持续流动已经使得地区间资本生产率的差距出现缩小的趋势；这个趋势，加上西部大开发战略的实施，可能在未来逐步改变资本流动的格局，使之较有利于中西部的发展。但生产率的地区差距还没有出现缩小的趋势，说明要缩小地区差距还要经历一个相当长期的过程；在这个过程中，迫切需要尽快改善中西部地区投资的软环境，包括推进市场化改革，促进非国有经济的发展，提高企业管理水平和政府服务水平，改革科研开发体制，以及加速城市化建设的步伐等。

一国内经济的一体化是现代国家经济的基本特征之一，地区差距的变化也与经济一体化的演变有关。经济一体化要求生产要素和产品能在地区间自由流动，形成地区间合理的产业分工和有效的资源配置。长期以来，由于法律和政策的限制，特别是地方保护主义的约束，要素和产品在地区间的流动一直不自由，中国经济处于严重的地方割据状态，严重制约了统一市场的形成和地区优势的发挥。那么，改革开放以来，随着经济自由化政策的推进，特别是在中国加入世界贸易组织之后，中国在经济一体化方面取得了什么样的进步？中国地区间的产业分工格局有些什么变化？这些变化是什么因素导致的？这些问题不仅是经济学界关注的问题，也是政府部门所关注的。

范剑勇的《市场一体化、地区专业化与产业集聚趋势——兼谈对地区差距的影响》在一个简单的分析框架基础上，利用两位数水平的制造业数据，实证分析了中国 1980 年、2001 年地区专业化和产业集中度的变化。作者发现，改革以来中国地区间的专业化水平和市场一体化水平已有提高，产业布局发生了根本改变，绝大部分行业已经或正在转入东部沿海地区。基于国际的经验，作者同时认为，中国现阶段仍处于“产业高集聚，地区低专业化”的状态，国内市场一体化水平总体上仍然较低，且低于对外的一体化水平，这一现状使得制造业集中于东部沿海地区，无法向中部地区转移，进而推动了地区差距的扩大。

地区间要素生产率的趋同是经济一体化的重要标志。龚六堂和谢丹阳的《我国省份之间的要素流动和边际生产率的差异分析》通过估算我国28个省份的生产函数得到了资本存量和劳动的边际生产率的差异的变化趋势。他们发现，资本存量的边际生产率的差异趋势在1970—1989年间下降，之后保持在比较稳定的水平；而劳动的边际生产率的差异在1970—1993年下降，而1993年之后反而上升，甚至在1999年，这个差异水平回到了1970年的水平。从美国等发达国家的经验，我们知道，经济发展过程中劳动的边际生产率差异应该是下降或者稳定的，为什么中国的情况与此不一致？作者认为，是因为资本和劳动的流动性都得到了提升的结果，而这种流动性可能取决于不同省份不同的税收优惠政策。

在中国经济学界，有关地方保护主义对地区间贸易和专业化的影响，一般性讨论很多，但对此问题的系统的实证研究很少，白重恩等人的《地方保护主义及产业地区集中度的决定因素和变动趋势》可以说填补了这方面的空白。作者实现建立了中国29个省级地区32个产业的13年间(1985—1997)的数据库，用动态估计的方法研究了中国产业地域专业化的决定因素，其关注的重点是地方保护主义对区域专业化的影响。他们发现：产业区域专业化水平在以往享有较高税率和国有成分比例较高的行业里，其程度较低，反映了地方政府有动机保护这两类产业。这篇文章还提供了较强的证据来支持规模经济理论对专业化的解释，对外部经济理论对专业化解释的支持则相对较弱；进一步，地方保护主义的作用在决定专业化水平中超过了外部经济性和规模效应，仅次于历史影响的作用。

市场分割的一个重要表现是同种产品地区间的价格差异。李杰和孙群燕的《从啤酒市场整合程度看 WTO 对消除地方保护的影响》一文利用中国 40 个城市啤酒市场的月度价格资料，运用协整分析方法，对中国啤酒业的市场整合趋势作了较深入的分析。作者的研究表明：(1)从 1997 年 1 月到 2003 年 3 月整段时间看，中国啤酒市场的市场整合程度不高，市场分割的现象比较普遍；(2)从分时期看，在中央政府出台取消地方保护壁垒的措施之前，啤酒市场的市场分割比较普遍；政策出台之后，啤酒市场分别以北京和青岛为中心出现了区域性的整合趋势；(3)加入 WTO 对于中国的市场整合产生了较大的影响，它促使中央政府和地方政府相应地调整自己的政策趋向，消除地区间的贸易壁垒。

中国社会正处于从农业社会向工业社会转变的过程中，有关农村问题的研究自然是中国经济学界最重要的研究领域之一。本书收录了 4 篇与农村问题有关的研究。

自上世纪 80 年代中期以来，以县为单位的扶贫项目一直是中央政府解决贫困问题的主要政策之一。扶贫项目能否取得预期的成效，很大程度上取决于贫困县的选择，也就是说，是不是能将有限的扶贫资金用于真正的贫困县。岳希明和李实的论文《中国农村扶贫项目的目标瞄准分析》使用国家统计局收集的分县数据，围绕农村扶贫项目的目标瞄准问题，主要讨论了以下两方面的论题：(1)在国定贫困县的认定过程中是否发生了目标瞄准上的失误？(2)扶贫资金是怎样在省、县、农户之间分配的？分析表明，在目标瞄准的准确性上，2001 年重点县的选择较 1993 年贫困县指定有了相当的改善，在全国范围内，各贫困县得到的扶贫资金与县人均纯收入有明显的负相关性；但是，当具体到省一级时，扶贫资金的分配与县人均纯收入没有相关关系的省份很多;另外,没有证据表明,贫困户较非贫困户有更多的机会得到贴息贷款。

人力资本是决定经济发展的重要因素,也是决定农民收入水平的重要因素。陈玉宇和邢春冰在《农村工业化以及人力资本在农村劳动力市场中的角色》中考察了人力资本(尤其是教育水平)在农村工业部门中的回报以及教育在农村劳动力转移过程中的作用。利用农村地区家庭人均年收入等数据进行分析,结果表明,尽管从1990年到1996年间教育年限对农村工业部门内部的工资水平没有显著影响,但教育年限可以显著地提高农民在工业部门就业的机会,从而可以贡献于农民收入的增加,并推进农村劳动力的转移。比如说,在1990年和1992年,在工业部门工作可以使家庭人均收入分别提高56%和47%,而教育每增加一年,人们到工业部门工作的机会增加2.3%和3.2%左右,这意味着使得家庭人均收入增加1.2%和1.5%,也相当于给个人带来5%—7%的回报。利用1989年的数据,这篇文章还分析了农村工业部门内部的工资机制并发现,教育水平低的人接受计件工作的多,而计时工资的整体水平高于计件工资。

近年来,健康作为人力资本的重要因素,其对经济发展的影响越来越受到经济学界的关注。魏众的《健康对非农就业及其工资决定的影响》一文探讨了中国农村地区健康对非农就业及其工资决定的影响,试图从微观层面揭示中国农村地区健康与收入之间的关系。利用1993年中国营养调查数据的分析表明,健康状况对劳动力参与非农就业的机会有显著影响,但在传统的种植业领域,健康并不是劳动参与的决定因素;同时,在农村中的非农就业者中,健康并不是劳动力市场表现的重要因素。尽管如此,作者认为,由于非农就业机会对家庭收入的重要性,我们仍然可以发现健康在提高农村家庭收入方面有显著的作用。这篇文章所发现的健康的作用与陈玉宇和邢春冰的文章发现的教育的作用非常类似。

有关家庭健康投资决策，国外经济学界已有不少研究，但这些研究忽略了不同家庭成员在非市场活动中的专业化分工比较优势，特别是在非市场活动中不同性别家庭成员的优势。高梦滔和姚洋的《性别、生命周期与家庭内部健康投资——中国农户就诊的经验证据》一文使用来自中国8省份农户的数据，从家庭内部资源分配框架出发对处于不同性别、生命周期的家庭成员的健康投资进行经验研究，试图弥补现有文献的不足。他们发现，在两周就诊概率和费用方面，处于生育期和抚养期的女性往往在健康投资上获得优先地位。这一结论拓展了已有的家庭内部成员人力资本投资的研究成果，揭示了家庭人力资本投资导向必须同时考虑市场因素和非市场的经济机会，尤其是女性在抚育后代方面的比较优势，对女性的健康投资至关重要。

2004年中国媒体上展开了一场有关国有企业改革的轰轰烈烈的大讨论，这场讨论在一定程度上影响了政府部门国有企业改革的政策。与此形成强烈反差的是，这一年，中国经济理论界关于国有企业改革的理论文章并不多，一个可能的原因是，经济学界普遍认为，国有企业改革该说的都说了。林毅夫和李志赟合作的《政策性负担、道德风险与预算软约束》一文是2004年少数有关国有企业改革的理论文章之一。这篇文章延续了林毅夫教授的一贯观点，即国有企业的低效率不在企业所有权本身，而在于由企业的政策性负担导致的软预算。文章在一个动态博弈的框架下，考察了政策性负担与转轨经济中企业的预算软约束问题。文章认为，在信息不对称情况下，政策性负担将导致国有企业经理的道德风险，从而导致国有企业的低效率；当市场竞争达到一定程度时，政策性负担必然带来国有企业的预算软约束；而且，预算软约束同企业的共有性质无关，在同样承担政策性负担的条件下，私有企业比国有企业更容易产生预算软约束，并且要求政府提供更多的补贴。当国有企业承担政策性负担时，政府剥夺企业的生产自主权往往是一种次优的制度安排。

与一般行业的国有企业改革不同，伴随2003年底政府对中国银行和中国建设银行的财政注资，国有银行的改革在2004年提上了新的议事日程，股份制改造和海外上市成为国有银行改革的主要方向。张杰在《注资与国有银行改革：一个金融政治经济学的视角》一文中，试图从金融政治经济学的视角解读国家通过注资方式推动国有银行改革的意图与绩效，作者观察到，政府推动的银行改革有一个共同的特征，就是一般都受到某种外部因素的刺激并追求短期见效的效果。作者认为，中国国有银行的问题是经济改革过程诸多矛盾与利益博弈的长期积淀，解决方案须基于演进主义的方法论，仅仅做到外观和技术参数上接近国际水准并不能解决实质问题。特别是，在微观经济基础未能得到有效调整的情况下，单方面改变银行资本结构的行动注定会无功而返，通过人为方式降低国有银行比例以提高整体银行效率是一种逻辑误导；中国国有银行低效率运行的根据不在出资人本身，而在于出资人获取回报的特殊经济流程；而且，若考虑到被巴塞尔协议剔除的一些无形资产可以在国有银行的资本结构中得到确认，则国有银行出资人的资本压力就没有人们想象的那么大。

中国的银行一直以大量不良贷款和效率低下而著称，怎样提高效率是国内银行尤其是国有商业银行生存和成功的关键。一般认为，所有制改革和硬化预算约束有助于提高中国的银行效率。姚树洁、冯根福和姜春霞合作的《中国银行业效率的实证分析》一文使用了22家银行1995—2001年期间的一组数据，利用随机前沿生产函数研究了所有制结构和硬预算约束对银行效率的影响。经验结果表明，非国有银行比国有银行效率高11%—18%；面临硬预算约束的银行的绩效比国家和地方政府投入大量资本的银行的绩效好。

近年来，中国经济学界在运用经济学理论分析政府行为和法律制度方面取得了不少有价值的研究成果。本书收入了2004年发表的三篇这方面的论文。杨瑞龙和卢周来《正式契约的第三方实施与权力最优化——对农民工工资纠纷的契约论解释》一文，运用契约理论解释农民工工资纠纷的成因，提出如下观点（理论假说）：首先，农民工工资被拖欠的主要原因并非农民工与直接“关系”雇主（包工头）之间的非正式口头契约无法有效履行，而恰是国家明文规定的、应该由国家作为第三方强制执行的建设方和总承包商以及总承包商与分包商（包工头）之间的正式合同无法得到有效执行；其次，正式合同无法得到国家有效执行的原因在于，一方面，政府机关拥有的部分绝对权力在追求租金最大化的动机下被滥用，另一方面，作为国家强制实施的直接工具的司法体系的相对权力又被强势利益群体所削弱，无法有效进行强制；再次，国家作为第三方在保护农民合法权益方面的失败，导致农民工选择契约的其他执行方法，使得契约的实施由“公共强制”倒退回“私人强制”，进而可能导致私人暴力的无序使用，危及社会稳定，反过来又迫使政府只能选择更大力度地实际使用权力。作者认为，国家要重新建立国家作为强制实施第三方在保护农民工权益中的权威，就必须考虑“第三方权力的最优化”问题。

近年来，中国农村有两个看似相互矛盾的现象同时发生：一方面，自1998年《村委会组织法》正式颁布以来，农村基层民主化建设工作以由上至下的方式在农村全面展开；另一方面，农民税费负担变得更加严重。这后一现象意味着基层民主化建设在约束地方政府方面并没有取得我们所希望的结果。章奇、刘明兴和单伟在《政府管制、法律软约束与农村基层民主》一文中试图用“法律软约束”的概念解释这一矛盾。他们认为，基层民主建设之所以不能有效约束基层政府对农民利益的侵害，是因为《村委会组织法》对基层政府的约束是软的；而法律约束之所以是“软”的，是因为中央政府给基层政府施加了太多的负担，不得不默认基层政府的某些行为。对中央政府来说，它需要地方基层政府来执行自己所下达的各项管制任务，却又不提供资金，这样，地方政府就有理由自行收费以弥补成本；进一步，由于信息不对称，地方基层政府所收的费用，可能大大超过实施中央政府管制政策所要求的水平。如果完全实现村级民主自治，地方基层政府搭便车收费的行为会导致很高的成本，这样，地方基层政府就很有可能出于自身利益考虑而不支持甚至消极对待村级民主自治。中央政府为使地方基层政府完成管制任务，也可能默许基层政府的“反”民主行为，从而出现“法律软约束”问题。作者还用所收集的数据验证了自己的理论假说。

西方经济学界发展起来的激励理论是以企业作为分析对象的。事实上，不仅企业，所有组织都存在激励问题，特别是，政府官员的激励制度对经济社会发展具有重要影响。在我国，由于地方政府长期以来一直对地方经济发展具有至关重要的影响力，地方官员的激励与行为一直备受关注。但是，过去大量的研究主要强调的是行政分权和财政包干制度下地方官员的财政激励对区域经济发展及其互动的影响，而对政府内部晋升制度这一最重要的激励机制研究甚少。周黎安的《晋升博弈中政府官员的激励与合作——兼论我国地方保护主义和重复建设问题长期存在的原因》一文开创了这方面研究的先河。作者建立了一个地方官员政治升迁博弈的简单模型，用于分析地方官员的晋升激励如何影响地区间的竞争与合作。分析表明，由于政治晋升博弈是一个零和博弈，即一个官员的升迁直接降低另一个官员升迁的机会，使得同时处于政治和经济双重竞争中的地方官员有更大的积极性相互阻碍对方的发展，而不是相互合作。周黎安的理论模型为我们理解我国区域经济竞争与合作提供了一个新的视角和框架，特别有助于我们理解我国长期存在的地方保护主义、"大而全，小而全"的地区发展战略和地区间形形色色的产业大战和恶性竞争。

在城市化的过程中，中国面临的一个重要问题是农地的转让和征用，这一问题不仅影响城市化的进程，而且涉及农民与国家之间的收入分配，影响土地资源的合理配置和经济发展。周其仁《农地产权与征地制度——中国城市化面临的重大选择》一文根据中国近年经济增长和制度变迁的经验，集中研究了城市化过程中的农地转让权，探讨了在现存土地转让权的法律安排下人们的实际行为以及这些行为的经济含义，并讨论了将要修订的《宪法》和《土地法》面临的主要选择。作者认为，城市化要求加快土地资源的转让，但现行的法律制度并没有对土地的转让权做出清楚的界定。这时，如果不终止违法行为，经济秩序就会受到冲击；但是同时，依靠执行原有的土地产权制度来消除混乱则不得不以限制土地资源的转让为代价。解决这个矛盾的办法是适时改变法律关于土地转让权的界定；特别是要修改"城市土地属于国家"的宪法准则，结束单一国家征地制度，发展农地转用市场。

《中国经济学——2004》所选的 17 篇论文，分别来自《经济研究》、《世界经济》、《经济学(季刊)》、《中国社会科学》、《中国社会科学评论》等，另有 24 位学者参与推荐，在此一并致谢。

浅释中国地区收入差距:1952—2002*

董先安

(北京大学中国经济研究中心)

一、文献综述

对于中国地区收入差距问题的研究,尤其是针对改革开放以来的变化趋势,已经积累了大量的文献。与大量文献相对应的,是对中国地区收入差距问题提出的各种各样的解释,本节将对现有的文献做一个简要的回顾。

Tsui(1991)发现,尽管20世纪80年代以前中国中央政府作出了种种再分配努力,其缩小地区差别的实际效果却并不明显。Duncan和Tian(1999)针对1952—1995年间数据进行的实证研究发现,中国的产出和消费的地区差距在改革前后呈相反方向变动。他们提出的解释认为,产出的倒U形曲线是由改革前后工业化的不同特征所决定的,改革以后实行外向型经济并推行民营化缩小了产出差距;而U形省际消费差距的出现,则主要是因为中央政府对地区收入差距在不同时期的干预程度不同。改革以来,在产出差距缩小的同时,随着地方自主权扩

* 本文为博士论文稿其中一章的压缩稿。感谢林毅夫老师、殷韦、李志赟、陶然、刘明兴、章奇、孙希芳、李永军以及北大经济研究中心学生讨论会其他参与人对文章的批评与建议。

大，中央政府在收入分配方面的干预不力，使得消费差距扩大了。他们因而强调说，如果要缩小地区差距，则应该采用有效方法来加强政府转移支付。

Chen 和 Feng(2000)的文章，对 1978—1989 年间中国 29 个省份的数据进行了回归分析，他们发现中国区域的经济在 20 世纪 80 年代呈现出了收敛的趋势，并且认为私有化是促进经济增长的主要原因。Young(2000)则提出了不同的观点，他认为地区性保护政策是地区差距扩大的关键，因为地区性的市场保护会使本地企业的资源配置状况偏离本地的比较优势。

蔡昉和都阳(2000)的实证研究表明人力资本上的差异是造成地区差距的主要原因。Wang 和 Yao(2001)等也持类似观点。

Lee(1995)、Dayal-Gulati 和 Husain(2000)的研究都提出了相似的观点，他们认为不同地区的外商直接投资规模的差异导致了不同区域之间的经济差距。后者对 1978—1997 年数据进行了分析，发现投资、国有企业集中度和银行存贷比是决定经济增长与收敛的重要因素。

王小鲁、樊纲(2004)考察了上世纪 80 年代和 90 年代地区收入差距的变动趋势，认为我国东部沿海地区和中西部内陆地区之间，在经济发展水平方面，无论是绝对差距还是相对差距都还在扩大。这主要是由于生产率的差别以及由此引起的资本流动所导致。资本的持续流动已经使地区间资本产出率的差别出现了缩小的趋势，但是生产率的地区差距还没有出现缩小的趋势。

Li 等人(1998)的文章则采用 Augmented Solow-Swan 模型来分析 1978—1995 年的数据，他们的结果也证实了条件收敛假说。他们估计条件收敛速度高达每年 4.75%。同时，他们也注意到 1990 年以后收入的差距扩大了。他们认为，经济改革促进了各省份分别朝着稳态水平收敛，却扩大了不同省份稳态水平的差距;但由于存在着绝对收敛,所以即使各省份稳态差距扩大,总的来说也出现了收敛现象。

Jian 等人(1996)的文章对 1978—1993 年期间的数据进行了分析,他们发现地区收入差距来源于沿海与内陆的收入差距拉大,而不是沿海内部、内陆内部的差距扩大。他们认为这是由于中央政府给予沿海的特殊优惠政策造成的。他们的发现与 Chen 和 Fleisher(1996)针对同样时期数据采用附加的 Solow 增长模型进行分析的结论相似,即经济条件收敛于沿海位置。

Démurger 等人(2001)将数据扩展到 1952—1998 年,他们的实证研究可以说是针对 1952 年以来中国地区收入差距的研究当中迄今最为完整的分析。他们发现,在 1952—1978 年期间,省际收入差距主要是体现了高收入的京津沪与其他地区之间的差距,这是政府"重工业优先"与"城市偏向"的政策所导致的。改革以前,三大直辖市以及黑吉辽等工业重镇的收入水平位居全国排行榜前列。他们已经注意到政府为了实施重工业优先发展战略,通过人为压低农产品价格、提高工业品价格为工业部门提供资金支持;在农村实行农业集体化等配套政策,其目的也是将农业剩余用于工业投资。这些政策都影响到地区收入差距与城乡差距。他们将改革以来影响地区收入差距的因素归结为两大类,即地理条件以及政府的相关政策。Fleisher 和 Chen(1997)也持有相似的观点。他们认为:第一,沿海地区的快速发展不能全部归功于中央政府的优惠政策,沿海地区比较有利的地理条件对其快速发展同等重要;第二,虽然自 1992 年以来,政府对于内地外商直接投资(FDI)和国际贸易的管制明显放松,但是 1996—1998 年期间沿海与内地在优惠待遇方面的差别仍然很大,这导致了沿海、中部、西北、西南 1%的差距。此外,他们还认为中国区别于美国经验的重大制度差异在于中国的户籍制度与国有银行体系。美国经验表明，人口从北部到东西海岸的逐步迁移对于美国国内的经济收敛至关重要。然而，中国特有的户籍制度却成为地区收入差距扩大的主要原因。根据内生经济增长理论，持续的技术创新会使投资回报率保持较高，所以资本并不会明显地从高工资地区流向低工资地区。在这种情况下劳动力流动便是缩小地区收入差距最容易的办法。但是由于户籍制度，这种收敛的途径在中国并不存在。不仅如此，中国垄断的国有银行体系以及各种地方保护主义的存在也阻止了资本在地区间的流动。但是，他们并未对上述假说进行实证检验，其实证检验的重点是地理条件和优惠政策。

龚六堂、谢丹阳(2004)讨论了我国各省份之间的生产要素配置的有效性问题。他们发现，从1970—1989年，资本的边际生产率的差异水平在缩小，从1989年起，边际生产率的差异水平保持在一个稳定水平；劳动的边际生产率的差异从1970—1993年也在缩小，但是，从1994年开始，劳动的边际生产率的差异水平反而开始上升。

而刘树成等(1994)、陆大道等(1997，2000)、胡鞍钢等(1995)、国家计委(1997)以及国务院发展研究中心课题组(1994)的研究成果，对于中国的地区收入差距都给出了百科全书式的解释，这些研究把地区差距扩大的原因归结为经济发展起点低下、市场失效、政策失效、中央财力下降、工农差距与城乡差距扩大、不同发展模式等。①

二、主要假说的简要评判

(一) 人力资本

对单个人而言，人力资本的初始条件是按随机概率而不是按地区分布的。教育与“边干边学”促进了人力资本的积累，前者的地区差异造成人力资本分布的地区特征。人力资本的增加对于经济增长的贡献率可以由扣除物质资本积累与全要素生产率提高贡献率之后的剩余部分来代表。教育内生于省级经济体的经济与财政状况，可以预期人力资本与经济增长正相关。此外，改革前后人力资本市场从无到有，从严重分割到逐步融合，这方面的制度变迁影响人力资本的差异。总体来看，人力资本与经济增长和市场化程度之间的正相关现象较稳定地存在了很多年。但相对而言，人力资本的基本趋势一直以来并未发生较大的波动，何以解释变动频繁的地区收入差距呢？这有待随后的实证工作来检验。

（二）物质资本

改革以前，各省级经济体的投资决策附属于中央财政的全国投资计划；金融市场完全由国家控制，同时金融系统也完全附庸于财政部门。因此，整个计划经济时期的物质资本投资往往是出于各个时期的不同战略考虑（比如：“大跃进”、备战备荒、三线建设等等）。笔者预期在计划经济时期，物质资本投资战略的改变会对地区收入差距变动产生重要影响，从而资本作为重要的生产要素之一被中央政府牢牢控制，其遵循行政命令而进行的跨区域转移可能是该时期地区收入差距波动的重要原因。一个合理的预期是，在资本市场流动性较强的情况下，资本要素的流动能够促进经济收敛。但是，一个不能忽略的事实是，改革开放以来资本市场逐渐开放，金融市场化步伐也逐渐加快，而改革后期地区收入差距却明显扩大了。

（三）中央政府针对沿海的优惠政策

毋庸置疑，特殊的关税、地方政府更大的自由度以及能源交通投资等方面的偏向政策，促进了受益地区的经济增长。但是，藉此来解释改革开放以来地区收入差距的变动显得较为勉强。如果说优惠政策是地区收入差距扩大的原因，那么，上世纪 90 年代政策范围扩大了，一个必然的推论应该是支持经济收敛的，而这与事实并不相容。

(四) 地理因素

地理因素通过市场可及性、交通成本与技术扩散成本等对经济增长产生影响。在所考察的一段较长时期内，地理因素的变化相对较少。从逻辑上讲，用一个相对不变的变量更适用于解释持续的收入差距本身，而不是这个差距的变动。

三、提出解释性假说

首先有必要简要回顾一下过去半个世纪的中国经济史。1952—1978 年中国处于典型的计划经济时期，中央政府对产品与要素市场实行严格的管制政策。改革开放以来，我国逐步放开产品与要素市场。迄今，政府除了对少数产品与要素的生产、价格与流动仍然实行严格控制以外，中国已经基本上是一个市场化国家。

所以，对于中国地区收入差距演变特殊性的一个合乎情理的猜测就是：

假说一：中国经济制度过去 50 年的演变，尤其是政府对于产品市场与要素市场的控制范围与力度的演变，对于各省级经济体的经济增长绩效和收敛特征可能产生重要影响。

在新古典经济增长框架下，产品市场与要素市场的开放性是经济收敛现象发生的前提条件。但是在中国，该条件并没有得到很好的满足。改革开放以来，在很长一段时期内仍保留着对政府认为特别重要的产品（比如粮食、棉花和某些矿产品）的生产控制和垄断收购，以及对重要的生产要素（劳动力）流动的限制。上述控制对于不同省级经济体的影响有很大差别。根据假说一，结合对于中国经济史的观察，并与不同的时期相对应，可以得出下述推论：

（一）计划经济时期（1952—1978年）

推论一：1952—1966年期间，中央政府通过计划与行政命令的方式实施全国统一的价格控制与资源调配，些微缩小了地区收入差距。其间，1958—1960年由于“大跃进”产生了扰动。

推论二：1966—1976年期间，“文化大革命”对地区收入差距再次产生扰动，“备战备荒”政策扩大了地区收入差距。在此期间，中国地区差距扩大的趋势主要由直辖市、工业重镇与其他地区的收入差距扩大造成，这部分归因于直辖市、工业重镇所享受到的特殊政治与经济优惠待遇，部分归因于直辖市、工业重镇农业人口比重相对较低，以及农产品价格与工业品价格存在“剪刀差”以支持重工业导向的发展战略。

（二）改革前期（1978—1989年）

推论三：1978—1984年期间，发轫于农业的改革开放政策迅速缩小了地区收入差距。实施“家庭联产承包责任制”等制度创新所产生的改革红利令偏重农业的中西部获得了实惠。这一时期的收敛现象主要来源于农业生产率的提高。

推论四：1985—1989年期间，中国地区收入差距缩小由直辖市与其他地区的收入差距缩小驱动。虽然农业改革发挥的作用渐少，但其他地区的轻工业迅速发展在一段时期内弥合了与大都市工业化程度的差距。

（三）改革后期（1989—2002年）

1990年至今，中国地区收入差距进一步扩大。而同期在绝大多数产品与要素市场领域内，市场化改革在继续推进。一个重要的例外是，中央政府迄今仍未放弃全球各国中最为苛刻的对于国内人口流动的户籍控制。该控制不仅扭曲了所有受过高等教育的新增劳动力的就业选择，而且阻碍了普通劳动力的迁徙过程，尤其是位于社会最底层、现阶段数量最庞大的非熟练劳动力。Barro 等人(1995)的实证研究显示，迁徙是发达国家经济收敛的重要条件。针对该时期的主要特征，假说一可以进一步具体化为假说二。

假说二：在产品市场与资本要素市场具备相对更加自由的流动性的条件下，劳动力要素市场的流动性一旦受到压抑，集聚效应就有可能使得经济发生两极化。

可以用一个两地区—两部门模型来说明上述机制。假设一个经济体有东、西两个地区，两地区内部进一步分为城市与农村。假定两种消费品由完全竞争的追求利润最大化的厂商生产，并在东部与西部地区间和地区内部的城乡之间自由贸易。假定传统部门 X 的生产函数如下：

$$X^i = (L_x^i)^\alpha (H_x^i)^{1-\alpha},\ 0 < \alpha < 1 \tag{1}$$

其中 L 和 H 分别代表非熟练劳动力与熟练劳动力；$i \in \{u, r\}$ 分别表示城市与农村。为了简化，舍掉资本因素并假定传统部门的全要素生产率为 1。现代部门 Y 的生产函数如下：

$$Y = NL_y^\beta H_y^{1-\beta},\ 0 < \beta < 1 \tag{2}$$

假定现代部门只存在于城市地区，N 代表现代部门的全要素生产率，服从下述过程：

$$\frac{\mathrm{d}N}{\mathrm{d}t}\frac{1}{N} = \left(1 + \phi \frac{N^*}{N}\right) q_y \tag{3}$$

其中，$q_y \equiv H_y / L_y$，表示现代部门熟练工人与不熟练工人的比例；N^* 是东部地区现代部门的全要素生产率；$\phi \in [0, 1]$ 测度从东部向西部技术扩散的速度。假定 N 的变动与熟练工人比重、东西部的技术差距以及技术扩散速度正相关。给定产品价格与现代部门的全要素生产率，两个部门的厂商分别最大化利润；消费者最优化其效用，代表性消费者的效用函数为：

$$U_0=\int_0^{\infty}\mathrm{e}^{-\delta t}\left[\gamma^{1/\theta}C_y^{(\theta-1)/\theta}+(1-\gamma)^{1/\theta}C_x^{(\theta-1)/\theta}\right]^{\theta/(\theta-1)}\mathrm{d}t,\ \gamma\in(0,\ 1) \tag{5}$$

效用依赖于传统部门产品 C_x 与现代部门产品 C_y 的消费组合。δ 表示贴现率，θ 表示两种产品的替代弹性，假定大于1。消费者的区别在于劳动禀赋及所在地区。消费者拥有所在地区企业的全部股份并享有利润 π。为了简化，假定不存在跨期借贷，消费者不跨期平滑消费。并假定存在户籍制度管制，非熟练劳动力不能流动，熟练劳动力能够在城乡之间流动，而不能跨地区流动。

两地区模型的均衡条件为：(1)消费者在给定价格下最优化效用；(2)厂商在给定要素价格下最优化利润；(3)两类劳动力均被完全雇用。东部与西部地区劳动力市场均出清；(4)产品市场出清；(5)全要素生产率分别满足(3)式所描述的过程。均衡时，熟练劳动力工资在地区内部一样，但是在不同地区不同；不熟练劳动力工资则不仅在不同地区有差别，而且在地区内部城乡之间也有差别。可以证明：如果东西部城市之间存在发散，进而在东西部之间产生发散，那么经济会逐渐收敛到一条平衡增长路径，西部地区完全集中在传统部门的生产，东部地区完全集中在现代部门生产，即：

$$H_y^{r}=0,\ \frac{\mathrm{d}N}{N}=0;\ H_y^{*r}\rightarrow\bar{H},\ \frac{\mathrm{d}N^*}{N^*}\rightarrow\frac{\bar{H}}{\bar{L}^u}$$

接下来，需要对主要的竞争性或互补性假说进行一番检验，考察人力与物质资本、地理禀赋、经济的主要结构特征如产业结构、产权结构、政府规模以及企业规模结构等因素的影响，同时希望通过实证分析直接或者间接地验证前述假说与推论的真实性。

四、实 证 分 析

(一) 数据

本文采用两套面板数据进行研究，即数据甲(1952—1998年)和数据乙(1985—2002年)，分别包括30和28个省、自治区、直辖市。由于从官方统计年鉴上数据不可得或者不匹配，数据甲不包括重庆，在1952—1969年期间不包括西藏和新疆，在1970—1977年期间不包括新疆；数据乙不包括西藏和青海，重庆的数据全部并入四川。数据来源于《新中国五十年统计资料汇编》(1949—1998年)与中经网数据库(1985—2002年)。

(二) 初步检验

初步检验控制了地区虚拟变量与影响经济收敛的主要结构因素，主要针对假说一及其推论。σ收敛指数变动的基本事实表明:1952—1978年期间，地区差距扩大的趋势主要由直辖市与其他地区收入差距扩大造成。1978—1984年期间，发轫于农业的改革开放政策迅速缩小了地区收入差距。1985—1989年期间，地区收入差距缩小由直辖市与其他地区的收入差距缩小驱动。1990年至今，中国地区收入差距进一步扩大。其间，“大跃进”、三线建设与邓小平“南方谈话”等都对收敛系数产生了强烈的扰动。在整个时期，只有中部地区内部收入差距呈现连续缩小趋势；在1974年以前(尤其在后半段)，东部与西部地区内部收入差距显著扩大；在后一时期发生“收敛俱乐部”现象。三大区域之间的差距拉大，同时东部与中部地区内部收入差距显著缩小，但西部地区内部收入差距虽然在 1974—1979 年期间也显著缩小，之后则逐渐扩大。

β 收敛初步检验结果表明：在 1978—1984 年期间存在显著的绝对收敛现象；计划经济时期绝对收敛并不存在。其中，在“文革”时期显著发散；但在 1958—1966 年期间，地区收入差距受到了激进的绝对平均主义政策的强烈扰动；通过控制 6 地区虚拟变量，β 收敛检验证实了计划经济时期地区收入差距扩大主要是工业重镇与其他地区之间的差距扩大造成的；控制 3 区域虚拟变量证实了 20 世纪 90 年代初期以来“经济收敛俱乐部”的存在。

控制了产业结构与产权结构的 β 收敛初步检验结果表明，在改革前后农业比重与国有比重分别显示了截然相反的影响，都是影响地区收入差距的重要因素。在 1952—1998 年期间，农业产值比重与地区经济增长之间存在负相关关系，说明政府工业化地区布局显著地影响到各地区的经济发展速度。但是，在 1978—1998 年期间，市场化改革使得原先以农业为主的一些欠发达地区如粤闽浙追赶上来，农业比重系数的符号也转而为正。初步检验结果中，国有比重估计值的符号在改革前后截然相反。其中，在 1952—1978 年期间，享有绝对垄断地位和投资偏好的国有企业的存在对于地区经济发展无疑有正的影响；改革开放以后，国有企业密集地区的经济发展相对落后。这一趋势在 1992 年以后表现非常明显。可见，国有企业的地区布局直接影响地区收入差距。从上述初步检验的结果来看，假说一以及相应的 4 个推论均得到了较好的验证。

(三) 中国地区经济增长因素的弹性分析

针对上述各种竞争性与互补性假说，接下来的实证检验通过弹性分析与条件收敛分析两步进行，分别以人均国内生产总值增长率及其变动为被解释变量。首先，利用数据乙(1985—

2002 年)对影响经济增长的各种因素进行简化式分析。

$$\log y_{it} = a + \phi \log S + \varepsilon_{it}, \text{其中 } a = u_i + v_t \tag{11}$$

常数项 a 可以分解为时间和地区特定(固定或随机)效应。这里用时间特定效应来控制经济周期以及改革不同时期的特殊性,用地区特定效应控制地理特征。在上式中,S 代表所要考察的影响因素。本文的实证检验控制了包括人力资本、物质资本、市场密度、农业生产、农业结构、城乡差距、产业结构、产权结构、政府规模、企业规模、户口结构等多组变量(参见表 1 变量目录)。简化式的弹性分析直观地得出了上述解释变量对经济增长是否存在显著影响以及影响力的大小。表 2 列出了中国地区经济增长因素弹性分析的 OLS 估计的主要结果(共 5 列),前 4 列分别是单向固定时间不控制地区以及控制 3 区域、6 区域与区域重合的估计,最后是对时间和地区进行双向固定估计的结果。[②]

表 1　中国地区收入差距实证检验的解释变量目录

H1 学龄儿童入学率
H2 人口自然增长率
K1 全社会固定资产投资总额/GDP
M1 耕地人口密度
A11 水产品产量/农业人口
A12 猪牛羊肉产量/农业人口
A13 水果产量/农业人口
A14 大牲畜年底头数/农业人口
A21 农林牧渔业总产值/GDP
A22 农业总产值/农林牧渔业总产值
A23 牧业总产值/农林牧渔业总产值
R11 东部 R12 中部 R21 直辖市
A24 渔业总产值/农林牧渔业总产值
D1 城镇居民家庭平均每人全年可支配收入/农村居民家庭平均每人全年纯收入
S1 农业人口/年底总人口

（续表）

I1 第一产业增加值/GDP
I2 第二产业增加值/GDP
P1 国有经济单位职工人数/职工人数
P2 其他经济单位职工人数/职工人数
G1 地方财政支出/GDP
Z1 大型工业企业总产值/工业总产值
Z2 小型工业企业总产值/工业总产值
R22 东北 R23 沿海 R24 中部 R25 西南

（四）中国地区收入差距的条件收敛分析

条件收敛分析以人均国内生产总值增长率的变动为被解释变量，解释变量中增加了初始年份人均国内生产总值。

$$(1/T)\log(y_{iT}/y_{i0}) = a - [(1-\mathrm{e}^{-\beta T})/T]\log(y_{i0}) + \phi S + u_{i0,T} \tag{12}$$

常数项 a 和解释变量中 S 的含义与(11)式中一致。与按时间段估计的初步分析不同，这里解释变量增加了很多，为了充分利用数据信息，令 $T=1$。同时控制了包括人力资本、物质资本、市场密度、农业生产、农业结构、城乡差距、产业结构、产权结构、政府规模、企业规模、户口结构等多组变量，也即收敛条件。条件收敛分析得出了上述解释变量对经济收敛是否存在显著影响，并估计其影响力。表 3 列出了中国地区经济增长因素弹性分析的 Nonlinear FIML 参数估计的主要结果(共 5 列)。各列的排列次序与表 2 相同。

（五）实证结果解读

首先，通过弹性分析发现，与预期相一致，人力资本的增加与经济增长之间存在显著的正相关。在表 2 的多数估计中，控制住其他变量之后，代表人口质量的学龄儿童入学率(H1)每提高 1%，会使得经济增长率增加 1.02%—1.08%；不过，从数据

表 2　中国地区经济增长因素的弹性分析(1985—2002)

解释变量	单向固定(时间)				双向固定
	分省份	三区域	六区域	区域重合	(时间、地区)
H1	1.054416***	1.076128***	1.02127***	1.022565***	−0.13633
H2	−0.00477	0.008181	0.023634	0.033149	0.018241
K1	0.079685	0.062843	0.070908	0.072128	−0.06828*
M1	−0.11966***	−0.10357***	−0.18864***	−0.20168***	0.084707
A11	0.007256	0.006771	−0.00797	−0.00248	−0.01673
A12	0.032008	0.037523	0.030827	0.033186	0.133378**
A13	−0.00979	−0.01375	−0.00753	−0.00433	−0.01494*
A14	0.114506***	0.128561***	0.076364***	0.085363***	0.182965***
A21	−0.27089***	−0.29554***	−0.30042***	−0.30727***	−0.24368***
A22	−0.32288**	−0.33678**	−0.46695***	−0.5044***	−0.45577***
A23	−0.10541	−0.11396	−0.15194**	−0.14699*	−0.25585***
A24	0.029633	0.030769	0.031682	0.034308	0.002287
D1	−0.2651***	−0.29541***	−0.1827**	−0.22395**	−0.23646***
D2	−0.16994***	−0.18525***	−0.12056*	−0.08794	−0.08047
S1	0.467804***	0.452456***	0.314936**	0.300438**	0.661956***
I1	−0.53764***	−0.52893***	−0.41479***	−0.43328***	−0.32595***

（续表）

解释变量	单向固定(时间)				双向固定
	分省份	三区域	六区域	区域重合	(时间、地区)
I2	0.102602	0.022898	0.088714	0.030886	0.215575***
P1	−1.89928***	−1.74068***	−1.7364***	−1.71746***	−0.68707***
P2	−0.59899***	−0.51587***	−0.54117***	−0.50261***	−0.36166***
G1	−0.19422***	−0.23658***	−0.23121***	−0.27299***	−0.04559
Z1	0.002813	0.006496	0.004053	0.003231	−0.00553
Z2	−0.14889**	−0.11892*	−0.08915	−0.08209	0.0811**
R11		−0.0446		−0.11275	
R12		−0.09076*		−0.04248	
R21			0.114755	0.140365	
R22			0.131946*	0.129457	
R23			−0.02798	−0.0026	
R24			−0.09085*	−0.11346	
R25			−0.04637	−0.06785	
Adj R^2	0.9445	0.9455	0.9471	0.9474	0.9798

注:(1) *、**、*** 分别表示显著性在10%、5%、1%的水平。(2)共325个样本。

来看，代表人口数量的人口自然增长率(H2)对于经济增长影响较为不明显。条件收敛分析的结果也与预期一致(但显著性较差)。可见发展初级教育提高人口质量(而不是增加人口数量)对于经济收敛的重要性。从表3可见，人口自然增长率对于经济收敛存在显著负影响，是造成地区经济差距的重要原因之一。

物质资本积累对于经济增长显示出正向影响，但与人力资本影响力相比较不显著。使用全社会固定资产投资总额占GDP比重(K1)来控制实物与无形资本的影响，弹性分析发现虽然我国的物质资本投资率很高，但其边际回报率并不高，平均而言物质资本投资比例每增加1%，能够带动0.06%—0.08%左右的经济增长。而完全控制住时间与地区效应之后，物质资本投资率相对经济增长率的弹性竟然为负。条件收敛分析则显示物质资本投资并非重要的收敛条件。

鉴于我国各省级经济体在地理特征方面的巨大差异，特别是西部地带不适宜居住的面积较大，因此，剔除人烟特别稀少的地区来统计人口分布更能反映主要经济活动地区的实际人口稠密度。使用单位耕地人口密度(M1)来反映人口密度，弹性分析发现人口密度与经济增长率显著负相关，耕地人口密度每增加1%，经济增长率减少0.1%—0.2%。该现象进一步表明，在现阶段人口数量与经济发展之间单纯看确实存在某种负向联系。从条件收敛的实证结果看，人口密度与经济收敛的关系并不显著，可能是同样人口稠密的沿海地区与西南地区的经济表现差距太大所造成。

在农业生产方面，本文尝试用农业人口的平均水产品产量(A11)、猪牛羊肉产量(A12)、水果产量(A13)、大牲畜年底头数(A14)等变量来控制各经济体的农业发达程度。检验结果表明，总体上农业生产能力与经济增长之间关系不明显。但其中

表 3　中国地区收入差距的条件收敛分析(1985—2002)

解释变量	单向固定(时间)				双向固定
	分省份	三区域	六区域	区域重合	(时间、地区)
β	0.091413***	0.098987***	0.095389***	0.096063***	0.240268***
H1	0.000339	0.000315	0.000282	0.000385	—0.0001
H2	—0.00445***	—0.00437***	—0.0044***	—0.0045***	—0.00655***
K1	0.030243	0.025209	0.058975	0.029561	—0.08475
M1	0.00695*	0.006464*	—0.00101	0.00249	0.020556**
A11	—0.56687**	—0.52728**	—0.68116**	—0.67291**	—0.40277
A12	0.37909	0.350401	0.200186	0.124692	0.166468
A13	—0.00238	—0.0516	—0.03434	—0.111	—0.18488
A14	0.167826***	0.154513***	0.156259***	0.180496***	0.336924
A21	0.001901	—0.00275	—0.00246	—0.02483	—0.04481
A22	0.159774	0.174858	0.176068	0.146177	0.168231
A23	0.037688	0.016313	0.040011	0.015058	—0.03919
A24	0.578804***	0.524297**	0.622418***	0.518627**	0.302055
D1	—0.03349***	—0.03067***	—0.03647***	—0.03568***	—0.04964***
D2	—0.01183	—0.01348	—0.01012	—0.01354	—0.00704
S1	0.163283***	0.153444***	0.139146	0.176817*	0.425711

（续表）

解释变量	单向固定(时间)				双向固定
	分省份	三区域	六区域	区域重合	(时间、地区)
I1	−0.3425***	−0.30399**	−0.4368***	−0.41379***	−0.61361***
I2	−0.07778	−0.05997	−0.17709*	−0.17483*	−0.09973
P1	−0.28965**	−0.30276**	−0.345***	−0.3857***	−0.29501*
P2	−0.53632***	−0.57435***	−0.62018***	−0.65514***	−0.66189***
G1	−0.30908***	−0.25163**	−0.29744**	−0.2544*	−0.25957
Z1	−0.02489	0.011479	0.018123	0.003957	−0.08803
Z2	0.02921	0.05708	0.047263	0.045773	0.057224
R11		0.024079		0.011881	
R12		0.007101		−0.02426	
R21			−0.03114	−0.01089	
R22			0.000382	0.01782	
R23			−0.01688	−0.01009	
R24			−0.01604	0.018053	
R25			−0.04379	−0.02848	
Adj R^2	0.5849	0.5865	0.5969	0.5987	0.6458

注：(1) *、**、*** 分别表示显著性在10%、5%、1%的水平。(2)共308个样本。

大牲畜年底头数和粮食与油料产量与经济增长之间存在较为显著的正相关，而水果产量与经济增长之间负相关(不显著)。由于检验结果比较稳定，笔者倾向于认为是外部因素(比如没有控制价格扭曲、生产受干预程度与市场竞争状态)导致了上述“增产不增收”的结果。从收敛分析的角度来看，水产品与大牲畜生产是经济收敛的重要条件，也即这两类生产活动可以部分地解释地区经济差距，它们都是经济发散的原因。

弹性分析结果表明GDP中农林牧渔业总产值比重(A21)越高，经济增长率越低，前者每降低1%导致经济增长率显著提高0.24%—0.3%。可见，经济增长主要由非农产业驱动。在农林牧渔业内部，农业的产值比重(A22)越高，经济增长率越低，1%的农业比重降低显著地导致0.32%—0.5%的经济增长率提高。牧业比重(A23)的影响与农业方向一致，但影响力约为后者的1/2—1/3。相反，渔业比重(A24)对经济增长的影响为正，但影响力不及农业比重的1/10。从收敛分析的角度来看，在农林牧渔业内部渔业比重与经济收敛呈显著的正向关系。换言之，控制住渔业因素，显著利于条件收敛。

本研究同时考虑了经济体内部的城乡差距对于经济增长和收敛的影响。弹性分析与条件收敛分析都证实了城乡差距的显著负面影响。分别用城镇居民家庭平均每人全年可支配收入与农村居民家庭平均每人全年纯收入之比(D1)和城乡居民消费水平之比(D2)来控制城乡差距的影响(由于城乡居民消费倾向差异两者并不相同)，发现前者每扩大1%，经济增长率下降0.18%—0.3%；后者每扩大1%，经济增长率下降0.08%—0.19%。相应地，以收入代表的城乡差距对于经济收敛的影响力是消费差距影响力的3倍左右。上述分析显示，缩小城乡差距能够显著地促进经济收敛。

中国存在着严厉的户籍管制，这一点从实证分析中也得到显示。使用农业人口占总人口的比例（S1）来刻画户口结构，发现该比例与经济增长存在显著的正相关，这与前面控制农林牧渔业产值比重（A21）的结果背道而驰！固定了时间效应以及双向固定的检验结果表明，农业户籍人口比例每上升1%，经济增长率增加0.3%—0.66%。这个现象间接地反映了户籍制度与实际经济活动的背离，而不是说农业户籍人口越多，经济增长率越高。实际上，越来越多的农业户籍人口的主要经济活动是在经济相对发达的异地。户口结构同时也是条件收敛的一个较为显著的影响因素，且与预期相反，符号为正，这间接说明数据所显示的经济发散程度由于户籍人口统计的原因而在一定程度上被高估了。[③]上述检验实际上间接验证了假说二。

再使用第一产业增加值占GDP比重（I1）和第二产业增加值占GDP比重（I2）来控制产业结构对经济增长和收敛的影响，[④]弹性分析表明，第一产业比重越高，经济增长越慢；第二产业比重越高，经济增长越快。其中，第一产业比重相对经济增长率的弹性远超过后者（分别为－0.33—－0.54、0.02—0.22），而且间接显示了第三产业比重也具有较大的正弹性（第一产业弹性与第二产业弹性之和的相反数，约0.11—0.50）。第一产业比重对于经济增长的显著负面影响以及后者的正面影响与预期一致。条件收敛的结果显示，第一、第二产业比重同是经济收敛的条件，前者显著性更佳。而且，第一、第二产业比重越高，经济越不容易收敛。这间接显示第三产业的发展能够显著地促进经济收敛，而第二产业比重提高虽然促进经济增长，但对于经济收敛的影响并不积极。

本文的初步分析结果已经证实，在中国经济转型过程中，一个相当重要的因素是国有企业在整个经济中所扮演角色的转换。使用国有经济单位职工人数占全部职工人数的比例(P1)以及其他经济单位职工人数比例(P2)来控制产权结构的影响，弹性分析表明在产权结构中国有比例每增加1%，经济增长率显著地降低1.69%—1.9%；其他经济单位职工人数比例的负面影响力约为前者的1/3—1/2。间接表明城镇集体经济单位职工人数比例变化对经济增长有显著正的影响。但是，由于其他经济单位职工人数比例是由总职工人数剔除国有与城镇集体经济单位职工人数得来，而笔者认为除了国有企业人数与实际误差不大以外，由于统计原因改革时期其他经济单位职工人数与真实值有较大差距，尤其是灰色经济的大量存在使得后者不足为信。与初步的收敛分析结论基本一致，改革时期国有企业比重对经济收敛存在显著的负影响，是经济收敛必须控制的条件之一。

为了检验政府规模与经济增长的关系，本文控制了地方财政支出占GDP的比重(G1)。弹性检验显示政府规模每扩大1%，经济增长率降低0.04%—0.27%。条件收敛的检验结果也表明，简政放权是经济收敛的重要条件之一。

这里一并考察了企业规模结构对于经济增长率和条件收敛的影响，分别控制了大型工业企业总产值占工业总产值比重(Z1)和小型工业企业总产值占工业总产值比重(Z2)。弹性分析结果显示，单向固定结果是小型企业产值比重变动对经济增长率有较显著的负影响，而双向固定结果显示小型企业比重变动相对经济增长率弹性系数为正(0.08)，大型企业的影响则并不明朗。如果用大型与小型企业比重的弹性间接计算中型企业的弹性，得到后者相对经济增长率弹性的绝对值小于小型企业的弹性。条件收敛分析表明，大、小型企业比重对于经济收敛的影响不太显著，后者不明显地促进了经济收敛。鉴于大小企业人均产值的较大差异，而人均工资差距则相对要小，因此如果用不同类型企业的雇员比重来控制企业的规模结构可能得到更真实的结果。

在单向固定的弹性与条件收敛分析中，根据 3 地区地理区划控制了东部(R11)与中部(R12)地理位置，以及根据 6 地区地理区划控制了直辖市(R21)、东北(R22)、沿海(R23)、中部(R24)以及西南(R25)等经济区位。结果发现这种控制并不影响上述各种解释变量参数估计的稳定性。而且，就地理区位本身的参数估计而言，尽管其显著性并非良好，系数值仍然能够显示出，相对而言，东部与沿海区位对经济增长和收敛分别拥有更积极的影响力。

五、结　　论

本文对解释中国半个世纪以来地区收入差距演变的各种假说进行了归纳、分析与检验，同时提出并检验了 2 个主要假说和 4 个推论。通过控制人力资本、物质资本、市场密度、农业生产、农业结构、城乡差距、产业结构、产权结构、政府规模、企业规模、户口结构等多组变量，弹性分析与条件收敛分析均证实上述解释变量对经济增长与收敛存在显著影响，本文同时还估计了其影响力。上述检验结合初步检验较好地验证了各种竞争性与互补性假说以及本文提出的假说与推论。

人力资本的增加与经济增长之间存在显著的正相关。人口自然增长率对于经济收敛存在显著负影响，是重要的收敛条件。分析结果显示虽然我国的物质资本投资率很高，但其边际回报率并不高，且非重要收敛条件。

总体上农业生产能力与经济增长之间关系不明显，确实存在"增产不增收"现象，间接表明价格扭曲、市场垄断以及农业生产的低市场化程度阻碍了经济增长。检验结果表明，第一产业比重越高，经济增长越慢；而第三产业则具有较大的正弹性；产业结构是经济收敛的重要条件。

城乡差距对经济增长与收敛均存在显著负面影响。收敛分析显示，缩小城乡差距能够显著地促进经济收敛，分析还证实了户籍制度与实际经济活动存在严重的背离，并直接妨碍经济收敛。

在产权结构中，国有比例每增加1%，经济增长率显著地降低1.69%—1.9%。与初步分析结论一致，改革时期国有企业比重对经济收敛存在显著的负影响，是经济收敛必须控制的条件之一。弹性检验还显示政府规模每扩大1%，经济增长率降低0.04%—0.27%。条件收敛分析也表明，简政放权是经济收敛的重要条件。

地理区位也显示了稳定影响，相对而言，东部与沿海区位对经济增长和收敛分别拥有更积极的影响力。

注　释

① 其他对中国地区发展差距的解释还包括：林毅夫等(1998)从发展战略的角度进行的解释；Zhang 和 Zou(1998)；Jin、Qian 和 Weingast(1999)从财政分权角度进行的解释；林燕平(2000)从产业结构、人口结构与教育水平角度进行的解释。

② 在初步估计时，笔者尝试了用 Pooled DATA 进行弹性与收敛估计(因变量为省级经济体 1985—1991、1992—1998、1999—2002 年平均增长率)，但发现即使控制了地理因素，条件收敛系数仍表明经济显著发散。这一发现与 Démurger 等(2001)针对 1979—1984、1985—1991、1992—1998 年数据的发现不同，后者主要控制地理与优惠政策即得出了显著的条件收敛结果，并认定 Pooled DATA 估计比固定或随机的 individual 效应估计优越。笔者认为除了数据的原因，是解

释变量的选择导致了这个差异，而不认为他们的研究具有稳定性。此外，Hausman 检验非常显著，显示固定效应估计比随机效应估计更合适。

③ 实际的地区收入差距多大程度上不如数据所显示的严重尚无法确定。由于农业人口基数庞大，这方面应当不存在明显高估。实行更加灵活的户籍制度，乃至最终取消所有附加在户籍之上的就业、教育与福利等方面的不公平政策，对于缩小中国地区差距与城乡差距、促进经济增长而言至关重要。

④ 国家统计局数据中第一产业与农林牧渔业总产值口径并不相同。在新制定的《三次产业划分规定》中，三次产业划分的具体范围是：第一产业包括农、林、牧、渔业及农、林、牧、渔服务业；第二产业包括采矿业，制造业，电力、燃气及水的生产和供应业，建筑业；第三产业包括除第一、二产业以外的其他行业，具体内容略。

参考文献

蔡昉、都阳，2000：《中国地区经济增长的趋同与差异——对西部开发战略的启示》，《经济研究》第 10 期。

龚六堂、谢丹阳，2004：《我国省份之间的要素流动和边际生产率的差异分析》，《经济研究》第 1 期。

国家计委国土地区司、国家计委国土开发与地区经济研究所，1997：《1996 中国地区经济发展报告》，改革出版社。

国务院发展研究中心课题组，1994：《中国区域协调发展战略》，中国经济出版社。

胡鞍钢、王绍光、康晓光，1995：《中国地区差距报告》，辽宁人民出版社。

林燕平，2000：《中国地区国民收入差距研究》，北京大学出版社。

林毅夫、蔡昉、李周，1998：《中国经济转型时期的地区差距分析》，《经济研究》第 6 期。

刘树成、李强、薛天栋主编，1994：《中国地区经济发展研究》，中国统计出版社。

陆大道等著,2000:《2000 中国区域发展报告:西部开发的基础、政策与态势分析》,商务印书馆。

陆大道、薛凤旋等著,1997:《1997 中国区域发展报告》,商务印书馆。

王小鲁、樊纲,2004:《中国地区差距的变动趋势和影响因素》,《经济研究》第 1 期。

Barro, R., and Sala-i-Martin, X., 1995, *Economic Growth*, New York: McGraw-Hill.

Chen, B. Z., and Feng, Y., 2000, "Determinants of Economic Growth in China: Private Enterprise, Education and Openness", *China Economic Review*, 11(1):1—15.

Chen, J., and Fleisher, B. M., 1996, "Regional Income Inequality and Economic Growth in China", *Journal of Comparative Economics* 22, 141—164.

Dayal-Gulati, A., and Husain, A. M., 2000, "Centripetal Forces in China's Economic take-off", IMF Working Paper 00/86.

Démurger, S., Sachs, J. D., Woo, W. T., Bao, S. M., Chang, G., and Mellinger, A., 2001, "Geography, Economic Policy and Regional Development in China", CID Working Paper No. 77.

Duncan, R., and Tian, X. W., 1999, "China's Inter-provincial Disparities: An explanation", *Communist and Post-Communist Studies* 32, 211—224.

Fleisher, B. M., and Chen, J., 1997, "The Coast-Noncoast Income Gap, Productivity and Regional Economic Policy in China", *Journal of Comparative Economics*, 25(2):220—36.

Jian, T. L., Sachs, J. D., and Warner, A. M., 1996, "Trends in Regional Inequality in China", *China Economy Review*, 7(1), 1—21.

Jin, H. H, Qian, Y. Y., and Weingast, B. R., "Regional Decentralization and Fiscal Incentives: Federalism, Chinese Style", *Working Paper*, Hoover Institution, Stanford University, March, 1999.

Lee, J. Ch., 1995, "Regional Income Inequality Variations in China",

Journal of Economic Development, 20(2), 99—118.

Li, H., Liu, Z. N., and Rebelo, I., 1998, "Testing the Neoclassical Theory of Economic Growth: Evidence from Chinese Provinces", *Economics of Planning*, 31, 117—132.

Tsui, K. Y., 1991, "China's Regional Inequality, 1952—1985", *Journal of Comparative Economics*, 17, 1—21.

Wang, Y., and Yao Y. D., 2001, "Sources of China's Economic Growth, 1952—99: Incorporating Human Capital Accumulation", *WBI Working Paper*, The World Bank.

Young, A., 2000, "The Razor's Edge: Distortions and Incremental Reform in the People Republic of China", *Quarterly Journal of Economics*, CXV:1091—1135.

Zhang, T., and Zou, H. F., 1998, "Fiscal Decentralization, Public Spending, and Economic Growth in China", *Journal of Public Economics*, 67:221—40.

（原载《经济研究》2004 年第 9 期）

中国地区差距的变动趋势和影响因素*

王小鲁　樊　纲
（中国改革基金会国民经济研究所）

一、地区经济差距研究的理论框架

在改革以前，中国在东、中、西部地区之间就存在显著的经济差距。① 就总体而言，东部沿海地区和一部分中部地区的经济发展水平和人均收入均高于西部地区。为了缩小地区差距，中央政府在20世纪50年代到70年代之间实行了转移财政支付、平衡收入差距的政策，并在中西部地区进行了大量投资，但这并没有显著缩小东西部地区间在经济效率方面的差距。

20世纪80年代，为了扩大地方政府和企业的经济自主权和积极性，中央政府对各省（自治区、直辖市，下同）实行了财政"分灶吃饭"，减小了经济较发达地区的财政上缴比重，从而在一定程度上减小了东西部之间财政转移支付的力度。这促进了东部地区的经济发展，特别是首先享受到这项政策的广东省在整

* 本文是国民经济研究所的研究课题："中国地区差距：20年变化趋势和影响因素"的总报告压缩。文中引用了该课题一系列专题报告的研究成果。这些专题报告的作者有：蔡昉、王德文、都阳、郭金龙、王宏伟、武剑、姚枝仲、王美艳、陈渝、樊纲、王小鲁。所援引的专题报告列在结尾处的参考文献中。本课题得到了中国经济改革研究基金会和德国阿登纳基金会的资助。

个改革时期取得了突飞猛进的发展。

尽管各地区在改革期间都有不同程度的经济增长加速，但就总体而言，东部沿海地区的经济增长率在过去 20 年中显著高于中西部地区。因此出现了区域间收入差距扩大的趋势。特别是在 20 世纪 90 年代，差距扩大非常明显。表 1 列出了按两种不同方法计算的东中西三个地区在 20 世纪 80 年代和 90 年代(至 2001 年)的年均 GDP 增长率。20 世纪 80 年代中西部比东部平均增长率低约 1 个百分点，90 年代则低 2—3 个百分点。按照第二种方法，80 年代中西部比东部平均增长率低不到 1 个百分点，而 90 年代则低 2 个百分点左右。②

表 1　改革期间东中西部 GDP 增长率比较(1981—2001 年)

地　区	1981—1990 年	与东部差距	1991—2001 年	与东部差距
按统计局可比价格				
东部	9.98		12.94	
中部	8.75	−1.23	10.70	−2.24
西部	9.12	−0.86	9.63	−3.31
按作者计算的不变价格				
东部	8.80		11.68	
中部	7.85	−0.95	9.64	−2.04
西部	8.71	−0.09	9.69	−1.99

注：第一种方法来自国家统计局按可比价格计算的分省 GDP 年度增长率。第二种方法是作者根据国家统计局公布的分省 GDP(当年价格)加权平均并进行价格平减后得出的。GDP 价格平减指数由居民消费价格指数、工业品出厂价格指数、农产品收购价格指数、固定资产投资价格指数合成。

资料来源：王小鲁(2000)，根据国家统计局(1999，2001，2002)计算。

东中西部经济增长率的差别也导致了人均 GDP 和人均可支配收入(农村居民按人均纯收入计)差距的明显扩大。1980 年，中、西部人均 GDP 按各省区加权平均计相当于东部的 65%

和53%。到2002年，它们占东部的比例分别降到了49%和39%(表2)。从表中还可以看出，差距的扩大主要发生在20世纪90年代。由于转移支付的作用，人均可支配收入的地区差别相对小些，但相对差距扩大的趋势也很明显。1980年，中、西部人均收入各自相当于东部的78%和70%。到2000年，它们占东部的比例分别降到了62%和54%(国家统计局，不同年份)。

表2　东中西部人均GDP和相对比例的变化(元/人，当年价格)

人均GDP(元/人)	1980年	1990年	2000年	2002年
东部	598	2240	11334	14363
中部	391	1338	5982	7047
西部	308	1156	4687	5536
中部/东部	65%	60%	53%	49%
西部/东部	53%	52%	41%	39%

资料来源：国家统计局(1999, 2001, 2003)。

东西部收入差距扩大的趋势，更集中地表现在区域间农村居民收入差距的扩大。从城镇居民收入的差距来看，1980年西部相当于东部的85%，2002年下降到71%，下降了14个百分点；而从农村居民收入差距来看，在同一时期西部与东部之比由70%下降到46%，下降了24个百分点。

根据新古典增长模型的推论，收入水平较低的国家总体上经济增长速度会比较快，因此穷国和富国的收入水平会逐渐接近。这被称为“趋同”理论(Solow, 1956; Swan, 1956)。但内生增长理论证明，人力资本对经济增长有显著的贡献，而发达国家人力资本存量较高，因此穷富国家收入水平可能不会趋同(Romer, 1986; Lucas, 1988)。在不加选择地使用世界各国数据进行的实证分析中，一般性的趋同并没有被证实。但是一些研究发现趋同确实存在于某些类别的国家和地区之间，例如东亚国家和地区间，以及经合组织国家间。进一步的研究还发现，如果排除了人力资本、储蓄率等某些条件的差别，各国间的确存在趋同现象。因此这些影响条件就导致了国家间的经济差距。上述研究结果被称为“俱乐部趋同”和“条件趋同”理论（Barro and Sala-i-Martin，1995）。

在我国，上述增长理论已经开始应用于区域经济差距的研究中。蔡昉和都阳（2000）发现，我国东中西三个地区分别存在内部趋同，但地区间的差距却扩大了。而在控制了初始人力资本、投资率等变量时，各地区间存在有条件的趋同。

有哪些因素影响地区经济增长？我们可以看到，地区间的资本和劳动力流动、人力资本在各地区分布的差异、各地区的城市化程度、农村工业化程度，以及制度和政策因素的差别等等，都可能成为影响因素。这些因素怎样影响地区经济增长？它们使地区间的经济差距发生了哪些变化？这些问题对于研究地区差距的成因和变动趋势至关重要。在本文的以下部分将分别对这些因素进行考察，试图在此基础上对区域差距的形成和变动趋势进行比较完整的描绘，并就如何缩小区域差距得出一些政策性结论。

二、地区间的资本流动和外资的地区分布

资本在各地区间的配置和流动是影响区域经济增长，从而影响地区差距的一个关键因素。改革以前，地区间资本流动完全是一种计划行为，受中央政策支配。改革以来的这二十多年间，资本流动一方面受财政分配资金和国家银行政策性资金分配的制约，另一方面又受到市场的引导。对外资而言，还受到地域性优惠政策的影响。财政体制、银行政策、市场条件、外资优惠政策等因素使得区域间资本流动呈现出复杂的格局。其总体

流向如何？今后的变动趋势又如何？以下分别从不同方面对此进行考察，以期大致刻画出一个过去若干年间资本跨地区流动的整体趋势（另见郭金龙、王宏伟有关计算和分析，2003）。

（一）固定资产投资在地区间的分布

表3计算了1980年以来全社会固定资产投资在东中西三个地区之间分布的情况。在改革初期的1980年，西部地区的固定资产投资只相当于东部的48%，但西部的投资率（固定资产投资与本地区GDP的比例）是22%，高于东、中部的18%。这提示当时投资是向西部倾斜的。这也基本反映改革以前投资的分布情况。在改革期间东部地区投资率迅速提高，超过了西部。只是到20世纪90年代末实行西部大开发之后，西部投资率才又超过了东部，2002年更是达到了42%的历史高点（但规模只相当于东部的35%），可见投资在改革期间直到西部大开发之前是向东部倾斜的。这显然是导致东中西部区域经济差距扩大的重要原因。

表3　东中西部固定资产投资的变化（按当年价格，亿元）

	1980年	1985年	1990年	1995年	2000年	2002年
固定资产投资总额	911	2543	4517	20019	32918	43500
投资相对比例（东部＝100%）						
中部	61%	55%	45%	34%	38%	38.6%
西部	48%	36%	34%	26%	33%	35.2%
投资率（固定资产投资/当地GDP）						
东部	18%	29%	25%	38%	34%	35%
中部	18%	28%	20%	27%	28%	31%
西部	22%	30%	21%	30%	37%	42%

资料来源：国家统计局（1999，2003）投资比例和投资率使根据各省市区投资额计算。

为了搞清导致区域间投资率差距的原因，以下将对区域间不同类型的资本流动进行考察。这些计算受到数据准确度的影响，有的还需要借助于假设条件，误差是难以避免的。因此这里提供的只是非常粗略的估计。

（二）对国内跨地区资本流动总量的估计

这里我们对整个20世纪90年代国内跨地区资本流动总量进行估计。根据宏观经济学原理，各省的资本净流入（流出）应当等于投资与储蓄之差。我们以各省农业和非农业人口为权重计算了各省城乡居民储蓄率，并用它近似代表各省总储蓄率，从各省GDP推算出各省储蓄总额。以各省的国内固定资产投资总额减去储蓄总额，再扣除误差分配，就是近似的跨地区国内资本流动额。再加上外资投入，就反映出各地区净流入（流出）资本的总量。表4列出了按3个地区汇总的计算结果，并据此计算了资本净流入（流出）占各地区GDP的比重。

我们还采用另一种计算方法对上述结果进行验证。根据支出法GDP核算，各省的GDP可分解为最终消费C、资本形成I、货物与服务净出口X三项（这里的"净出口"应理解为"净出省"）。假定初始阶段某省的跨省贸易是平衡的（但该假设会带来误差），那么$X=0$，$C+I=\text{GDP}$。当发生资本净流入而其他条件不变时，$C+I>\text{GDP}$，$X<0$。此时资本形成中包含省外资本的流入，其值与X相等，符号相反。此时用X扣除对国外净出口后的负值可近似表示各省国内资本流入（或流出）的毛值。各省合计数不为0的部分为误差部分，进行分配和剔除后可近似得到各省国内资本流动净值。后一种方法的结果与前一结果有一定出入，但在总的资本流动方向上与前者相当一致，因此起到了互相验证的作用（结果从略）。按三个地区汇总的数据，两组结果关联显著，相关系数为0.841；OLS回归的t值为7.777，$R^2=0.708$。

表 4　跨地区资本流动总表(亿元)

	1991 年	1992 年	1993 年	1994 年	1995 年	1996 年	1997 年	1998 年	1999 年	2000 年
国内资本跨地区流动额										
东部	9	13	−151	−300	−408	−709	−586	−904	−595	−1227
中部	−121	−114	−153	−199	−332	−375	−681	−519	−939	−567
西部	112	101	303	499	740	1083	1267	1423	1534	1794
资本净流入(包括外资)合计										
东部	226	557	1175	2146	2261	2302	2652	2445	2373	1795
中部	−111	−73	−18	23	−50	−49	−285	−156	−628	−262
西部	121	122	418	699	897	1230	1478	1618	1686	1947
资本净流入比 GDP(%)										
东部	2.0	4.0	6.1	8.4	7.0	6.1	6.2	5.3	4.8	3.2
中部	−1.9	−1.1	−0.2	0.2	−0.3	−0.3	−1.4	−0.7	−2.8	−1.1
西部	3.0	2.6	7.1	9.1	9.5	10.0	10.8	11.0	11.0	11.7

资料来源:根据国家统计局(2001、1999)计算。

根据以上结果(以第一种方法为准),东部地区在20世纪90年代经历了国内资本净流出,多数年份有数百亿的规模,在2000年达到1200多亿元。但加上规模巨大的外商投资,东部一直是资本净流入,多数年份超过2000亿元。中部每年有几百亿元的资本净流出。加上外资后,也没有改变流出的格局。西部地区在20世纪90年代一直是资本净流入,后期突破了1000亿元(不包括外资)。加上外商投资,资本流动的格局变化不大,每年仅增加100多亿元。

(三)对跨地区资本流动的分解

以下从几个方面对跨地区资本流动进行分解,以考察它的构成。在国内资本方面,包括财政转移支付,银行信贷的转移,通过国内资本市场的资本流动,以及其他渠道(包括民间渠道)的资本流动。此外,还需要考虑外商投资。

财政资金在各地区间的转移支付缺乏完整的统计,现行财政支出统计中的"支援经济不发达地区支出"远没有包括全部的财政转移支付。在现行财政体制下,中央政府对地方政府有大量财政收入返还。它的分配不取决于中央财政从该省取得的税收,而在很大程度上取决于区域发展政策和历史分配格局的延续性,实际上执行了财政转移支付的功能。我们以各省市区财政支出与收入之差作为毛转移支付,扣除中央从各省取得的待返还收入,得到近似的净财政转移支付。

净财政转移支付在20世纪90年代始终是由东部向中西部(主要是西部)转移,由于财权下放,其力度逐渐减弱;但由于西部开发而在2000年显著回升,东部付出超过1000亿元,中西部分别收入近800亿元和200亿元(未包括中央直接投资)。

银行资金在地区间的转移可能通过以下途径实现:商业银行在下属分支行之间调拨资金、银行间的跨地区拆借等等。作者近似地用各省银行贷差代表累计资金流入(存差代表流出),在将全国存差(贷差)总额分配到各地区并作为不相关因素剔除后,推算出累计的银行资金跨地区流动。其年度增量就是当期的银行资金净转移。

银行资金转移在20世纪90年代的基本方向是由东部流向中西部,主要是流向中部(2000年除外),1999年规模超过1000亿元。这可能是因为中部地区国有企业较为集中,其中许多严重依赖银行贷款维持,吸纳了较多的资金,也产生了大量呆坏账。此外中部粮食主产区的国有粮食企业可能也占压了相当多的粮食收购资金。这说明银行资金的跨地区流动在20世纪90年代主要不是受市场引导,而是受政策和体制的牵制。

上述格局在2000年发生了变化,东部的净转移由负转正,而中部则相反。这看来与银行规避风险的政策有关。为避免不良贷款,各银行近年来实行了较审慎的信贷政策,减少了向高风险地区的投放。但同时,中西部地区中小企业融资难的问题也加剧了。

资本市场跨地区融资很难按来源进行划分。假定其来源基本上与各地区的GDP成比例,那么按来源划分和按去向划分的差额就近似等于跨地区融资。按此推算,在资本市场上的资本流动在20世纪90年代是由中西部流向东部,但只有几十亿元的流动规模,因此对地区差距的影响不大。

国内其他渠道的跨地区资本流动主要包括通过民间渠道的资本流动,也包括不通过地方财政的中央直接投资和不按分省统计的银行贷款在地区间的转移。这些方面缺乏数据,我们以国内跨地区资本流动总量减去通过财政、银行、资本市场三个渠道的资本流动,残差部分就是通过其他渠道的资本流动。该项资本流动,东部地区在整个20世纪90年代是流入区,中部是流出区(2000 年除外),规模在几百亿元到上千亿元不等;西部则在 20 世纪 90 年代前期为流出区,后期变成了流入区。由此可以推测,通过民间渠道的资本流动基本流向是从中西部到东部,但这个趋势在 20 世纪 90 年代末西部大开发时期被同样包括在“其他”项下的中央在中西部的直接投资等所抵消。

外商投资是各地资本投入的一项重要来源,在整个 20 世纪 90 年代,外资 85%以上都集中在东部地区,直到 2000 年也没有改变。按汇率折算,20 世纪 90 年代后期东部地区吸收的外资每年超过 3000 亿元,相当于东部地区 GDP 的 5%—8%。显然,外商投资的地区差异是导致 20 世纪 90 年代地区差距扩大的一个重要因素。根据武剑(2003)的分析,这是导致区域经济差距仅次于国内投资的地区差距(包括数量差距和效率差距)的次重要因素。

(四) 资本流动的变动趋向

综上所述,在整个 20 世纪 90 年代,市场主导的资本流动(包括外资、通过民间渠道和资本市场渠道的资本流动)和政府主导的资本流动(财政资金,某种意义上也包括银行信贷资金)呈两个不同的方向。前者在利润引导下主要流向东部地区。这种流动改善了资本的配置效率,带动了经济增长,但也扩大了地区差距。外资优惠政策的地区差别也对资本投向有影响。这个差别如果长期保持下去,不利于资源的优化配置,也不利于缩小地区差距。相反,政府主导的财政转移支付主要着眼于缩小地区差距,并受到以前财政分配格局惯性的影响,较多地照顾西部地区。西部大开发以来,转移支付增加较快,使西部的投资率超过了东部,2002 年达到了 42%的历史高点。东西部地区的增长率仍然存在明显差距。这说明减小地区差距主要不能依赖政府主导的资本转移。

至于银行信贷资金的分配，居主导地位的国有银行在一定程度上沿袭了首先满足国有企业资金需求的模式，政策性贷款更是直接服从政府的政策目标，使银行贷款在20世纪90年代更多地向中部地区倾斜，也在一定程度上照顾了西部。在过去，由于银行体系改革滞后，资金的使用效率很低并产生了大量不良信贷，银行资金在地区间的转移基本上无助于消除地区差距。在2000年已经出现了银行资金向东部转移的趋势。

由于市场导向的资本流动(包括外资在内)超过了政府导向的资本流动，地区间资本流动的整体趋势是向东部地区倾斜。这是导致地区差距扩大的关键原因。而市场导向的资本流动的决定因素是资本回报率的差别。

可以预见在不久的未来，上述资本流动格局将发生一定程度的变化。首先是地区间资本边际收益差距缩小的趋势。根据蔡昉、王德文(2003)的计算，在改革初期(1978年)，东西部资本的边际产值相差一倍以上，经过了20年东部地区的持续大量投资后，资本边际收益递减规律的作用已经使两者趋于接近。这在资本充分流动的条件下是必然趋势，它预示着资本在地区间的配置将逐渐趋于平衡，从而阻止地区差距的继续扩大。其次，随着西部大开发政策的实施，原来只给予一些东部地区的外资优惠政策已部分地扩大到中西部地区，在一定程度上加强了后者对外资的吸引力。第三，中西部地区的基础设施条件和投资环境也在改善。上述变化有利于缩小投资回报率的地区差距，从而逐渐改变市场导向的资本一边倒地流向东部的局面。此外，政府资金支持中西部地区的力度还将继续保持。这些因素的综合作用可能使地区差距不断扩大的趋势逐步得到遏制。

但是，实现上述转变还需要一个较长的过程。首先这取决于资本回报率的地区差别进一步缩小的速率，而后者又依赖于中西部地区投资环境的改善和投资效率的提高。其次还取决于一些不确定因素的影响，例如今后银行体制的改革方向。一方面，银行商业化和贷款利率市场化可能继续引导资金向东部地区流动；另一方面，如果银行业能够逐步形成多元竞争的局面，将产生一批地方性中小金融机构，这将有利于中西部地区中小企业融资而减缓资金向东部地区的流动。两者都将有利于提高中长期经济效益，特别是后一个因素将有利于缩小地区差距。

三、地区间的劳动力流动

经济学理论能够证明，在市场条件下，劳动力总是从边际劳动生产率低的地区流向高的地区，这有助于提高劳动力资源的利用率，缩小地区间的劳动报酬差距和人均GDP差距（姚枝仲，2003）。劳动力流动不但为流入地提供丰富的劳动力，使之保持较低的工资成本和较高的国际竞争力，同时还提高迁徙者和流出地的人均产出水平，改善资源配置状况。实证分析也发现，劳动力市场发育程度直接影响各地区的经济增长率（蔡昉、王德文、都阳、王美艳，2003）。下面将对跨地区劳动力流动的规模进行描述，并就其对地区经济差距的影响作一粗略估计。

（一）跨地区流动劳动力的规模

根据劳动和社会保障部以及国家统计局在全国6万多农户抽样调查基础上进行的推算（见2002年报告，以下简称劳动部），截至2000年，农村转移到非农产业的劳动力总数为1.13亿人，占农村劳动力总量的23.6%。其中在城镇就业的占65.8%。跨省流动劳动力（外出半年以上）约为2825万人，其中90%来自中西部（中部56%，西部34%）；82%流向东部地区，而且主要是流向城镇。农村劳动力在三个地区之间流动的矩阵由

表5列出。表中各列表示各地区的劳动力流出(按去向划分),各行表示各地区的劳动力流入(按来源划分)。

表5 农村劳动力跨地区流动2000年存量矩阵

	东部	中部	西部	总量
数量(万人)				
东部	212	1370	735	2317
中部	51	172	68	291
西部	20	40	155	215
总量	283	1582	958	2822
构成(%)				
东部	7.5	48.5	26.0	82.0
中部	1.8	6.1	2.4	10.3
西部	0.7	1.4	5.5	7.7
总量	10.0	56.0	34.0	100

资料来源:根据劳动部(2002)数据计算。

最主要的劳动力流入地是广东,占全国跨省流动就业的农民工总数的一半。其他主要有浙江、上海、北京、福建、江苏。这6个省市加起来占跨省农民工的3/4。主要的劳动力流出地有四川、安徽、湖南、河南、江西、广西、重庆等;它们占了跨省流动劳动力来源的77%。

为了验证以上数据的准确度,作者将1999年劳动部数据与中共中央政策研究室和农业部的全国固定跟踪调查数据进行了对比(两个样本互相独立;后者包括2万多农户)。根据两个样本推算总体,1999年农村劳动力跨省流动总量分别为2115万人和1894万人,相差10%。差别不太大,说明基本上可信。

应当说明,两个抽样调查都是通过入户方式进行的,不可能包括已经全家迁徙到其他地区的原农村住户,因此以上流动数据可能偏小。如果假定跨省流动的农村劳动力中有15%是举家搬迁，那么跨省流动的劳动力在2000年可能已达到3300万人。按同比例估计，从中西部流到东部的劳动力接近2500万人。

(二) 跨地区劳动力流动对产出的贡献

农村劳动力从中西部流向东部地区对经济带来了什么影响？以下进行简要的估计。第一步需要估计这些劳动力在流出地和流入地的边际产出。根据国家统计局的农村居民收入调查，2000年东、中、西三个地区农村居民人均纯收入（按各省算术平均值）分别为3476、2075、1632元。假定劳动回报占纯收入的50%，其余部分为资本和土地的报酬。再根据经济活动人口占总人口的比重将人均收入折算为劳动力的人均劳动报酬。考虑到外出劳动力以青壮年为主，将该报酬按1.2的系数进行调整。根据经济学理论，这个劳动报酬近似等于外出劳动力在原住地的边际产出水平。同样可以假定，外出劳动力在流入地的边际产出等于他们的工资水平。我们知道外来劳动力在流入地区的工资一般低于当地的平均工资。由于没有相关数据，作者采用各地区城镇集体所有制企业平均工资水平（这在各类企业中工资水平是最低的）来近似代表外来劳动力的工资水平。

表6列出了这些劳动力在东中西部地区边际产出的差异。2000年中西部农村劳动力的年边际产出分别只有1773元和1434元，而他们在东部城镇地区打工的边际产出达7837元，两者相差约5倍，平均每人多创造收入6224元。按2500万人计，中西部农村到东部打工的劳动者额外创造了约1556亿元的价值，大约相当于中西部农业增加值的18%（而他们只占中西部农村劳动力数量的8%）。

表6　流动劳动力在东中西部地区边际产出的差异

	农村劳动边际产出(元)	城镇劳动边际产出(元)	城乡边际产出之比
东部	2862	7837	2.74
中部	1773	4980	2.81
西部	1434	5902	4.12
东部城镇比中西部农村			4.86

资料来源:根据国家统计局(2001)数据计算。

地区间和城乡间的劳动力转移,当然也对输入地的就业状况产生一定的压力。不过,外来劳动力从事的工作大多数仍然是东部地区和城镇居民不愿意从事的脏、累、苦、低报酬的劳动,因此对当地就业的替代率显然远低于1∶1。他们填补了市场空缺、活跃了当地经济,对东部地区的经济增长作出了贡献。

(三)跨地区劳动力流动对缩小地区差距的贡献

劳动力流动缩小地区差距的作用主要发生在两个方面。首先,中西部低收入地区的劳动力外流,会缓和这些地区农村人口对土地的压力和就业压力。由于劳动边际报酬递减规律的作用,这些地区的劳动生产率会随劳动力数量的减少而提高,从而提高人均收入水平。在种植业这方面的作用更加突出,劳动力减少会提高人均耕地面积,有利于土地规模经营。根据姚枝仲的计算,1998年劳动报酬的变异系数C＝0.493,基尼系数Gini＝0.258。若没有劳动力流动,则C＝0.529,Gini＝0.272。劳动力流动使C降低了0.036,Gini降低了0.014。可见,尽管跨省流动的规模还小,如果同劳动力不流动的情况相比,区域收入差距还是明显缩小了。

另外,劳动力流动还为中西部地区带来了大量的汇款。

根据劳动部(2002)数据,2000年农村转移劳动力人均寄带回家庭的款额为4522元。推算总体,汇寄款总额达5128亿元,因此对流出地区农民收入的增长起了直接支撑作用。推算中西部跨省转移的农村劳动力汇款,当接近1000亿元。这相当于将5亿多中西部农村居民的人均纯收入水平提高了约10%。对那些相对贫困、外流劳动力多的区域来说,提高收入的作用尤其明显。③

(四) 跨地区劳动力流动的潜力

尽管跨地区流动的劳动者对经济作出了巨大贡献,但由于其对输入地就业的某种程度的竞争性,以及对城市基础设施和生活环境产生的压力,仍然频繁地受到输入地设置的行政性限制甚至歧视。与农村劳动力的巨大数量相比,目前跨地区劳动力流动的规模还小。除了广东省和少数大城市,其他较发达省份和城市吸纳的劳动力还比较有限。上述这些劳动力迁移带来的问题有些是被人为夸大了,有些则是可以通过改善服务和管理来解决的。事实上仅广东一个省就吸纳了全部跨省流动劳动力的一半,并没有带来严重的社会问题和高失业现象,相反这些源源不断的劳动力供应使得广东经济一直走在全国前列,而且在国际市场上保持了强大的产品竞争力。可见,如果未来出现几个类似广东的省份,将使劳动力的跨地区流动大大扩展,从而有效地减小地区间的收入差距。

妨碍劳动力流动的另一重要因素是我国城市化程度较低,服务业发展空间不足。我国目前仍有61%的人口居住在镇以下的农村,居住在50万人口以上城市的人口还不到全国人口的10%。这是改革前实行的城乡分割政策,和一段时期内实行的限制大中型城市发展政策的结果。现代化过程必然伴随着持续的城市化过程。这将为劳动力的流动提供更加广阔的空间。今后还需要进一步打破城乡壁垒，为劳动力流动提供必要的条件，完善职业培训和就业服务体系，改善城市基础设施建设和城市的市场环境，从而推进城乡一体化的发展。

四、人力资本的地区分布

根据新古典增长理论和内生增长理论，资本和劳动存量的变动会在短期内影响经济增长率（Solow，1956；Swan，1956），而人力资本存量的差异却有可能直接影响全要素生产率，从而影响长期的经济增长率（Romer，1986；Lucas，1988）。这就是说，其他条件相同时，人力资本存量较大的先进国家或地区有可能在长时期内保持相对较高的经济增长率。因此人力资本是影响地区差距长期趋势的因素。在研究资本和劳动对地区经济差距的影响时，我们应当侧重流量的分析；而在研究人力资本的影响时，则需要更加侧重对其存量差别的分析。

衡量人力资本的存量，有若干不同的角度。例如 Romer (1986)用从事研究和开发的科技人员数量来表示人力资本，而 Lucas(1988)用劳动者的受教育程度来表示人力资本。以下我们使用现有的数据，从不同角度对各地区的人力资本存量进行描述。

（一）劳动者的受教育程度及教育的规模

表 7 列出了 1996—1999 年期间分地区从业人员的平均受教育年限。1999 年，东部地区劳动者的平均受教育年限为 8.1 年，中部是 7.7 年，西部是 6.9 年，东西相差 1.2 年；而且在 1996—1999 年间两地区差距扩大了。关于人力资本的跨地区流动我们没有准确的数据，但是经验观察说明受过高等教育者有从中西部向东部流动的明显趋向。

表7　从业人员平均受教育年限(年)

	1996年	1997年	1998年	1999年
东部	7.64	7.89	7.92	8.10
中部	7.49	7.73	7.70	7.72
西部	6.64	6.77	6.81	6.90
西部与东部之差	1.00	1.12	1.11	1.20

注:受教育年限是根据各不同学历的从业人员人数加权平均推算的。三个地区的平均数分别是根据各省平均数加权计算的。

资料来源:各年《中国统计年鉴》。

我们还可以用下列指标衡量东中西部地区教育规模或教育能力的相对差别:在校学生数占人口的比例、教职工人数占人口的比例、教育经费占GDP的比例、按人口平均的教育经费等等(计算结果从略)。这些指标都反映三个地区的相对教育规模有一定差距,其程度与从业人员的受教育程度差距基本一致(西部大约是东部的62%—88%)。但特别需要指出的是,西部中学教育普及率低于东部,即使差距不大(按在校学生占人口比例,西部为东部的88%),持续下去将严重影响西部地区的人力素质。

(二) 专业技术人员和研究开发经费

关于各地区专业技术人员数量目前没有全社会范围的统计,我们只能近似地使用国有企事业单位专业技术人员数。目前非国有经济部门在研发和教育方面的发展还很有限,因此上述指标能够大致反映地区间的差别。按专业技术人员在人口中的比例,东中西部地区间的分配还是相对平衡的,西部相当于东部的91%。但是按研发经费支出占GDP的比例看,差距较大。在东部,研发经费占GDP的1.1%,而中西部分别只有0.6%和0.8%(国家统计局,2002)。

（三）科技成果的市场化

如果从科技成果的角度来看地区差距，差别就远远超过了上面这些指标所反映的程度。按每万名专业技术人员申请专利件数，东部为 140 件，中部和西部只有 39 和 35 件，西部相当于东部的 25％（国家统计局，2002）。如果看平均每名专业技术人员的技术市场成交额，中西部也仅相当于东部的 31％和 29％，而且这个差距似乎还在扩大（表 8）。

表 8　按专业技术人员数平均的技术市场成交额（元/人）

	1995 年	1998 年	2000 年
东部	2212	3732	5883
中部	931	1479	1827
西部	805	1139	1696
西部与东部之比（％）	36.4％	30.5％	28.8％

资料来源：国家统计局（各年份）。

以上情况说明，尽管以教育程度和专业技术人员来衡量，东西部之间的人力资本存量都有一定的差距，但更为突出的差距是中西部地区科技成果向市场转化的程度太低，在人力资本的产出率方面无法与东部竞争。这显然是制约中西部技术进步和经济发展的一个关键因素。

五、各地区市场化程度的差异

影响地区差距的因素，除了生产要素在地区间的配置和流动，还有制度和政策因素。我国经济改革期间，经济增长显著加快，最主要的推动力就是中国经济从计划体制转向市场体制的改革。但是市场化的进程在各地差别仍然很大。根据国民经济研究所市场化指数课题使用25项客观指标进行度量的结果，东部沿海地区的市场化程度远远超过中部和西部地区（樊纲、王小鲁、朱恒鹏，2003）。各省、自治区、直辖市2000年的市场化指数（记分区间0—10分），按东中西3个地区分组平均，分别为7.16、5.47、4.71。这反映出绝大部分东部省份不仅经济发展程度比较高，而且在市场化进程中也走在中西部前面。中西部省份市场化程度与东部差距较大的方面主要是非国有经济的发展和要素市场的发育程度，但在政府与市场的关系、产品市场发育、市场中介组织和法律制度环境等方面也都存在明显差距（见表9）。

表9　各地区市场化指数的平均得分

	政府与市场的关系	非国有经济的发展	产品市场的发育程度	要素市场的发育程度	市场中介组织和法律制度环境
平均	6.05	5.34	7.44	3.60	5.26
东部	7.52	7.73	8.80	5.64	6.44
中部	5.77	4.41	7.25	2.75	4.94
西部	4.78	3.63	6.21	2.19	4.31
东西差距	2.74	4.10	2.59	3.45	2.13

资料来源：根据樊纲、王小鲁、朱恒鹏（2003）计算。

樊纲和陈渝的研究进一步发现，各省市场化程度对全要素生产率（TFP）的提高有明显的贡献。他们使用国民经济研究所的分省市场化指数和技术进步变量（用技术发明专利表示）对各省的TFP进行回归，两个解释变量在不同模型中都有显著的正效应。这说明市场化程度和技术进步是两个影响全要素生产率、从而影响经济增长率的重要指标。他们指出，TFP可以通过下面5个方面的改革来提高：(1)精简政府机构和转变政府职能以减少其对资源配置的直接干预，提高市场配置资源的比重，发挥企业作为市场主体的作用;(2)鼓励非国有部门的发展;(3)大力培育产品市场,提高市场在价格决定中的作用,减少商品市场上的地区贸易壁垒;(4)促进要素市场的发育,鼓励银行部门的竞争,加速信贷资金分配的市场化,吸引更多的外国直接投资,提高劳动力的流动性;(5)改善法律制度环境以更好地保护产权和保证合同的履行,提高市场中介组织(如律师事务所、会计师事务所和独立审计机构等)的质量和数量。

这一发现证实,地区间市场化程度的差异是导致地区间经济差距的一个重要因素。在改革期间,中西部地区与东部地区之间差距的扩大,与前者在市场化改革中相对滞后有密切关系。因此,加速推进欠发达地区的市场化改革进程,对于缩小地区间的经济差距将有重要的意义。

六、城市化和农村工业化发展水平的区域差异

本文前面曾指出,东西部的收入差距突出表现在东西部农村居民收入的差距。而影响农村居民收入的关键在于大量农村剩余劳动力能否尽快地向城乡非农产业转移。因此欠发达地区的城市化和农村工业化对于缩小地区差距具有非常重要的意义。

在农村工业化方面,中西部的发展程度远低于东部。以乡镇企业从业人数占农村从业人数的比例衡量,2000 年东部平均为 36.8%,中部 24.2%,西部只有 18.9%,东西部相差一半(国家统计局,2002)。研究还发现,各省乡镇企业的发展水平与农村人均收入水平之间有显著的关联,说明乡镇企业的发展对提高农村居民收入起了重要作用(王小鲁,2003)。据国家统计局数据,2002 年全国农村居民人均工资性收入为 840 元,而西部 12 省(区、市)平均仅为 483 元。不难看出,中西部地区农村工

业化程度落后是导致地区经济差距的一个重要因素。

但这种落后并不仅仅意味着时间上的滞后。今天中西部已经不太可能简单重复东部走过的农村工业化道路。改革初期，市场供给存在大量空缺，而占主导地位的国有企业因为体制障碍而缺乏竞争力，不能适应市场的需要，使乡镇企业凭借较低的劳动力成本和市场导向的优势占领市场。今天随着市场竞争的加剧，消费者对产品质量、技术含量、品牌、相关服务的要求越来越高，而乡镇企业在人力资本、技术、管理、基础设施、企业布局等方面的先天劣势越来越制约着它们的发展。它们已经很难再像过去那样以两位数的增长率扩展。

城市经济在基础设施、人力资本和技术供应、市场集中度、服务业发展空间等方面都给现代产业发展提供了必不可少的条件。经济改革期间，城市化发展速度有了明显的加快。但中西部地区目前在城市化方面发展同样滞后，而且与东部的差距在继续扩大。从1982年到2000年，东部城镇化率上升了22个百分点，西部只上升了12个百分点(见表10)。

表10 各地区城镇化率的变化

	城镇化率(城镇人口/总人口,%)		
	1982年	2000年	变动率
东部	24.1	46.1	22.0
中部	19.9	33.0	13.1
西部	16.6	28.7	12.1

数据来源:根据国家统计局(1999a, 2001b)计算。

城市化水平的差距还集中地反映在大中型城市不足。在我国，规模在50万人口以上的城市(按市区非农业人口计)只有92座，只容纳了全国9.6%的人口。在这方面东西部差距更大。

在东部，50 万人口以上的城市有 42 座，人口有 6500 万，占东部人口的 13.3%；而西部只有 14 座，人口还不到 2000 万，只占西部人口的 5.6%。

模型分析发现，东西部城市化的差距可以解释 0.5 个百分点的经济增长率差距(王小鲁，2003)。因此目前东西部地区差距扩大的趋势，部分源于城市化水平的差距。西部的发展，在很大程度上要靠振兴城市经济来带动。

七、主要结论

本文分别考察了影响地区经济差距的各主要因素，包括资本、人力资本和劳动力在各地区间的流动和配置状况、制度变革(主要是市场化进程)在各地区间的差异、结构变动(城市化是最主要的因素)对地区经济差距的影响。这些因素在过去若干年中主导了地区间的相对变动趋势。主要结论可概括如下：

(1) 在过去 20 年的经济改革期间，市场导向的外商直接投资以及民间资本流动使资金大量流向东部，加速了东部地区的经济增长，同时也扩大了地区差距。财政和银行资金的流向基本不受市场调节，主要向中西部转移。但由于外资数量巨大，东部地区仍然有大量的资本净流入。

(2) 东部持续的资本流入同时也在逐渐缩小东西部的资本边际生产率差距。这将在未来减弱民间资本从中西部向东部流动的趋势，并改变外资一边倒地向东部倾斜的投资格局，从而减少东部和中西部之间的增长率差距，减缓地区间人均收入差距逐渐扩大的趋势。西部大开发战略的实施，给这种转变创造了一定的条件。不过，这个转变将是一个缓慢的过程。

(3) 政府转移支付有助于改善中西部软硬基础设施条件，

但缩小地区差距主要不能依赖政府主导的资金转移，而要着眼于提高效率，改善投资环境。

(4) 东部地区长期以来享受的外资优惠政策，是导致地区间经济差距的一个原因。长期保持区域性的优惠政策不利于资源在地区间的优化配置和缩小地区差距，应当逐步向全国统一的国民待遇靠拢。

(5) 推进银行业的改革，发展区域性金融机构，改善中小企业特别是小企业的融资环境，从而提高资本使用效率和就业水平，也将对中西部地区的发展产生重要的作用。

(6) 受收入和就业机会差距的吸引，农村劳动力有从中西部向东部地区流动的趋势，这有利于缩小地区间人均收入的差距、同时也有利于提高效率。由于区域间劳动的边际生产率差距仍然很大，这方面还有巨大的潜力，需要进一步消除障碍，提供更完善的服务和培训，发挥劳动力流动的潜力。

(7) 东部与中西部之间在人力资本存量方面存在差距。但更重要的差距在于中西部科技成果市场化程度很低，严重影响了人力资本的生产率。因此改革科研体制，促进科技成果市场化、产业化，对提高中西部地区的生产率和缩小地区差距有重要意义。

(8) 中西部地区的经济增长率与东部的差距在很大程度上是由于要素生产率低。而这主要取决于技术进步和市场化程度的差异。在市场化方面，东西部差距明显，尤其是在非国有经济的发展和要素市场发育方面差距非常突出。这是制约中西部地区经济发展的一个关键因素。进一步转变政府职能，鼓励非国有企业发展，促进要素市场发育，改善法律制度环境等将对中西部的发展起到重要作用。

(9) 东西部地区间发展程度差异的另一个重要原因是西部地区城市化程度低。在市场导向的基础上推进城市化发展将是西部发展的一个推动力。但这需要合理规划,全局统筹,发挥市场机制的作用,防止不顾条件的一哄而上。

概括来说,我国东部沿海地区和中西部内陆地区之间,在经济发展水平方面,无论是绝对差距还是相对差距都还在继续扩大。这主要是由于生产率的差别以及由此引起的资本流动所导致。但资本的持续流动已经使得地区间资本生产率的差距出现了缩小的趋势。这个趋势,加上西部大开发战略的实施,可能在未来逐步改变资本流动的格局,使之较为有利于中西部的发展。但是生产率的地区差距还没有出现缩小的趋势,说明要缩小区域差距还要经历一个相当长期的过程。在这个过程中,迫切需要尽快改善中西部地区投资的软硬环境,包括推进市场化改革,促进非国有经济发展,提高企业管理水平和政府服务水平,改革科技开发体制,以及加速城市化建设的步伐。这些将推进中西部的发展步伐,促使缩小区域差距的目标尽早实现。

注　释

① 在本文中东部地区包括京、津、冀、辽、沪、江、浙、闽、鲁、粤、琼11省市;中部包括晋、吉、黑、皖、赣、豫、鄂、湘8省;西部包括蒙、桂、渝、川、黔、云、藏、陕、甘、青、宁、疆12省区。

② 根据某些证据,各地区经济增长数据存在不同程度的失真(主要是偏高)的现象(Maddison, 1998;孟连、王小鲁,2000)。这种情况在中西部可能比东部更严重些。因此东中西部实际经济增长率的差距可能会比表中两种方法所反映出的更大些。

③ 上述计算仅指跨东中西地区和跨省劳动力流动,未包括省内劳动力流动部分。后一部分目前占大多数。

参考文献

蔡昉、都阳,2000:《中国地区经济增长的趋同与差异》,《经济研究》第

10期。

蔡昉、王德文,2003:"中国地区比较优势:差异、变化及其对地区差距的影响",工作论文。

蔡昉、王德文、都阳、王美艳,2002:《技术效率、配置效率与劳动力市场扭曲——解释经济增长差异的制度因素》,工作论文。

都阳、王美艳,2003:《人力资本投资及其对中国地区差距的影响》,工作论文。

樊纲、陈渝,2003:《中国的地区差异:体制改革、技术进步与全要素生产率的相关性分析》,工作论文。

樊纲、王小鲁、朱恒鹏,2003:《中国分省市场化指数——各地区市场化相对进程报告(2001)》,经济科学出版社。

国家统计局,不同年份:《中国统计年鉴》,中国统计出版社。

国家统计局,1999:《新中国50年统计资料汇编》,中国统计出版社。

国家统计局,2001:《中国城市统计年鉴》,中国统计出版社。

郭金龙、王宏伟,2003:《区域间资本流动与区域经济差距》,工作论文。

劳动和社会保障部就业培训司、国家统计局农村调查总队,2002:《2000年中国农村劳动力就业及流动状况》,劳动与社会保障部"中国劳动力市场"网,http://www.lm.gov.cn/。

孟连、王小鲁,2000:《对中国经济增长统计数据可信度的估计》,《经济研究》第10期。

中国金融年鉴编辑部,2001:《中国金融年鉴》,中国金融年鉴编辑部出版。

王小鲁,2003:《农村工业化和城市化在区域发展中的作用》,工作论文。

武剑:2003:《外国直接投资的区域分布及其经济效应》,工作论文。

姚枝仲,2003:《劳动力流动与地区差距》,工作论文。

Barro, R. and X. Sala-i-Martin, 1995, Economic Growth, McGraw-Hill, London.

Lucas, R. E., 1988, "On the Mechanics of Economic Development", *Journal of Monetary Economics*, 22, 3—42.

Maddison, A., 1998, *Chinese Economic Performance in the Long Run*, OECD publication, France.

Romer, P. M., 1986, "Increasing Returns and Long-run Growth", *Journal of Political Economy*, 94, 1002—37.

Solow, R. M., 1956, "A Contribution to the Theory of Economic Growth", *Quarterly Journal of Economics*, 70, February, 65—94.

Swan, T. W., 1956, "Economic Growth and Capital Accumulation", *Economic Record*, 32, 334—61.

（原载《经济研究》2004 年第 1 期）

市场一体化、地区专业化与产业集聚趋势*

——兼谈对地区差距的影响

范剑勇

（浙江工商大学经济学院）

一、引　　言

在保持经济可持续发展的过程中，中国经济面临着一系列巨大的问题和挑战，其中之一便是如何遏制日益扩大的东西部地区差距。对如何解决地区差距扩大问题，多数学者认为，乡镇企业发展、沿海偏向的对外开放政策、外国直接投资、地方自主性增强或投资政策的倾斜、人力资本，以及包括交通在内的基础设施的地区差异等因素，是导致地区差距扩大的原因。①但是，大多数研究都是从新古典增长理论出发，无法解决生产函数（$Y = AF(K, L)$）中代表技术进步的内部机制，而且它的微观基础是建立在规模报酬不变的假定之上，因而无法解释产业在空间上的集聚。这一先天性的缺陷致使多数研究无法找到产业集聚和地区差距扩大的真正机制，也就没有办法提出正确的、切

* 本文得到国家社会科学基金（项目批准号03BJY009）资助，王进教授、宋铮博士、陆铭博士、张吉鹏博士等对本文初稿提出了有益的评议，刘小寒、石灵云两位同学计算了部分数据，特此感谢！

实可行的政策建议。

传统的新古典增长理论或比较优势理论为我们分析现实贸易格局提供了一个参照系。但是,却无法解释现实经济世界中的许多现象,如产业集聚、地区间的要素价格不均等、发达国家间的贸易流量远远大于发达国家与发展中国家的贸易流量等。为此,本文放弃这些传统的分析框架,转而在以报酬递增和存在运输成本为假设前提的新经济地理学基本框架中来分析地区间市场一体化引致的地区专业化与产业集聚的变化趋势。②

已有研究显示,改革以来中国整体上发生了产业在空间上的转移与集聚,而地区差距扩大与产业集聚有密切关系。地区差距扩大的推动力在1995年以前表现为以第二产业高份额为主的结构效应,而在1995年以后转变为结构效应与以产业集聚为主的集中效应并重。③以人口密度为衡量指标的本地市场规模、中西部地区农村劳动力向沿海地区转移和外商直接投资涌入东部沿海地区是解释产业在东部沿海地区集聚的重要因素。④同时,产业在东部沿海地区的集聚持续地吸引了中西部农村劳动力的流入,反过来又进一步推动了集聚优势在东部沿海地区的循环累积。⑤本文的研究则进一步表明,地区差距持续扩大突出表现在产业集聚的整体性累积,因此深入探讨这种集聚背后的机制是解决地区差距扩大问题的基础性研究工作。

同时,从地区市场一体化与地区专业化研究成果看,存在以下主要贡献和争论。陈东琪与银温泉、吴敬琏分别从制度条件、财政分权与分税制的实施角度就地方市场分割的成因、危害、表现形式等方面作了详细的阐述。⑥另外,国外学者对国内市场一体化研究存在着正反两方面意见。一是认为国内商品市场处于越来越严重的分割状态,以 Young 和 Poncet 为代表⑦,Poncet 甚至认为如果将当前省际间的贸易壁垒折算成隐含的关税率来看,1987 年和 1997 年的关税分别达到 35%和 46%,这一水平已达到当前欧盟内部各国之间的关税水平;二是以 Naughton 和 Bai 等为代表[⑧],认为国内市场一体化水平已有提高,其中 Naughton 通过 1992 年的投入产出表,分析 1987 年和 1992 年各省制造业产品的贸易流量在这一期间有明显的提高,从而表现出国内市场一体化水平的提高,Bai 等发现 1985—1997 年的各省制造业两位数水平上的行业空间基尼系数呈上升趋势,表明国内市场的一体化水平已有提高。另外有必要述及的是,与本文实证研究结论部分相似的是,赵伟认为在改革以前和初期中国几乎不存在区际贸易[⑨],但存在人为计划安排下的区际分工;在 1978 年以后中国政府强调对外开放甚于对内开放,导致中国在国际分工中的地位迅速确立,而国内区际贸易的局限使得地方重复建设现象普遍。

需要事先说明的是,根据自然条件和体制转轨差异,我们将中国(除港澳台地区)分为六大区域,分别为直辖市、东部沿海地区、东北三省、中部地区、西北地区与西南地区。[⑩]同时,除非特别说明,本文应用的数据取自第二次工业普查资料中 1980 年各省制造业两位数行业的从业人员数、第二次全国基本单位普查资料中 2001 年各省制造业两位数行业的从业人员数。由于 1980 年全国基本没有跨区域的农村劳动力流动,2001 年基本单位普查资料调查的从业人员数又涵盖了农村劳动力流动的部分,因此我们认为跨越 21 年各省的行业从业人员数可以衡量各地区制造业发展变化的真实情况。

本文的结构如下:第二部分为分析市场一体化与地区专业化、产业集聚的关系提供一个简单的理论框架,第三部分实证分析改革 21 年来地区专业化水平的变化情况,第四部分计算分析了同期制造业的产业集聚变化状况,第五部分根据上述计算结果并结合国际经验作进一步的讨论，第六部分是结论。

二、分 析 框 架

进入正式论述之前，我们不妨先从传统新古典理论来回顾市场一体化与地区专业化、产业集聚之间的关系。在这一理论框架下，李嘉图模型揭示的是在完全一体化条件下各国专业化生产与产业集聚的贸易格局，即各国专门生产自己机会成本最低的产品，从而实现完全专业化和产业集聚，它与各产业相互之间的上下游联系、运输成本大小没有直接关系。这是一种简单的一体化与产业分布的关系，即只要是在完全一体化条件下，各地区就有可能根据机会成本高低选择适合自己的产业进行专业化生产。在赫克歇尔—俄林模型中，各国之间的贸易流量实际上是取决于各自的资源禀赋差异，即进口含自己稀缺要素的产品而出口自己富含要素的产品，从而通过商品的流动达到两国之间的要素报酬均等。在这种情况下，市场一体化虽是地区专业化的前提条件，但两者没有必然的联系，因为地区有选择的专业化是由各地区要素禀赋差异决定的，而不是市场一体化决定国家之间的分工格局。

新经济地理学主要的两个假定是：垄断竞争的市场结构与制造业产品跨地区销售具有运输成本。新经济地理学认为制造业产品具有差异性，其差异性大小由产品间的替代弹性σ表示，σ越小，则产品差异性越大，制造业产品的种类数越多。垄断竞争市场结构规定了规模报酬递增是在单个厂商水平层次上的，这一内生的厂商水平的规模报酬递增特性决定了某一制造业产品的生产只能由一家垄断厂商或少数厂商来完成，因为随着单个厂商规模的扩大，产品的平均成本和售价降低，直至厂商经济利润为零和打败其他竞争对手为止；同时，一个地区内制造业产品的种类数与既定地区内的制造业劳动力数量成正比，而制造业种类数恰恰是一个地区市场规模效应的表现，因此，市场规模效应与地区内制造业从业人员数量有紧密的联系。⑪

新经济地理学另一个重要的假定是任何制造业产品跨地区销售都具有运输成本。这一运输成本是广义的，它既包括看得见的运输网络形成的有形运输成本，也包括地方保护引起的贸易壁垒等因素，因此运输成本不但是市场一体化的反义，而且对地区专业化、产业集聚来说始终是外生的。从直观上看，制造业之间有上下游联系的产业如果集聚在一起，则能减小中间投入品的在途损耗、缩小运输成本，从而降低中间投入品的价格，由此导致厂商有内在的冲动集聚在同一区域内共同分工协作，这种产生集聚效应的力量我们称作"价格效应"或"制造业前向联系"。另一方面，厂商具有内在冲动以集聚在一起生产，形成产业集群，各专业化分工的工人也集聚在同一区域内，产品种类数增多、市场规模扩大；制造业产品从出厂到消费者手中，运输成本降低，工人的名义、实际工资均高于其他非产业集聚区，非产业集聚区的劳动力受产业集聚区的高工资诱惑，也向产业集聚区内迁移，这一引起产业集聚的力量被称为"市场规模效应"(home market effect)或"制造业后向联系"。由此可见，制造业后向联系使新进入的边际制造业厂商总是选择市场规模效应大的地区进行投资设厂。因此从理论上讲，产业集聚背后的两种力量分别是"制造业的前向联系"和"制造业的后向联系"。⑫

报酬递增与运输成本结合起来，制造业厂商总是选择最接近于大市场空间的某一点进行制成品生产，当许多厂商都有相同的决策时⑬，"空间外部性"或称"产业集聚的正外部性"就被创造出来了。在这种情况下，由运输成本引起的产业集聚向心力导致一个具有初步制造业优势的地区可以通过累积循环机制使得这一优势逐渐放大和巩固，直到别的地区制造业逐渐消失，这时产业分布就呈现出“制造业中心—农业外围”格局。几乎所有的产业都集中在制造业中心地带，这一地区的产业平均集中率、制造业中心值、地区间专业化指数都处于极高的水平。[14]因此，伴随着运输成本的最初降低，即一体化水平从低水平向中级水平跨越，地区的产业集聚现象发生，地区差距扩大、极化效应开始显现。

随着地区间的一体化进一步提高，地区的产业集聚状况将发生显著变化，此时极化效应弱化，扩散效应开始显现。因为在这一情况下，产业集聚到一定程度后产生的诸如非贸易品价格居高不下、环境污染等拥挤成本，往往超过了引向集聚的向心力，部分技术含量低、劳动密集型产业将不得不率先从原制造业中心向周边地区转移，而原制造业中心可能会衰落，或者发展成为技术或资本密集型产业中心，或者纯粹成为技术创新或者贸易、金融服务等中心。因此，可以想象此时地区之间实现了产业梯度转移和分工协作。

如果将地区间市场一体化水平推进到一个极致的情况，即达到完全一体化的理想状况。此时地区专业化分工是根据各自的要素禀赋差异(即要素价格差异)来选择生产，真正实现了“你有我无、我有你无”的完全专业化分工格局。

我们可以将上述思想用图1来表示。

具体来讲，假设一国存在资源禀赋完全一样的两个地区，同时又没有发生国际贸易：

(1) 在地区间一体化水平很低的情况下，两地区没有发生贸易往来，生产都处于自给自足状况，地区产业平均集中率相

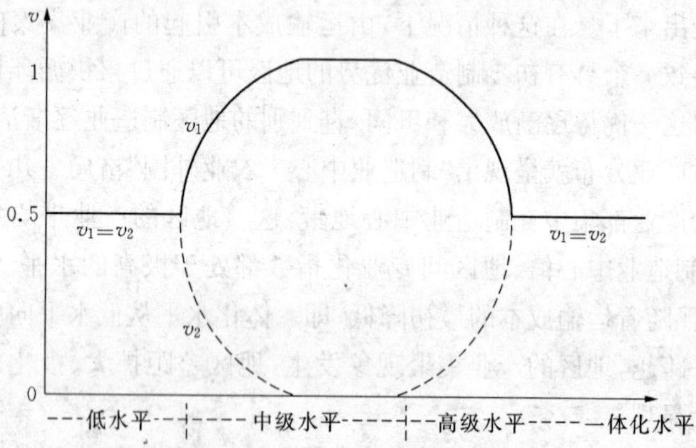

图 1　地区一体化水平增强对产业集聚的影响

等（$v_1 = v_2$），地区间的产业结构没有差异，地区间专业化指数为 0。

（2）当一体化水平从低水平向中级水平推进时，由于历史的偶然因素使得某一地区的制造业具有初步优势，则这一地区将通过吸收另一地区的要素而使制造业优势逐渐扩大，并通过累积循环机制，最终出现两地区的"制造业中心—农业外围"产业布局；在这一过程中，地区 1 逐渐成为制造业中心（v_1 逐渐趋向于 1），而地区 2 的制造业逐步被掏空和边缘化（v_2 趋向于 0），地区 1 的产业平均集中率上升，衡量地区间的产业结构差异水平的地区专业化指数上升。

（3）当地区间一体化水平从中级水平向高级水平推进时，原制造业中心将出现产业的外移，原农业外围地区接受了转移过来的产业，开始实现工业化起飞并与原制造业中心实现有效的产业分工协作。此时，地区 1 的产业集中率、地区专业化水平都有所下降，地区专业化生产的内容取决于地区间的要素价格差异。如果两个地区原先资源禀赋相同，则两地区的制造业平均集中率重新趋于相等（$v_1 = v_2$）。

本部分关注的重点是地区间的一体化增强了对产业的地区分工与集聚的影响，这对中国区域经济的协调发展具有重要的启示意义。在改革开放初期，由于历史的因素使得各地区基本处于一种自给自足的状况，制造业的集中程度、地区专业化水平都较低；而在市场化改革不断取得进展后的今天，尽管存在种种地方市场分割引起的非一体化因素，但随着市场在资源配置中主导地位的确立，各种资源纷纷向效率高的部门和地区流动，从而地区专业化水平和制造业的空间集中率不断提高，同时地区差距也持续扩大。

三、地区专业化水平变化情况

地区专业化水平，又称地区间的产业结构差异程度，本文用以衡量的指标是地区相对专业化指数、地区间专业化指数，分别用以下两个公式表示：

$$K_i = \sum_k \left| s_i^k - \bar{s}_i^k \right| \text{，其中 } \bar{s}_i^k = \frac{\sum_{j \neq i} E_i^k}{\sum_k \sum_{j \neq i} E_i^k} \tag{1}$$

$$K_{ij} = \sum_k \left| s_i^k - s_j^k \right| \tag{2}$$

其中，i、j、k 分别为地区 i、地区 j、行业 k，E_i^k 为地区 i 行业 k 的从业人员数，s_i^k 等于 $E_i^k / \sum_k E_i^k$。(1)式表示地区相对专业化指数，即某一地区各行业的专业化系数与全国其余地区相应行业的专业化系数差的绝对值之和，测度的是第 i 地区与其余地区平均水平的产业结构差异程度，或称第 i 地区的专业化程度。(2)式表示地区间专业化指数，直接衡量的是两个地区间产业结构的差异程度，取值范围为0—2，数值越大代表两地区的产业结构差异越强。[15]地区相对专业化指数与地区间专业化指数是从两个不同角度描述地区间的产业结构差异程度，其作用可以相得益彰。同时，从(1)式和(2)式来看，在制造业两位数水平上，地区i专业化指数在下述情况下应该引起注意：地区i的专业化指数处于较高水平，有可能是地区i的确实现了与别的地区较大差异的专业化生产，即"我有你无、我无你有"格局；但也有可能是地区i集聚了所有产业，而别的地区一无所有。

图2是根据(1)式计算出的1980年与2001年各主要地区相对专业化指数。图2显示，2001年的地区专业化指数比1980年有了显著的提高，从1980年均值为0.216、标准偏差为0.051的范围提高到2001年的均值为0.422、标准偏差为0.062的范围。因此，从地区的专业化指数提高这一指标上反过来推测，改革以来地区间的一体化水平已有较大的提高。[16]但是单从图上我们无法区分地区的专业化指数提高是由于所有产业都集中到了少数地区，还是各地区实现了有差异的产业结构，也就是说，我们还无法判断2001年是处于图1中倒U形曲线的前半段还是后半段。另外，图2还显示，2001年东部沿海地区与西南地

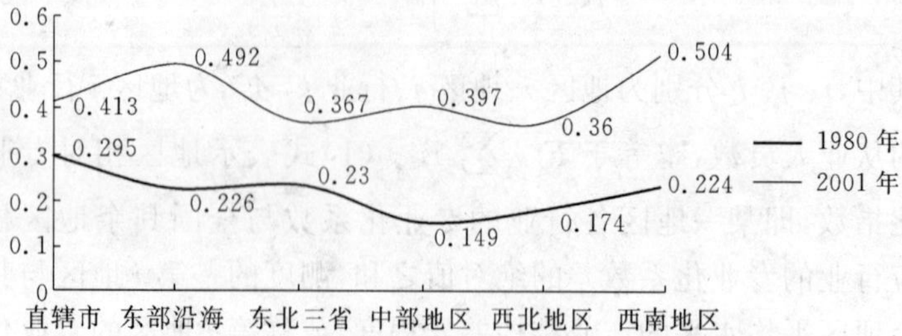

图2　1980年、2001年各地区相对专业化指数比较

区的地区专业化指数都处于0.49以上的最高水平，而这两个地区恰恰是制造业最为发达和最不发达的地区，因此我们初步推测中国绝大多数制造业都集中在东部沿海地区。这一推测从以下证据中得到了印证：2001年地区专业化指数最高（在0.60以上）的省份是广东、海南、山西、西藏、青海、宁夏、新疆、贵州、云南，可以看到除了广东以外[17]，其余省份都是全国制造业最不发达地区和在地理上属于"老、少、边"地区。因此，改革以来中国的制造业极有可能都已转移或正在转移到东部沿海地区，即处于图1中的倒U形曲线的前半段。

根据(2)式我们得到表1的计算结果。从两个时间横截面看，两位数行业的地区间平均专业化水平是上升的，从1980年的0.287上升到2001年的0.455[18]，这也证实了Naughton和Bai等人所言的改革二十多年来地区间的市场一体化水平是提高的。但我们还无法确切区别两位数行业地区专业化指数上升的两种子情况，因此，我们还必须深入到各个省份或各主要地区的层面上了解各地区间的专业化指数（见表1）。

表1　1980年、2001年制造业两位数的地区间专业化指数比较

	直辖市	东部沿海	东北三省	中部地区	西北地区	西南地区	平均水平
1980年							
直辖市	0.000	0.332	0.371	0.325	0.357	0.395	0.356
东部沿海	0.332	0.000	0.327	0.205	0.295	0.335	0.299
东北三省	0.371	0.327	0.000	0.244	0.214	0.183	0.268
中部地区	0.325	0.205	0.244	0.000	0.191	0.212	0.235
西北地区	0.357	0.295	0.214	0.191	0.000	0.187	0.249
西南地区	0.395	0.335	0.183	0.212	0.187	0.000	0.262
全国							0.287

（续表）

	直辖市	东部沿海	东北三省	中部地区	西北地区	西南地区	平均水平
2001 年							
直辖市	0.000	0.383	0.479	0.631	0.619	0.665	0.555
东部沿海	0.383	0.000	0.557	0.549	0.577	0.674	0.548
东北三省	0.479	0.557	0.000	0.354	0.355	0.302	0.409
中部地区	0.631	0.549	0.354	0.000	0.163	0.278	0.395
西北地区	0.619	0.577	0.355	0.163	0.000	0.242	0.391
西南地区	0.665	0.674	0.302	0.278	0.242	0.000	0.432
全　　国							0.455

1980 年，地区间专业化指数有以下几个特点需要把握：(1)直辖市的平均专业化水平(0.356)显著高于其他地区，说明改革初期直辖市的制造业领先于其他地区；而直辖市又与东北三省、西南地区的产业结构差异最大，分别达到 0.371 和 0.395，说明直辖市的产业结构可能更偏重于轻工业，东北三省、西南地区主要侧重于重工业。(2)东部沿海地区的平均专业化水平(0.299)仅略高于除直辖市以外的地区，显示出改革初期由于长期以来的计划经济体制，除直辖市以外的各地区基本都处于自给自足的状态，地区间的市场一体化水平低，地区间的产业结构变异程度小。(3)东北三省、中部、西北与西南这四个地区间的产业结构较为类似，它们之间的专业化指数都在 0.183—0.244 之间小幅波动。

2001 年，地区间的产业结构和改革初期相比发生了较大的变化。除了整体上地区间的产业结构发生变化以外，直辖市、东部沿海地区与其余地区的产业结构差异凸现出来，平均专业化水平分别达到 0.555 与 0.548，其中直辖市与中部地区、西北地区、西南地区的结构差异均在 0.62 以上，东部沿海地区与中部地区、西北地区、西南地区的结构差异达到 0.55 以上。而中部地区与西北地区、西南地区之间的结构差异系数只在 0.39—0.43之间，说明改革二十多年来这些内陆地区之间的产业结构差异程度不是很大。因此，制造业两位数行业的地区间专业化指数上升，主要体现为沿海地区与内陆地区的产业结构差异，特别是东部沿海地区的平均专业化水平上升幅度达到了 83.4%（表 1）。从这一结果看，中国的制造业很有可能转移到了东部沿海地区或直辖市。当然，进一步的举证还需视地区的产业集中率情况而定，第四部分将作出证明。

从本部分的实证结果看，改革二十多年来地区间的专业化水平和市场一体化水平已有提高，但同时对地区经济协调发展产生潜在威胁的是，大部分制造业都已或正在转移进入东部沿海地区，这导致了地区差距的持续扩大。

四、地区的产业集中率变化情况

改革以来地区间的市场一体化水平提高，会影响产业的集中率，而地区产业集中率的变化对于理解产业的空间分布和地区差距更为直观。本部分应用两个指标来衡量地区的产业集中率，分别是地区的产业平均集中率和制造业中心值：

$$v_i = \frac{\sum_k (v_i^k)}{k}, \text{其中 } v_i^k = \frac{E_i^k}{\sum_i E_i^k} \tag{3}$$

$$\text{Central}_i = \frac{1}{N}\left(\sum_j \frac{\sum_k v_j^k}{\delta_{ij}} + \frac{\sum_k v_i^k}{\delta_{ii}} \right) \tag{4}$$

其中，k 为产业数量，N 为省份数量，v_i^k、v_j^k 分别为第 i、j 省份的第 k 产业就业占全国该行业全部就业的份额，δ_{ij} 为第 i 与 j

省份之间的距离，这里以各省省会城市之间的距离来衡量，δ_{ii} 为第 i 省内距离，计算公式为$\frac{1}{3}\left(\frac{省面积}{\pi}\right)^{0.5}$。⑲ (3)式 v_i 表示地区 i 的产业平均集中率，直接衡量该地区所有产业的平均占有率，它的范围在0—1之间，该值越接近于1，则该地区的制造业平均占有份额越高、制造业越发达。

(4)式地区 i 的制造业中心值区别于(3)式的是引入了空间距离维度，即(4)式结合了产业集中的绝对水平和空间距离两个因素综合考察了某一地区产业集聚状况，这样就更客观地描述了产业的空间分布情况和地区的市场规模大小。例如，假设一国存在两个以上的地区，如果根据(3)式得出其中有两个地区的产业平均集中率相同，但这两个地区与其余地区距离不等的话，则在空间上显示这两个地区的产业集中程度应该是不一样的。

利用(3)式我们直接计算得到各大地区和省份的产业平均集中率(表2)，得出以下几个明显的特点和结论：

(1) 即使是在改革初期的计划经济时代，东部沿海地区的制造业平均来说也是高于其他地区的，它的平均集中率达到0.3228，这纠正了我们以往认为在计划时代制造业平衡分布的概念，即在改革初期制造业的地区分布就已不平衡，东部沿海地区占有初步优势。

(2) 经过二十多年的发展，产业的地区集中更加明显，大部分制造业集聚到具有初步优势和地理位置优势的东部沿海地区，该地区的平均集中率从1980年的0.3228上升到2001年的0.4947，上升幅度达53%；相应地作为零和游戏，其他地区的平均集中率纷纷下降，其中东北三省下降幅度最大，从0.1608下降到0.0889，降幅达45%。这就印证了图1关于地区一体化从低水平向中级水平转化时，制造业将向具有初步优势和地理位置优势的地区转移和集聚的理论预期。

表 2　1980 年、2001 年各地区的产业平均集中率比较

1980 年											
直辖市	0.1393	东部沿海	0.3228	东北三省	0.1608	中部地区	0.1981	西北地区	0.0691	西南地区	0.1091
北京	0.0358	河北	0.0384	辽宁	0.0845	山西	0.0224	内蒙古	0.0167	广西	0.0168
天津	0.0313	山东	0.0591	吉林	0.0331	河南	0.0413	西藏	0.0004	重庆	—
上海	0.0722	江苏	0.0886	黑龙江	0.0432	安徽	0.0279	陕西	0.0231	四川	0.0607
		浙江	0.0496			湖北	0.0447	甘肃	0.0166	贵州	0.0155
		福建	0.0252			湖南	0.0377	青海	0.0026	云南	0.0162
		广东	0.0620			江西	0.0241	宁夏	0.0025		
		海南	—					新疆	0.0073		
2001 年											
直辖市	0.0925	东部沿海	0.4947	东北三省	0.0889	中部地区	0.1861	西北地区	0.0506	西南地区	0.0871
北京	0.0231	河北	0.0430	辽宁	0.0481	山西	0.0245	内蒙古	0.0089	广西	0.0151
天津	0.0217	山东	0.0901	吉林	0.0179	河南	0.0550	西藏	0.0003	重庆	0.0146
上海	0.0477	江苏	0.1013	黑龙江	0.0229	安徽	0.0268	陕西	0.0191	四川	0.0315
		浙江	0.0843			湖北	0.0330	甘肃	0.0122	贵州	0.0116
		福建	0.0368			湖南	0.0278	青海	0.0016	云南	0.0143
		广东	0.1369			江西	0.0190	宁夏	0.0034		
		海南	0.0022					新疆	0.0053		

(3) 从分省的角度看，1980—2001年间，东部沿海诸省的平均集中率均出现上升趋势，如广东从0.062上升到0.1369，浙江从0.0496上升到0.0843，山东从0.0591上升到0.0901，上升幅度都接近50%，而在东北三省，辽宁从0.0845下降到0.0481，吉林从0.0331下降到0.0179，黑龙江从0.0432下降到0.0229，下降幅度均在50%以上。因此，制造业从东北三省转移到东部沿海地区省份的趋势比较明显。如果联系到这些省份的相对专业化指数，则可以发现除了广东有明显的提升外，其余东部沿海地区的专业化指数没有明显的上升，表明多数沿海地区省份吸收内地省份产业转移的方式是整体式的，而不是有选择地进行产业专业化的地区分工。

(4) 对于西北地区和西南地区，无论是改革初期还是现在，其制造业的产业平均集中率均处于全国最低水平，而且随时间的推移呈进一步下降的趋势。2001年，西藏、青海、宁夏、海南、新疆等地的产业平均集中率均低于0.005，因此，这些地区基本是制造业的空白地。对于中部地区，二十多年的改革开放使这一地区的产业平均集中率略有下降，从0.198下降到0.186。

从上面分析可以看出，二十多年来地区的制造业分布已经出现剧烈的改变，原来具有初步优势的沿海地区因优越的地理位置和本身具有的人口规模优势，其制造业通过累积循环机制而进一步取得了压倒性的优势，而这一优势的取得是以东北三省、西部地区制造业的相应萎缩为代价的。同时，产业集聚与地区间一体化水平的提高是分不开的，这与Naughton等人的结论是一致的。但是这种一体化水平的提高还仅是本分析框架所示的中级水平。

表3是根据(4)式将各省中心值与各省地理位置相结合得出的各省制造业中心值。透过这些经验数据可以看出，制造业

正向以长江三角洲、珠江三角洲和环渤海湾地区为中心的东部沿海地区集聚，而地区间的一体化水平仅处于中级水平。具体说来，有以下特征值得关注：

表 3　1980 年、2001 年各省份制造业中心值

较高水平								
北京	21.9	(31.5)	上海	46.0	(67.5)	广东	22.7	(16.4)
天津	24.5	(33.7)	江苏	30.9	(32.4)			
河北	19.1	(21.1)	浙江	28.1	(26.7)			
山东	24.0	(23.6)	安徽	22.9	(24.8)			

中间水平			较低水平								
山西	16.5	(18.4)	辽宁	14.0	(22.1)	内蒙古	10.1	(12.2)	广西	9.9	(10.3)
湖北	17.6	(20.8)	吉林	10.0	(15.4)	西藏	4.1	(4.7)	重庆	12.0	(—)
湖南	15.2	(17.6)	黑龙江	7.9	(11.9)	陕西	12.6	(14.7)	四川	10.0	(13.0)
江西	16.5	(18.6)				甘肃	8.5	(10.3)	贵州	10.2	(11.6)
福建	15.7	(15.1)				青海	7.2	(8.7)	云南	7.6	(8.7)
河南	19.8	(20.5)				宁夏	9.0	(10.4)	海南	8.6	(—)
						新疆	3.6	(4.4)			

注：括号外为 2001 年，括号内为 1980 年；较高、中间、较低水平均以 2001 年的制造业中心值为分类依据。

(1) 改革以来，制造业中心值上升的省份只有广东、浙江、福建、山东四个，其中广东上升的幅度最大，从 1980 年的 16.4 上升到 2001 年的 22.7，而福建与山东上升的幅度仅在 0.4—0.6之间，表明广东在改革开放二十多年期间制造业的蓬勃发展和快速集中的趋势。(2)直辖市因集聚后本身产生的拥挤成本，使其有选择地退出部分制造业行业，导致制造业中心值下降；江苏虽然中心值略有下降，但仍处于所有省份的最高水平，2001 年达到 30.9。(3)尽管广东许多制造业领先于其他省份，但由于公式含有空间距离的因素，而其周边没有发达省份，因而使得中心值没有其地区专业化指数那样突出；相反，安徽、河北等省份由于靠近上海、北京等发达地区，其中心值自然也“水涨船高”，安徽作为一个农业大省，其中心值也达到 22.9 的高水平。(4)从制造业中心值较高省份所处的区域看，更进一步印证了制造业向东部沿海地区集聚的趋势，具体说来我国已经形成了三大中心，它们分别是北京、天津、河北、山东环绕的环渤海湾区域，以上海为龙头、以浙江、江苏为腹地的长江三角洲区域，以及广东省内的珠江三角洲。(5)与产业平均集中率相对应，中部地区的制造业中心值处于中间水平，2001 年在 15.2—19.8 的小幅范围内波动，与 1980 年相比略有下降，这一地区在改革开放二十多年中所受的影响显然没有东北三省、西南和西北地区所受的影响大。(6)制造业中心值水平最低的仍然是新疆、西藏、青海、海南、云南、宁夏等地，均在 10 以下；而在 1980—2001 年期间制造业萎缩最强的地区仍是东北三省，尤其是辽宁，从 1980 年的 22.1 下降到 2001 年的 14.0。

从上述这些特征可以看出，各省制造业中心值实际上也衡量了其市场规模的大小和制造业的产业竞争力。经过二十多年的改革开放和制造业的空间转移调整，惟有东部沿海省份的制造业规模与竞争力是上升的，东北三省的制造业萎缩最甚，西南与西北地区仍是制造业最不发达的地区。因此，国内一体化水平的提高和市场化改革不仅改变了计划经济体制下原有的制造业集聚状态，而且使得中国大部分制造业都集中到最接近于国外高收入市场的东部沿海地区。

五、相关国际经验和进一步的讨论

在进一步讨论之前，我们先看看美国和欧盟地区市场一体化过程中的地区专业化与产业集中率的变化情况：

（1）美国的地区差距在其历史上呈现出典型的倒U形曲线关系，其地区间专业化指数、各行业的平均基尼系数恰恰也都呈现着类似的倒U形曲线关系（图3）。只不过有一点需要倍加注意，在1860—1967年的多数年份，其地区间专业化指数都大于0.57，远远高于中国现阶段相应的地区间专业化指数水平（见表1），而同时期相应的行业未加权平均基尼系数却都低于0.32，远远低于中国2001年的各行业未加权平均基尼系数0.498。[20]

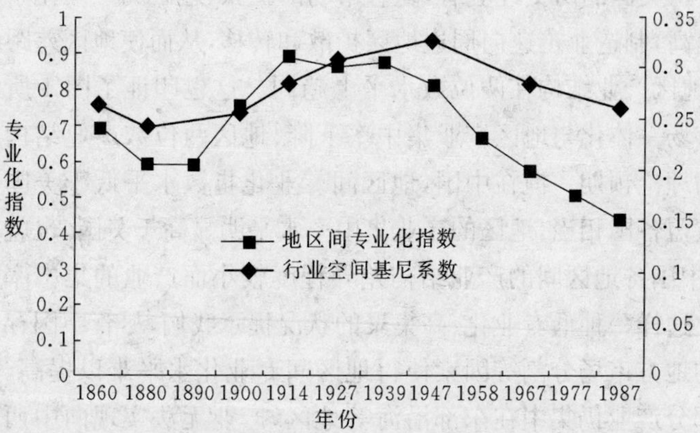

图3　1860—1987年美国地区间专业化指数与产业集中变化趋势

注：地区间专业化指数是按各地区间平均的制造业两位数水平计算的；行业空间基尼系数也是按制造业两位数行业的各行业未加权平均值计算。

资料来源：Sukkoo Kim, "Expansion of Market and the Geographic Distribution of Economic Activities: The Trends in U. S. Regional Manufacturing Structure, 1860—1987", *Quarterly Journal of Economics*, 110, 1995, pp. 881—908.

（2）美国早期制造业集中区域的改变与一体化之间也存在密切关系。美国早期制造业都集中在东北地区、大西洋中部沿海地区，从19世纪后半叶开始，随着以交通运输为主要内容的一体化水平迅速提高，美国早期制造业开始沿着交通线向以五大湖为中心的中西部地区迅速扩散，到20世纪初美国制造业中心已经转移到了东北地区、大西洋中部沿海地区、五大湖地区。[21]

(3) 欧盟各国在20世纪70年代初、80年代初、80年代末、90年代中期的专业化指数分别为0.432、0.404、0.436、0.471[22]，即随着欧盟一体化取得进展，各国的专业化水平略有提高。但其总体水平与2001年中国地区专业化水平相当。如果联系到欧盟内部是各国之间的联盟，而中国是在一个主权国家内，则可以轻易判断中国地区间一体化水平仅处于中级水平。

从美国的历史经验看，随着市场的扩张、地区间一体化水平的提高，制造业迅速向周边地区扩散和转移，从而使地区差距缩小、地区产业结构在两位数水平上趋同。这也印证了图1所示的市场一体化与地区产业集中率下降、地区两位数产业结构趋同的理论预期。但在中国，地区间专业化指数水平低于美国但与欧盟各国相当，地区的产业集中率水平明显高于美国，也就是说，中国各地区间的产业结构差异程度较小而产业的集中率较大。这样一种低专业化、高集聚的状况提示我们，尽管中国存在着的地方市场分割等因素使得地区间专业化水平难以提高，但大部分产业仍集中在东部沿海等地区，产业无法实现向中西部地区有梯度的扩散和转移，由此导致地区间无法进行合适的分工与合作。这种状况更进一步提示我们，虽然改革以来地区一体化水平已从初期的低水平向中级水平迈进，各地区自给自足的状态已经基本被打破，地区之间的贸易往来有很大的提高，但由于偏向于地方的财政分权体制、地方政府的业绩考核等软环境因素约束，地区间的一体化水平已无法向高级水平挺进，各种形式的地方市场分割极大地限制了国内统一大市场的建立，从而无法完成产业的跨地区转移，也就无法缩小地区间的收入差距。

与国内一体化水平提高受到很大局限形成鲜明对比的是，对外一体化水平在这二十多年的时间内有了极大的提高。改革开放以来，我国平均关税税率从1982年的55.6%下降到2000年的15.3%，加入WTO的缓冲期结束时，平均关税税率将降到8.9%的低水平。伴随着平均关税水平的不断下调，非关税壁垒也出现了一个不断消除的曲折过程。进口许可证和配额、对外经贸权的限制、进口替代的名录使用、特定进口商品的登记和招标制度等形式的非关税壁垒将逐渐被消除。以进口许可证和配额制度为例，20世纪80年代后期，许可证商品在所有进口商品中的比重为46%，到了90年代末，这一比例下降到了4%。[23]在这一背景下，大量劳动密集型产业纷纷从国外转移到中国国内，进出口贸易总额、FDI都有极大的提高，从而确立了中国在国际分工中的地位。进出口贸易总额从20世纪70年代末的约200亿美元增加到2003年的8512亿美元，中国成为世界第四大贸易国。[24]在20世纪90年代的大部分年份，中国一直是世界第二大引资国，到90年代末，中国累计吸收的外国直接投资相当于全部发展中国家累计引资额的三分之一。这种FDI大量涌入的结果是，中国经济日益融入世界经济之中，加工贸易成为对外贸易的一种主要形式。1985年以前，外资企业出口占总出口的比重低于1%，进口占总进口的比重低于5%，到2000年，这一数值分别增长到48%和52%。但是，从外资企业的地域分布来看，80%以上的外资企业和本地企业对外贸易的加工点都集中在东部沿海地区，这一区域正在逐渐成为世界制造业中心。因此，从理论上总结，如果说图1中的横轴代表对外一体化水平，则纵轴中的v_2就是中国在世界制造业的份额，现在中国正处于v_2不断提高、对外一体化水平从中级水平向高级水平过渡的阶段。

从上面可以看出，中国的对内、对外一体化进程是非常不对称和不一致的，这种情况对地区差距产生了极大的负面影响。

一方面，东部沿海地区正在成为世界制造业中心，而且这是以不断出现的都市圈形式出现的，它不但可以包含技术与资本密集型的制造业产业，而且也可以包含技术含量低、劳动密集型的制造业产业；另一方面，横在东西部之间的对内地区一体化滞后，使得东部地区的劳动密集型产业被就地消化在都市圈内的中小城市，无法转移到中部地区实现产业的梯度转移，导致中西部地区无法公平地享受经济增长果实。因此，东部沿海地区都市圈的形成、劳动密集型制造业的就地消化、产业无法实现跨区域的转移等等，都可以归结为国内一体化水平总体偏低，而这很有可能就是目前地区差距持续扩大的症结所在。

六、结　论

本文在新经济地理学关于地区间市场一体化与地区专业化、产业集聚之间关系的一个理论分析框架基础上，通过计算1980年、2001年中国各地区的相对专业化指数、地区间专业化指数、地区的产业平均集中率、制造业中心值等指标，发现改革以来国内地区一体化水平正在提高，制造业的地区分布已发生很大的变化，绝大部分制造业已经或正在转移进入东部沿海地区。同时，结合国际经验的进一步讨论认为，国内的一体化水平在现阶段仅处于中级水平，而这与一个主权国家内地区间一体化的程度是不相符合的，从这一意义上说，Poncet和Young坚持认为中国国内市场有走向非一体化的危险是非常有道理的。而与此形成对比的是，对外一体化水平已经取得了非常大的进展，大量FDI涌入东部沿海地区、进出口贸易持续增长，使得东部沿海地区正在成为世界制造业中心。这两种不相对称的一体化，使得中国出现了这样一个产业布局：东部沿海地区成为制造业中心，中西部地区成为低效率的农业与采掘业外围区域。这种极不平衡的产业空间布局对经济的可持续发展、社会稳定和国家安全构成了严重威胁。

基于本文的研究结论，我们认为：应当进一步深入进行政府间的财政体制改革，取消一切不利于国内市场一体化的各类制度和政策障碍，如限制劳动力流动的各类显性和隐性的制度和政策、地区偏向的经济政策等；政府也有责任通过一揽子宏观政策来改变中国制造业的不合理布局，如通过诸如当初中央政府对东部沿海地区采取地区倾斜政策那样来扶持中部有条件的省份主动吸收、承接东部沿海地区转移的制造业，加速省际交通建设等。同时，国际经验表明㉕，只有通过迅速达到高水平的一体化才能缩短地区产业集中的阵痛期，加快产业转移时刻的到来，地区经济增长才有可能收敛，地区收入差距才有可能缩小。因此，推动国内一体化建设，是解决目前收入差距过大的一个有效途径。

总之，正如世界银行报告所建议的㉖，建立一个有效的、灵活的国内统一市场，将东部沿海地区部分制造业有选择地转移到中部地区是十分必要的，只有这样，才能让经济增长果实惠及中西部地区，实现中国经济的可持续增长。

注　释

① 参见魏后凯《中国地区经济增长及其收敛性》，载《中国工业经济》1997 年第 3 期；万广华《中国农村区域间居民收入差异变化的实证分析》，载《经济研究》1998 年第 5 期；Martin Raiser, "Subsidising Inequality: Economic Reforms, Fiscal Transfers and Convergence across Chinese Provinces", *The Journal of Development Studies*, vol. 34, no. 3, 1998, pp. 1—26; Jian Tianlun, Jeffrey Sachs and Andrew M. Warner, "Trends in Regional Inequality in China", *NBER* working paper no. 5412, 1996; Sylvie Demurger, "Infrastructure Development and Economic Growth: An Explanation for Regional Disparities in China?", *Journal of Comparative Economics*. vol. 29, no. 1, 2001, pp. 95—117。

② 本文所指地区间市场一体化,简称市场一体化,它既包括商品和劳务市场、金融市场等的一体化,也包含国内市场的一体化与国外市场的一体化,后者就是融入世界经济的水平。地区专业化有两层含义,一是衡量某行业在地区诸产业中的地位,在(1)式或(2)式中以 s_i^k 表示,二是从总体上衡量各地区之间的产业结构差异程度,以(1)式或(2)式表示,在本文中是指第二层含义。产业集聚也有两层含义,一是衡量某地区的某一行业占全国同行业的份额,以(3)式中 v_i^k 表示,二是从总体上衡量各地区的产业集中率,以(3)式或(4)式表示,在本文中也为第二层含义。

③ 集中效应是指,由构成总产出或总收入的分项部分的内部集中率,或者内部不平等程度的变化,导致总基尼系数的变化。结构性效应是指,在各分项部分的内部集中率不变的情况下,仅仅因为各分项部分的结构变化,带来的对总基尼系数变化的影响。范剑勇、朱国林:《中国地区差距的演变及其结构分解》,《管理世界》2002 年第 7 期。

④ 范剑勇:《产业集聚与地区差距:来自中国的证据》,《中国社会科学评论》,法律出版社,2004 年第 1 卷第 1 期,第 22—40 页。

⑤ 范剑勇、王立军、沈林洁:《产业集聚与农村劳动力跨区域流动》,《管理世界》2004 年第 4 期。

⑥ 陈东琪、银温泉:《打破地方市场分割》,中国计划出版社,2002 年,第 20—50 页;吴敬琏:《试论政府在体制转轨中的作用》,《中国党政干部论坛》1997 年第 4 期。

⑦ Alwyn Young, "The Razor's Edge: Distortions and Incremental Reform in the People's Republic of China", *Quarterly Journal of Economics*, vol. 115, no. 4, 2000, pp. 1091—1135; Poncet, Sandra:《中国市场正在走向"非一体化"?——中国国内和国际市场一体化程度的比较分析》,《世界经济文汇》2002 年第 1 期。

⑧ Barry Naughton, "How Much Can Regional Integration Do to Unify

China's Markets?", *Conference for Research on Economic Development and Policy Research*, 1999, Stanford University; Bai, Chong-En, Yingjuan Du, Zhigang Tao and Sarah Y. Tong, "Protection and Regional Specialization: Evidence from China's Industries", *Working Paper*, Feb. 2003.

⑨ 赵伟:《区域开放:中国的独特模式及其未来发展趋向》,《浙江学刊》2001 年第 2 期。

⑩ 除直辖市(未包括重庆,将重庆纳入四川省分析)外,剩余五个地区包括:(1)东北三省:黑龙江、吉林、辽宁;(2)东部沿海地区:河北、山东、江苏、浙江、福建、广东、海南;(3)中部地区:山西、河南、安徽、湖北、湖南、江西;(4)西北地区:内蒙古、陕西、宁夏、甘肃、青海、新疆、西藏;(5)西南地区:四川、云南、贵州、广西。

⑪ Avinash Dixit, Joseph Stiglitz, "Monopolistic Competition and Optimum Product Diversity", *American Economic Review*, vol. 76, 1977, pp. 297—308.

⑫ Paul Krugman, "Increasing Returns and Economic Geography", *Journal of Political Economy*, vol. 99, 1991, pp. 483—499.

⑬ 这里的制造业厂商不仅是具有上下游联系的厂商,也可以笼统地指制造业厂商。根据新经济地理学理论,市场规模效应往往取决于外部需求强度和产品的规模与多样性,因此应该包括所有制造业厂商。具有上下游联系的厂商可能是更直观的理解。

⑭ 这些指标的解释见本文第三、第四部分。

⑮ 对(2)式需略加说明的是,地区间专业化指数不仅与地区间一体化水平有关,还与行业层次 k 取值有关。从本文分析框架看,当地区间一体化处于较高或很高水平时,产业从原制造业中心转移到周边地区,用二位数行业衡量的地区间专业化指数可能会下降,但用三位数行业衡量的地区间专业化指数仍会很高,因为从专业化生产或产业分布看,一个更细的行业往往是一个地区独家生产。

⑯ 需要加以说明的是,从地区生产的专业化水平变化来判断地区一体化水平是否提高,这一方法经常应用于欧盟、美国地区间一体化水平

的判断上，如 Knarvik Midelfart-Knarvik, Henry Overman, Stephen Redding and Anthony Venables, "The Location of European Industry", http://www.econ.lse.ac.uk/staff/ajv/fineuloc.pdf, 2000; Sukkoo Kim, "Economic Intergration and Convergence: U.S. Regions, 1840—1987", *Journal of Economic History*, vol. 58, no. 3, 1998, pp. 659—683。在中国的案例中，Bai 等也应用了这一方法，参见 Bai, Chong-En, Yingjuan Du, Zhigang Tao and Sarah Y. Tong, "Protection and Regional Specialization: Evidence from China's Industries", *Working Paper*, Feb. 2003。

⑰ 广东省在 1980 年的专业化指数仅是 0.407，而在 2001 年提高到 0.781。

⑱ 全国地区间的平均专业化水平是通过算术平均各地区的平均专业化水平得出，而地区的平均专业化水平是由它与其余地区间的专业化指数通过算术平均计算得来的。

⑲ (4)式直接取自 Bluhar 关于欧盟产业分布的计算公式，它最初实际上是来自 Harris 关于中心市场(MP)大小的概念。参见 Marius Brulhart, "Evolving Geographic Concentration of European Manufacturing Industries", *Weltwirtschaftliches Archiv*, 137, 2001, pp. 215—243; Cruis Harris, "The Market as a Factor in The Location of Industry in U.S.", *Annals of Association of American Geographers*, 64, 1954, pp. 315—348。

⑳ 数据来源为第二次全国基本单位普查资料中各省制造业两位数行业的从业人员数，计算方法为各行业基尼系数的算术平均，计算方法详见崔启源《测算中国省际地区差距问题》，载刘树成、李强、薛天栋主编《中国地区经济发展研究》，中国统计出版社，1994 年，第 70 页。

㉑ 范剑勇、杨丙见：《美国早期制造业集中的转变及其对中国西部开发的启示》，《经济研究》2002 年第 8 期。

㉒ Knarvik Midelfart-Knarvik, Henry Overman, Stephen Redding and Anthony Venables, "The Location of European Industry", http://www.econ.lse.ac.uk/staff/ajv/fineuloc.pdf, 2000.

㉓ 尼古拉斯·拉迪:《中国融入全球经济》,经济科学出版社,2002 年,第 49 页。

㉔ http://info. news. sinobnet. com/HTML/001/002/003/013/41752. htm。

㉕ Sukkoo Kim, "Expansion of Market and the Geographic Distribution of Economic Activities: The trends in U. S. Regional Manufacturing Structure, 1860—1987", *Quarterly Journal of Economics*, 110, 1995, pp. 881—908.

㉖ 世界银行:《中国:推动公平的经济增长》,清华大学出版社,2004 年,第 43—50 页。

(原载《中国社会科学》2004 年第 6 期)

我国省份之间的要素流动和边际生产率的差异分析*

龚六堂
（北京大学光华管理学院）

谢丹阳
（国际货币基金组织）

一、引　　言

对任何一个经济来讲，有效配置生产资源是它走向繁荣的一个重要步骤，因此对资源配置的有效性的研究一直是经济学家研究的热点。目前，这方面已经有了大量的研究，如 Barro 和 Sala-i-Martin（1991，1992），Jian 等（1996），Chen 和 Fleisher（1996），Aziz 和 Duenwald（2001），以及姚洋（1997）和张军（2002）等等。但是，在这些研究中，他们关注的是不同产业之间或者不同国家之间生产资源的配置问题，很少有文献来研究不同省份（州）之间的生产资源的有效配置问题。虽然，也有经济学家曾经利用基于省份（州）的水平上的数据来研究人均收入的收敛性问题和省际收入的收敛性与地区发展差异性问题，如

* 本研究受国家教育部人文社会科学十五规划项目资助。作者感谢香港大学阮志华教授和匿名审稿人的有益建议。

Barro 和 Sala-i-Martin (1991, 1992), Jian 等(1996), Chen 和 Fleisher (1996)以及 Aziz 和 Duenwald (2001),但也很少关注不同省份(州)之间的生产要素配置的有效性问题。至于中国经济的研究方面,近年来,已经有许多经济学家进行了系统的研究。Chow (2002)对我国改革开放以来的经济进行了系统研究。他的研究涉及到当初是什么原因使得新中国首先选择了计划经济以及计划经济是如何运作的,是什么力量促使中国进行经济改革,为什么中国成功地从计划经济转向了市场经济,中国市场经济包含的具体内容是什么,现在中国经济存在的主要问题是什么,以及中国经济发展的走向等。高坚(2000a, 2000b)讨论了我国经济的发展趋势、科技对经济增长的影响等。至于对资源配置的研究,姚洋(1997)研究了地权残缺对土地资源配置效应的影响。张军(2002)在讨论工业化中也涉及到要素配置问题。但是,在他们的讨论中都没有涉及到省份之间的生产要素的配置有效性问题。本文的目的就是要讨论一个国家中不同省份之间的生产资源配置的有效性问题,特别是讨论我国经济中不同省份之间生产资源配置的有效性问题,从而来研究改革开放以来我国经济的资源配置是否得到了改善。①

从理论上讲,资源配置的有效性条件从任何一本经济学教科书中都可以得到答案,那就是各个要素的边际生产率相等。因此,考虑不同省份之间的生产资源配置的有效性是否得到改善只需要考虑省份之间的资本存量和劳动的边际生产率变化。为此,研究不同省份之间的生产资源配置的有效性问题的步骤是:首先,根据省份的数据来估计每个省份的生产函数;第二,根据定义计算资本存量和劳动的边际生产率;第三,比较不同省份之间的资本存量和劳动的边际生产率差异的变化趋势。一般来讲,如果生产要素的边际生产率差异变小就表明了资源配置的有效性得到改善。但是,这个结论的成立需要以下条件:(1)经济中只有一个要素是自由流动的。(2)生产函数以常数规模回报。当这两个条件之一不成立时,就可能出现资源配置的有效性提高和生产要素的边际生产率差异同时增加的情形。如果资本和劳动都是可以自由移动的,这样条件(1)不成立时,我们可以给出例子说明资源配置的有效性提高,可能同时使得资本和劳动的边际生产率的差异增加。如果生产函数对资本存量是凸的(Romer, 1986),这样条件(2)不满足,同样也可能出现资源配置的有效性改善和资本存量的边际生产率差异同时增加的情形。对此,我们会在正文较详细地论述。

为了研究边际回报差异的变化趋势,本文定义了刻画差异的指标。基于这个指标,通过分析发现从1970年到1985年资本存量的边际生产率的差异下降,从1985年以后资本存量的差异水平就保持在一个较稳定的水平上。劳动的边际生产率的差异从1970年到1993年同样是下降的,但从1993年开始,劳动的边际生产率差异反而上升。分析上面的结论,资本存量和劳动的边际生产率差异下降表明了资源配置的有效性增加。但是,劳动的边际生产率差异水平上升就需要详细的解释。本文给出了三种解释:(1)政策驱使的劳动力流动增加了劳动市场的无效性;(2)出现了劳动力的规模回报递增;(3)在1993年以后出现了资本存量和劳动力可以同时流动的情形。这里只指出可能出现的上面三种情形,将来进一步的工作和更细致的研究则要区分到底是什么因素导致了1993年以后的边际生产率差异上升的现象。

本文的结构安排如下:第二部分,讨论边际回报差异变化趋势与资源配置的关系,指出资源配置的有效性提高与边际生产率的差异增加同时存在的情形。同时,定义了刻画边际回报差异的指标。第三部分，说明数据来源和构成，构造了省际水平的资本存量水平、劳动力水平和产出。第四部分，估计各个省份的生产函数，给出资本存量和劳动的边际回报差异的变化趋势。最后，给出本文的结论。

二、边际回报差异与资源配置有效性的关系

在本节，我们将考虑边际回报率差异变化趋势与资源配置的关系；同时，也将给出度量边际回报的差异的指标。

对于传统的严格凹的生产函数来讲，资源配置的最优条件要求在每种资源上面的边际回报相等，但是，这不能直接地表明边际生产率的差异变小可以改善资源配置的有效性。我们可以证明这个结论，也可以简单地通过例子来说明。为简单起见，我们通过例子来说明。下面是两个都具有 Cobb-Douglas 生产函数形式的经济，我们讨论了生产要素的边际回报差异与资源配置的有效性的关系。对于 n 个省份的经济，我们构造了一个指标来度量要素的边际回报的差异程度。

(一) 两个省份的经济

考虑一个具有两个省份(简记为 $i=1,2$) 的经济，假设它们的生产函数分别为：

$$Y_i = A_i K_i^{\alpha} L_i^{\beta},\ i=1,2$$

假设总量的资本存量和劳动为 $K=K_1+K_2$ 和 $L=L_1+L_2$。进一步地，假设生产函数对于资本存量和劳动力水平是严格凹的，即 $0<\alpha_i<1$ 和 $0<\beta_i<1$，$i=1,2$。

为简单起见，我们用图 1-a，1-b，1-c，1-d，1-e 来表示要素回报差异的变化与资源配置有效性的关系。其中图 1-a，1-b 和 1-c 给出的是两个省份具有相同产出的情形；图 1-d 给出的是两

个省份具有不同产出的情形；图 1-e 给出的是生产函数对于资本存量是凸的情形。

图 1-a，1-b 和 1-c 分别给出的是常数规模回报、规模回报递减和规模回报递增经济情形下的资本的边际回报的差异与总产出的关系。从中可以看到，如果只有资本或劳动中一个要素是自由流动的，则两个省份的资本存量的边际回报的很小的差异就可以导致更高的总产出。在图中，实线上的点表示劳动不能自由流动，虚线上的点表示资本不能自由流动。同时，我们也看到，不管 $\alpha_i+\beta_i$ 是大于、小于或者等于 1，两种情形时的曲线都是向下的。也就是说，资本的边际回报的差异较小对应总产出很大。

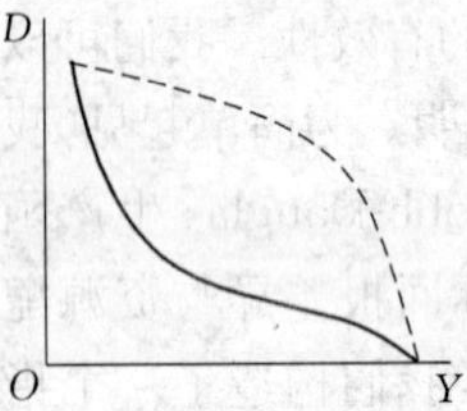

图 1-a　常数规模回报

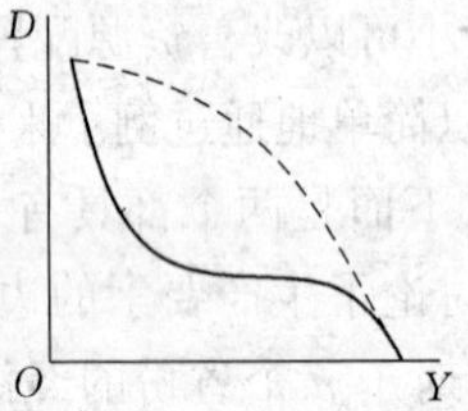

图 1-b　规模回报递减

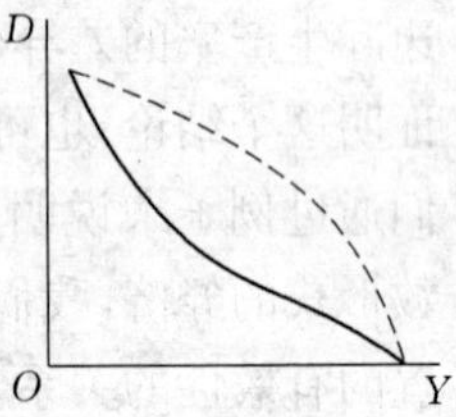

图 1-c　规模回报递增

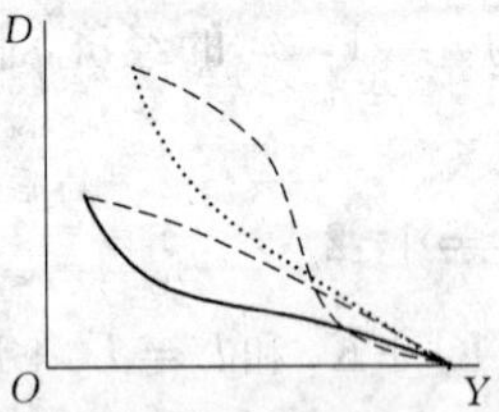

图 1-d　常数规模回报（生产水平不同）

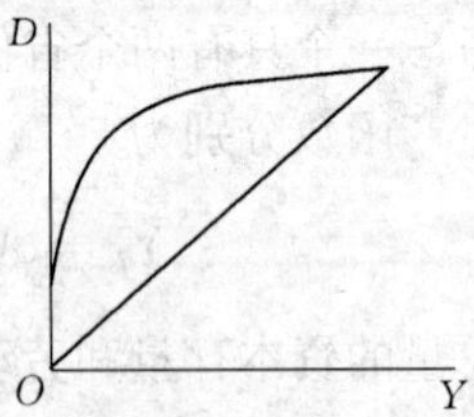

图 1-e　生产函数对资本存量是凸的

通过图 1-a，1-b 和 1-c，可以很清楚地看到当两种要素都是自由流动时，总产出的提高和资本存量的边际生产率的绝对差异变大是可以同时存在的。至于劳动的边际生产率与总产出的关系也可以通过类似的分析得到。

至于两个省份的产出存在差异的情形，通过图 1-d 也给出了类似的总产出的提高和资本存量的边际生产率的绝对差异变大的情形。对于具有凸的生产函数的经济，通过图 1-e，我们也发现了当生产函数对于资本存量是凸的时候，总产出的提高和资本存量的边际生产率的绝对差异变大并存的情形。（在图中，D 表示资本存量的边际回报差异的绝对值，Y 表示总的产出。）

（二）*n* 个省份的情形：差异程度的衡量指标

对于具有 n 个省份的经济，在考虑要素的边际回报差异之前必须给出一个度量要素的边际回报率的差异的指标。对于一组数据，它们的差异可以有很多种度量方式，本文采用比较简单但又合理的形式。[②]

假设 n 个省份的资本存量的边际生产率已经给出，分别记为 $r_1, r_2, \cdots, r_n$。按照下面的步骤来定义它们的差异。首先，把 $r_1, r_2, \cdots, r_n$ 按照从大到小排序，记排序后的边际生产率为 $\hat{r}_1, \hat{r}_2, \cdots, \hat{r}_n$。这样，离差指标定义为：

$$D=\frac{2}{n^2\bar{r}}\sum_{i=1}^{n}i\hat{r}_i-\frac{n+1}{n}$$

其中 $\bar{r}$ 是 $r_1, r_2, \cdots, r_n$ 的平均值。通过简单的计算可以把这个指标改写为：

$$D=\frac{2}{n^2\bar{r}}\sum_{i=1}^{n}i(\hat{r}_i-\bar{r})$$

显然，如果每个省份的资本的边际回报都一致，那么 $D=0$；同时，可以看到 D 也是零次齐次的，即如果每个省份的资本的边际回报同时提高相同的倍数，那么它们的差异程度是不会改变的。

用类似的方法可以定义劳动的边际回报率 $w_1, w_2, \cdots, w_n$

的差异程度。

为了计算我国各省份的资本和劳动的边际回报率，我们需要各个省份的生产函数，下面的主要工作就是要估计出各个省份的生产函数。

三、中国经济的省份数据

在本节，我们来说明数据的来源。从1998年开始，我国除港澳台外共有31个省份。因为时间关系，海南、重庆的数据很短，因此，我们没有考虑海南和重庆③，同时因为西藏的数据问题，我们也没有考虑西藏。这样，在我们的样本中包括28个省、自治区和直辖市，它们分别是：(1)北京，(2)天津，(3)河北，(4)陕西，(5)内蒙古，(6)辽宁，(7)吉林，(8)黑龙江，(9)上海，(10)江苏，(11)浙江，(12)安徽，(13)福建，(14)江西，(15)山东，(16)河南，(17)湖北，(18)湖南，(19)广东，(20)广西，(21)四川，(22)贵州，(23)云南，(24)山西，(25)甘肃，(26)青海，(27)宁夏和(28)新疆。④

我们要估计每个省份的生产函数，就需要每个省份的人均实际产出、人均实际资本存量和劳动力数据。它们的来源是：

(1) 各省份的人均GDP数据。

各省份的人均GDP数据来源于中国统计出版社1990年出版的《全国各省、自治区、直辖市历史统计资料汇编1949—1989》和1983年到2000年历年出版的《中国统计年鉴》。

(2) 人均实际资本存量数据。

为得到人均实际资本存量数据，我们首先考虑的是投资的平减指数(RPI)和投资的数据，投资的平减指数由《中国国内生产总值核算历史资料：1952—1995》中给出的资本存量形成指数值计算得来。在1996—1999年，所有省份的投资平减指数值均不存在，因此(固定)资本形成按照各省份固定资产投资指数平减，存货按照RPI平减。

在上述数据中，天津缺少全部的指数值，因此，我们只有直接分别计算投资的平减指数。主要依据天津市区的RPI。江西缺少所有1952—1978年的投资数据，但并不缺少指数。我们按照积累占国民收入的比例，乘以1.3，即资本形成占GDP支出的比重高于前者的程度，再乘以江西每年的GDP，得到资本形成的估计值。假定固定资产投资占固定资本形成的比例一定，则1978—1980年的比例为0.86，以此值乘以1952—1977年的资本形成估计值，得到固定资产投资的估计值。广东缺少1952—1977年所有数据，因此只好按照江西的做法估算投资数据，且按照RPI进行平减。我们注意到，存货增加的数据的平减指数比较异常，例如青海。

基于对投资数据的整理，我们计算了各省份的实际资本存量，具体方法是：先按照各省份的固定资产投资平减指数将固定资产投资统一折算到1978年不变价的数据。然后，按照折旧率10%累计计算资本存量，所以资本存量均按照1978年不变价计算。各省份人均资本存量是按照劳动力总数计算出来的。邹至庄(Chow, 1993)曾经按照这种方法计算各省份的人均资本存量。

(3) 劳动力数据。

在中国工业的统计数据中，从业人数和职工人数差异巨大。且在1995年以前的数据中，中国工业经济统计年鉴中的职工人数与中国统计年鉴中的职工人数，及从业人数均不相同。由此，我们在计算选择指数时，分别按照职工人数和从业人数进行了两次计算。其中，职工人数的数据全部来源于《中国工业交通能源50年统计资料汇编1949—1999》。中国各省份的工业从业人数1985年以后采用了中国统计年鉴中的数据，但1978—1984年间，缺少从业人数统计。因此，我们将“改革开放17年来的中国经济”中的“第二产业从业人数”数据，按其和“工业从业人数”在1985—1987年的差异比例的平均值，再乘以“第二产业从业人数”1978—1984年的数据，以估算出所缺损的工业从业人数数据。

表1　中国各省份的生产函数的估算

代码	省份名称	α_j	β_j	代码	省份名称	α_j	β_j
1	北京	0.314467	0.685533	15	山东	0.468865	0.531135
2	天津	0.47763	0.52237	16	河南	0.200188	0.799812
3	河北	0.501975	0.498025	17	湖北	0.747166	0.252834
4	山西	0.328888	0.671112	18	湖南	0.158933	0.841067
5	内蒙古	＃N/A	＃N/A	19	广东	0.74472	0.25528
6	辽宁	0.473177	0.526823	20	广西	0.254311	0.745689
7	吉林	0.4875	0.5125	21	四川	0.409874	0.590126
8	黑龙江	0.522405	0.477595	22	贵州	0.384443	0.615557
9	上海	0.351412	0.648588	23	云南	＃N/A	＃N/A
10	江苏	0.744048	0.255952	24	陕西	0.167243	0.832757
11	浙江	0.457956	0.542044	25	甘肃	0.432584	0.567416
12	安徽	0.688869	0.311131	26	青海	0.205105	0.794895
13	福建	0.715138	0.284862	27	宁夏	0.86996	0.13004
14	江西	0.430638	0.569362	28	新疆	0.659603	0.340397

四、边际生产率的差异变化趋势

在本节，我们利用第三节给出的数据来估计每个省份的生产函数。我们按照下面的方式估计生产函数[⑤]，$j=1, 2, \cdots, n$。

$$\ln Y_t^j = \ln A_o + g_j t + \alpha_j \ln K^j + \beta_j \ln L^j$$

这里,我们强加条件⑥ $\alpha_i + \beta_i = 1$,而且假设技术进步率为 g_j。

在得到 α_j 的估计后,通过 $\beta_j = 1 - \alpha_j$ 得到相应的生产函数中劳动力水平的回归系数,从而我们可以计算这些省份的资本和劳动的边际回报。在 Cobb-Douglas 生产函数的假设下,第 j 个省份的资本存量的边际回报率 r_t^j 可以表示为:

$$r_t^j = \alpha_j Y_t^j / K_t^j$$

第 j 个省份劳动的边际回报率 w_t^j 可以表示为:

$$w_t^j = \beta_j Y_t^j / L_t^j$$

通过上面的计算公式可以给出 26 个省份的资本存量和劳动的边际回报率。为了直观地了解这些数据,我们选择几个省份,在图 2-a 和图 2-b 分别给出了资本存量和劳动的边际回报率的变化趋势。通过比较发现,江苏在 1989 年前的资本存量的边际生产率最高,之后是福建的资本存量的边际生产率最高。至于劳动的边际生产率,上海始终最高。

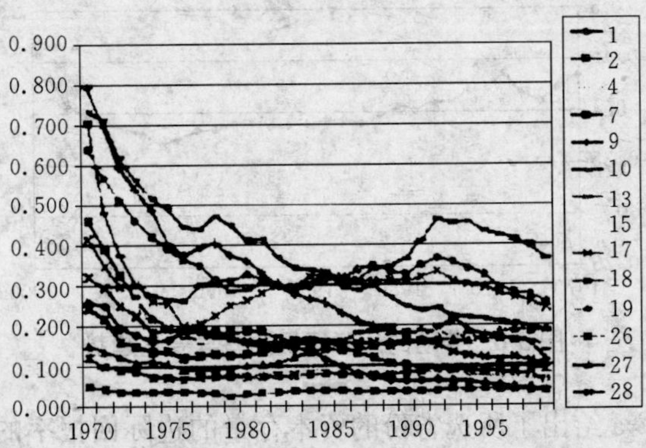

图 2-a 资本存量的边际回报率的变化趋势

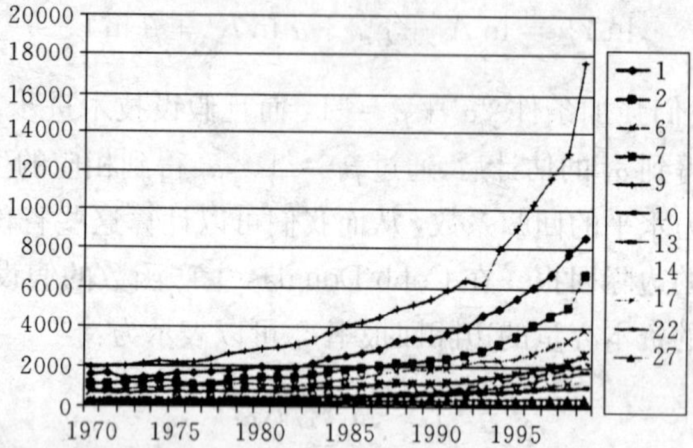

图 2-b　劳动的边际回报率的变化趋势

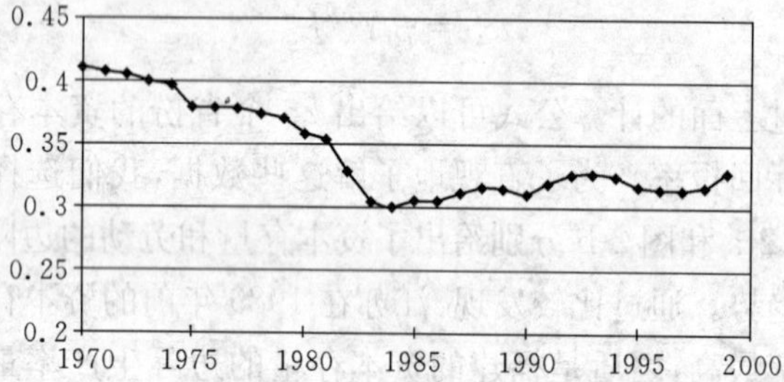

图 3-a　资本的边际回报的差异变化趋势

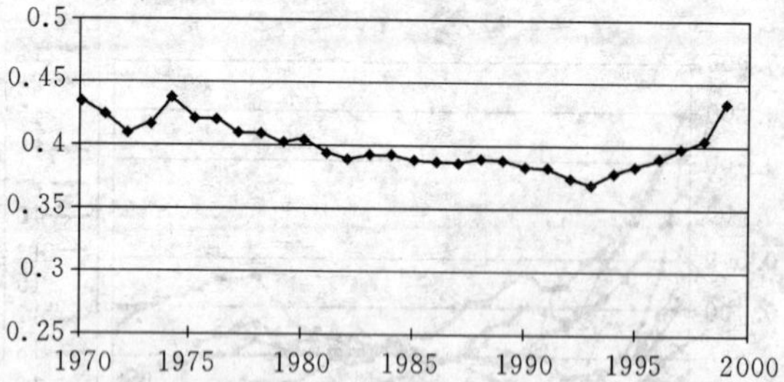

图 3-b　劳动的边际回报的差异变化趋势

图 2-a 给出了所选省份的资本存量的边际回报率的变化趋势。从图中可以看到，对于大多数省份来讲，资本存量的边际生

产率是下降的。通过方程(3)计算的资本存量的边际生产率的离差在表2和图3-a中表示出来。我们发现1970—1984年这26个省份的资本存量的差异趋势在减小,在此之后,资本存量的边际回报的差异水平稳定在这个水平。

图2-b给出了所选省份的劳动的边际回报的变化趋势。从图中看到,劳动的边际回报率在增加。它们的差异程度在表2和图3-b中表示出来。我们发现1970—1993年劳动的边际生产率的差异在减小,但是1994年后,这个差异趋势正好相反,甚至在1999年,这个差异水平回到了1970年的水平。

表2 中国资本和劳动边际生产率的差异水平

年份	资本	劳动	年份	资本	劳动
1970	0.411495	0.434383	1985	0.305618	0.389747
1971	0.407663	0.425001	1986	0.304083	0.388444
1972	0.405919	0.408603	1987	0.310807	0.386136
1973	0.400768	0.416884	1988	0.316018	0.389989
1974	0.397223	0.43798	1989	0.314966	0.389007
1975	0.379691	0.422035	1990	0.309923	0.384509
1976	0.378744	0.421092	1991	0.31691	0.384271
1977	0.378094	0.410619	1992	0.324955	0.375621
1978	0.374735	0.41011	1993	0.326177	0.369663
1979	0.369819	0.402787	1994	0.323144	0.378794
1980	0.357715	0.404684	1995	0.316036	0.384144
1981	0.351884	0.39483	1996	0.3137	0.390109
1982	0.327491	0.388846	1997	0.313179	0.396875
1983	0.304296	0.392839	1998	0.314636	0.404381
1984	0.298928	0.393248	1999	0.326887	0.434478

1970—1984年资本存量的边际回报率差异水平下降,说明了资本存量的配置有效性增加,之后处于稳定的水平,表明资本

存量配置的有效性处于稳定状态。1970—1993年,劳动的边际生产率差异水平下降,同样表明了劳动力资源的配置有效性提高。但是,1993年以后,劳动的边际生产率却上升了。如何解释这个现象呢?一般地,出现这种现象有下面三种情形:

第一,从1994年后劳动力市场出现了扭曲、变坏。我们认为这种情形似乎是不可能出现的。虽然,我国对于流动人口来讲有严格遣返制度,但改革开放以后劳动力的流动自由程度应该是得到了很大的改善。我国的经济日益市场化的事实告诉我们,劳动力的配置也日益由市场来决定。因此,这种情形的出现是不可能的。

第二,生产函数对于劳动力是凸的。这样,劳动的边际生产率是劳动力的单调递增函数,因此,劳动力越来越向边际生产率较高的省份流动,从而边际生产率的差异增加表明资源配置的有效性得到提高。⑦和我们想象的一致,这种情形也不可能出现,因为从生产函数对于劳动力是凸的可以知道产出对劳动力水平的弹性是大于1的,这是和已知的经验结论不一致的。在已知的研究中,如Young(1995),Iwata, Khan和Murao(2002)研究东亚经济得到的产出对劳动力的增长弹性在0.34(Philippines)和0.81(Korea)之间,Hu和Khan(1996)用0.411和0.453之间的数来研究中国经济的产出对劳动力的弹性,Li et al (1993)用0.462和0.536之间的数来研究不同样本中的产出对劳动力的弹性。Iwata, Khan和Murao(2002)利用非参数估计甚至得到了高达0.95的产出对劳动力的增长弹性。但是,这些估计都不可能出现产出对劳动力的弹性大于1的情形,从而不可能出现生产函数对劳动力水平是凸的情形。

第三,劳动的边际生产率差异变化趋势上升的现象是资本和劳动力的流动性都得到了提高的结果。我们认为从1993年出现的劳动力的边际生产率差异的增加可以解释为这种情形。这是因为，虽然户籍制度还存在，但是很多省份已经从原来的户籍制度中解脱，因此劳动力的自由流动已经得到了大大的改善，同时，资本的流动性也是得到了大大的改善。因此，正如前面图1给出的那样，当资本和劳动力都可以自由流动时，边际回报率的差异增加正是表明了资源配置的效益得到提高。在图1-b中，差异变大就像从一条斜率向下的线上面的一点向下跳到下面一点。为了极大化产出，可能出现向下跳到右边，也就是差异指标对于最有效的配置来讲是下降的。但是，暂时向东北方向的流动仍然表明了资源配置的有效性得到改善。这种流动可能取决于不同省份的不同的优惠政策。如果一个省份的税收是基于收入来源的，而不是基于当地居民的，则要素的流动将由要素的税后边际回报来决定(Razin and Yuen, 1996)。基于这种要素的税后边际回报率，我们也可以类似地讨论上面的问题。

五、结　论

通过估算我国28个省份的生产函数得到了资本存量和劳动的边际生产率的差异程度的变化趋势。我们发现资本存量的边际生产率的差异趋势在1970—1989年间下降，之后保持在比较稳定的水平，而劳动的边际生产率的差异在1970—1993年下降，而到1993年后反而上升。从美国等发达国家的经验中，我们希望看到劳动的边际生产率差异是下降或者稳定的，但是我们得到的结论和此不一致。我们讨论了到底是什么原因导致了这种现象的出现。⑧

虽然劳动的边际回报率差异水平的上升可能是由于我们希望的资本和劳动的流动性加强，但是我们也应该监控这个指标的进一步发展。这是因为我们通过下面的回归得到了边际生产率的差异(记为 D_L)与人均 GDP 的增长率(记为 g)成显著的负相关:

$$g = 160 - 130.9D_L, R^2 = 0.34, \text{DW} = 1.93$$
$$(-2.34)$$

其中括号内为 t 统计量。其他变量,如价格水平等等可以加入上面的回归方程,但是不具有统计意义。

最后,我们通过图 4-a 和图 4-b,可以发现在西部大开发中,山西和青海从劳动力的流入中可以得到很大的利益,而宁夏和广西从资本的流入中可以得到很大的利益。

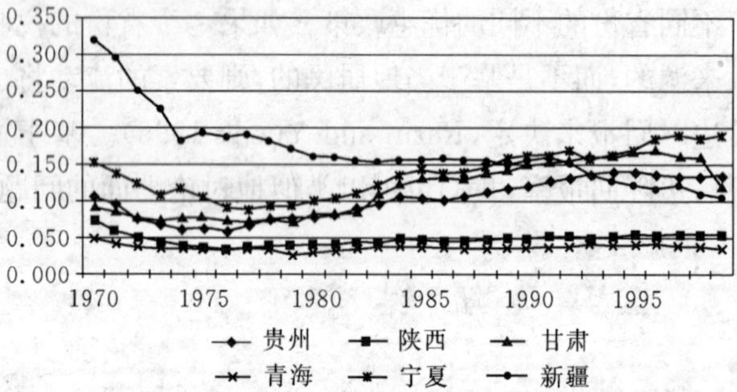

图 4-a　西部省份的资本边际回报趋势

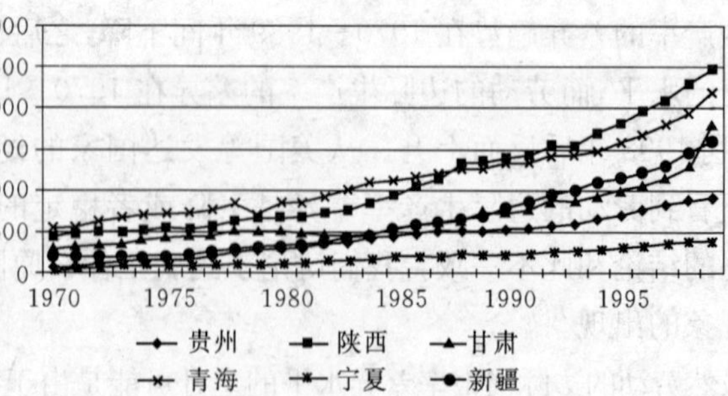

图 4-b　西部省份的劳动边际回报趋势

本文提出了一种重要的经济学现象，并给出了初步的解释。进一步探讨的工作包括：(1)劳动边际生产率差异增大与我国目前的收入分配差异增大的关系，是否这种差异会导致收入分配差异的增加等。(2)本文的分析方法可以用来分析世界上很多国家的经济，考察其资源配置的有效性是否得到改善，并和中国经济进行比较。(3)本文采用的研究同一个国家不同省份之间的资源配置有效性问题的方法可以推广来研究不同国家之间的资源配置的有效性问题。事实上，早在1989年，Lucas就已经研究了两个国家之间的资源配置问题，研究为什么资本不会很快地从富裕国家流动到贫穷国家。但他只是简单地比较了两个国家(美国和印度)的经济，而我们这里采用的是横截面数据的研究。

注　释

① 为方便起见，我们把中国内地的31个省、自治区和直辖市统统用“省份”这个词来代替。

② 这个指标来源于Resa Corporation (2002)给出的“Gini-Coefficient”的思想。

③ 根据审稿人的意见，我们把海南和重庆建省或直辖市后的数据分别加入广东和四川来考虑。

④ 其中括号为该省份的代码。

⑤ Chow(2002)按照这个方程估计了中国总体生产函数。我们考虑资本存量和劳动力外部性问题时，回归方程为

$$\ln Y_t^j = \ln A_j + \eta_j t + \alpha_j \ln K_t^j + \beta_j \ln L_t^j + \gamma_j \ln \bar{K}_t + \theta_j \ln \bar{L}_t$$

我们同样可以得到相应的回归方程，求出资本存量和劳动力水平边际回报差异的变化趋势。我们发现在这种回归下得到的结论和文中得到的类似，因此，我们没有在文中写出。

⑥ 高坚(2000a, 2000b)基于类似的方程估计了中国经济的总体生产函

数。对基于省份的生产函数的估计，Chow(1993)曾经研究过，在这里，我们也进行了很多不同的估计，对于这些不同的估计，我们发现要素的边际生产率的差异的变化趋势是不改变的。同时，我们发现在对生产函数做常数规模回报的约束后，给出的估计结果更稳定，而其余的估计可能出现一些问题，如对某些省份的生产函数回归时，出现了资本存量或劳动的边际生产率为负的问题。

⑦ 细心的读者可能会发现，在劳动力的边际生产率是递增的情形下的离差指标还是通过上面的计算得到的。此时实际上应该通过假设生产函数对劳动力是凸的得到。事实上，我们也进行了这方面的计算，发现得到和上面分析一致的结论。因此，我们这里不再详细论述。如果需要，读者可以向作者索取。

⑧ 在 Aziz 和 Duenwald(2001)的工作中，他们发现相对收入的分布成双塔型的分布，他们的发现和我们的一致。

参考文献

高坚，2000a:《科技进步对中国经济的影响》，国家开发银行政策研究室工作报告，No. 59。

高坚，2000b:《中国经济发展的基本趋势》，国家开发银行政策研究室工作报告，No. 58。

姚洋，1997:《农地制度与农业绩效的实证研究》，北京大学中国经济研究中心。

张军，2002:《资本形成、工业化与经济增长:中国的转轨特征》，《经济研究》第 6 期。

Aziz, Jahangir and Christoph Duenwald, 2001, "China's Provincial Growth Dynamics", IMF Working Paper, No. 01/3.

Barro, R. J. and Xavier Sala-i-Martin, 1991, "Convergence across U. S. States and Regions", *Brookings Papers on Economic Activity*, Ⅰ: pp. 107—182.

Barro, R. J. and Xavier Sala-i-Martin, 1992, "Regional Growth and Migration: A Japan-U. S. Comparison", *Journal of the Japanese and In-*

ternational Economies, No. 6, pp. 312—346.

Chen, Jian and B. M. Fleisher, 1996, "Regional Income Inequality and Economic Growth in China", *Journal of Comparative Economics*, Vol. 22, pp. 141—164.

Chow Gregory C. 1993, "Capital Formation and Economic Growth in China", *Quarterly Journal of Economics*, pp. 809—842.

Chow Gregory C. 2002, *China's Economic Transformation*, Oxford: Blackwell Publisher.

Garofalo G. and S. Yamarik, 2001, "Regional Convergence: Evidence from a New State-by-State Capital Stock Series", Forthcoming in *Review of Economics and Statistics*.

Hu, Zuliu and M. S. Khan, 1996, "Why is China Growing so Fast", IMF Working Paper, No. 96/75.

Iwata Shigeru, M. S. Khan and H. Murao, 2002, "Sources of Economic Growth in East Asia: A Nonparametric Assessment", IMF Working Paper, No. 02/13.

Jian, Tianlun, J. D. Sachs and A. M. Warner, 1996, "Trends in Regional Inequality in China", NBER Working Paper, No. 5412.

Li, J., D. Jorgenson, Y. Zheng, M. Iuroda, 1993, *Productivity and Economic Growth in China, United States and Japan*, Beijing: Chinese Social Science Press.

Rawski, Thomas, 2001, "What's Happening to China's GDP Statistics?", *China Economic Review*.

Razin, Assaf and Chi-wa Yuen, 1996, "Capital Income Taxation and Long-run Growth: New Perspectives", *Journal of Public Economics* 59, pp. 239—263.

Resa Corporation, 2002, "*Gini Coefficient*", *in Statistics Resources-Econometrics-Forecasting*, http://www. xycoon. com/gini. coefficient 1. htm.

Romer, P., 1986, "Increasing Returns and Long Run Growth", J.

Pol. Econ., 94: pp. 1002—1037.

Young A., 1995, "The Tyranny of Numbers: Confronting the Statistical Realities of the East Asian Growth Experience", *Quarterly Journal of Economics*, pp. 641—680.

（原载《经济研究》2004 年第 1 期）

地方保护主义及产业地区集中度的决定因素和变动趋势*

白重恩

（清华大学经济系和香港大学经济金融学院）

杜颖娟　陶志刚

（香港大学商学院）

仝月婷

（新加坡国立大学经济系）

一、引　言

贸易有助于专业化，而反向来看，专业化也将增加人们从贸易中的收益。为了揭示地区间的贸易形式，我们需要研究国际以及地区专业化的决定因素。正是由于这个原因，对生产地区集中性的研究已经成为国际经济学和区域经济学研究中的一个重要领域。实质上，这方面的很多实证研究都是使用一个国家

* 我们向陈松年、Michael Enright、孔笑微、李稻葵、陆毅、Barry Naughton、方博亮、魏尚进、王于渐、郑京海、朱力径，以及AEA年会的参加者致谢，他们提供了十分有价值的意见。感谢查志民、陈小洪、周学文等在确认数据方面所提供的慷慨帮助。同时感谢香港大学和香港经济与商业战略研究所在研究经费方面的支持。

内的数据，因而集中在对于经济活动区域专业化的研究[参见Hanson(2001)对此的最新综述]。这种方法有两方面的优势：一是在一个国家内能够比较容易地获得具有可比性的数据，另一个优势是它避免了在国际研究中衡量国家间制度差异的困难(O'Connell and Wei, 2002)。

经济学家提出了一系列理论来解释经济活动中的区域专业化的现象。有的理论强调地区之间资源禀赋的差异性(Ohlin, 1933)；有的理论强调规模报酬递增的作用，即对于那些规模报酬递增的行业，将生产集中在少数的地方而不是分散在各地，是一种自然的趋势(Krugman, 1991)；而另一些理论则认为，即使对于那些规模报酬不变或者规模报酬递减的行业，一个企业的生产成本(或者其推出新产品和服务的能力)也可能会由于本地区存在其他同行业企业而降低(或增加)，这种溢出效应，或者说经济外部性，可能造成生产集中在个别地区(Marshall, 1920)。

尽管贸易和专业化的优势是很清楚的，但是实现这些优势的前提条件，却并不总能得到满足。由于国际上和地区中所存在的保护主义，商品和服务的自由流通往往难以实现。地区保护主义为贸易设置壁垒，使自由贸易变得困难，从而削弱了专业化本应具有的优势。因而，地方保护主义对专业化的形成起了很大的阻碍作用。

然而，地方保护主义与地区专业化的关系在现有文献中还没有得到应有的重视。据我们所知，至今还没有系统的、特别是实证方面的研究。①这个课题缺乏国际范围的研究，可能是因为前面提到过的数据问题；而关于一国内的研究也没有取得很多成果，这是因为在很多国家，例如美国，地区间贸易壁垒是受到政府管制的，因此地区保护主义并不是一个影响因素。但是中国的情况比较特别，它为我们提供了研究区域专业化中保护主义作用的难得机会。1978年以来的中国经济改革采取了财政分税制度，这使得地方政府存在出于保护税收基础的强烈动机，采取措施保护当地企业免受跨地区竞争威胁。除了财政收入，出于对政权基础和私人利益的考虑，地方政府也有保护地区内的国有企业的动机。另一方面，在改革初期中央政府没有颁布禁止地区间贸易壁垒的条例，后来也缺乏对条例的有效实施。因此，地方保护主义成为影响中国产业区域专业化形成的重要原因。

对于中国地方保护主义的程度存在着广泛的争议。Young(2000)提供了中国在改革期间地方保护主义上升的结论，他通过对各地区国民收入的五个部分（农业、工业、建设、交通和贸易）以及国民生产总值中三个部分（第一产业、第二产业和第三产业）相对比重演变的分析，得出地区专业化降低的结论。但是另一方面，Naughton(1999)通过使用中国省市投入—产出表的数据所作的研究指出，1992年中国的地区专业化与1987年相比增加了许多。我们相信，对于地方保护主义在地区专业化中作用的系统研究以及对中国地区专业化趋势的深入分析将能更清楚地解决这个争论。

鉴于1998年后的部分数据尚未出版，同时部分数据的格式与前13年不一致，我们构建了1985—1997年13年间中国29个省份的32个行业的数据集②，具体的数据集来源参见表1。我们使用的区域专业化数据比Young(2000)使用的数据更加细化，而比Naughton(1999)所使用的数据时间跨度更长，数据也较新。本文不仅研究区域专业化的总体趋势，也分析影响其变化的决定因素。除了资源禀赋、规模报酬递增及外部经济性的作用之外，我们特别关注地方保护主义的作用。具体地说，我们推测地方政府将对以往取得高利税的行业采取保护，因而降低这些行业的地区集中度。③同时国有成分较高的行业中地方保护主义的程度也将较高。

表 1　数据附录:数据和测量值的索引

	1985 年	1986 年	1987 年	1988—1989 年	1990—1994 年	1995 年	1996 年	1997 年
HOOVER 地方化系数(以产出值计算)								
各地区行业的产出值	2	2	2	1	1	3	5	1
HOOVER 地方化系数(以就业人数计算)								
各地区行业的就业人数	4	NA	NA	1	1	NA	5	1
SCALE 规模(总产出/企业数/deflator)								
行业的总产出	1	1	1	1	1	3	1	1
行业总企业数	1	1	1	1	1	3	1	1
价格通缩	2	2	2	2	2	2	2	2
TPM(税收和利润的加总率=(税收+利润)/销售额)								
行业的税收和利润	1	1	1	1	1	3	1	1
行业的销售额	1	1	1	1	1	3	1	1
SSOE(产出中国有企业所占的份额)								
行业总产出	6	6	6	6	6	6	6	6
行业总产出中国有企业所占份额	6	6	6	6	6	6	6	6
ET(总就业人数中工程师和技术人员比例)								
行业大中型企业中的总就业人数	4	NA	5	5	7	7	7	7
大中型企业工程师和技术工人的人数	4	NA	5	5	7	7	7	7

资料来源:《中国工业经济统计年鉴》;《中国统计年鉴》;《中国工业普查 1995》;《中国工业普查 1985》;中国国家统计局;国务院发展研究中心;《中国科技统计年鉴》。

因为产业活动分布的重新调整是一个缓慢的过程，跨地区之间的产业分布除了要受上述因素的影响，还要受历史发展的影响。出于这方面的考虑，我们对数据进行动态估计，也就是说因变量（区域专业化程度）的滞后值，将与解释变量一同出现在方程右边，我们在分析中采用了 Arellano and Bond（1991）建立的估算过程。

实证分析的结果支持我们对于地方保护主义作用的推测。当其他条件相同时，那些在过去取得高利税以及国有企业比重大的行业，地区集中度低。同时，在对区域专业化的解释上，我们的研究有力地支持规模报酬递增理论，而对外部经济性理论的支持则相对有限。因为我们没有找到一个令人满意的方法来测度产业对不可移动资源的依赖度，所以本文没有检验资源禀赋理论。关于各因素的相对重要程度，地方保护主义的影响超过了规模效用和外部经济。最后，中国产业的区域专业化整体趋势在经历了 20 世纪 80 年代中期的些微降低后发生了逆转，近年来出现了显著的增加。这个发现有助于解释关于中国地区专业化趋势的争论。

本文的结构如下：第二部分详细介绍地区专业化的相关理论，并在此基础上建立理论假设；第三部分构建了检验这些假设的重要变量；第四部分对关键变量进行统计描述；第五部分通过模型估算对假设进行计量检验，并探讨各理论对于中国情况的适用性；第六部分是全文的结论。

二、理论和假设

在一国内产业生产的区域专业化与国际专业化有很多的共同之处，并成为国际贸易和区域经济学研究的热点。

第一种解释在一国内生产的区域专业化的理论是由国际贸易和专业化理论衍生而来(Ohlin, 1933)。不同国家具有自然资源、物质资源和人力资源禀赋的不同组合,如果地区间实现贸易,每个地区将会集中从事某类产品和服务的专业化生产,专业化的类型是由资源禀赋和技术能力所导致的相对优势而不是绝对优势所决定的。需要指出的是,这种理论的关键假设是生产要素是不可移动的。因此,我们提出以下假设:

假设1:使用大量不可移动资源的行业应集中在个别地区。

第二种解释区域专业化的理论是直接由新贸易理论衍生而来,它是建立在某些行业具有规模报酬递增的技术特征基础之上的(Krugman, 1991)。比如,对某些行业的生产来说,当产量增加时,固定生产成本或平均生产变动成本显著下降,也就是说,规模报酬递增。在这种行业中,当企业生产大量商品和服务时,它们的平均生产成本相对较低,这也将进一步增加该企业在市场中的竞争优势和产品需求,这种良性的反馈最终将形成生产的高度集中。于是我们有下述假设:

假设2:地区集中化更容易出现在规模报酬递增的行业中。

第三种区域专业化理论是经济外部性(Marshall, 1920)。Marshall认为存在三种体现经济外部性的渠道,使得同一地区同一行业的企业之间存在正的溢出效应。这三种渠道包括:通过行业聚集可以支持供给的专业化、鼓励专业化劳动力市场的产生以及促进支持知识的溢出效应(Krugman and Obstfeld, 2000)。前两种渠道中企业的生产成本因为有同行业其他企业的存在而降低,第三种渠道表明企业在集群中将更易于开发新的产品和服务。有关理论的实证检验,可参阅Dumais等(2002)和Rosenthal和Strange(2001)等人被广泛引用的研究成果。以上所述归纳为下面的假设:

假设3:区域专业化将在拥有重要经济外部性的行业内存在。

在所有上述三种区域专业化理论的背后是关于商品和服务在地区间贸易的重要假设。如果所有的地区都是孤岛,那么即使存在资源禀赋的显著差异、行业的规模报酬递增或者外部经济性,也无法形成任何地区间行业生产的专业化。一般而言,地区间商品和服务的贸易是存在的,但是其自由程度,除了受其他因素影响之外,还依赖于地方保护主义的程度。所以,专业化的程度受制于地方保护主义的程度。

几乎所有的地方政府,不论是经济发达国家的还是发展中国家的,都存在保护地方行业的动机。这是由于地方政府依赖于来自地方行业的税收。它们同样也关心地方的就业情况,在许多发达国家,这直接关系到选票,而在转轨经济国家,则关系到社会稳定(Bai, Li, Tao and Wang, 2000)。为了保证税收基础和确保地方就业率,地方政府可以构建各种贸易壁垒以保护地方行业免于外部的竞争。这与国际贸易中的保护主义相似,但有一点重要的不同,与国家间的国际贸易相比,要保证畅通的地区间贸易容易得多,这是由于国家政府对地方政府有控制权。如在美国,联邦法律禁止各州之间的关税,这极大促进了跨地区商品和服务的贸易,从而促进了行业生产的地区专业化。

尽管地方保护主义在中国一直是一个严重的问题,但是数据显示地区间始终存在大量的商品和服务的流通。严重地方保护主义的出现主要来源于1978年改革后的各种经济政策的不匹配。改革开放以前,中国存在一个高度集权的财政体制。所有的税收首先上交中央政府,中央政府的计划委员会决定地方政府财政预算和向地方分配国库收入(Qian, 2000)。这种制度切断了地方税收收入和地方政府财政支出的联系,地方政府对地方保护的积极性不大。自1978年以来，中国开始采取财政的分权制度，即允许地方政府保留一定比率的税收收入，这使得它们有了保护地方行业的强烈意愿(Li et al., Forthcoming)。财政体制改革中的缺陷是：中央政府没有在改革初期颁布，以及在后期有效实施限制国内贸易壁垒的有关政策。

我们难以直接度量中国国内贸易保护主义的程度，因为贸易保护并非采取对跨地区贸易征收关税或者发放许可证的形式，而是有时利用表面上为其他目的所制定的行政性法规。例如，某地政府为了保护本地汽车行业，采用了只适合本地生产客车技术标准的环境法规。这说明地方保护主义本质是意识形态上的，难于建立对所有行业都适用的衡量标准。④

为了建立对地方保护主义的检验假设，我们关注地方政府能够从建立跨地区竞争壁垒中获得的利益，从而来寻找哪些行业是地方政府愿意保护的。首先，像前面指出过的，地方政府的税收收入依赖于本地行业。可以推测地方政府倾向于保护高税收的行业。此外，尽管经过二十多年经济改革，国有企业对地方政府仍然具有十分重要的地位，因此地方政府倾向于保护国有企业的利益。由于缺乏法律条款的有力约束，私人企业的利润也受到地方政府通过各种税收和收费形式的不同程度的征收。综上所述我们得到下面的假设：

假设4：地区集中度在过去取得高利润和(或)高税收的行业较低。

应该注意到地方政府要花时间了解哪些行业具有高的利税率(TPM)，所以在前面的假设中使用了利税率的滞后值。应该强调的是，尽管地方政府也关心本地企业创造就业机会，但是更加注重利税率。因为仅仅为了保证就业去支持亏损行业的行为是不能长久的。只有盈利行业才能提供稳定的就业，从而给地方政府带来长期持续的利益。越来越多的证据显示,地方政府急于摆脱亏损企业,以避免解决它们最终带来的失业问题。因而,我们把地方政府从当地就业中获得的利益包括在利税率的假设之中。

中国的地方政府从国有企业中获得的利益远超过其他类型的企业,这是一个无法否认的事实。因为地方政府/官员有权任免国有企业的主管人员,所以比起其他类型企业,他们有更多方法可以从国有企业捞取好处。比如,地方政府官员可以为他们的亲戚、朋友和支持者在国有企业找到就业及升迁机会。地方政府还可以甚至公开地把资本从国有企业转移出去,或者挪用于其他项目,或者中饱私囊。国有企业对政府领导的活动进行广告赞助,则被视为正确的表现从而被大力提倡。由于国有企业带来的特殊好处,地方政府有更强烈的动机保护它们。因此我们提出:

假设 5:区域专业化在那些国有企业所占比重高的行业中程度较低。

三、数据和测量

在本节中我们首先将讨论如何对生产的区域专业化进行测量。接着我们将定义和测量其他的变量,来检验我们在上节中提出的五个假设。最后,我们将提出一些统计结果,特别是我们将探讨中国区域专业化的总体趋势,并对 Naughton(1999)和 Young(2000)的论文进行评述。

(一) 区域专业化的测度

测度区域专业化的一种方法是确定专业化所形成的地区间贸易的类型。这种方法在研究全球经济分工和专业化中被广泛地使用。但是与国家间贸易相比,一个国家内地区间贸易的数据更难取得。因此我们在本文中采取更直接的方法来测量不同行业中地区集中性的程度，即先计算出每个行业中各地区的产出比重，然后与各地区全部产出的比重进行比较。

我们从《中国统计年鉴》、《中国工业经济统计年鉴》，以及《中国工业普查资料》等资料中收集了29个地区中32个行业的产出数据，并根据产出数据，可以构建称为Hoover地方化系数(Hoover, 1936)⑤的区域专业化指数。我们首先计算各地区在各行业的相对比重，定义为：

$$L\_OUTPUT_{ij} = (OUTPUT_{ij}/OUTPUT_i)/(OUTPUT_j/OUTPUT)$$

其中 $OUTPUT_{ij}$ 是行业 i 在地区 j 的产出，$OUTPUT_j$ 是地区 j 的总产出，$OUTPUT_i$ 是行业 i 的总产出，OUTPUT 是中国的总产出。如果 L_OUTPUT_{ij} 大于1，那么地区 j 于行业 i 中在全国所占的比重超过地区 j 的总产出在全国总产出所占的比重。同样的，如果 L_OUTPUT_{ij} 小于1，地区 j 于行业 i 中在全国所占的比重低于地区 j 的总产出在全国总产出所占的比重。给定行业 i 在所有 $j=1, \cdots, R$ 的地区份额，我们进行降序排列，得到地区的序列组合。接着，我们计算行业 i 产出在各地区的累计百分比(y 坐标轴)和所有行业产出在各地区的累计百分比(x 坐标轴)，由此构建行业 i 的地方化曲线。如果行业 i 在地区间均匀分布，那么地方化系数对所有行业都为1，同时地方化曲线为45度的直线。另一方面，行业越是地方集中，地方化曲线也就越弯曲。Hoover地区化系数与Gini系数有些相似，它是定义为由45度直线和地方化曲线所围成的区域相对面积。Hoover系数越高，行业地区集中程度越高。

Hoover地方化系数同样可以从就业数据中构建得到。事实上，这种方法被许多经济学家在研究美国经济地方专业化中使用，包括Kim(1995)，Ellison和Glaeser(1997)。在本文中，我们将只使用根据产出数据计算的Hoover地方化系数。原因有两点:第一,就业的数据比产出的数据少。29 个地区中 32 个行业的就业情况数据只有从 1988—1994 年和 1997 年的《中国行业经济统计年鉴》中获得。其他年份的就业情况只有行业的总体数据,而没有按地区分的行业数据。因此,估计 Hoover 系数是不可能的。13 年中缺失 3 年数据(1985 年、1986 年和 1995 年),对通过动态分析方法进行计量研究(比如 Arellano-Bond procedure)产生了严重的影响。其次,就业数据可能会受到国有企业中特别严重的劳动力过剩问题的影响。由于各地区和行业的过剩劳动力问题严重程度不一,根据就业数据计算出来的 Hoover 系数将会是有偏差的。事实上,我们发现以下两个特点:其一,根据产出数据和就业数据计算出的 Hoover 系数之间有很高的相关性,相关系数达到 90%以上;此外,两者的相关系数呈现随时间持续递减的趋势,从 1988 年的 96.89%缓慢降低到 1997 年的 92.39%。这表明,由于不断增加的剩余劳动力问题,根据就业数据来估算的 Hoover 系数,其偏差程度在逐步增加。

另一个度量地方化程度的方法是 1997 年由 Ellison 和 Glaeser 建立的。他们建立的序数中用分解 Herfindahl 相关产业序数的方法,并控制工厂规模分布的差异。由于我们没有可以用来计算 Herfindahl 系数的数据,我们无法使用 Ellison-Glaeser 系数,因此我们把一个行业的平均企业规模作为地方化程度的一个解释变量,用来控制行业间的规模差异(参考假设 2)。

(二) 其他变量

下面我们将定义用来检验上文所提出的五个假设的变量。我们曾指出资源禀赋理论解释区域专业化的一个关键的前提是这些资源是不可移动的。然而我们难于找出一个合适的方法度量资源的不可移动性。Kim(1995)使用的方法不适合于中国(Bai, et al., 2002),同时,另一种度量方法——能源消耗度,由于缺乏数据也不能使用。因此我们决定放弃检验区域专业化的资源禀赋假设。不过,这个牺牲是可以接受的,因为本文的重点集中在讨论地方保护主义对区域专业化的影响。

为了验证规模报酬递增的行业相对集中的假设,我们使用一个行业的平均企业规模作为规模经济性的测量。我们用产出的数据来计算企业的平均规模,以保证与测量地区集中度方法的一致性。行业层面的产出数据和企业数量取自《中国工业经济统计年鉴》和《中国工业普查资料》。我们构建了1986—1997年32个行业平均企业规模的数据集,用SCALE表示,定义其为一个行业的总产出除以行业企业的总数量。

外部经济性主要是原料提供商、劳动市场和知识溢出效应,它通常很难直接测量。本文中,我们使用一个行业中工程师和技术工人的数量占总就业的比重代表行业的外部经济性。根据Dumais等(2002)和Rosenthal和Strange(2001)[⑥]的研究,我们认为可以用这个变量代表劳动市场和知识溢出。32个行业不同年份的大中型企业工程师、技工和总职工人数数据,来自《1985年中国工业普查》和《中国科技年鉴》等。我们构建了32个行业工程师和技工占职工比例的数据集,用ET表示。

在1978年之前,大多数企业都是国有企业,因此它们的利税都被计算为政府的收入。官方统计数据仅仅将税收与利润的总和作为一个项目报告,在我们的样本时期的最初几年中没有单独的关于利税率数据的报告。我们从《中国工业普查资料》以及各年《中国工业经济统计年鉴》中获得32个行业的税收利润总和以及总销售额的数据,构建了1985—1996年间32个行业的利税率数据集,用税收与利润加总率除以总销售额来定义利税率,表示为TPM。

国有成分比例(SSOE)可以从许多方面度量,可以是一个行业内国有企业的产出、销售和就业占行业总人数的百分比。我们的分析主要用总产出计算国有成分的比重，并通过与国务院研究发展中心和国家统计局有关部门的合作，获取了1985—1997年间32个行业国有企业在总产出中比率的有关数据。

四、统 计 概 要

图1是Hoover地方化系数随时间变化的趋势。1985年各行业的简单平均值是0.313，在1987年略有下降，随后平稳上升到1997年的0.434。用加权平均值计算出的趋势也很类似，1985年为0.256，在1988年下降到0.250，在随后的年份中又上升，1997年达到0.304。这种趋势显示，中国的区域专业化程度在1985—1997年的13年间有了相当大的提高。我们的结果与Young(2000)的结果截然相反，而与Naughton(1999)的结论一致。

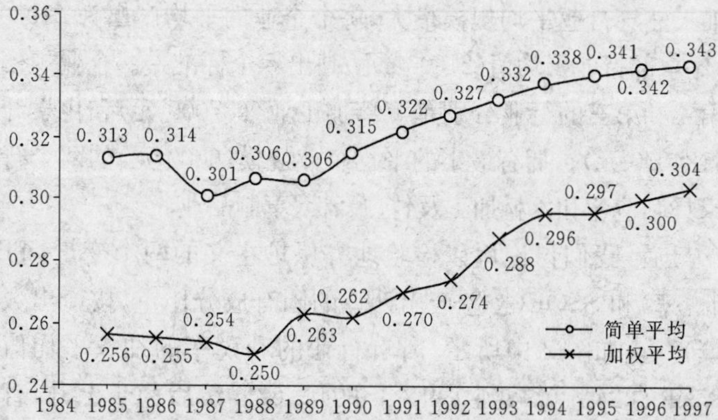

图1　跨行业平均Hoover地方化系数的时间趋势

另一个检验Hoover地方化系数的方法是对各行业的比较。表2显示，不同行业的Hoover系数有很大差异，最低的是金属制品业，仅为 0.146，最高的是木材和竹材采运业，高达 0.847。采矿业由于对资源的依赖程度较高，其地方化程度高于制造业：1985—1997 年，采矿业的平均 Hoover 系数是 0.656，而制造业则仅为 0.328。⑦即使在制造业内部，也存在显著的差异。烟草加工业的地区化程度最高，其次是文教体育用品制造业以及电子及通信设备制造业。金属制品业、机械和设备制造业、化学原料及化工产品是制造业中地区化程度最低的三个行业。

对于外部经济理论的测量指标（工程师和技术人员比重）和规模经济的测量指标（平均规模），行业之间也有很大差异。电子通讯业的工程师与技术工人的比例最高（占总职工人数的 13.99%）；其次是仪器仪表文具制造业（12.63%）；然后是医药业（10.85%）；煤炭矿采掘加工业拥有的工程师和技术工人比例最低（2.73%）；服装和其他纤维制品业与纺织业略高一些，分别是 2.85%和 3.22%。下一步我们比较行业间企业平均规模的差异。石油天然气行业平均规模最大，每个企业的平均产出为 5103000 元，比全部行业平均值（216000 元）高出 5 个标准差。企业规模位于第二和第三的行业分别是烟草加工业（687000 元）和化学纤维业（184000 元）。拥有最小的平均企业规模（6000 元）的两个行业是家具制造业和木材加工及竹、藤、棕、草制品业。

最后，我们讨论用以检验地方保护主义的两个变量，TPM（利税率）和 SSOE（按总产出计算的国有成分比重，按产出数据计算）。正如图 2 中所示，所有行业的利税率的加权平均值从 1985 年的 21%锐减到 1990 年的 11.6%，然后稳步上升，直到 1996 年又一次下降到 9.1%，这是 1978 年后期开始的中国经济改革的结果。在 1949 年到 1978 年间，中国的经济是中央计划经济体制。计划经济的两个重要特征是缺乏竞争和抑制原料价格，这都确保了行业的高利润率。但是经济改革所释放的市场

表 2　主要变量的平均值及排序

行业代码	行 业 名 称	HOOVER	排序	规模	排序	ET	排序	TPM	排序	SSOE	排序
6	煤炭开采加工业	0.579	3	0.0024	15	2.73	32	2.0%	32	79.34	7
7	石油天然气开采业	0.744	2	0.5103	1	8.91	7	16.1%	6	98.24	1
8	金属矿采及加工业	0.578	4	0.0018	19	4.94	18	14.1%	12	66.58	12
10	非金属矿采及加工业	0.319	12	0.0007	30	4.19	25	15.4%	9	36.13	25
12	木材竹材采运业	0.847	1	0.0040	10	4.38	24	15.0%	11	96.55	3
13	食品加工及制造业	0.199	24	0.0019	18	4.73	19	5.9%	31	68.23	11
15	饮料制造业	0.238	20	0.0018	22	6.31	13	18.8%	5	65.51	14
16	烟草加工业	0.537	5	0.0687	2	4.69	20	56.1%	1	97.37	2
17	纺织业	0.283	15	0.0047	8	3.22	30	7.4%	29	50.85	21
18	服装及纤维制品制造业	0.277	17	0.0016	23	2.85	31	7.6%	28	11.73	31
19	皮革毛皮羽绒及其制品业	0.279	16	0.0018	20	3.33	29	6.0%	30	22.06	29
20	木材加工及竹藤棕草制造业	0.348	10	0.0006	31	4.58	22	7.7%	27	35.95	26
21	家具制造业	0.219	22	0.0006	32	3.89	26	8.1%	26	10.95	32
22	造纸及纸制品业	0.197	25	0.0018	21	4.50	23	11.0%	20	51.00	19
23	印刷及记录媒体制造业	0.183	27	0.0008	29	3.65	28	13.8%	14	55.30	18
24	文教体育用品制造业	0.476	6	0.0014	24	3.87	27	12.1%	18	26.84	27
25	石油加工、炼焦产品、煤气生产和供应业	0.391	8	0.0148	4	10.18	4	19.9%	3	92.47	4
26	化学原料及制品制造业	0.154	31	0.0036	13	7.96	10	13.1%	15	69.38	9

（续表）

行业代码	行业名称	HOOVER	排序	规模	排序	ET	排序	TPM	排序	SSOE	排序
27	医药制造业	0.159	29	0.0055	7	10.85	3	13.9%	13	69.10	10
28	化学纤维制造业	0.387	9	0.0184	3	6.90	12	15.4%	8	66.29	13
29	橡胶制品业	0.192	26	0.0036	12	5.07	17	15.0%	10	56.91	17
30	塑料制品业	0.264	18	0.0014	25	5.96	15	8.8%	25	19.45	30
31	非金属矿物制造业	0.161	28	0.0011	27	4.68	21	12.3%	16	44.47	23
32	金属冶炼及研压加工业	0.332	11	0.0143	5	6.03	14	15.5%	7	79.05	8
34	金属制品业	0.146	32	0.0012	26	5.96	16	10.0%	24	22.28	28
35	机械与设备制造业	0.154	30	0.0022	16	8.18	9	10.8%	22	58.78	16
37	交通运输设备制造业	0.302	14	0.0042	9	9.66	6	10.8%	21	64.68	15
40	电器机械及器材制造业	0.229	21	0.0032	14	8.52	8	11.5%	19	39.34	24
41	电子及通信业	0.414	7	0.0068	6	13.99	1	10.2%	23	50.72	22
42	仪器仪表及文化办公用品制造业	0.308	13	0.0020	17	12.63	2	12.3%	17	50.88	20
44	电力蒸汽热水生产和供应业	0.207	23	0.0039	11	9.93	5	22.7%	2	90.02	5
46	自来水生产和供应业	0.252	19	0.0008	28	7.21	11	19.8%	4	89.58	6
均值		0.324		0.0216		6.39		13.7%		57.38	
标准差		0.174		0.0900		2.93		9.0%		25.68	

注：计量单位：亿元人民币每企业；ET：每百人的技术人员；TPM：利税率；SSOE：国有成分比例。

力量增加了市场的竞争，提高了原料的价格，导致了行业利润率的全面下降。中央计划体制的退出使得地方政府和私人企业更容易进入各种行业，从而加剧了产品市场的竞争。同时，对原料价格的各种限制的逐步取消，导致了市场价格的增长和波动性的增加，从而增加了大多数行业生产的成本。1991年起，利税率逐步趋向稳定，这意味着中国市场竞争的逐步成熟。⑧国有成分比重的时间趋势如图3中所示，清楚地显示了改革开放后国有企业比重的显著下降。国有成分比重的跨行业加权平均值先从1985年的73.11%下降到1990年的68.00%，然后猛降到1997年的40.92%。

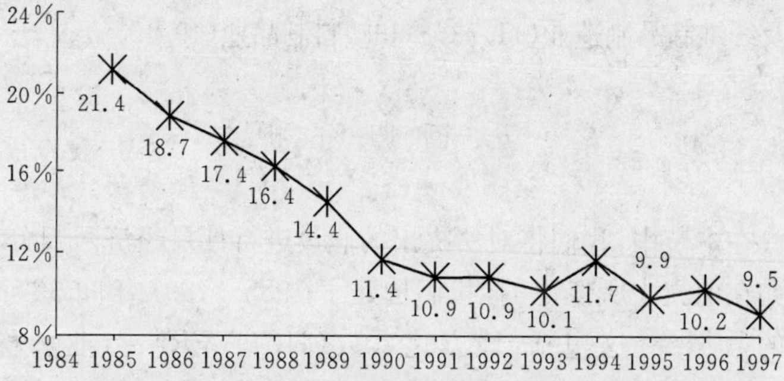

图2　跨行业平均税收和利润加总率的时间趋势(%)

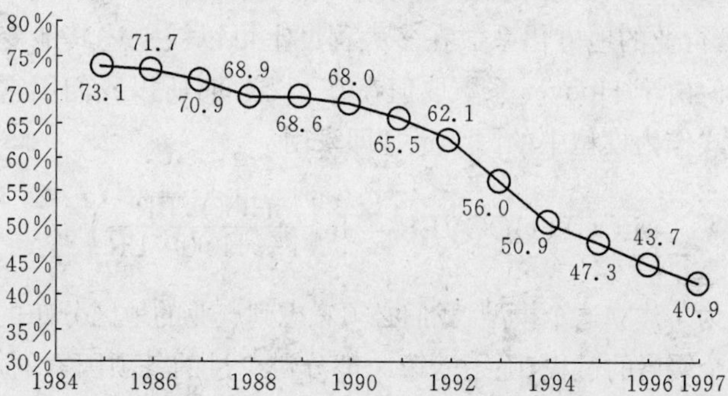

图3　跨行业的平均国有企业比重的时间趋势(%)

尽管行业利税率和国有企业比重随时间变化的趋势非常明显，但是表 2 显示这两项指标在行业间存在显著的差异。首先，平均税收和利润率是 13.7%，其中烟草加工业的利润率最高(56.1%)，随后是电力、蒸汽和热水生产和供应业，石油加工、炼焦产品和煤气生产和供应业，分别为 22.7%和 19.9%。税收和利润率低的行业包括煤炭开采和加工业(2.0%)，食品加工和制造业(5.9%)，皮革、毛皮、羽绒及其制品业(6.0%)。其次，平均国有企业产出比重是 57.38%。其中石油天然气开采业最高(98.24%)，随后是烟草加工业(97.37%)和木竹采伐运输业(96.55%)。国有企业比重低的行业包括家具制造业(10.95%)，服装及纤维制品制造业(11.73%)和塑料制品业(19.45%)。

五、回 归 分 析

在本节中，我们将对所提出的假设进行计量经济回归分析。正如在前文中所谈论的，我们构建了 1985—1997 年间 32 个行业的数据集，这包括：地方化系数(HOOVER)、行业利税率(TPM)、平均企业规模(SCALE)、国有成分比率(SSOE)和工程师与技术人员占行业职工比例(ET)。使用这些数据，我们可以估算，行业的地方化系数在多大程度上可以被上述其他变量所决定。由于 Hoover 系数取值在 0—1 之间，所以我们用它的对数形式作为模型中的因变量。即采用：

$$\mathrm{LOGITHOOVER} = \ln\left(\frac{\mathrm{HOOVER}}{1 - \mathrm{HOOVER}}\right)$$

为了建立这个模型，我们必须考虑到产业的地区分布的调整是一个缓慢的过程，除了受第二部分讨论过的各项因素的影响，还要受到历史传统的作用。因此，我们将运用下面的动态模型：

$$\begin{aligned}\text{LOGITHOOVER}_{it} = {} & \delta_1 \text{LOGITHOOVER}_{i,\,t-1} \\ & + \delta_2 \text{LOGITHOOVER}_{i,\,t-2} \\ & + \beta_l \text{TPM}_{i,\,t-l} + \beta_2 \text{SSOE}_{it} \\ & + \beta_3 \text{SCALE}_{it} + \beta_4 \text{ET}_{it} \\ & + \alpha_i + \gamma_t + \varepsilon_{it} \qquad (1)\end{aligned}$$

其中 α_i 是行业的特殊效应，β_t 是时间的特殊效应，ε_{it} 是误差项，l 是利税率变量滞后的年数，我们考虑 $l = 1, 2, 3$ 的情形。我们使用滞后的利税率值的原因是，地方政府需要时间来辨别哪些行业能够带来更多的财政税收，也因此更值得保护。为了保留足够的样本数量，我们不考虑三年以上的滞后。

使用对利税率滞后变量的另一个好处是可以减轻有可能存在的利税率是内生变量的问题。比如，Hoover 和利税率可能同时受一个没有被模型包括的变量的影响，利税率变量就会与回归中的误差项有相关关系，这样用最小方差法所估算的结果就是有偏差的。例如，如果某个行业在每一个地区都只有一个企业供应当地需求，而且产品不容易在地区之间流通，那么，由于垄断的存在，该行业将同时表现出较低的地区专业化程度和较高的行业利润率。在这种情况下，地区专业化的低水平就不是因为地方保护主义，而是垄断结果。如果这类因素不随时间变化，当我们加入行业特定变量后，这种内生性问题就可以得到解决。如果这类因素随时间变动，同时其变动是没有自相关的，那么同时使用滞后一年的利税率和行业特定变量，就可以解决这个内生的问题。如果这个共同的因素随着时间变动，而且其变动是呈现一阶自相关的，那么使用滞后两年的行业利税率和行业特定变量，就可以解决这个内生的问题。更高阶的自相关情况依次递推。如果对方程进行一阶差分消除了行业特殊效应，对于给定的自相关阶数，需要利税率的更大的阶数的滞后值。

方程(1)不能直接估计,因为滞后的因变量与误差项 ε_{it} 相关,即使 ε_{it} 不是自相关的(Greene, 2000)。

我们使用 Arellano 和 Bond(1991)建立的动态估计过程,在这个估算过程中,行业特殊系数在上述方程式的一阶差分中被消去,得到的方程中使用因变量和事先给定变量的各阶滞后值,用外生变量的差值作为工具变量。Arellano 和 Bond 估算过程允许我们把利税率的滞后值或者作为给定变量或者作为外生变量来使用。

表 3 总结了方程(1)的估计结果,利税率(TPM)的滞后值被作为预先给定的变量,在表中,无论滞后的时期为多少,利税率的相关系数都是负的。当利税率滞后一年或两年,统计显著水平分别为 10%或 15%。这样的结果显示,地方政府倾向于保护能带来较高利润和税收的行业,支持前面讨论的第四个假设。

表 3 方程(1)的估计结果

因变量:Hoover 地方化系数的对数形式 TMP 被当作预先决定的变量

解释变量	1	2	3
LOGITHOOVER			
Lag1	0.4665*** (0.0915)	0.4491*** (0.0891)	0.4707*** (0.0958)
Lag2	0.2145*** (0.066)	0.2316*** (0.0662)	0.2286*** (0.0669)
TPM			
Lag1	−0.3068* (0.2123)		
Lag2		−0.4867* (0.2624)	
Lag3			−0.1257 (0.248)
SSOE	−0.0024* (0.0016)	−0.0030* (0.0017)	−0.0034** (0.0014)

（续表）

解释变量	1	2	3
SCALE	0.5616*** (0.1478)	0.5457*** (0.1341)	0.6103*** (0.1776)
ET	0.0021 (0.0033)	0.0019 (0.0031)	0.0026 (0.0028)
CON	0.0011 (0.0055)	−0.0020 (0.006)	−0.0038 (0.005)
# of obs.	306	306	280
显著性检验			
Wald Chi^2	444.20	345.17	592.47

注：***，**，* 和 # 分别表示 1%，5%，10%和 15%的显著性水平；括号里的数值是标准差；年份作为虚拟变量包括在计算中，但是它们的系数没有列入表内；LOGITHOOVER = ln[HOOVER/(1 − HOOVER)]。

国有企业比重(SSOE)的系数，无论利税率滞后阶数为多少，也都是负的。当利税率滞后 1、2、3 年时，显著性水平分别为 5%、10%和 15%。这个结果对第五个假设的支持是显著的，也就是说地方政府倾向于保护国有成分比例较高的行业。

SCALE 的系数始终都是正的，显著性水平一直保持在 1%。这个结果支持第二个假设，即说明一个行业的平均企业规模越大，它的区域专业化程度越高。

ET 的系数虽然在任何情况下都是正的，但是统计显著性水平太低。这个结果对第三个假设提供了有限的支持。行业拥有的工程师和技术人员比例越高，则区域专业化的程度越高。

LOGITHOOVER 一阶滞后值的系数是正的，并且在各种情况下都十分显著。二阶滞后值也是同样的，这说明一个行业的区域专业化程度深受历史影响。对行业其他条件的变化的调整反应过程也是较慢的。

表 4 列出了把利税率的滞后值作为外生变量时的方程(1)的估计结果。结论和表 3 相似,只是利税率系数 3 年的滞后值的检验显著性水平提高了,但是在使用利税率的一年期滞后值时国有企业比重的显著性水平却恶化了。为了测量地区专业化的不同因素的经济意义,我们计算每一个自变量变动一个标准差时因变量随之变动几个标准差。我们用使用两年的滞后变量并把它作为预先给定的变量的结果来做估算,因为在这个模型中大多数变量是统计上显著的。在这个模型中,变量的时间范围是 1987—1997 年,这个时期里 LOGITHOOVER 的标准差是 0.8246,同一时期利税率的标准差是 0.1005,每当利税率变化 1 个标准差,LOGITHOOVER 变动 5.9%个标准差;当 LOGITHOOVER_1、LOGITHOOVER_2、SSOE、SCALE 和 ET 分别变动一个标准差时,LOGITHOOVER 分别变动 45.4%、23.7%、10.2%、6.0%和 0.8%个标准差。这些数字显示:历史对中国产业地区专业化程度有着决定性的影响,在其他的因素中,最重要的是地方保护主义,科技人员比重的影响相对最小。

表 4 方程(1)的估计结果

因变量:Hoover 地方化系数的对数形式 TMP 被当作预先决定的变量

解释变量	1	2	3
LOGITHOOVER			
Lag1	0.4430*** (0.0897)	0.4429*** (0.0918)	0.4213*** (0.0979)
Lag2	0.2136*** (0.0639)	0.2374*** (0.0628)	0.2327*** (0.0629)
TPM			
Lag1	0.4291* (0.2423)		
Lag2		−0.5318* (0.2589)	

（续表）

解释变量	1	2	3
Lag3			−0.1753 (0.2602)
SSOE	−0.0024 (0.0018)	−0.0030* (0.0017)	−0.0032** (0.0015)
SCALE	0.4933*** (0.1298)	0.4338*** (0.1015)	0.5984*** (0.1507)
E	0.0019 (0.0034)	0.0027 (0.0027)	0.0030 (0.0026)
CON	0.0004 (0.0057)	−0.0022 (0.0059)	−0.0025 (0.0058)
# of obs.	306	306	280
显著性检验			
Wald Chi^2	356.09	320.83	534.49

注：***，**，* 和 # 分别表示 1%，5%，10%和 15%的显著性水平；括号里的数值是标准差；年份作为虚拟变量包括在计算中，但是它们的系数没有列入表内；LOGITHOOVER = ln[HOOVER/(1 − HOOVER)]。

总而言之，上述各个研究影响产业地区专业化的不同因素的结果是明显一致的，我们先前的假设得到了有力的验证：产业区域专业化的水平在以往高税利的行业、国有成分比例较高的行业里比较低；而这两个指标体现了地方政府有动机保护这两类地方产业。结论还较强地支持了规模经济理论对专业化的解释，对外部经济理论对专业化的解释也提供了有限的支持。在区域专业化程度决定中，地方保护主义的作用超过了外部经济性和规模效用，仅次于历史影响的作用。

六、结　　语

尽管地方保护主义是贸易和专业化的重要决定因素，但是至今还没有对这方面系统的实证研究，本文试图填补这方面空白。我们首先建立了中国 29 个地区 32 个产业的 13 年间(1985—1997 年)的数据集，用动态估计的方法研究中国产业区域专业化的决定因素，关注的重心是地方保护主义。我们发现：产业区域专业化的水平在以往享有较高利税率和国有成分比例较高的行业里比较低，反映了地方政府有动机保护这两类地方产业。本文还提供了较强的证据来支持规模经济理论对专业化的解释，对外部经济理论对专业化解释的支持则相对较弱。地方保护主义的作用在决定区域专业化水平中超过了外部经济性和规模效用，仅次于历史影响的作用。

除了提供地方保护主义重要性的证据，本文还考察了中国产业区域专业化水平的整体趋势，在经历了早期的微弱下降后，在经济改革的近几年来有显著的提高。这个结论与 Young(2000)相反，却与 Naughton(1999)一致。我们使用的数据比 Young(2000)更加细化，比 Naughton(1999)时期跨度更长、数据更新，所以我们的工作将会有助于中国区域专业化时间趋势方面问题的解决。

注 释

① 沈立人和戴园晨(1990)提到了地方保护主义和产业结构趋同之间的关系，但没有进行实证分析。

② 样本包括 29 个省、自治区和直辖市。虽然海南在 1988 年建省，但是在本文中它的数据被归在广东省中。

③ 银温泉和才婉茹(2001)也对我国地方市场分割的成因进行了理论探讨。他们认为地方市场分割的基础是行政性分权。我们的实证结果也是对他们的理论的支持。黄肖广(1996)也探讨了财政体制与地方保护主义的关系。

④ 臧跃茹(2000)介绍了地方保护的更多形式。

⑤ 由于中国行业中企业层面的数据有限，我们无法使用最近由 Ellison 和 Glaeser(1997)建立的地方化指数。

⑥ Dumais 等(2002)采用美国统计局分纬度调查数据库，去建立区域专业化的外部经济 3 种方式的代表，Rosenthal 和 Strange(2001)主要依赖美国经济分析局的数据。在对中国的产业地区专业化的研究中，我们严格地保持在数据可获得的范围之内。大多数美国经济分析局的统计数据，在中国没有相对应的经济统计。中国统计局只是在行业水平上有可以得到的调查数据。所以我们采用技术人员比例的变量，与 Rosenthal 和 Stranger(2001)使用的具有博士、硕士和学士学位的工人比率作为劳动力指标相似，也与 Dumais 等(2002)使用的雇员教育水平作为知识溢出效应的指标变量相似。

⑦ 这个数据是从表 2 的相关样本数据中获得。开采业包括从 6—12 的 7 个行业，制造业包括 13—42 的 30 个行业。

⑧ 尽管这里是对于利润率的讨论，税收与利润的加总率也有相同的趋势。

参考文献

黄肖广，1996：《财政体制改革与地方保护主义》，《经济研究》第 2 期。

沈立人、戴园晨，1990：《我国"诸侯经济"的形成及其弊端和根源》，《经济研究》第 3 期。

银温泉、才婉茹，2001：《我国地方市场分割的成因和治理》，《经济研究》第 6 期。

臧跃茹，2000：《关于打破地方市场分割问题的研究》，《改革》第 6 期。

Arellano, M., Bond, S., 1991, "Some Tests of Specification for Panel Data: Monte Carlo Evidence and an Application to Employment Equations", *Review of Economic Studies*, 58, 277—297.

Bai, C. E., Li, D. D., Tao, Z. G., Wang, Y. J., 2000, "A Multitask Theory of State Enterprise Reform", *Journal of Comparative Economics*, 28, 716—738.

Bai, C. E., Du, Y. J., Tao, Z. G. and Tong, Y. T., 2002, "Protectionism and Regional Specialization: Evidence from China's Industries", The University of Hong Kong Mimeo.

Dumais G., Ellison, G. and Glaeser, E., 2002, "Geographic Concentration as a Dynamic Process", *Review of Economics and Statistics*, 84, 193—204.

Ellison, G. and Glaeser, E., 1997, "Geographic Concentration in US Manufacturing Industries: a Dartboard Approach", *Journal of Political Economy*, 105, 889—927.

Greene, W. H., 2000, *Econometric Analysis*, Prentice-Hall, Upper Saddle River.

Hanson, G. H., 2001, "Scale Economies and the Geographic Concentration of Industry", *Journal of Economic Geography*, 1, 255—276.

Hoover, E. M., 1936, "The Measurement of Industrial Localization", *Review of Economics and Statistics*, 18, 162—171.

Kim, S., 1995, "Expansion of Markets and the Geographic Distribution of Economic Activities: The Trends in US Regional Manufacturing Structure, 1860—1987", *Quarterly Journal of Economics*, 110, 881—908.

Krugman, P., 1991, "Increasing Returns and Economic Geography", *Journal of Political Economy*, 99, 483—499.

Krugman, P., Obstfeld, M., 2000, "International Economics: Theory and Practice", Addison-Wesley, Reading, MA. Kung, J. K.-S., 1999, The Evolution of Property Rights in Village Enterprises: The Case of Wuxi County.

Li, J., Qiu, L. D., Sun, Q. Y., Forthcoming, "Interregional Protection: Implications of Fiscal Decentralization and Trade Liberalization", *China Economic Review*.

Marshall, A., 1920, *Principles of Economics*. MacMillan, New York.

Naughton, B., 1999, "How much can Regional Integration do to

Unify China's Market", University of California at San Diego Mimeo.

O'Connell, P. G. J., Wei, S. J., 2002, "'The Bigger They are, The Harder They Fall': Retail Price Differences Across US Cities", *Journal of International Economics*, 56, 21—53.

Ohlin, B., 1933, *Interregional and International Trade*, Harvard University Press, Cambridge.

Qian, Y. Y., 2000, "The Process of China's Market Transition (1978—1998): The Evolutionary, Historical, and Comparative Perspectives", *Journal of Institutional and Theoretical Economics*, 156, 151—171.

Rosenthal, S. S., Strange, W. C., 2001, "The Determinants of Agglomeration", *Journal of Urban Economics*, 50, 191—229.

Young, A., 2000, "The razor's Edge: Distortions and Incremental Reform in The People's Republic of China", *Quarterly Journal of Economics*, 115, 1091—1135.

（原载《经济研究》2004 年第 4 期）

从啤酒市场整合程度看 WTO 对消除地方保护的影响*

李　杰　孙群燕

（中山大学岭南学院）

一、引　　言

关于贸易保护，中外学者主要研究了不同国家间的贸易壁垒问题，但对于一个国家内不同地区间的贸易保护，学者们没有给予足够的关注。中国地区间的贸易保护是一个普遍的现象，汽车、烟草、服装等产品的跨地区销售，在不同程度上面临着地方保护的重重障碍，啤酒行业是其中表现突出的一个行业（Gilley, 2001）。

目前，对中国地区间贸易保护问题的研究，比较有代表性的论文有 Young（2000）、银温泉和才婉茹（2001）以及陈抗等（2002），前两篇文章提供了大量关于中国地区间贸易保护的事实，后一篇文章则从中央与地方之间分配财政资源的不同方式

---

* 本文的研究得到国家自然科学基金之金融数学重大项目（项目号：10131030）以及中山大学笹川优秀青年基金之博士生重要创新项目提供的资助，特此致谢。在本文的写作过程中，王美今提供了许多有价值的参考意见，在此表示感谢。

入手，考察了财政集权程度的变化对地方政府保护行为的影响。以上文章都认为，行政性分权是造成地区间高贸易壁垒的重要原因。Li 与 Zhang(2003)在完全竞争的模型框架内，建立了一个中国地区间贸易保护的经济模型，分析中国在加入 WTO 后，各地区贸易保护壁垒对地区经济福利，进而对整个国家福利状况的影响。文章认为，加入 WTO 并对外实行自由贸易，有助于消除地区间的贸易保护壁垒。Li 等(2003)通过构建一个寡头垄断竞争模型，从理论上分析了地方政府设立地区贸易保护壁垒的激励与中国税制改革以及贸易自由化进程的关系。文章认为，低的中央税率和高的对外贸易保护，是促成地区间形成贸易保护壁垒的重要原因。到目前为止，从经验分析的角度来研究中国地区间的保护问题的文章尚不多见，即便涉及这一问题的文章，通常也只是把地方保护作为其中的一个影响因素，如 Bai 等(2002)主要研究地区间分工专业化与地方保护之间的关系，其分析的重点是分工专业化而非地方保护行为。Ha 与 Fan (2003)用 ADF 方法研究了香港与内地四个城市价格序列的收敛趋势，其基本结论是，这些价格序列之间具有一致收敛的趋势。但该文的研究重点在于四个城市价格收敛的一致性如何影响香港特区的价格变动趋势。据笔者所知，到目前为止还没有文章从经验分析的角度考察中国加入 WTO 对地方政府保护行为的影响，本文试图沿着这个方向做一些尝试性的研究工作。

鉴于中国各行业都存在不同程度的地方保护行为，而且受到数据资料方面的限制，要对所有行业做一个全面的分析是不可行的。因此，本文仅仅以啤酒行业作为一个切入点，采用1997—2003 年全国 40 个主要的大中城市 640 mL 当地主销啤酒价格的月度数据，着重分析以下两方面的问题：中国地区间是否存在贸易保护壁垒？加入 WTO 是否有助于消除地区间的贸易壁垒？本文的基本结论是：从1997年1月到2003年3月，中国啤酒市场的整合程度不高，市场分割的现象比较普遍。从分时期的结果看，在中央政府出台取消地方保护壁垒的措施之前（无论有没有考虑政策出台的事前效应），中国啤酒市场的市场分割现象比较普遍；但在这一政策措施出台以后，啤酒市场却出现了明显的整合趋势。同时，以北京和青岛为中心，中国的啤酒市场出现了区域性的整合趋势。但是，北京与青岛这两个最大的啤酒生产地的啤酒价格序列之间，无论是从整段时期看，还是分时期看，都不存在协整关系。

文章的第二部分回顾了中国啤酒行业的发展状况及所存在的地方保护行为；第三部分提出研究的理论框架与研究方法；第四部分具体考察中国最大的两个啤酒产地与其他城市在啤酒价格方面的协整关系，据此分析中国地区间在啤酒行业方面的贸易保护程度及变化趋势；第五部分对基本结论提供一个合理的经济学解释。

二、地方保护与中国啤酒行业的发展状况

中国地区间的商品流动存在壁垒限制是一个众所周知的事实，这在很大程度上源于长期以来形成的地方保护主义，其表现形式主要是当地政府直接在当地投资设厂，并通过使用贸易壁垒，阻碍外地生产同类产品的企业进入本地市场。这种政府行为在啤酒行业表现得尤为突出。在新中国建立后，国家对啤酒行业采取了扶持政策，新建了一批啤酒厂，使啤酒业取得了一定的发展，但由于受当时购买能力和消费习惯的限制，啤酒的消费市场不大，全国多数地区啤酒生产为空白。改革开放后，国家出台了一些政策，鼓励啤酒业快速发展。在这样的形势下，地方政

府纷纷投资建立自己的啤酒厂，啤酒企业的数量与产量迅速扩张。到1988年，全国有啤酒企业813家，产量656.4万吨，仅次于美国和德国。但企业规模非常小，大多年产1—2万吨，并且在地域上高度分散。

从20世纪90年代初期开始，啤酒产量以年均20%的速度增长，到1997年，全国啤酒总产量达到了1888.5万吨。在产业竞争格局上，各地政府纷纷扶持自己的啤酒品牌。在这一阶段，全国啤酒企业基本分化为三个层次：以青岛、燕京和珠江三大集团为第一层次；地方名牌啤酒企业为第二层次，如沈阳华润雪花啤酒、重庆啤酒、河南金星啤酒、哈尔滨啤酒、钱江啤酒、圣泉啤酒等；其他市县啤酒企业为第三层次。值得注意的是，啤酒行业的产业集中度仍然偏低，到1997年底，在全国500多家啤酒企业中，没有一家年产量超过100万吨，即使是产量最大的燕京和青岛啤酒，其产量总和也只占全国总产量的5%左右。全国的啤酒市场仍处于群雄逐鹿的市场分割状态。导致这种局面出现的一个重要原因，在于各地政府保护本地企业利益的动机。这种动机的产生源于啤酒企业在地方财政收入中的重要地位。尤其在几次重大的税制改革之后，地方政府支配自身财政收入的权限大大增加，而啤酒企业历来是地方的利税大户，为了维护自身的利益，地方政府都会千方百计地保护当地的啤酒厂。它们通过设置各种有形或无形的进入障碍，如设置质量检测标准和各种税费，提高外地啤酒企业的销售成本，甚至通过明令禁止外地啤酒在本地的销售等手段，把外地品牌阻挡在当地市场之外(Li et al., 2003)。

出于加入WTO的需要，从1995年开始，中央政府多次表示要取消地区间的贸易保护壁垒。2001年4月21日，国务院发布了《关于禁止在市场经济活动中实行地区封锁的规定》，明确规定“市场交易中的地区封锁”是违法行为。这一措施意在规范市场竞争，打击行政垄断，根除地方保护，为建立市场经济新秩序保驾护航。与此同时，由于中国啤酒消费进入年均5%的低增长状态，啤酒产能过剩，竞争激烈，行业盈利能力下降，出现大面积亏损。为增强自身的竞争实力，青岛和燕京啤酒集团开始在全国进行大规模的资本圈地运动，拉开了战略竞争和行业大整合的进程。它们通过并购地方名牌企业，使产销区域不断扩张。到目前为止，青岛啤酒的产销区域已经向西延伸到陕西，向南延伸到广东，并打入香港特区市场，形成了很高的知名度；燕京啤酒也不甘示弱，先后进入湖南、湖北与江西，两者同时发展成为中国最大的啤酒生产厂家。近年来，两大啤酒集团的产能规模位次交错变化，燕京啤酒1995—1998年产量和市场占有率均居全国第一，1999年以后，青岛啤酒上升为第一，燕京退居第二。到2002年底，青岛啤酒在全国啤酒市场所占有的份额已经达到11%，而燕京为10%左右。总体上看，这两大啤酒集团在国内的啤酒市场上基本处于寡占的地位。

三、研究的理论框架、方法和数据说明

地区间贸易壁垒的主要表现形式是市场分割。所谓市场分割，是指一个市场商品价格的变化，不能及时有效地传递到另一个市场，市场间的价格信息不存在相互或共同决定的趋势。市场分割是与市场整合相对的一个概念。市场分割往往会导致商品的低效率流通，损害消费者的利益。

一般来说，从经验分析的角度研究市场分割问题的方法有很多，如相关分析法、Ravallion模型法(Ravallion procedure)，协整分析方法(co-integration approach)及Parity Bounds模型法(Parity Bounds model)。鉴于本文搜集的数据资料主要为城

市的月度价格数据，同时缺乏城市间的运输成本资料，在这种情况下，我们选择采用协整分析方法是比较合适的。①

运用协整分析方法研究市场分割问题，首先必须检验单个市场商品价格的时间序列是否平稳。平稳性检验通常采取 Augmented Dickey-Fuller 方法（ADF 法）。ADF 法是依据对以下模型中的统计值的显著性来判定：

$$\Delta P_t = r_0 + r_1 P_{t-1} + \sum_{k=1}^{N} \delta_k \Delta P_{t-k} + \varepsilon_t \qquad (1)$$

其中，$\Delta P_t = P_t - P_{t-1}$ 表示当期价格与上一期价格的差，ε_t 为误差项，N 表示滞后期数。在方程(1)中，零假设 H_0 为序列$\{P_t\}$具有一阶单整，即经过一阶差分后变平稳，用数学方法表示为 $P_t \sim I(1)$。如果 r_1 为负数并且在统计上显著，则拒绝零假设，序列为零阶单整，即 $P_t \sim I(0)$。如果 r_1 在统计上不显著，则不能拒绝零假设，这说明序列$\{P_t\}$可能在更高阶上实现整合，我们应继续对方程(1)进行回归，做二阶平稳的单位根检验。

$$\Delta^2 P_t = \varnothing_0 + \varnothing_1 P_{t-1} + \sum_{k=1}^{N} \theta_k \Delta^2 P_{t-k} + \eta_t \qquad (2)$$

与方程(1)相比，方程(2)用 ΔP_t 代替了方程(1)中的 P_t。如果仍无法拒绝 $\varnothing_1 = 0$ 的零假设，我们还需进一步用 $\Delta^2 P_t$ 代替 ΔP_t，对序列$\{P_t\}$进行三阶平稳检验，并继续重复上述过程，直到能拒绝相应的零假设，得到一个平稳的序列为止。

在对单个价格序列进行了平衡性检验后，就可以进一步考察不同市场的商品价格之间是否具有协同变化的趋势。价格序列之间存在协同关系的一个基本前提，是价格序列必须同阶单整。如果不存在同阶单整性，则谈不上讨论序列间的协整关系问题。在两个市场的价格序列存在同阶单整的前提下，就可以分析它们之间的协整关系。

研究人员通常采用 E-G 两步法或 Johansen 方法来测定两个市场的价格序列之间的协整关系。本文采用 Johansen 方法来进行测定。Johansen 方法的基本原理是:采用最大似然法估计包含有关变量一阶差分滞后项和水平量滞后项的向量自回归(VAR)模型。依据 Johansen(1988)及 Johansen 和 Juselius(1990)的方法,可以利用特征根最大值统计量 $-T\ln(1-\lambda)$ 即 λ_{max} 和迹统计量 $-T\sum\ln(1-\lambda)$(其中 T 为样本数,λ 为对应于不同秩数的特征根),来判断是否存在协整关系。

采用 Johansen 方法进行协整分析时,会涉及确定解释变量的最大滞后期数问题。我们的处理方法是:通过估计相应的 VAR 系统,并根据赤池(Akaike)信息准则(AIC)或者施瓦茨(Schwartz)准则(SC),确定适当的最大滞后期数。由于我们采用的是啤酒价格的月度数据,如果不存在区域性的贸易壁垒,价格信息的传递是比较迅速的,因此选取的最长滞后期不超过 3 期。

如果两个不同市场的价格序列之间存在协整关系,则这种关系可表述如下:

$$P_{it} = \alpha_0 + \sum_{k=1}^{N} \alpha_k P_{j,\,t-k+1} + \mu_t \tag{3}$$

其中 P_{it}、P_{jt} 分别表示市场 i、j 在时期 t 的价格,μ_t 表示误差项,N 表示滞后期数,α_0 表示除另一个市场的商品价格以外的所有影响价格变化的因素,如运输、加工成本、销售收入、政策因素等。

四、中国最大的两个啤酒产地与其他城市在啤酒价格方面的协整关系

下面我们主要研究两个问题:全国最大的两个啤酒生产地,

即北京和青岛，与其他主要城市的啤酒市场之间是否存在市场分割？如果存在的话，中国加入 WTO 是否有助于消除这种地区性的市场分割？我们首先对这些数据的总体变动趋势做一个粗略的描述，然后运用第三部分讨论的分析方法，构建经济计量模型，并对估计结果进行经济学解释。本文的数据分析结果主要通过使用计量分析软件 E-views 3.1 计算得到。

（一）数据来源及基本分析

本文采用 1997 年 1 月至 2003 年 3 月全国 40 个主要的大中城市 640 mL 当地主销啤酒价格的月度数据，数据来源于中国价格信息中心提供的工业消费品零售价格数据库。

由于我们使用的是月度数据，很有可能存在季节性波动，必须首先对其进行判别，在此基础上，再进一步考察数据波动的基本趋势。

图 1 显示了北京与青岛这两个城市 640 mL 当地主销啤酒价格随时间的变动趋势，表 1 给出各个城市啤酒价格数据的描述性统计量。

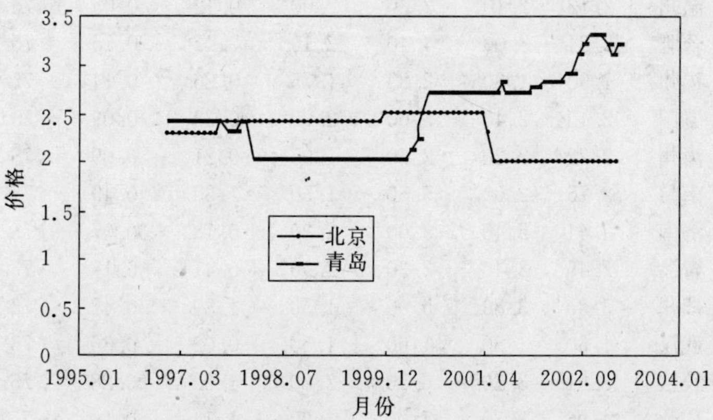

图 1　北京—青岛啤酒价格变化趋势(1997.1—2003.3)

表 1　各城市啤酒价格序列的统计描述

城市	均值	中位数	最大值	最小值	标准差	标准差/均值	观察值个数
北京	2.29	2.40	2.50	2.00	0.20	0.09	75
天津	1.65	1.70	1.75	1.50	0.09	0.06	75
石家庄	3.21	3.20	4.90	2.00	0.78	0.24	75
唐山	1.48	1.50	1.60	1.30	0.06	0.04	75
太原	2.14	2.20	2.40	1.80	0.15	0.07	75
呼和浩特	2.84	3.00	3.10	2.50	0.27	0.09	75
沈阳	2.86	3.00	6.00	1.50	1.34	0.47	75
大连	1.84	1.80	1.90	1.70	0.05	0.03	75
锦州	2.26	1.70	3.60	1.50	0.85	0.38	75
长春	2.74	3.20	3.60	2.00	0.59	0.21	75
哈尔滨	1.79	1.60	3.60	1.50	0.63	0.35	75
佳木斯	1.97	2.00	2.10	1.80	0.07	0.04	75
上海	2.88	3.00	3.60	1.30	0.43	0.15	75
南京	2.77	2.70	3.60	2.40	0.18	0.07	75
杭州	1.56	1.55	1.70	1.50	0.06	0.04	75
宁波	2.30	2.00	3.50	1.80	0.49	0.21	75
温州	2.12	2.10	2.30	2.00	0.12	0.05	75
合肥	2.84	3.00	4.40	2.10	0.42	0.15	75
福州	1.90	1.80	2.83	1.75	0.26	0.14	75
厦门	2.43	2.40	3.00	2.00	0.23	0.09	75
漳州	2.22	2.20	2.50	1.95	0.21	0.09	75
南昌	2.76	2.00	5.50	1.50	1.35	0.49	75
济南	2.44	2.40	3.00	2.20	0.18	0.07	75
青岛	2.46	2.40	3.30	2.00	0.41	0.17	75
郑州	3.30	3.80	5.00	1.50	1.39	0.42	75
武汉	1.50	1.50	1.60	1.50	0.02	0.36	75
长沙	3.91	3.20	6.50	2.80	1.39	0.28	75
广州	4.06	3.70	7.00	3.00	1.14	0.16	75

（续表）

城市	均值	中位数	最大值	最小值	标准差	标准差/均值	观察值个数
深圳	4.18	3.80	5.20	3.40	0.65	0.06	75
南宁	2.40	2.40	2.90	2.20	0.14	0.22	75
海口	4.33	3.80	5.70	3.50	0.96	0.10	75
成都	2.69	2.70	3.00	2.00	0.26	0.26	75
重庆	2.78	2.80	3.50	1.80	0.72	0.09	75
贵阳	2.37	2.50	2.55	2.00	0.21	0.18	75
昆明	3.46	3.50	4.90	2.50	0.63	0.06	75
拉萨	4.00	4.00	5.00	3.20	0.22	0.16	75
西安	3.34	3.00	5.60	2.50	0.53	0.14	75
兰州	2.37	2.50	3.00	1.98	0.34	0.19	75
西宁	2.71	2.40	3.50	2.00	0.50	0.06	75
银川	2.24	2.30	2.60	2.00	0.14	0.01	75

根据这些数据，可以初步得出以下几点结论：

（1）各城市的啤酒价格基本不存在季节性波动趋势，无须引入季节性虚拟变量对数据进行修正。

（2）从1997年1月至2001年3月，各城市的啤酒价格差异比较大，城市间的啤酒价格变化缺乏趋同性；2001年4月以后，除少数城市以外，如长沙、海口、郑州，各城市的啤酒价格变化趋势趋于一致，价格差异比较稳定。

（3）北京与青岛在啤酒价格方面的变化趋势差异较大，基本上不存在共同变化的趋势。

（4）从基本的统计指标看，均值最小的城市是唐山，只有1.48元，均值最大的城市是海口，达到4.33元；从标准差这一指标看，价格波动比较大的城市是沈阳、南昌、郑州、长沙和广州；变异系数（标准差/均值）的分布范围从0.01到0.49。这些基本的统计指标同样表明，各地价格波动的差异比较大，价格分散化的趋势明显，地区间的价格信息不易于沟通。

（二）单位根检验

根据上面提到的单位根检验方法，需要对价格序列的平稳性进行测定，这里采用了 ADF 检验方法。由于本研究使用的价格序列数据并没有明显的随时间变动的趋势，同时考虑到如果在平稳性分析中包含截距项这个外生变量，会降低 ADF 检验的能力。因此，从增强 ADF 检验能力的角度考虑，我们只选择进行不包含截距和时间趋势项的 ADF 检验。我们首先进行序列的水平值测试，其零假设为各城市的啤酒价格水平序列存在单位根。结果见表 2。

表 2　各城市啤酒价格序列的单位根测试

城市	水平值测试		一阶差分测试	
	ADF 测试 (1)	滞后值 (2)	ADF 测试 (3)	滞后值 (4)
北京	－0.670	2	－5.557*	1
天津	－0.559	2	－6.058*	1
石家庄	－2.657	1	－5.495*	1
唐山	－3.313	2	－4.123*	2
太原	－1.186	1	－7.572*	1
呼和浩特	－1.380	1	－8.485*	0
沈阳	－2.155	1	－6.390*	0
大连	－1.181	0	－8.544*	0
锦州	－1.672	1	－8.322*	0
长春	－1.059	5	－8.134*	0
哈尔滨	－0.451	0	－8.523*	0
佳木斯	－1.013	0	－8.485*	0
上海	－1.998	2	－7.941*	1
南京	－3.145	2	－7.495*	2
杭州	－1.758	1	－5.289*	2
宁波	－0.157	1	－5.847*	0

（续表）

城市	水平值测试		一阶差分测试	
	ADF 测试 （1）	滞后值 （2）	ADF 测试 （3）	滞后值 （4）
温州	−0.113	4	−4.495*	3
合肥	−0.586	1	−8.333*	0
福州	−0.372	1	−7.796*	0
厦门	−0.821	0	−8.485*	0
漳州	−1.559	1	−5.867*	1
南昌	−0.669	3	−3.977*	2
济南	−2.285	2	−8.672*	0
青岛	−0.190	2	−4.156*	2
郑州	−0.630	3	−4.099*	2
长沙	−0.473	1	−8.458*	0
广州	−0.581	1	−7.265*	0
深圳	−1.261	1	−9.302*	0
南宁	−1.462	3	−6.411*	2
海口	−0.648	4	−3.938*	3
成都	−2.144	1	−5.968*	1
重庆	−1.687	2	−4.031*	1
贵阳	−2.487	2	−5.799*	2
昆明	−1.667	1	−5.824*	1
拉萨	−6.011*	1	n. a.	n. a.
西安	−3.016	1	−8.322*	1
兰州	−0.663	1	−7.965*	0
西宁	−1.150	1	−6.414*	1
银川	−0.832	0	−6.933*	1

说明：加 * 表示通过显著水平为 5%的 ADF 单位根检验。

从表 2 可以看出，在 5%的统计水平上，只有拉萨的价格序列水平平稳，其他城市的价格序列都不能拒绝存在单位根的零假设。因此，我们必须做进一步的单位根检验，继续对除拉萨以外的城市的啤酒价格序列做一阶单整测试。一阶单整测试的零假设为经一阶差分后各城市的价格序列存在单位根。在5%的水平上，所有城市的价格序列都在统计上显著，拒绝零假设。即除拉萨外的其余39个城市的价格序列均为一阶单整序列，服从 $I(1)$过程，因此可以对这39个城市的啤酒价格序列进行协整检验分析。

（三）协整分析结果

因为这39个城市的啤酒价格变量序列都是服从 $I(1)$过程的同阶序列，可运用Johansen方法来测定各配对价格序列的协同变化程度。由于北京和青岛是中国最大的两个啤酒生产基地，它们的销售网络遍布全国，分别考察其余城市与这两个城市之间在啤酒价格序列方面的协同趋势，可在相当大程度上反映中国啤酒市场总体的整合或分割情况。首先对1997年1月至2003年3月整个时期的所有价格序列进行一个长周期的协整检验，考察这段时期内啤酒行业的总体市场整合情况。然后我们再区分两个阶段，即1997年1月到2001年3月以及2001年4月到2003年3月，分别进行阶段性的协整检验，考察中国加入WTO这个事件是否对中国啤酒行业的市场整合趋势产生影响。表3、表4及表5、表6列出了北京（青岛）啤酒市场与其他城市的啤酒市场从1997年1月到2003年3月间的整合情况及以2001年4月作为分界点的整合情况。

表3　以北京市当地主销640 mL的啤酒市场价格作为参考（1997.1—2003.3）

时　期	与北京存在协整关系的城市	与北京不存在协整关系的城市
1997.1—2003.3	呼和浩特、上海、南京、济南、武汉、长沙、南宁、海口、西安、银川	天津、石家庄、唐山、太原、沈阳、大连、锦州、长春、哈尔滨、佳木斯、杭州、宁波、温州、合肥、福州、厦门、漳州、南昌、青岛、郑州、广州、深圳、成都、重庆、贵阳、昆明、兰州、西宁

表 4　以青岛市当地主销 640 mL 的啤酒市场价格作为参考（1997.1—2003.3）

时　期	与青岛存在协整关系的城市	与青岛不存在协整关系的城市
1997.1—2003.3	天津、长春、南京、温州、合肥、福州、厦门、济南、武汉、南宁、西安	北京、石家庄、唐山、太原、呼和浩特、沈阳、大连、锦州、哈尔滨、佳木斯、上海、杭州、宁波、漳州、南昌、郑州、长沙、广州、深圳、海口、成都、重庆、贵阳、昆明、兰州、西宁、银川

表 5　以北京市当地主销 640 mL 的啤酒市场价格作为参考（以 2001 年 4 月为分界点）

时　期	与北京存在协整关系的城市	与北京不存在协整关系的城市
1997.1—2001.3	长春、佳木斯、南京、厦门、济南、武汉、南宁、银川	天津、石家庄、唐山、太原、呼和浩特、大连、锦州、哈尔滨、上海、杭州、宁波、温州、福州、漳州、南昌、青岛、郑州、长沙、广州、深圳、海口、成都、重庆、贵阳、昆明、西安、兰州、西宁、沈阳、合肥
2001.4—2003.3	天津、石家庄、唐山、太原、呼和浩特、沈阳、大连、上海、宁波、温州、福州、厦门、漳州、南昌、济南、武汉、长沙、广州、深圳、南宁、海口、重庆、贵阳、昆明、西安、兰州、西宁、银川	锦州、长春、哈尔滨、佳木斯、南京、杭州、合肥、青岛、郑州、成都

表 6　以青岛市当地主销 640 mL 的啤酒市场价格作为参考（以 2001 年 4 月为分界点）

时　期	与青岛存在协整关系的城市	与青岛不存在协整关系的城市
1997.1—2001.3	长春、佳木斯、上海、南京、温州、合肥、厦门、武汉、南宁	北京、天津、石家庄、唐山、太原、呼和浩特、沈阳、大连、锦州、哈尔滨、杭州、宁波、漳州、南昌、济南、郑州、长沙、广州、深圳、海口、成都、重庆、贵阳、昆明、西安、兰州、西宁、银川、福州
2001.4—2003.3	天津、石家庄、唐山、太原、呼和浩特、沈阳、大连、锦州、长春、佳木斯、南京、宁波、合肥、福州、漳州、南昌、济南、郑州、武汉、广州、深圳、海口、成都、贵阳、兰州	北京、哈尔滨、上海、杭州、温州、厦门、长沙、南宁、重庆、昆明、西安、西宁、银川

从整段时期看，中国啤酒市场整合的总体趋势并不明显，具有较明显的市场分割趋势。具体而言，与北京存在协同价格变动趋势的城市只有 10 个，与青岛存在协同价格变动趋势的城市也只有 11 个。而与北京邻近的城市如天津、石家庄和唐山，基本上与北京不存在价格变动方面的协同趋势；与青岛邻近的城市中，除了济南外，基本上与青岛也不存在价格变动方面的协同趋势。另外，一个值得注意的趋势是，北京与青岛这两个最大的啤酒生产地的啤酒价格序列之间并不存在协整关系。

中国政府为了加速中国的贸易自由化进程，在 2001 年 11 月正式加入 WTO，出台了一系列旨在取消地方保护壁垒的措施，其中最有影响的一项措施，是国务院于2001年4月公开发文到各级政府，明令禁止区域间的贸易封锁行为。所以我们首先选择2001年4月作为分界点，分两阶段进行协整分析。我们发现，两段时期所呈现的啤酒市场整合趋势存在显著的差异。从1997年1月至2001年3月，与北京存在协整关系的城市个数只有8个，而从2001年4月至2003年3月，这一数字却上升到了28个。青岛与其他城市的市场整合情况也呈现出类似的趋势，在前一时期只有9个，而从2001年4月开始的后一时期却上升到了25个。所以上述协整变化的趋势说明，中国在加入WTO后，市场整合的趋势在加强。另外，与北京邻近但在前一时期不存在协整关系的城市，如天津、石家庄、唐山、太原、呼和浩特，在后一时期都与北京市场的价格变动呈现协同趋势。与青岛邻近的城市也有类似的结果。这说明，以北京和青岛为中心的区域性整合趋势在不断增强。但是，北京与青岛的啤酒价格序列，无论是从整段时期看，还是分时期看，都不存在协整关系。

在一个政策出台以前，下级政府可能在事先就得到相关的信息，从而对其做出反应，调整自己的政策措施。考虑到政策出台的事前效应，我们分别选择了以2001年4月往前倒推三个月和六个月作为分界点，分两个时期进行协整测试。我们发现，往前倒推三个月及六个月作为分界点的测试结果，与以2001年4月作为分界点的测试结果差异不大。也就是说，我们以2001年4月作为分界点的处理是合理的。我们在表7和表8中列出了以2000年10月作为分界点的协整测试结果。当然，对以2001年4月和以2000年10月作为分界点的两个测试结果进行比较后我们看到，前者所体现的市场整合趋势比后者更明显。

表 7　以北京市当地主销 640 mL 的啤酒市场价格作为参考（以 2000 年 10 月为分界点）

时　期	与北京存在协整关系的城市	与北京不存在协整关系的城市
1997.1—2000.9	长春、佳木斯、南京、厦门、济南、武汉、南宁、银川	天津、石家庄、唐山、太原、呼和浩特、沈阳、大连、锦州、哈尔滨、上海、杭州、宁波、合肥、温州、福州、漳州、南昌、青岛、郑州、长沙、广州、深圳、海口、成都、重庆、贵阳、昆明、西安、兰州、西宁
2000.10—2003.3	天津、石家庄、唐山、太原、呼和浩特、沈阳、大连、上海、宁波、温州、福州、厦门、漳州、南昌、济南、武汉、广州、深圳、南宁、海口、重庆、贵阳、西安、兰州、银川	锦州、长春、哈尔滨、佳木斯、南京、杭州、合肥、青岛、郑州、长沙、成都、昆明、西宁

表 8　以青岛市当地主销 640 mL 的啤酒市场价格作为参考（以 2000 年 10 月为分界点）

时　期	与青岛存在协整关系的城市	与青岛不存在协整关系的城市
1997.1—2000.9	长春、佳木斯、南京、温州、福州、厦门、武汉、南宁	北京、天津、石家庄、唐山、太原、呼和浩特、沈阳、大连、锦州、哈尔滨、上海、杭州、宁波、合肥、漳州、南昌、济南、郑州、长沙、广州、深圳、海口、成都、重庆、贵阳、昆明、西安、兰州、西宁、银川
2000.10—2003.3	石家庄、唐山、太原、大连、锦州、长春、佳木斯、南京、合肥、福州、厦门、南昌、济南、郑州、武汉、深圳、成都、贵阳、兰州、西宁	北京、天津、呼和浩特、沈阳、哈尔滨、上海、杭州、宁波、温州、漳州、长沙、广州、南宁、海口、重庆、昆明、西安、银川

五、结论及其经济解释

本文利用来自中国40个城市的月度市场价格资料,以啤酒市场为例,运用协整分析方法,对中国啤酒市场的市场整合趋势作了较深入的分析。结果表明:

(1) 从1997年1月到2003年3月整段时期看,中国啤酒市场的市场整合程度不高,市场分割的现象比较普遍。

(2) 从分时期讨论的结果看,在中央政府出台取消地方保护壁垒的措施之前(无论有没有考虑政策出台的事前效应),中国啤酒市场的市场分割现象比较普遍;政策出台以后,啤酒市场分别以北京和青岛为中心出现了区域性的整合趋势。

(3) 北京与青岛这两个最大的啤酒生产地的啤酒价格序列之间,无论是从整段时期看,还是分时期看,都不存在协整关系。也就是说,这两个啤酒市场基本上处于分割状态。

从以上结论看,中国加入WTO对于中国的市场整合产生了较大的影响,它促使中央政府及各级地方政府相应地调整自己的政策取向,消除地区间的贸易壁垒。我们可以结合中国的税制改革与贸易自由化进程,对政府的这种政策取向变化给出合理的经济学解释。1994年的税制改革,明确了中央与地方政府之间的税收分配按照分税制的原则进行,地方的税收留成比例大大增加,这就给地方政府提供了进行地方保护的激励。微观经济学的基本理论告诉我们,一个政府在考虑实施一项政策决策时,它必须同时兼顾厂商与消费者两方面的利益。实施地方保护政策往往会增加厂商的利润,但同时也会损害消费者的利益。在中国,从政绩考核的角度考虑,同保护消费者利益相比,地方政府会更倾向于保护当地企业的利益。并且,如果国家对外保持比较高的关税水平，外国企业对本国企业的竞争压力就会比较小，因而实行地区间的贸易保护政策就会比较奏效。这就能够在一定程度上解释，为什么中国的啤酒行业在中国加入 WTO 之前市场分割现象如此普遍，其主要的影响因素是分税制的作用。

中国于 2001 年 11 月正式成为 WTO 的成员，在中央政府与各成员方签订的协议中，其中一项重要的承诺，就是逐年降低各类产品的关税。也就是说，要逐步实现贸易自由化，这意味着外国企业进入本国市场的成本降低，竞争力加强。此时，设置地区间的贸易壁垒只是在一定程度上给外地企业进入本地市场造成了障碍，但由此让渡出来的市场份额很有可能被进入成本日益降低的外国企业所攫取。这样，地方政府在设置地区间的贸易壁垒时，就必须考虑这一做法是否能够增加本地企业的利润，这种增加是否足以抵偿消费者的利益损失，如果这种增加不能抵偿消费者的利益损失，地方政府就有可能会自动放弃地区间的贸易保护壁垒。这能够在一定程度上解释为什么中国啤酒市场的整合趋势日益明显。

对于北京与青岛的啤酒价格序列之间不存在协整关系这一结论，我们提供的一个解释是，由于燕京和青岛啤酒边际生产成本都不高，运输成本在总成本中就成为比较重要的一个因素。燕京和青岛啤酒都是以本地市场为生产基地、并逐渐向外地市场辐射而发展起来的，它们在本地市场的影响根深蒂固，其他品牌的啤酒往往难以进入当地市场。这样，它们在当地就具有足够的市场势力，并导致北京和青岛这两个啤酒市场的价格决定具有相对独立性。

本研究仍然存在许多有待改进之处。首先，由于数据的原因，本文只采用了协整分析的方法，分析市场整合的变化趋势，而没有采用更多的方法对市场整合趋势作相应的检验。其次，由于缺乏财税改革方面的相关数据，我们没有验证税制改革对市场整合的具体影响。这些都是我们今后进一步研究的方向。

注　释

① 关于市场整合分析方法的比较，可参阅周章跃、万广华(1999)。

参考文献

北京市经济信息中心，2001：《中国啤酒：从"春秋"到"战国"》6月4日。

陈抗、Arye L. Hillman、顾清扬，2002：《财政集权与地方政府行为变化——从援助之手到攫取之手》，《经济学季刊》第2卷第1期。

银温泉、才婉茹，2001：《中国地区间市场分割成因和治理》，《经济研究》第6期。

喻闻、黄季焜，1998：《从大米市场整合程度看中国粮食市场改革》，《经济研究》第3期。

周章跃、万广华，1999：《论市场整合研究方法》，《经济研究》第3期。

Bai, Chong-En et al., 2002, "Protectionism and Regional Specialization: Evidence from China's Industries", Working paper, Mimeo.

Gilley, B. 2001, "Breaking Barriers", *Far Eastern Economic Review*, July 12, pp. 12—19.

Greene, William H., 2003, *Econometric Analysis*, Fifth Edition.

Ha, Jiming and Fan, Kelvin, 2003, "One Country, Two Prices? A Study of Deflationary Effect of Price Convergence on Hong Kong", Working Paper, Mimeo.

Johansen, S., 1988, "Statistical Analysis of Cointegration Vectors", *Journal of Economic Dynamics and Control*, 12, pp. 231—245.

Johansen, S. and Juselius, K., 1990, "Maximum Likelihood Estlmation and Inference on Cointegration, with Applications for the Demand for Monet", *Oxford Bulletin of Economics and Statistics*, 52, pp. 169—210.

Li, Jie and Zhang, Anming, 2003, "WTO Accession and China's Domestic Regional Liberalization: A Theoretical Analysis", *Pacific Economic Review*, 8(2), pp. 127—141.

Li, Jie; Qiu, Larry D. and Sun, Qunyan, 2003, "Interregional Protection: Implications of Fiscal Decentralization and Trade Liberalization", *China Economic Review*, 14(3), pp. 227—245.

Young, Alwyn, 2000, "The Razor's Edge: Distortions and Incremental Reform in the People's Republic of China", *Quarterly Journal of Economics*, 115(4), pp. 1091—1135.

（原载《世界经济》2004 年第 6 期）

中国农村扶贫项目的目标瞄准分析*

岳希明　李　实

（中国社会科学院经济研究所）

一、引　言

1978年农村改革以来，虽然农村贫困的发生率显著下降，但是当前的贫困规模仍然很大，尤其在广大的西部地区，农村贫困仍然是一种普遍的现象。根据国家统计局的估计，2001年中国农村贫困人口为2927万人（国家统计局农村社会经济调查总队，2002）。但是，这只是根据官方的较低的贫困线确定的数字（2001年官方农村贫困线是每人每年630元）。如果贫困线采用每人每天1美元的国际标准，1999年的中国农村贫困人口将达到1亿人（World Bank，2001），比根据官方贫困线估计出来的贫困人口多出近6000万人。同时应该注意的是，中国是一个在收入水平、经济和社会发展以及自然禀赋方面有着明显地区差异的国家，农民人均纯收入和农村贫困发生率的地区差异尤其严重（Gustafsson and Li，1998；Gustafsson and Wei，2000）。考虑到农村贫困人口主要集中在一些特定的省份和县，把扶贫

---

* 本文的英文稿曾是作者提交给2002年9月瑞典哥德堡第一届亚太研究年会（The First SSAAPS Asia-Pacific Annual Conference）的会议论文。岳希明、丁赛将英文稿翻译成中文，由李实做了最后修订。

资金集中使用在这些地区，是提高扶贫资金的使用效率，使有限的扶贫资源最大限度地消除贫困人口的一种选择。基于这样一种考虑，中国政府在 1986 年划定 258 个县为国家重点扶贫县，并把扶贫资源集中使用在被划定的贫困县上。然而，这一战略也有其自身的局限性，它忽略了生活在贫困县以外的广大贫困人口。Riskin(1994)批评说，这一战略过分强调了贫困县的贫困人口的扶贫问题，而忽视了其余地区的贫困人口。实际上，在 20 世纪 80 年代，后者的贫困规模要大于前者。

一旦一个县被划定为国家贫困县之后，随之而来的是享受一系列的优惠政策，如获取贴息贷款、发展资金以及以工代赈等扶贫专项资金的支持。也就是说，获得国家贫困县的身份同时意味着可以得到了可靠的资金来源，于是，争取被列入贫困县对低收入县来说就成了一种政治上的竞争(Park et al., 2002)。继 1986 年第一次国家认定贫困县，中国政府又于 1993 年和 2001 年分别进行了两轮贫困县的重新认定。在贫困县认定过程中，除了考虑农民人均纯收入水平以外，是否为革命老区、是否为少数民族地区等政治因素也是中央政府考虑的重要因素(Ravallion and Jalan, 1999; Park et al., 2002)。

Park 等(2002)对最初两轮贫困县认定的目标瞄准问题进行了研究，发现对革命老区、少数民族县等政治上考虑在贫困县划定过程中起了重要的影响作用，而对人均收入重视不够。也就是说，在三项扶贫资金的分配上，扶贫资金的多少与县人均纯收入没有明显的负相关关系。人均纯收入低的县未必得到更多扶贫资金，而革命老区和少数民族地区几乎在扶贫资金的分配上都得到了优惠。

本文将在大量详实数据的支持下，对我国农村扶贫项目的瞄准问题进行深入的分析。本文的研究内容主要有两个。第一是分析2001年国家扶贫工作重点县划定中的目标瞄准问题。这里要回答的问题是，在目标瞄准的准确性上，2001年国家扶贫工作重点县的划定与1993年相比是否得到了改善？[①] 或者说，收入水平低的县一定能被划定为国定贫困县吗？影响划定国家贫困县的因素都有哪些？第二个研究内容是扶贫资金在国定贫困县之间的分配问题。要回答的问题是扶贫资金是如何分配的。我们通过三种不同层次的分析来回答这一问题：第一层次是分析三种不同的扶贫资金是如何在省际间分配的；第二层次是讨论扶贫资金是如何在省份内的各个贫困县之间分配的；第三层次是集中讨论贴息贷款在农户之间分配的决定因素。

如下各部分的内容是这样安排的：第二部分简单介绍政府扶贫计划；第三部分介绍数据来源及其可靠性；第四部分对2001年贫困县认定的目标瞄准问题进行分析；第五部分是讨论扶贫资金在省、县和农户之间的分配情况；最后一部分给出了本文的结论。

二、农村扶贫开发历史演变与扶贫资金规模

扶贫战略有各种可选择的方式。最理想的是，首先从总人口中界定出所有的贫困人口，然后对这些贫困人口加以扶持，以此来消除贫困。但是，由于界定每一个贫困人口所花费成本太高，这种直接瞄准贫困人口的扶贫战略虽然是最理想的，但通常是不可行的。贫困人口在地理上集中在少数区域的情况下，一种可选择的扶贫战略是，首先根据一定的标准把贫困人口集中的地区与其他地区区分出来，划定为重点扶贫地区，然后对这些地区集中加以扶持，也就是以这些地区的全部人口为扶贫对象。与直接瞄准贫困人口的最理想的扶贫战略相比，这是一种地区

瞄准的扶贫战略。这种战略虽然有其不可替代的优点，但是也有其不可避免的局限性。一种局限性是它必然发生扶贫资金的目标瞄准的偏离问题。首先，因为所有的贫困人口不是都集中在被划定的重点扶贫地区，因而生活在这些地区之外的贫困人口的扶贫问题往往被忽视。其次，这种地区瞄准的扶贫战略在扶贫资金使用上通常是以被划定地区的全部人口为扶贫对象，因此常常对这些地区的贫困人口注意不够。尽管在项目执行过程中有时对贫困人口给予特殊考虑，但是同样是由于识别贫困人口的困难性，以及非常有限的扶贫资金的支持力度，最终非贫困人口占有大部分扶贫资金的现象也是常有的。尽管如此，在贫困人口高度集中的情况下，地区瞄准的扶贫战略仍不失为一种可行的扶贫战略。中国从 20 世纪 80 年代中期开始实施的农村扶贫战略就是考虑到农村贫困人口主要集中在山区、少数民族和边疆地区而采取的地区瞄准的扶贫战略。具体地说，首先由政府把一部分县划定为国定贫困县，然后把所有的扶贫资金都集中使用在国定贫困县上。

1986 年中央扶贫开发领导小组及其办事机构国务院扶贫开发办公室(通常简称为扶贫办)成立。为了在管理和实践上切实可行，同年扶贫领导小组认定了 258 个国家贫困县。贫困县的选择基于 1985 年的人均收入，也有一些政治上的考虑，对一般地区采用了较低的收入标准(低于 150 元为贫困县)，对少数民族和边疆地区采用了较高的标准(低于 200 元为贫困县)，进而对革命老区使用了更高的收入标准(低于 300 元为贫困县)。尽管对不同类型的县规定了明确的收入标准，但这并不意味满足该标准的县都自动地被认定为贫困县。或许是因为各省份政府讨价还价和游说能力的差异，地处云南和贵州等省的一些低收入县，实际已符合收入标准，但并未能被划定为贫困县。Park

等(2002)证实,如果按1986年县人均纯收入将全部县分为十等分组,在最低收入组中,有100多个县未能被认定为贫困县。

贫困县的第一轮认定工作之后,政府并没有停止对贫困县数目的调整。到1988年,扶贫领导小组将国家贫困县增加到了328个。同时,又有370个县被确定为省级贫困县。1993年,政府开始实施"国家八七扶贫攻坚计划",力争在未来的7年中消除8000万贫困人口,并对国定贫困县重新进行了调整。此一轮国定贫困县总数增加到592个县,这意味着有更多的县被划定为国定贫困县。按理说,前一轮被划定的贫困县,如其人均纯收入高于本次确定的收入标准(320元),则不应当再被划定为国定贫困县,应当从贫困县"出列"。但是,由于各种因素的影响,"出列"的县很少。可以说,这一轮国定贫困县的认定,虽然在贫困县的覆盖面上有所改进,但存在着遗漏问题,因为它认定了一些并不贫困的县,却遗漏了一些实际上的贫困县(Park et al., 2002)。

最后一轮对贫困县的调整,或者说第三轮国定贫困县的认定发生在2001年。此次调整的背景是,中国已经完成了"八七扶贫攻坚计划",除了居住在西部边远地区、少数民族地区、革命老区等地区的3000万贫困人口以外,我国基本上消灭了农村贫困。为了巩固扶贫成果,防止刚刚脱贫人口的返贫,提高低收入人口的收入水平,以及最终消灭剩余的3000万贫困人口,中央政府开始新一轮的扶贫开发计划。2001年随着"中国农村扶贫开发纲要(2001—2010年)"的出台,政府对国定贫困县进行了调整,这就是我们所说的第三轮国定贫困县的认定。此次的国定贫困县的总数与第二轮保持不变,仍然保持了592个县。但在总数不变的情况下,对构成进行了较大调整。调整内容包括以下三项。

第一，东部地区的贫困县由东部省份自己负责解决，中央政府不再将东部的县划定为国定贫困县。上一轮中33个东部地区的国定贫困县由此失去了国定贫困县的身份。这一举措主要基于东部各省份经济发展水平相对较高，自己可以筹集一定量扶贫资源来解决本省份的人口脱贫问题。这样一来，中央扶贫资源就可以更有效地集中到贫困人口聚集的中西部地区；第二，西藏自治区的贫困县由中央另行考虑，不再列入新一轮划定的范围之内。由此，又有5个县的名额空出来给其他中西部地区；第三，除东部各省份以及西藏以外，在其他省份的国定贫困县中，由于收入水平的提高而被摘掉了贫困县帽子，即所谓的“出列”的县有51个。因此，在第三轮国家贫困县划定中，共有89个中西部县被认定为新的国定贫困县，成为国家重点扶贫开发对象。本文内容之一就是要探讨新一轮国定贫困县认定中的目标瞄准问题。

上面已经谈到，伴随国定贫困县的划定而来的是中央政府扶贫资金的集中投入。把扶贫资金集中到国定贫困县上是我国扶贫开发事业最显著的特点之一。据估计，1986—1999年间中央政府投入的扶贫资金总额大约为200亿美元（World Bank，2001）。如图1所示，按固定价格计算，资金总额自1997年以来迅速增加。历年的增长速度是：1997年52%，1998年23%，1999年为39%。

表1　中央政府扶贫资金的支出情况（百万元）

年份	扶贫资金总计(1)		贴息贷款(2)	财政部发展资金(2)	以工代赈资金(2)
	可变价	不变价			
1986	4800	14583	8811	3038	2734
1987	4900	14018	8582	2861	2575

（续表）

年份	扶贫资金总计[1]		贴息贷款[2]	财政部发展资金[2]	以工代赈资金[2]
	可变价	不变价			
1988	4050	9860	7425	2435	0
1989	4150	8469	6224	2041	204
1990	4650	9081	5956	1953	1172
1991	6410	12237	6777	2024	3436
1992	6270	11432	6473	2042	2917
1993	7730	12396	5693	1892	4811
1994	9790	12722	5913	1611	5198
1995	9850	10894	5032	1438	4424
1996	9800	10045	5638	1333	3075
1997	15265	15265	8450	2815	4000
1998	18315	18773	10250	3398	5125
1999	24800	26056	10191	3483	5253
总计	130780	185830	101415	32363	44924

资料来源：(1) World Bank (2001)，*China*：*Overcoming Rural Poverty*。
(2) 根据 World Bank (2001)中可变价数字，换算成 1997 年不变价的数字。

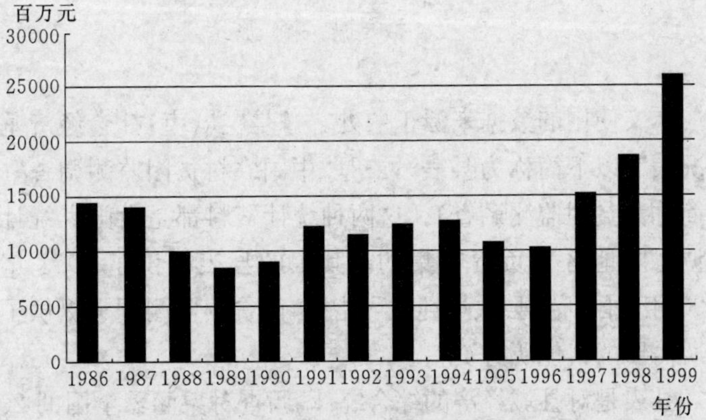

图 1　中央政府扶贫资金支出情况(以 1997 年不变价)

资料来源：The World Bank (2001)，*China*：*Overcoming Rural Poverty*。

中央政府筹集的扶贫资金是通过三个渠道分配的:贴息贷款、发展基金和以工代赈资金。贴息贷款具体由农业发展银行管理实施,以工代赈资金由国家计委负责实施,发展基金由财政部提供。表1给出了自1986年到1999年的每年每项扶贫资金总额。以1999年为例,我们可以从不同的角度了解扶贫资金的规模。1999年的资金总额为250亿元,平均每个国定贫困县可获资金超过4000万元,人均可得资金大约130元,相当于当年全国农村人均纯收入的10%,大约相当于这些国定贫困县的年人均财政收入(国家统计局农村社会经济调查总队,2001)。1999年国定贫困县的贫困人口为1800万,如果把扶贫资金平均分配给贫困户的话,每人可得到大约1380元的扶贫资金,相当于当年农村贫困线的2倍以上。另外值得注意的是,除了政府组织的扶贫资金以外,尚有各种非政府募集的扶贫资金(World Bank, 2001)。因此,从某种意义上讲,中国用于扶贫开发上的资金规模已经达到了相当大的程度。

三、数 据 来 源

本文使用的数据来源于两处。一是“县(市)社会经济基本情况表”(以下简称为县表),二是“中国农村贫困监测调查”(以下简称为贫困监测调查)。这两种统计资料都是由国家统计局农调总队地区处负责收集的。其中的县表提供了1993年和2000年全国所有县人均纯收入指标,而贫困监测调查提供了本文所需要的其他所有资料。

县表是对县域经济的综合统计,调查对象涵盖全国的2000多个县,统计指标120个,包括人口、劳动力、财政收支、产业、文化、人民生活等多方面的信息。统计数据是首先由县以及县级市统计局根据相关资料编制之后，然后逐级上报形成的。本文所使用的县农民人均纯收入是根据住户调查数据计算的。

中国农村贫困监测调查的目的是通过收集扶贫资金来源和去向、地理环境和社区基础设施、住户的人口、教育、收入、消费等信息，监测国定贫困县的贫困规模及其变化，评价扶贫资金的使用效率，为提高扶贫资金的使用效率提出建议。基于贫困监测调查结果形成的研究报告集中在每年出版的《中国农村监测报告》中。

贫困监测调查的调查内容由5张表组成:《贫困县调查表》;《住户基本情况调查表》;《住户收支情况调查表》;《调查户家庭成员个人调查表》(简称《个人表》)以及《社区调查表》。《贫困县调查表》主要包括扶贫资金来源、使用以及反映扶贫资金使用效果的一系列指标。《住户基本情况调查表》包括住户的财产及资产拥有、土地承包、基础设施、技术培训及无劳动力户的社会保障等情况。《住户收支调查表》包括住户收入来源、支出去向、主要食物消费、储蓄借贷等状况。《个人调查表》包括家庭成员年龄、性别、就学以及就业等情况。《社区调查表》包括社区环境、交通、文教卫生、人口、土地资源等主要指标。

贫困监测调查沿用了中国目前农户住户调查的做法。每个调查县的样本规模大致在100户左右。但是，根据县人口的多少，县样本数有所不同。人口多的县，样本多于100户，多到150户或200户;人口少的县，样本不足于100户。贫困监测调查的总样本在5万户左右。调查样本的选择取决于该贫困县是否是国家住户调查点。是国家住户调查点的贫困县，调查网点以及样本户等均使用住户调查点的网点和样本，对其不做任何调整。对于国家住户调查中所缺少的指标，则另行组织调查。这一原则同样适用于有地方调查网点的贫困县。对于没有任何住户调查网点的国定贫困县，则建立新的调查网点。抽样方法与国家住户调查的样本抽样方法完全相同。

四、目标瞄准的分析

本部分将对2001年国家贫困县的认定过程中的目标瞄准的准确性进行分析。我们试图要回答的问题是：国定贫困县认定中是哪些因素在起作用？认定过程中发生了哪些偏差？换句话说，认定过程中是否存在遗漏问题，即在将一些低收入县排除在外的同时，却把一些收入水平较高的县划定为贫困县？我们同时对1993年和2001年两轮贫困县的认定结果进行分析，旨在通过比较，观察贫困县认定的目标瞄准的准确性是否有所提高。为了回答这些问题，我们使用两种分析方法。一个是Probit模型，另一个是由Cornia和Stewart（1995）提出的测量目标瞄准的准确性的方法。

Probit模型是处理被解释变量为离散变量时所使用的一种分析手段。在我们日常经济分析中所碰到的被解释变量为离散变量的情况中，一种最常见的是被解释变量本身是双值变量，也就是被解释变量只取1和0两个值，如果某一事件发生了，被解释变量取值为1，而没发生时，被解释变量取值为0。具体在我们对贫困县认定的目标瞄准分析中，被解释变量就是根据某个县是否被认定为国家贫困县而取1和0两个值，即国定贫困县为1，否则为0。解释变量包括了县人均纯收入、革命老区身份和少数民族自治县和反映县财力的人均财政收入。这些因素一般被认为是政府在划定国家贫困县时优先考虑的因素。另外，我们还把省份作为虚拟变量引入解释变量，目的是观察哪些省份在贫困县认定过程中被优先考虑，这同时也部分反映了各省份的游说能力。表 2 给出 Probit 模型的估算结果。

表 2　国家贫困县认定中的决定因素——Probit 模型的估算结果

	1993 年	2001 年	1993 年	2001 年
县人均纯收入(对数值)	−0.767	−0.656	−0.612	−0.686
	(22.32)**	(20.66)**	(19.82)**	(19.48)**
县人均财政收入(对数值)	−0.02	−0.123	−0.035	−0.118
	(1.92)	(6.64)**	(3.69)**	(6.85)**
老区	0.216	0.18	0.183	0.248
	(6.90)**	(5.79)**	(5.69)**	(6.23)**
边区	0.048	0.01	−0.013	0.019
	(1.18)	(0.24)	(0.59)	(0.50)
少数民族地区	0.072	0.047	0.025	0.02
	(3.76)**	(2.28)*	(1.39)	(0.82)
山西			0.044	−0.06
			(1.31)	(2.30)*
内蒙古			0.581	0.056
			(6.34)**	(1.13)
辽宁			0.76	
			(6.84)**	
吉林			0.528	−0.032
			(4.91)**	(0.60)
黑龙江			0.578	0.03
			(6.03)**	(0.60)
浙江			−0.042	
			(1.15)	
安徽			0.011	0.063
			(0.33)	(1.38)
福建			0.649	
			(5.84)**	
江西			0.159	−0.07
			(2.71)**	(2.75)**

（续表）

	1993 年	2001 年	1993 年	2001 年
山东			0.089	
			(2.02)*	
河南			−0.001	−0.019
			(0.04)	(0.69)
湖北			0.025	−0.035
			(0.61)	(1.01)
湖南			−0.035	−0.077
			(1.61)	(3.43)**
广东			0.217	
			(2.26)*	
广西			0.219	0.118
			(3.03)**	(2.16)*
海南			0.298	0.018
			(2.77)**	(0.22)
重庆			−0.029	−0.022
			(1.04)	(0.42)
四川			−0.056	−0.11
			(4.82)**	(9.04)**
贵州			−0.028	−0.063
			(1.26)	(2.63)**
云南			−0.023	−0.067
			(0.97)	(2.77)**
西藏			−0.053	
			(2.75)**	
陕西			0.094	−0.085
			(2.38)*	(5.05)**
甘肃			0.068	−0.082
			(1.44)	(3.88)**
青海			0.014	−0.083
			(0.34)	(4.35)**

（续表）

	1993 年	2001 年	1993 年	2001 年
宁夏			−0.034	0.016
			(0.42)	(0.09)
新疆			0.237	−0.086
			(3.18)**	(3.95)**
样本数	2159	2106	2159	2106
Pseudo R2	0.51	0.52	0.63	0.60

注：(1) 括弧里的值为 z 统计量。

(2) * 和 ** 分别表示该估计值在 5%和 1%水平上显著。

表 2 中给出的不是估算系数，而是由估计系数换算出来的边际概率。当解释变量是连续变量时，边际概率表示当解释变量每变动一个百分点时，某县被认定为国定贫困县的概率变动几个百分点。当解释变量是虚拟变量时，以老区县为例，边际概率的意思是在其他条件相同的情况下老区的县与非老区的县相比被划定为国家贫困县的概率变化多少。② 表 2 显示，人均纯收入与被认定为与国定贫困县的概率负相关。这表明，人均纯收入增长了 10%，被认定为国定贫困县的概率 1993 年下降了7.7%，2001 年下降了 6.6%。这意味着由于人均纯收入和贫困线的提高，收入水平变量的影响随着时间的推移出现了弱化。但是，把省份变量放入模型后，县人均纯收入的影响在 2001 年要大于其在 1993 年的影响。这表明在 2001 年的国定贫困县的认定过程中县人均收入变量更多的是在省份内产生影响，而不是在省际之间发生作用。

还应该值得注意的是其他变量的边际概率在两轮认定过程之间的变化。如表 2 所示，革命老区作为解释变量，无论是否引入省份虚拟变量，两年模型中的系数估计值都是显著的。在 1993 年模型中老区县被划定为国家贫困县的概率与非老区县相比，高出21%，但在2001年模型中二者的差别下降了3个百分点。尽管如此，并未显示出革命老区的身份出现了贬值，因为在一些革命老区主要集中的省份，在2001年的国定贫困县的认定过程中革命老区身份仍被优先考虑。这一点可以从2001年的估计模型中引入省份虚拟变量后的估算结果中得到验证。与Park等(2002)不同的是，我们的估计结果显示，虽然在一般模型中少数民族县虚拟变量的系数估计值是显著的，但将省份虚拟变量引入模型后却变得不显著了。这表明在1993年的认定过程中，中央政府对少数民族地区给予了更多的关注，但是在省份内部却并非如此。更值得指出的是，在2001年国定贫困县的认定过程中，各省份对国定贫困县名额在各省份之间分配的影响力有所削弱。这一点可以从两年模型中省份虚拟变量的边际概率的下降趋势中看出。

下面使用Cornia和Stewart(1995)提出的测量目标瞄准准确性的指标对1993年和2001年国家贫困县认定中发生的失误进行分析。由Cornia和Stewart提出的指标可以通过表3来概括。从该表可以看出，当我们把全国所有的县按实际上是否是贫困县(按县农民人均纯收入是否低于贫困线来判断)和是否被划定为国定贫困县两个标准来划分时，可以得到四种不同类型的县：被认定为国定贫困县的贫困县、不被认定为国定贫困县的贫困县、被认定为国定贫困县的非贫困县、不被认定为国定贫困县的非贫困县。

表3　贫困县认定中发生的两种失误

	实际上的贫困县	实际上的非贫困县	合　计
被认定为贫困县	P^{c}	NP^{nc} (第二种失误)	c
不被认定为贫困县	P^{nc} (第一种失误)	NP^{nc}	nc
合　计	P	NP	N

在上述四种类型中，其中两类出现了目标瞄准的失误问题。一种失误发生在实际上的贫困县，却没有被认定为国定贫困县。我们把这种失误称为第一种失误。与第一种失误相反，另外一种失误是实际上的非贫困县，却被认定为国定贫困县。我们把这种失误叫做第二种失误。③将这两种失误结合起来考虑，可以得到目标瞄准失误的测量公式如下（Cornia and Stewart，1995）：

$$TCG = \frac{1}{N}\sum_{i=1}^{N}[I_{i1}(P_i = 0, Y_i < Z) + I_{i2}(P_i = 1, Y_i > Z)] \tag{1}$$

其中，I_{i1} 是第一种失误（不被认定为国定贫困县的贫困县数），I_{i2} 是第二种失误（被认定为国定贫困县的非贫困县数），N 是全部样本县，Y_i 是收入，Z 是贫困线。

Park 等（2002）利用上述公式计算了 1986 年和 1993 年两轮国定贫困县认定中发生的失误。为了与他们的计算结果加以比较，我们使用了同样的方法对 1993 年和 2001 年两轮认定中的失误进行了计算。计算结果显示在表 4-a 中。为了验证计算结果是否受贫困线高低的影响，我们分别使用了中国官方贫困线和世界银行的贫困线。

表 4-a　国家贫困县认定时发生的两种失误——以县为单位的计算结果

	1993 年	2001 年
中国官方贫困线	450 元	625 元
第一种失误	0.036	0.000
第二种失误	0.099	0.269
第一、二种失误合计	0.134	0.269
世界银行贫困线	559 元	875 元
第一种失误	0.139	0.007

（续表）

	1993 年	2001 年
第二种失误	0.040	0.235
第一、二种失误合计	0.179	0.242
TCE	0.247	0.260

表 4-a 中的计算结果给出的最重要结论是，与 1993 年的认定过程相比，在 2001 年的认定中第一种失误不再出现。与此同时，第二种失误却在增加。总的失误（即两种失误的加总）也呈现出增加的趋势。在 2001 年的认定中第一种失误消失而第二种失误增大的原因主要是国定贫困县的数额多于实际贫困县的数额。如果预定的国定贫困县数大于实际贫困县数，第二种失误也就必然要发生。相反，如果预定的国定贫困县数小于实际贫困县数，第一种失误注定要发生。为了克服上述测量指标的这种局限性，Park 等（2002）使用了新的测量指标。在预定的国定贫困县数给定的条件下（以 2001 年指定为例，592 个县），观察县人均纯收入最低的 592 个县是否全部被认定为国定贫困县。如果是的话，则认为目标瞄准完全准确，不存在认定失误的问题。否则，就发生了有些县应该被认定但没有被认定为国定贫困县的遗漏现象。这也意味着，与被遗漏的县同等数量的县，本不应当被认定为却被认定为国定贫困县。很明显，遗漏的县越多，意味着认定中失误的程度也就越大。Park 等（2002）把被遗漏县的个数占预定的国定贫困县个数的比重取名为瞄准计算误差（targeting counting Error，*TCE*）。其计算公式如下：

$$TCE = \frac{1}{D}\sum_{i=1}^{N} I_i(Y_i < Z^*,\ P_i = 0) \qquad (2)$$

其中 Z^* 是在完全瞄准的情况下最后一个贫困县的收入水平，D 是预定的国定贫困县的个数。

在此，我们也计算了 *TCE*，并放在表 4-a 的最后一行。从中可以看出，*TCE* 所测量的目标瞄准的准确性，在 2001 年的认定中比 1993 年的认定有所下降，*TCE* 值从 1993 年的 0.246 上升为 2001 年的 0.260。这一点也是和上面提到的两种失误的加总后的总失误上升的结果一致的。

应当注意的是，无论是 Cornia 和 Stewart(1995)所提供的测量指标(*TCG*)，还是 Park 等(2002)使用的 *TCE*，如果以县作为单位计算的话(Park et al.，2002)，都存在着一定的缺陷。以县为单位计算上述指标的话，忽略各县贫困人口规模的差异。如果能在上述测量指标中考虑县贫困人口的规模会更为理想。显然，在认定国定贫困县时，错误地认定了一个拥有一万贫困人口的县，和错误地指定了一个拥有十万贫困人口的县，其结果是完全不同的。下一部分的分析结果告诉我们，国定贫困县每年获得扶贫资金的规模，不仅与县人均纯收入有紧密的负相关，同时与县贫困人口的规模存在密切的正相关。这说明中央政府在分配扶贫资金时，不仅考虑县收入水平，同时也明显地考虑了贫困人口的规模。而这种考虑很可能同时体现在认定国家贫困县上。这样我们可以把上述公式(1)和公式(2)改写为：

$$TCG = \frac{1}{N}\sum_{i=1}^{N}[I_{i1}C_{i1}(P_i = 0, Y_i < Z) + I_{i2}C_{i2}(P_i = 1, Y_i > Z)] \tag{3}$$

其中 N 是农村总人口，I_{i1} 是某个不被认定为国定贫困县的贫困县(C_{i1})的人口。I_{i2} 是某个被认定为国定贫困县的非贫困县(C_{i2})的人口。

$$TCE = \frac{1}{D^*} \sum_{i=1}^{N} I_i C_{i1}(Y_i < Z^*, P_i = 0) \qquad (4)$$

其中 D^* 在完全瞄准的情况下国定贫困县的总人口，Z^* 具有与公式(2)相同的含义。

由于受到数据的限制，我们不可能获知每个县的贫困人口规模，取而代之，我们使用县人口总数重新计算了公式(3)和公式(4)，结果汇集在表 4-b 中。新的计算结果表明，第一种失误、第二种失误以及两种失误总计在两轮国定贫困县认定之间的变化趋势与上面的没有考虑人口规模的计算结果基本一致。然而，值得注意的是，新的 *TCE* 的计算结果与上面的计算结果正好相反。新的结果显示，2001 年与 1993 年相比，*TCE* 值下降了 40%以上。以县为单位计算的 *TCE* 和以人口规模为单位计算的 *TCE* 在趋势上出现了相反的结果，这表明 2001 年的认定中，本应被认定为国定贫困县而被遗漏的县，大多是人口较少的县，而那些被认定为国定贫困县的非贫困县却大多是人口大县。

表 4-b　国家贫困县认定时发生的两种失误——以县人口为单位的计算结果

	1993 年	2001 年
中国官方贫困线	450 元	625 元
第一种失误	0.027	0.001
第二种失误	0.074	0.214
第一、二种失误合计	0.101	0.214
世界银行贫困线	559 元	875 元
第一种失误	0.118	0.002
第二种失误	0.031	0.197
第一、二种失误合计	0.149	0.199
调整后 *TCE*	0.295	0.175

五、扶贫资金分配的分析

本部分主要讨论扶贫资金如何在省份、县和农户间进行分配。中国扶贫资金的分配机制是一个从上到下,逐级分配的过程,即首先中央政府根据贫困人口规模以及其他因素把扶贫资金分配到省份,然后由各省份再把扶贫资金分配给县,最后由县决定扶贫资金的最终使用,包括贴息贷款在农户之间的分配。鉴于扶贫资金是逐级发放的,因此我们也逐级讨论扶贫资金的分配问题。首先,讨论中央政府是如何在各省份之间分配扶贫资金的。表 5 给出了省份人均扶贫资金对其农民人均纯收入的回归分析结果。从该表中,我们至少得出两个重要结果。第一,正如我们所预料的,收入水平是中央政府分配扶贫资金时考虑的重要因素。人均纯收入越低的省份,得到人均扶贫资金也就越多。从 R^2 可以看出,人均纯收入的省际差距可以解释人均扶贫资金省际差异的 40%左右。第二,相关的系数估计值显示,2000 年三项扶贫资金的分配对低收入省份的倾斜程度大致相同。但是在 1999 年有些差异,其中以发展资金的倾斜程度最小,而贴息贷款的倾斜程度最大。

表 5　收入水平和人均扶贫资金之间的关系

	贴息贷款	发展资金	以工代赈资金	合计
2000 年				
省份农民人均纯收入的对数值	−7.932	−7.353	−7.132	−6.973
	(3.95)**	(3.97)**	(3.66)**	(3.42)**
常数项	66.462	61.203	60.068	60.284
	(4.57)**	(4.56)**	(4.25)**	(4.09)**
样本数	26	26	26	26
R^2	0.39	0.40	0.36	0.33

（续表）

	贴息贷款	发展资金	以工代赈资金	合计
1999 年				
省份农民人均纯收入的对数值	−8.549	−6.51	−7.48	−5.702
	(4.73)**	(4.13)**	(3.78)**	(3.53)**
常数项	71.41	5.316	62.744	51.593
	(5.44)**	(4.84)**	(4.37)**	(4.40)**
样本数	26	26	26	26
R^2	0.48	0.42	0.37	0.34

注：(1)被解释变量是省份人均扶贫资金的对数值。(2)括号里的数字是 t 统计值。(3) * 和 ** 分别表示该系数估计值在 5% 和 1% 统计水平上显著。

以上我们以省份为单位考察了扶贫资金是如何在不同省份之间分配的。进一步以县为单位考察县人均扶贫资金和县人均纯收入之间的关系是讨论扶贫资金分配的另外一种方法。很显然，二者之间的关系不仅受到中央政府在各省份之间分配扶贫资金的影响，同时也受到各省份在省份内分配扶贫资金办法的左右。表 6-a 给出了这方面的计算结果。我们分别对 1999 年和 2000 年的数据进行了估算，由于两年的估算结果极其相似，表 6-a 只给出了 2000 年的估算结果。当把分析对象具体到县一级时，我们可以引入更多的影响扶贫资金分配的解释变量。是否老区县，是否少数民族县，都可能会影响到扶贫资金的分配结果。另外，我们还把省份虚拟变量作为解释变量引入了模型。

表 6-a　扶贫资金在国定贫困县之间分配的决定因素(2000 年)

	贴息贷款	发展资金	以工代赈资金	合计
县人均纯收入的对数值	−0.52	−1.007	−0.457	−0.646
	(3.52)**	(5.98)**	(3.10)**	(5.36)**

（续表）

	贴息贷款	发展资金	以工代赈资金	合计
革命老区	−0.136	0.021	−0.087	−0.129
	(1.33)	(0.18)	(0.81)	(1.47)
边区	0.549	0.466	0.234	0.449
	(3.88)**	(2.72)**	(1.58)	(3.74)**
少数民族地区	0.449	0.581	0.37	0.445
	(4.83)**	(5.26)**	(3.86)**	(5.73)**
陕西	−0.201	−0.112	0.555	0.064
	(1.16)	(0.57)	(3.02)**	(0.43)
内蒙古	−0.771	−0.371	−0.054	−0.464
	(4.07)**	(1.73)	(0.27)	(2.87)**
辽宁	−3.928	−2.373	−1.037	−2.409
	(5.56)**	(6.29)**	(3.76)**	(10.62)**
吉林	0.06	0.471	0.888	0.312
	(0.18)	(1.12)	(2.48)*	(1.06)
黑龙江	0.202	0.319	0.969	0.402
	(0.78)	(1.14)	(3.72)**	(1.87)
安徽	−0.636	−0.903	−0.177	−0.497
	(3.04)**	(3.82)**	(0.79)	(2.73)**
福建	−2.967	−1.467	0.13	−1.018
	(6.92)**	(4.50)**	(0.43)	(4.08)**
江西	−0.523	−0.583	0.288	−0.225
	(2.37)*	(2.33)*	(1.23)	(1.17)
河南	−0.22	−0.181	−0.002	−0.12
	(1.26)	(0.91)	(0.01)	(0.79)
湖北	−0.359	−0.635	−0.415	−0.318
	(1.78)	(2.76)**	(1.85)	(1.81)
湖南	0.039	−0.6	0.015	−0.055
	(0.15)	(2.01)*	(0.05)	(0.25)

（续表）

	贴息贷款	发展资金	以工代赈资金	合计
广西	−0.159	−0.758	−0.313	−0.118
	(0.83)	(3.45)**	(1.53)	(0.71)
海南	−0.167	0.031	1.339	0.464
	(0.50)	(0.06)	(3.79)**	(1.59)
重庆	−0.071	−0.444	0.116	−0.023
	(0.28)	(1.56)	(0.44)	(0.10)
四川	0.375	−0.255	−0.161	0.246
	(2.04)*	(1.23)	(0.82)	(1.54)
贵州	−0.084	−0.814	−0.339	−0.178
	(0.51)	(4.30)**	(1.93)	(1.26)
云南	−0.333	−1.256	−0.71	−0.668
	(2.07)*	(6.38)**	(4.17)**	(4.89)**
陕西	0.201	−0.303	−0.121	0.074
	(1.21)	(1.58)	(0.68)	(0.52)
甘肃	0.001	−0.044	−0.383	−0.009
	(0.00)	(0.23)	(2.07)*	(0.06)
青海	0.972	−0.852	1.052	0.759
	(4.24)**	(2.58)*	(4.22)**	(3.80)**
宁夏	0.388	−0.042	0.23	0.362
	(1.34)	(0.13)	(0.72)	(1.44)
新疆	−0.389	−0.399	0.789	0.058
	(1.79)	(1.62)	(3.47)**	(0.32)
常数项	7.612	10.053	6.153	9.033
	(6.95)**	(8.08)**	(5.64)**	(10.12)**
样本数	537	503	539	565
R^2	0.42	0.4	0.37	0.49

注：(1)被解释变量是县人均扶贫资金的对数值。(2)括号里的数字是 t 统计值。(3) * 和 ** 分别表示该系数估计值在5%和1%统计水平上显著。

从表 6-a 给出的结果来看，我们可以得到以下几点结论。

首先，人均纯收入越低的县，获得的人均扶贫资金数额也就越多，如果县人均收入降低10%，人均扶贫资金就可以增加6.5%。在三项扶贫资金中，发展资金与农村人均纯收入之间的相关性是最强的。其次，革命老区身份对扶贫资金分配的影响并不显著，与此相反，少数民族县却在扶贫资金分配中得到优惠。少数民族县虚拟变量的估计系数表明，在其他情况相同的条件下，少数民族自治县能够得到比其他贫困县多出70%的扶贫资金。再次，我们的估计结果还显示，边远地区县也能得到较多的扶贫资金。最后，省份虚拟变量的估计系数显现了较大的差异性，这意味着在一些省份中政府在扶贫资金分配的过程中起到了较大的作用。

考察收入水平和人均扶贫资金之间的关系是理解扶贫资金的分配方式的方法之一。除此之外，还存在其他方法，其中之一是考察贫困人口规模和扶贫资金总额之间的关系。这二者之间的关系更能直接地反映扶贫资金的分配是否更准确地瞄准了贫困人口。为此，我们以县为样本进一步地分析了贫困人口规模和扶贫资金总额之间的关系。和上面回归模型的设定基本相同，除了贫困人口规模之外，作为解释变量的还有各种虚拟变量。表6-b给出了这种回归分析的结果。正如我们所期望的那样，贫困人口规模的估算系数为正数(尽管贴息贷款没有达到显著水平)，表明贫困人口规模大的县可以得到更多的扶贫资金。在验证了扶贫资金和贫困人口规模之间的正相关性之后，一个相应的问题是，扶贫资金的分配是按照贫困人口的规模等比例增加吗？换句话问，当一个县的贫困人口比另外一个县多出1倍时，前者所得到的扶贫资金也会比后者多出1倍吗？我们给出的回答是否定。这一点是不难从模型中的估计结果中找到答案。贫困人口规模的估算系数表明了当贫困人口增加1%时，得到的扶贫资金增加多少。贫困人口规模的估算系数均小于1，这意味着三大扶贫项目中的任何一项资金的分配规模都没有随贫困人口规模的增大而同比例地增加，扶贫资金的分配虽然向贫困人口规模有所倾斜，但是倾斜的力度显然是不够的，其结果是随着贫困人口的增加，人均扶贫资金反而下降。另外一个值得注意的估算结果是，老区、少数民族地区和边远地区等虚拟变量的估算系数值在统计上均不显著，然而估算系数显著的省份虚拟变量的数目却增多了。

表 6-b　扶贫资金分配与县贫困人口的关系(2000 年)

	贴息贷款	发展资金	以工代赈资金	合计
县贫困人口的对数值	0.142	0.401	0.191	0.155
	(1.56)	(3.73)**	(2.11)*	(2.45)*
革命老区	−0.053	−0.009	0.013	−0.052
	(0.23)	(0.03)	(0.06)	(0.32)
边区	0.042	0.216	0.000	0.012
	(0.20)	(0.90)	(0.00)	(0.08)
少数民族地区	0.472	0.186	−0.256	0.131
	(1.51)	(0.50)	(0.82)	(0.60)
陕西	0.655	0.904	1.877	1.477
	(1.88)	(2.19)*	(5.40)**	(6.07)**
内蒙古	0.625	1.183	1.602	1.499
	(1.54)	(2.48)*	(3.97)**	(5.31)**
辽宁	−5.199	−2.316	1.361	−0.065
	(8.91)**	(3.37)**	(2.34)*	(0.16)
吉林	1.97	0.92	3.08	2.449
	(2.64)**	(1.05)	(4.15)**	(4.72)**
黑龙江	1.148	2.024	2.882	2.24
	(2.16)*	(3.23)**	(5.45)**	(6.05)**

（续表）

	贴息贷款	发展资金	以工代赈资金	合计
安徽	2.071	1.729	2.761	2.326
	(4.53)**	(3.20)**	(6.07)**	(7.30)**
福建	－4.064	－0.024	1.834	0.423
	(6.48)**	(0.03)	(2.94)**	(0.97)
江西	1.566	1.698	2.619	2.009
	(3.26)**	(2.99)**	(5.47)**	(6.00)**
河南	2.165	2.258	2.668	2.377
	(5.72)**	(5.06)**	(7.08)**	(9.02)**
湖北	1.9	1.746	1.348	2.077
	(4.31)**	(3.36)**	(3.07)**	(6.76)**
湖南	2.528	1.183	2.699	2.587
	(4.52)**	(1.79)	(4.85)**	(6.64)**
广西	1.975	1.459	2.093	2.201
	(4.76)**	(2.98)**	(5.07)**	(7.62)**
海南	1.443	－0.27	3.236	2.219
	(1.92)	(0.30)	(4.32)**	(4.23)**
重庆	2.427	1.932	2.805	2.621
	(4.33)**	(2.92)**	(5.03)**	(6.71)**
四川	2.178	1.599	1.845	2.217
	(5.61)**	(3.49)**	(4.77)**	(8.19)**
贵州	2.159	0.713	1.861	2.228
	(6.31)**	(1.77)	(5.47)**	(9.35)**
云南	0.87	－1.237	1.281	1.552
	(2.69)**	(3.24)**	(3.98)**	(6.89)**
陕西	1.808	0.766	1.477	1.845
	(5.46)**	(1.96)	(4.48)**	(8.00)**
甘肃	2.017	1.752	0.92	2.179
	(5.97)**	(4.39)**	(2.73)**	(9.25)**

（续表）

	贴息贷款	发展资金	以工代赈资金	合计
青海	1.878	−1.944	1.753	1.845
	(3.76)**	(3.30)**	(3.52)**	(5.30)**
宁夏	2.417	1.896	1.568	2.581
	(3.77)**	(2.51)*	(2.46)*	(5.78)**
新疆	0.579	1.302	2.68	1.869
	(1.27)	(2.42)*	(5.91)**	(5.89)**
常数项	5.355	3.961	4.048	5.722
	(21.60)**	(13.54)**	(16.40)**	(33.11)**
样本数	577	577	577	577
R^2	0.41	0.29	0.21	0.31

注：(1)被解释变量是县人均扶贫资金的对数值。(2)括号里的数字是 t 统计值。(3) * 和 ** 分别表示该系数估计值在5%和1%统计水平上显著。

国家扶贫资金是通过省级政府分配给各国定贫困县，因此省级分配是其中的一个重要环节。那么，各省政府是否在分配扶贫资金时达到了目标瞄准的要求呢？为此，下面我们对各省份的扶贫资金分配加以考察，着重讨论各省份是否按人均纯收入标准在各国定贫困县之间分配了资金。表 7 分省份给出了人均扶贫资金对人均纯收入的回归分析结果。被列入估计的省份有 16 个，它们都是有足够样本的省份。从该表可以看出，16 个省份中只有 5 个省份的人均纯收入变量的回归系数为负数，而且是显著的。其他 11 个省份中，除了内蒙古，人均纯收入的回归系数，不论为负数或正数，均未达到统计上的显著水平。在内蒙古，收入水平的估计系数为正数，而且是显著的，这表明内蒙古的扶贫资金分配不仅没有向人均收入低的旗县倾斜，反而向收入高的旗县倾斜。总而言之，分省份的回归结果表明，多数省份在分配扶贫资金时并没有主要考虑各县的收入水平。这也意味着在部分省份内部扶贫资金分配存在着较为严重的目标瞄准问题,也影响到了扶贫资金分配的整体目标瞄准的准确性。

如果就人均纯收入的系数估计值而言,把全国的回归结果(表 6-a)和分省份的回归结果(表 7)加以比较,我们会发现一个有趣的结果。在全国范围内,每个国定贫困县得到的人均扶贫资金和县人均纯收入之间存在着明显的负相关关系,而且这种关系在统计上是显著的。这说明扶贫资金在中央政府一级目标瞄准得比较准确。但是,当扶贫资金到了省一级时,在绝大多数的省份中二者之间负相关关系不再存在了。也就是说,一些省份未必按着收入水平分配扶贫资金,导致扶贫资金部分地偏离最低收入的贫困县。扶贫资金的分配在中央政府一级瞄准得较好,而在省级政府一级瞄准较差,这样一种结果具有一定的政策含义。也就是说,为了使扶贫资金更好地瞄准低收入的贫困县,仅有中央政府的努力是远远不够的,必须保证各省级政府在资金分配瞄准低收入的贫困县,否则扶贫资金瞄准的准确性在整体上会受到影响。这也意味着扶贫资金瞄准的准确性可以通过省级政府把资金的分配更加向收入更低的国定贫困县倾斜而得以提高。

表 7　县农民人均纯收入和人均扶贫资金之间的关系——分省份分析

省份	县人均纯收入的对数值	t 值	常数项	t 值	样本数	R^2
河北	−0.85	(2.82)**	10.64	(4.81)**	37	0.18
陕西	−0.75	(3.12)**	9.84	(5.81)**	35	0.23
内蒙古	0.77	(2.24)*	−1.21	(0.49)	31	0.15
黑龙江	−0.19	(0.22)	6.39	(1.05)	11	0.01
安徽	−3.65	(2.85)*	30.54	(3.25)**	17	0.35
江西	−3.02	(1.94)	25.75	(2.30)*	18	0.19

（续表）

省份	县人均纯收入的对数值	t值	常数项	t值	样本数	R^2
河南	－0.54	(1.04)	8.09	(2.10)*	28	0.04
湖北	－1.37	(2.00)	14.08	(2.79)*	25	0.15
湖南	－4.14	(1.57)	33.76	(1.82)	10	0.24
广西	－0.81	(0.81)	10.59	(1.46)	28	0.02
重庆	－5.52	(1.81)	44.06	(2.02)	10	0.29
四川	－2.82	(12.23)**	24.82	(15.25)**	29	0.85
贵州	－0.20	(0.22)	5.96	(0.92)	48	0.00
云南	－0.89	(1.72)	10.51	(2.89)**	73	0.04
陕西	－0.93	(2.54)*	11.03	(4.30)**	50	0.12
甘肃	－0.54	(1.54)	8.42	(3.44)**	40	0.06
青海	0.20	(0.12)	4.18	(0.35)	14	0.00
新疆	0.68	(1.96)	0.60	(0.25)	25	0.14

注：(1)被解释变量是县人均扶贫资金的对数值。(2)括号里的数字是 t 统计值。(3) * 和 ** 分别表示该系数估计值在5%和1%统计水平上显著。

贫困监测调查还对农户是否得到以及得到了多少贴息贷款的情况进行了调查④，这使得我们有机会对贴息贷款在农户之间的分配结果进行分析。在全部农户调查样本中，只有 2.1% 农户得到了贴息贷款。如果对农户获得贷款的影响因素进行估计，由于绝大多数农户没有得到任何贷款，这样一种数据结构使得普通最小二乘法的估计结果产生一定的估计误差，而避免误差的一种办法是使用 Tobit 模型进行分析。于是我们决定使用了 Tobit 模型，试图从中发现贴息贷款分配的决定因素。

以农户为样本，取得贴息贷款的金额为被解释变量，绝大多数没有机会得到扶贫贴息贷款的农户的这一变量的数值为 0。解释变量除了包括农户的人均纯收入外，还有县人均纯收入，农户所在的县是否老区县、少数民族县、边远地区县，县人均贴息贷款，是否贫困户，家庭人数，农业收入占总收入的比重，人均健康支出额、人均教育消费额、劳动力/人口比率、户主的文化程度等等。之所以把许多解释变量引入模型，是因为要弄清这些住户特征是否对获得扶贫资金的机会和数量产生影响以及有多大的影响。最后，农户所在村与县城的距离，与最近乡镇的距离也作为解释变量引进了模型。

表 8　贴息贷款在农户之间分配的决定因素——Tobit 模型估计结果(2000 年)

解释变量	均值	估计系数	t 值
农户人均纯收入对数值	7.09	−0.163	(0.30)
县农民人均纯收入对数值	7.17	−6.535	(5.88)**
人均贴息贷款对数值	3.58	1.501	(6.53)**
贫困户(以 874 元为贫困线)		0.730	(1.13)
家庭人口数	4.41	0.267	(1.62)
总收入中农业收入的比重	0.21	−4.116	(3.84)**
家庭人均教育支出	2.31	0.229	(2.14)*
家庭人均健康支出	2.81	0.703	(7.13)**
劳动力与家庭人口比率	0.67	1.828	(1.64)
老区		−2.517	(4.35)**
边区		−1.219	(1.63)
少数民族地区		2.977	(4.92)**
户主受教育程度			
1—3 年小学		1.708	(2.24)*
4—6 年小学		−0.318	(0.38)
初中		0.602	(0.79)
高中		1.319	(1.36)
中专及中专以上		−3.266	(1.17)
到县城的距离(公里)			
2—5 公里		−0.430	(0.29)
5—10 公里		0.209	(0.15)

（续表）

解释变量	均值	估计系数	t 值
10—20 公里		−1.852	(1.34)
＞20 公里		1.428	(1.10)
到乡镇的距离(公里)			
2—5 公里		−1.657	(3.17)**
5—10 公里		0.641	(1.09)
10—20 公里		−0.908	(1.08)
＞20 公里		−4.541	(2.50)*
省份虚拟变量			
陕西		14.787	(11.60)**
内蒙古		−5.043	(2.14)*
安徽		12.381	(8.43)**
江西		4.279	(2.22)*
河南		3.962	(2.38)*
湖北		−11.556	(2.67)**
湖南		1.442	(0.69)
广西		2.226	(1.48)
海南		10.154	(4.97)**
重庆		−0.426	(0.18)
四川		−13.034	(3.96)**
贵州		10.484	(8.56)**
云南		6.923	(6.04)**
陕西		14.583	(11.94)**
甘肃		8.946	(7.07)**
青海		8.439	(4.22)**
宁夏		3.515	(1.71)
新疆		11.665	(7.56)**
常数项		−1.139	(0.14)
样本数		46833	

注：(1)被解释变量是农户获得的贴息贷款额。(2)括号里的数字是 t 统计值。(3) * 和 ** 分别表示该系数估计值在 5%和 1%统计水平上显著。

表8中给出了Tobit模型的计算结果，从中我们可以得出以下几种判断。(1)农户得到扶贫资金的机会和数量依赖于县人均纯收入以及所在县得到的扶贫资金的多少，而与农户本身的收入水平无关。(2)贫困户虚拟变量的系数估计值未达到统计上的显著水平，意味着与非贫困户相比，贫困户并没有获得更多的扶贫资金。(3)农业收入比重变量的估算系数为负数，而且统计上是显著的，说明从事非农活动的农户不仅更有机会获得扶贫资金，而且获得更多的扶贫资金。(4)农户人均健康支出和教育支出两个变量的估计系数不仅为正值，而且在统计上是显著的，这一结果需要慎重解释。也许农户在教育和健康方面投资越多越可能获得更多的扶贫资金，也许扶贫资金部分地分配给那些有教育和医疗需求的农户。[⑤](5)反映户主教育程度的几个虚拟变量的估计系数虽然都没有达到显著水平，但显示了这样一种倾向，教育水平越高的人越有机会获得扶贫资金。(6)少数民族县的农户能够获得更多的扶贫资金。然而，奇怪的是，老区的农户与其他地区的农户相比，获得扶贫资金的机会更小，并且获得的数额也较小。

六、结　论

本文使用国家统计局收集的分县数据，尤其是592个国定贫困县的分县数据和分户数据，围绕着农村扶贫项目的目标瞄准问题，探讨了以下两个方面的论题。第一，在国定贫困县的认定过程中是否发生了目标瞄准上的失误？与1993年的一轮贫困县认定相比，2001年的认定中发生的失误是减少了还是增加了？第二，扶贫资金是怎样在省份、县、农户之间分配的？也就是说，扶贫资金分配的决定因素是什么？

Probit 模型的估计结果显示，农民人均纯收入越低的县，被认定为国定贫困县的可能性也越大。收入水平的重要性在1993 年和 2001 年两次认定中并没有发生多大的变化。在其他情况相同的条件下，老区县以及少数民族县被认定为国定贫困县的可能性更大。通过计算 Cornia 和 Stewart（1995）和 Park 等（2002）提出的目标瞄准准确性的测量指数，我们对 1993 年和2001 年两轮国定贫困县的认定过程中的目标瞄准的准确性及其变化进行了讨论。结果显示，与 1993 年相比，2001 年国家贫困县的认定在目标瞄准的准确性上有了相当大的改进。

从扶贫资金目标瞄准准确性的角度，本文就中央政府对各省份扶贫资金的分配，以及各省级政府对各县扶贫资金的分配分别展开了讨论。结果显示，中央政府在把扶贫资金分配给各省份时，目标瞄准的准确度较高。与此相比，各省份在分配扶贫资金到县时，目标瞄准得不够准确。在我们分析的 16 个省份中，仅有少数几个省份按农民人均纯收入分配扶贫资金。而在更多的省份，县农民人均纯收入和县人均扶贫资金之间并不存在负相关性，有些省份甚至显示了正相关性。扶贫资金分配中这种目标瞄准的准确性的差异具有很强的政策性含义。它一方面表明，为了使扶贫资金更好地瞄准低收入的贫困县，仅有中央政府的努力是远远不够的，必须保证各省级政府在资金分配上瞄准低收入贫困县，否则扶贫资金瞄准的准确性在整体上会受到影响。另一方面也意味着，我们扶贫资金瞄准的整体准确性可以通过改善省份内的瞄准性而得到提高。

我们除了讨论了扶贫资金在省际之间，以及省内县际之间的分配问题之外，还讨论了贴息贷款如何在农户间进行分配。目的是为了了解哪些农户更容易得到贴息贷款，能够得到更多的贴息贷款。通过 Tobit 模型估计结果，我们发现农户获得的扶贫资金的数额主要依赖于所在县的收入而不是其自身收入。资金更倾向于分配给那些能够赚取非农劳动收入的农户。也就是说,纯农户很少有机会获得扶贫资金。我们原来期望贫困户更容易获得并且能够得到更多的扶贫资金。遗憾的是,我们并没有得到相应的经验分析结果。

注　释

① 1993 年被划定的国家贫困县通常被叫做国定贫困县,或者简称为国定县。而 2001 年被划定的国家贫困县叫做国家扶贫工作重点县,或者简称为重点县。本文更多的场合对国定县和重点县不加以区分地使用国定贫困县一词。

② 关于 Probit 模型估算系数的含义,参考 Greene(2000)第 824—825 页,或者 Maddala(2001)第 8 章。

③ Cornia 和 Stewart(1995)把第一种失误称为 F-mistakes,把第二种失误称为 E-mistakes。

④ 其他两种扶贫资金,因为直接分配到户的部分太少,所以在贫困检测调查中没有收集分户的有关信息。

⑤ 为了区分两种可能的效应,健康支出和教育支出变量需要进行内生化处理,这也是本文需要进一步研究的问题。

参考文献

国家统计局农村社会经济调查总队 2001,《2002 年中国农村贫困监测报告》,中国统计出版社。

国家统计局农村社会经济调查总队(2002),《2003 年中国农村贫困监测报告》,中国统计出版社。

Cornia and Stewart 1995, "Two Errors of Targeting", in Dominique van de Walle and Kimberly Nead, eds, *Public Spending and the Poor: Theory and Evidence*, Baltimore: John Hopkins University Press.

Greene, William H. (2000), *Econometrics Analysis*, fourth edition,

Prentice Hall International, Inc.

Gustafsson, Bjorn and Li Shi (1998), "Structure of Chinese Poverty 1988", *Developing Economies*, 36(4): pp. 387—406.

Gustafsson, Bjorn and Wei Zhong (2000), "How and Why Has Poverty in China Changed? A Study Based on Microdata for 1988 and 1995", *China Quarterly*, 164: pp. 983—1006.

Maddala, G. S. (2001), *Introduction to Econometrics*, third edition, John Wiley & Sons, LTD.

Park, Albert, Sangui Wang and Guobao Wu (2002), "Regional Poverty Targeting in China", *Journal of Public Economics*, 86(1): pp. 123—153.

Ravallion and Jalan (1999), "China's Lagging Poor Areas", *American Economic Review*, 89(2):301—305.

Riskin, Carl, 1994, "Chinese Rural Poverty: Marginalized or Dispersed?", *American Economic Review*, 84.

World Bank (2001), *China: Overcoming Rural Poverty*, The World Bank, Washington, D. C.

（原载《中国社会科学评论》第 1 卷）

农村工业化以及人力资本在农村劳动力市场中的角色

陈玉宇　邢春冰

(北京大学光华管理学院)

一、介　绍

提高农民收入、加快农村劳动力转移是当前政府工作的重中之重。① 提高农村劳动力的人力资本水平(尤其是教育),对于解决上述问题可以起到至关重要的作用。但是,这需要一个运行良好的劳动力市场——它不仅可以使人力资本得到相应的回报,反过来还可以激励农村地区的人力资本积累。本文通过估计教育回报率来考察教育在农村工业化过程中所发挥的作用,并据此来评价上世纪 90 年代中国农村的劳动力市场。

各种研究表明,中国农村教育回报率在 0—6%之间②,而 Psacharopoulos(1994)对世界范围内的总结表明,全世界的平均教育回报率为 10.1%,亚洲则为 9.6%。这与以下两个简单的事实很难协调。首先,中国是一个人力资本相对稀缺的国家,1995 年中国中等教育的毛入学率为 67%,美国则为 97% (World Bank, 2000)③。其次,中国家庭对人力资本的投资热情很高,1995 年教育④ 支出占到农村居民家庭人均生活消费支出的7.81%,仅次于食品(58.62%)和居住(13.91%)支出。如果教育的回报率低,便很难解释人们的教育投资行为。我们不认为人们的教育投资决策存在系统的对教育成本和回报的错误计算。本文认为,此前关于中国教育回报率的研究有两个弱点:一,人们往往基于农村工资收入者样本来估计农村的教育回报。二,以前的研究往往将注意力集中于工资水平本身[5],而缺乏对工资机制更加深入的探讨。针对此两点,本文将着重考察教育在提高人们到工业部门工作机会方面的作用,来更加全面地对人力资本回报率进行估计;而且,本文还将利用计时工资和计件工资的信息来讨论农村工业部门内部的工资机制问题。

利用美国北卡罗来纳大学 Chapel Hill 分校和中国预防医学会营养与食品卫生研究所的调查数据,本文考察了教育在农村男性劳动力市场中的作用。我们首先通过工资方程考察了工业部门内部的教育回报率问题。由于工资收入者只占整个农村劳动力市场的一部分,一个自然的考虑是样本选择问题。特别地,那些留在农业部门的劳动者(我们也无法观测到他们的工资水平)可能是那些能力比较低的人。如果我们关心的是整个农村劳动力市场的教育回报,忽略这个问题可能导致教育回报的低估。本文应用了 Heckman 样本选择模型来估计教育回报率。结果表明,1991 年到 1997 年,教育的工资回报率在 0—5%之间,但是并不显著,样本选择问题也不严重。

接下来的研究表明,教育在决定劳动力从农业向工业部门转移的过程中发挥了重要的作用。利用 Probit 模型,我们可以计算教育水平增加一年,劳动者到工业部门工作的机会增加1.5%—3.2%,这一结果在统计上是显著的。但是,如果无法衡量工资收入对于个人收入增加的影响,我们便无法知道教育在劳动力转移过程中带来的回报。本文采取的策略是,考察是否拥有工资收入对于家庭人均年收入的影响。结果表明，拥有工资收入使得劳动者的家庭人均年收入增加 50%左右。最后，我们通过综合考虑教育对于劳动力转移的作用、工资收入对于家庭收入的影响以及平均家庭规模，计算了教育通过增加人们到工业部门就业的机会给个人带来的回报。尽管依赖于很强的假设以及简单的计算，我们仍然可以看出，由于上世纪 90 年代农村农业部门与工业部门之间巨大的收入差距，教育在农村劳动力转移过程中带来的回报在 5%—7%左右。这是本文的主要结果和贡献之一。

本文的另外一个贡献在于，我们进一步讨论了农村工业部门内部的工资机制问题。1989 年的数据表明计时、计件工资作为不同的激励机制，与教育水平有着明显的关系。教育水平低的人接受计件工资的概率比较大。在计件工资的情况下教育回报率在 7.5%左右，而在计时工资的情况下为 3%左右。同时，计时工资的平均工资水平高于计件工资 22%(尽管统计上并不显著)。这一结果表明，拥有计时工资本身可能就是一种回报(相对于拥有计件工资)。因此只是考察工资水平而不关心具体的工资制度安排，可能成为低估教育回报率的另一个原因。

总之，农村的劳动力市场安排从多个渠道给教育带来了回报。这种安排可以激励农村劳动力提高他们的受教育水平。但是，由于工业部门内部工资制度的安排，导致了拥有较高人力资本水平的人没有足够的激励来利用自身的人力资本。这种状况在上世纪 90 年代没有明显的改善。

二、文 献 回 顾

人力资本与劳动者的收入以及经济增长之间存在着密切的

关系。本文的重点是从微观层面来研究教育的回报率，并由此来考察农村劳动力市场。⑥大量的研究表明，教育可以增进人们的知识、提高人们的技能，因此，在一个运行良好的市场，教育应该得到回报，估计教育回报率也就成了考察人力资本作用的重要途径(Schultz, 1961; Becker, 1993)。但是，估计教育回报率在技术上存在一个主要的问题：如果我们遗漏了能力这个变量，内生性问题会使OLS高估教育的回报率。人们往往通过三个途径来解决这个问题：利用教育系统的制度特征作工具变量；利用家庭背景作控制变量或工具变量以及将孪生子女或兄弟姐妹的相关变量进行差分之后再进行OLS回归或者利用工具变量。Card(1999)对上述方法以及发达国家的教育回报率进行了很好的总结，表明发达国家的教育回报率集中在5%—10%左右。⑦Duflo(2000)在控制了内生性和测量误差的问题之后，对印度尼西亚的估计结果表明，教育增加一年使得工资水平提高6%到10%。因此提高受教育水平成了提高人们收入和生活水平的重要途径。这也是我们在讨论农民收入时要考察教育回报率的原因之一。

关于中国农村劳动力市场在农村工业化过程中发挥的作用，不同的学者有不同的观点。其中一个重要的思路就是试图通过考察教育的工资回报率来评价中国农村劳动力市场。Meng(1996, 2000)的研究表明人力资本在工资中得不到相应的回报，而是一些非市场的因素在起作用。但是Meng没有将教育的回报问题放于二元经济的框架之中。Zhang等(2002)的研究表明，从20世纪80年代后期到90年代中期，教育水平在决定劳动力转移到工业部门方面发挥越来越重要的作用，而且教育的工资回报也从1988年和1992年的不显著变为1996年的6%—10%。因此得出结论，农村的劳动力市场有所改善。但是，他们的样本只来自于经济发达省份(江苏)的部分农村，不具有代表性。其次，该文没有分析农村中农业与工业部门之间的收入差距，也就无法得出教育在劳动力转移过程中给人们带来的回报。此外，魏众(2004)在分析健康对非农就业的影响时，也考察了教育的回报问题，结论是，即使在考虑了样本选择问题之后，教育的回报率仍然是比较低的，但没有分析教育对农村劳动力转移的影响。

二元性是发展经济的显著特征(Lewis, 1954)，部门与部门、地区与地区之间的收入水平存在着显著的差异。在这样的特征之下，劳动力在地域与部门之间的转移与教育水平存在着显著的关系。教育水平越高，对于工资差异带来的激励越容易产生反应。因此，地区和部门之间的工资(水平或机制)差异可能成为对于教育的回报。但是，与此相关的两个基本问题到现在还没有满意地解决。首先，是什么决定了部门之间的工资差异?⑧其次，教育在劳动力转移过程中到底发挥了什么作用?本文的目的不在于为这两个问题提供答案，而在于对于人们理解这个问题提供更多的证据。同时也指出，不考虑发展经济的二元特征，只是通过估计工资方程来考察教育的回报率，结果可能会误导人们对于中国农村劳动力市场的认识。

三、模型设定

为了考察农村地区的教育回报，我们分别构造了农村工业部门中的工资方程和劳动力转移模型。利用工资方程，我们可以考察工业部门内部的人力资本回报问题；而利用劳动力转移模型，我们可以考察教育对于农村劳动力转移的作用。

(一) 教育在农村工业部门内部的工资回报

1. 农村工业部门内部的工资方程

教育增加了劳动者的知识和技能，提高了他们创造财富的能力。不同国家和地区的研究证实：拥有更高教育水平的人，能够赚取更多的工资，较少受失业威胁，同时拥有更加体面的工作。我们首先考察教育对于工资水平的影响。我们在 Mincer 方程的基础上，设定模型的形式如下：

$$\ln(wage) = \alpha + \beta_1 S + \gamma X + u_1$$

S 代表教育，用劳动者受教育的年限来度量。此外，本文还考虑了其他变量(X)包括经验⑨、个人婚姻状况、家庭背景、是否是行政管理人员、是否是村级管理人员以及所在省份等其他变量，由于我们的样本中，企业的性质存在着显著的差异，我们还控制了工作单位的类型。

2. 考虑样本选择问题能否改善我们的估计？（Heckman 模型）

由于农村中存在大量没有工资收入的劳动者，因此便有样本选择的问题[关于这个问题更加严格的阐述见 Wooldridge (2001)第 561 页]。考虑到这一点，我们用 Heckman(1979)模型进一步估计工业部门内部的教育回报率。我们有：

$$\ln(wage) = \alpha + \beta_1 S + \gamma X + u_1 \tag{1}$$

$$wd = 1 \quad (\alpha + \beta_2 S + \lambda X' + u_2 > 0) \tag{2}$$

其中(2)式是表示工资收入是否被观测到的指示函数。假定(1) $(wd,\ S,\ X')$总可以被观测到，$\ln(wage)$只有在 $wd = 1$ 时被观测到；(2)$(u_1,\ u_2)$均值为零，与$(S,\ X,\ X')$独立；(3)$u_2 \sim N(0, 1)$；以及(4)$E(u_1 \mid u_2) = \eta_1 u_2$。

于是有：

$$E[\ln(wage) \mid S, X, wd = 1] = \alpha + \beta_1 S + \gamma X + \eta_1 m(\alpha + \beta_2 S + \lambda X') \tag{3}$$

其中 $m(\cdot) \equiv \phi(\cdot)/\Phi(\cdot)$。我们首先通过 Probit 模型得到 $m(\alpha+\beta_2 S+\lambda X')$，然后将其放入(3)式中，对(1)式进行 OLS 估计。如果 $m(\alpha+\beta_2 S+\lambda X')$的系数显著，则表明确实存在样本选择的问题；如果不显著则应该与直接对(1)式进行回归的结果是一致的。

(二) 从工业工作对于家庭人均年收入的影响来估计教育的回报率

上面的模型中，我们考虑的主要是工业部门内部的工资回报率问题。为了考察教育在整个农村劳动力市场中所扮演的角色，我们必须还要注意到如下两点事实。首先，拥有工资收入显著地提高了一个人(家庭)的收入水平；其次，教育显著地提高了劳动力赚取工资收入的概率。

1. *农村劳动力转移模型*

如果人力资本水平在劳动力转移过程中发挥作用，工业部门相对高的工资便是对人力资本的回报。我们首先用 Probit 模型考察教育在劳动力转移过程中的作用。我们关心的因变量是劳动力是否转移到工业部门($wd = 1$ 代表是，否则 $wd = 0$)，同时假定每个劳动者存在一个潜在决策方程。

$$y^* = \alpha + \beta_2 S + \lambda X' + u_2 \tag{4}$$

其中 y^* 为潜在变量(latent variable)，我们无法观测，但劳动者据此作出决策。S(教育水平)是我们主要关心的变量。教育水平高的人往往具有较高的生产力，更容易适应从农业部门到工业部门的转变(包括在找工作的过程中较强的信息处理能力以及适应工业生产环境的能力)，同时教育水平也为雇用者提供了劳动者能力的信号。X'控制了其他影响劳动者决策的因素，包括个人特征、家庭经济人口状况[10]、户主状况以及地域因素。此外为了控制遗漏变量的影响，还包括了户主的教育水平。u_2 为随机项，服从 $N(0, 1)$分布。因此，我们可以有：

$$wd = \begin{cases} 1 & \text{如果 } y^* > 0 \\ 0 & \text{如果 } y^* \leqslant 0 \end{cases} \tag{5}$$

进一步，

$$\begin{aligned} P(wd = 1 \mid S, X') &= P(u_2 > -\alpha - \beta_2 S - \lambda X') \\ &= \Phi(\alpha + \beta_2 S + \lambda X') \end{aligned} \tag{6}$$

因此，如果教育水平增加一年，劳动力转移概率增加的量为：

$$\Delta P(wd = 1 \mid S, X') \approx \phi(\cdot) \tag{7}$$

这是我们要估计的量。

2. 工业收入对家庭收入的影响

上面，我们考虑了教育对于劳动力转移的影响。接下来的问题是估计拥有工资收入在多大程度上提高了人们的收入水平。遗憾的是本套数据并没有关于个人收入组成的数据，有的只是以家庭为单位的数据。因此，我们只能考察拥有工资收入对于家庭人均收入的影响。模型的具体形式如下：

$$\ln pc = \alpha + \beta_3 wd + \theta_1 Y + \varepsilon \tag{8}$$

其中我们感兴趣的是 wd 如何提高了家庭的人均收入。向量 Y 控制了其他影响家庭收入的变量，包括土地数量、家庭中挣取收入的人数、家庭规模、性别比例、教育和经验以及户主的教育和经验。

如上小节分析的，wd 是教育水平的函数。为了叙述方便，我们采用线性概率模型的方式：[11]

$$wd = \alpha' + \gamma_0 S + \gamma_1 X' + u'_2 \quad (9)$$

则有，教育水平增加一年，拥有工资收入概率的概率增加 $\gamma_0[\gamma_0 = \phi(\tilde{\alpha} + \tilde{\beta}_2 S + \tilde{X}X')\tilde{\beta}_2]$。将(9)式代入(8)式，我们有：

$$\ln pc = \alpha + \beta_3\gamma_0 S + \beta_3\gamma_1 X + \theta_1 Y + (\beta_3 u'_2 + \varepsilon) \quad (10)$$

因此，教育水平增加一年，通过提高人们到工业部门就业的机会而使得家庭的人均年收入增加 $\beta_3\gamma_0$。值得注意的是，在(5)式中，教育通过两个途径来影响人均收入。一种途径是通过提高人们工业就业的机会；另外的途径可能是通过直接影响工资收入者的工资水平以及农业劳动者(以及自谋职业者)的劳动生产率而提高家庭的人均收入。

四、背景与数据

本文所采用的数据是由美国北卡罗来纳大学 Chapel Hill 分校和中国预防医学会营养与食品卫生研究所 1989 年、1991 年、1993 年和 1997 年所做的关于中国农村与城市 3000 多个家庭户的经济、人口、营养与健康调查(CHNS)中反映农村家庭收入、个人工资、教育水平以及其他一些反映家庭背景的数据。[12] 考虑到影响女性劳动参与的因素与男性劳动力不尽相同，本文将注意力主要集中在年龄在 16 周岁到 65 周岁的男性劳动力。[13]

为了准确地反映劳动生产率，我们计算了小时工资，1991 年、1993 年和 1997 年的数据中我们没有计时工资和计件工资的信息，但是 1989 年的数据提供了这方面的信息。我们在第五部分中讨论了工资的测度问题。由于本套数据没有关于教育年限的直接度量，我们根据不同阶段的教育年限进行计算。为了控制家庭背景的因素，我们根据家庭内部成员的关系把数据按照户主以及与户主的关系分成两个数据，分别包括户主的信息和儿子的信息，然后再进行合并。经这样的处理之后，样本有所减少。

表1中的A栏反映了农村中所有男性劳动力的情况。数据表明，1991—1997年间，男性劳动力的受教育水平不断上升，由1991年平均每人6.68年增加到1997年平均每人7.44年，6年间增长了11.45%。[14]与此同时，平均工资水平也有很大幅度的上升。1991年、1993年和1997年，农村地区的月平均工资分别为133.7元、176.4元和208.0元，1997年分别比1991年和1993年增长56%和18%。B栏反映了子女的情况。儿子的教育水平明显高于户主。1991年、1993年和1997年分别为7.43年、7.68年和8.39年；但是工资水平却低于户主。

为了客观地评价分析结果，有如下几点需要注意。首先，我们这里的农村是指广义的农村，样本中包括了农村地区的村庄和城镇，其中既有农业人口也有工业人口。其次，由于样本中82%左右的人全年都在家庭户中居住，这表明大部分农村劳动力是在农村内部的农业部门与工业部门之间转化。因此，我们的研究结果将主要对农村内部劳动力转移提供证据，而非劳动力在农村与城市之间的转移。但是，数据也表明，年轻人在外居住的月数多于年纪大的人。这也许表明，在农村发展的过程中，农村劳动力在地域间的转移越来越重要。但这不是本文的重点。

尽管教育和工资水平在不同的样本中呈现逐年增加的趋势，工业部门占整个农村劳动力的比重(拥有工资收入的人所占的比重)并没有明显的增加，1997年的比重甚至比1993年还要低。这可能与国家的整体经济形式有关。[15]此外关于工作月数的统计表明，在拥有工资收入的人当中，一年中劳动参与的情况也有很大的差异。全年(12个月)工作的只有70%左右。我们在本文的后面部分对教育水平与劳动参与率之间的关系进行了讨论。

表 1　主要变量的描述统计

主要变量		1991 年	1993 年	1997 年	1991 年	1993 年	1997 年
		A			B		
教育年限	样本量	2618	2617	2790	676	702	838
	均值	6.68(3.46)	6.76(3.38)	7.44(3.30)	7.44(2.80)	7.68(2.75)	8.39(2.63)
拥有收入	样本量	2622	2634	2800	678	707	843
	均值	27.8(44.8)	28.4(45.1)	27.7(44.7)	22.7(41.9)	27.0(44.4)	26.1(43.9)
月工资	样本量	950	981	1183	234	290	449
	均值	133(91)	176(153)	207(189)	124(87)	158(103)	198(129)
小时工资	样本量	933	922	1125	231	264	417
	均值	0.81(1.28)	0.97(1.12)	1.21(1.27)	0.66(0.5)	0.81(0.56)	1.14(1.02)

注:1991 年和 1993 年的工资数据按照调查提供的价格指数进行调整,其中 1997 年数据中的价格指数按照国家统计局公布的农村居民消费价格指数计算(1988=100);括号中为标准差。下同。

五、估 计 结 果

(一) 工业部门内部工资决定

1. 工资方程

表2的A栏报告了不考虑家庭背景的情况下的工资方程。工资方程中,教育水平的系数在1991年、1993年和1997年分别是−0.00566、0.0003和0.00976,而且均不显著。与教育水平的系数不显著相对,经验的系数在1991年和1993年比较显著,分别为0.021903和0.031948,1997年经验的系数为0.0132423,并不显著。

通过控制家庭背景,我们可以控制一些不可观测的变量(如能力)。[16]表2的B栏报告了控制户主教育水平之后的回归结果。教育水平的系数仍然都不显著,但是其系数水平的变化与我们的预测一致(1993年除外)。1991年和1997年教育的工资回报率变为−0.0205和−0.019。相反1993年的系数水平有所提高,变为0.024754。在不控制省份、工作单位性质和婚姻状况的情况下,模型调整后的R^2显著降低,但是教育系数没有显著的改变,表明这一结果是稳健的。

2. 样本选择模型

表2的C栏部分报告了利用Heckman(1979)的两步模型重新估计的结果(Probit部分将在下一节讨论)。我们在第一步的Probit模型中放入了人力资本、婚姻状况以及家庭和地域特征等变量,然后再利用第一步的结果重新对工资方程进行估计。教育的系数有所变化,1991年、1993年和1997年的系数分别为−0.00506、0.040355和0.02238[表2的C栏的(1)(3)(5)列中还报告了不考虑户主教育水平的估计结果,除1997年外,考虑户

表 2 工资方程

因变量=log(小时工资)	1991 年		1993 年		1997 年	
	(1)	(2)	(3)	(4)	(5)	(6)
	A(不考虑家庭背景)					
教育年限	−0.00566		0.0003		0.00976	
	(0.00907)		(0.01005)		(0.0099131)	
Adj. R^2[样本量]	0.1678[678]		0.1592[678]		0.0919[633]	
	B(考虑家庭背景)					
教育年限	−0.01815	−0.02052	0.025635	0.024754	−0.0115056	−0.019104
	(0.022430)	(0.030886)	(0.020728)	(0.029224)	(0.0184366)	(0.0251399)
Adj. R^2[样本量]	0.0107[152]	0.0994[126]	0.0173[176]	0.091[164]	−0.0117[178]	0.079[162]

（续表）

因变量＝log(小时工资)	1991 年		1993 年		1997 年	
	(1)	(2)	(3)	(4)	(5)	(6)
	C(Heckman 样本选择模型)					
教育年限	0.006143	−0.00506	0.050023	0.040355	0.014045	0.0223841
	(0.029185)	(0.038780)	(0.047839)	(0.050025)	(0.0371578)	(0.038591)
Lambda	−0.00682	0.032182	−0.08167	−0.08668	−0.38446**	−0.39081**
	(0.118013)	(0.149115)	(0.194706)	(0.220412)	(0.1905296)	(0.1950339)
样本量	572	555	518	512	448	447
Censored	469	469	425	425	400	400
Wald Chi^2	63.6{25}	158.43{36}	61.21{22}	321.45{30}	47.80{26}	47.46{32}

注：1. 表中 A 部分三次回归中均控制了经验、省份、单位性质和婚姻状况，以及是否是乡镇管理人员或者是否是村干部等变量，在这里没有报告。常数项也没有报告。2. B 部分控制了经验、家长的教育水平。其中的第(2)、(4)和(6)列还控制了省份、工作单位类型、婚姻状况以及户主的工作经验；常数项没有报告；3. C 部分我们只报告了工资方程的部分，Probit 部分没有报告；回归中均控制了经验、省份和单位性质的变量；其中第(2)、(4)和(6)列还控制了是否是管理人员、婚姻状况以及户主的教育水平和经验。Lambda 的系数反映了样本选择问题是否显著。{}中为自由度。4. *** 表示在 1%的水平上显著；** 表示在 5%的水平上显著；* 表示在 10%的水平上显著。圆括号中为标准差、方括号中为样本量。下同。

主的教育水平降低了教育的系数],单从数值上看,教育水平在1993年和1997年得到了一定的回报。但是,考虑到方差也变大了,单参数估计的结果并不显著。

从逆米尔斯比率(mills ratio)的系数来看,1991年和1993年,系数并不显著,这表明样本选择问题并不严重。但是到了1997年,系数变得显著,即便如此,工资方程中教育的系数也是不显著的(尽管数值变得比较大)。这与Zhang等(2002)的结果相差较大,他们应用同样的估计方法得出的结果是在1996年,增加一年的教育水平对于工资的贡献率为5%—9%。这也许与他们所采用的样本有关,因为他们所用的样本只是江苏省3个村庄的数据,而江苏是经济发展较好、乡镇企业较发达的地区。

本节的研究表明,农村中教育水平在工业部门的工资中没有得到很好的体现。这一结果与Meng(1996, 2000)以及Zhang等(2002)[17]的研究结果类似,但与Psacharopoulos(1994)以及Card(1999)总结的结果相去甚远。中国的教育回报率低有如下几种可能的解释:(1)农村劳动力市场机制不健全,劳动者的人力资本水平得不到反映;(2)农村产业结构低下,不需要更高的教育水平;(3)教育水平得到了回报,但是我们用来估计的数据中,没有准确地反映这些因素。我们将在第六部分详细讨论这几个问题。

(二) 从工业部门工作对于家庭人均年收入的影响来估计教育的回报率

1. 教育影响劳动力转移

这里重点考察教育通过提高人们到工业部门就业的机会而给人们带来的回报(劳动力转移回报)。首先,应用Probit模型,我们考察教育在农村劳动力转移过程中的作用。[18]利用是否拥有月度工资数据,我们生成了工资收入的虚拟变量($wd=1$或0分别对应有工资和没有工资)。样本总体是那些年龄在

16—65 岁之间、毕业离校同时在家庭中与户主属于子女地位的农村男性劳动力。

表 3 报告了估计的结果。教育水平在农村劳动力转移的过程中作用显著。在 1991 年、1993 年和 1997 年，增加一年的教育水平，使得一个人在工业部门工作的机会分别增加 2.2%、3.2%和 1.5%。尽管 1990 年代教育在农村的劳动力转移过程中发挥显著的作用，我们并没有发现其发挥越来越重要的作用。至于经验，除 1991 年外，系数均不显著。

表 3　劳动力转移模型

因变量＝是否有工资收入	1991 年	
	(1)	(2)
教育年限	0.020653***	0.02226***
	(0.007139)	(0.007116)
Pseudo R^2［样本量］	0.1658［599］	0.2597［590］
因变量＝是否有工资收入	1993 年	
	(3)	(4)
教育年限	0.033295***	0.03197***
	(0.008876)	(0.008918)
Pseudo R^2［样本量］	0.1408［545］	0.1985［540］
因变量＝是否有工资收入	1997 年	
	(5)	(6)
教育年限	0.01866***	0.015109**
	(0.00636)	(0.0062698)
Pseudo R^2［样本量］	0.1160［531］	0.1713［503］

注：1. 为了得到自变量变化对因变量的影响，我们采用了 stata 中的 dprobit 命令。2. 上述回归中均控制了经验(及其平方)、婚姻状况、家庭中贡献收入人数(1997 年缺乏相关数据)、土地数量以及省份变量；此外为了进行稳健性检验，第(2)、(4)和(6)列中还控制了户主的社会经济状况。

我们还控制了婚姻状况、教育水平、挣钱人数、土地数量以及户主的社会经济状况。结果表明,已婚劳动力倾向于没有工资收入,但是这种效应并不显著。关于家庭中挣钱的人数,我们只有 1991 年和 1993 年的数据。1991 年,家庭挣钱人数增加,对是否拥有工资收入没有显著的影响,到 1993 年,系数显著为负。也许是因为挣钱人数的增加,提高了人们的保留工资水平。土地数量的系数均为负值(除 1993 年外,系数均显著)。这表明土地数量的增加加大了对劳动时间的需求,因此也提高了人们到工业部门工作的保留工资水平。此外,我们还包括了一组反映户主社会经济特征的变量:户主是否在工业部门工作、户主的教育水平以及户主是否是乡镇或村级的管理干部。结果表明,那些户主在工业部门工作的家庭,户主的儿子在工业部门工作的机会增加 20%以上。户主的教育水平以及是否是行政管理干部并没有显著的影响。

教育对于劳动力转移的影响是强健的。当我们去掉反映家庭以及户主的社会经济特征的变量后,教育的系数没有发生显著的改变:教育的增加显著提高了一个人到工业部门就业的机会。如果拥有工资收入可以提高净收入水平的话,提高到工业部门就业的机会也可以看作是教育的回报。

2. 工业收入对于家庭人均年收入的影响

表 4 报告了拥有工资收入对于农村家庭人均年收入的影响。工资收入显著地增加了家庭的人均年收入。1991 年和 1993 年,拥有工资收入使得家庭人均年收入分别增加 56%和 47%。这说明这个时期农业部门和工业部门之间工资差异非常之大。由于数据的原因,我们没有考察 1997 年的情况,但是 Meng(2000)的结果表明,农村中农业与工业之间的收入有扩大的趋势,使得我们有理由相信,即使在 1997 年,工资收入对于家

庭人均年收入仍然有显著的影响。

表 4　工资收入对家庭人均收入的影响

因变量＝ ln(人均年收入)	1991		
	(1)	(2)	(3)
拥有工资收入	0.589289***	0.578621***	0.55899***
	(0.079595)	(0.090077)	(0.09519)
省份及家庭变量	No	Yes	Yes
人力资本	No	No	Yes
Adj. R^2[样本量]	0.1887[672]	0.1851[607]	0.2195[563]

因变量＝ ln(人均年收入)	1993		
	(1)	(2)	(3)
拥有工资收入	0.556252***	0.510194***	0.470868***
	(0.079256)	(0.091371)	(0.092798)
省份及家庭变量	No	Yes	Yes
人力资本	No	No	Yes
Adj. R^2[样本量]	0.1701[704]	0.1617[544]	0.1907[511]

注：家庭变量包括土地数量、贡献收入人数、家庭规模、性别比例以及户主是否拥有工资收入；人力资本包括所考察的男性劳动力及其户主的教育和经验。

此外我们还控制了家庭的土地数量、挣钱人数、规模、性别比例以及省份。土地数量增加一亩，家庭人均年收入减少1%—2%(1991 年不显著，1993 年显著)；挣钱人数的增加反而减少了人均年收入，这与我们直觉不相符。可能的原因是挣钱人数与家庭规模是正相关的；性别比例的系数为负，表明女性对于家庭收入的贡献要小于男性。

由于教育也可能提高农业劳动者或自谋职业者的生产率，

而我们关心的是教育在农村劳动力转移过程中给人们带来的回报,因此,我们也控制了户主及其儿子的人力资本。教育还可以通过其外部性的途径来影响家庭收入——一个人的教育水平高,可以影响其他家庭成员的生产率。1991 年和 1993 年教育水平(户主和儿子)的系数分别在 2.5%—2.8%(显著)和 1.7%—2.3%(不显著)之间。

通过添加控制变量,模型的整体解释能力有所增强,但是是否拥有工资收入对于家庭人均年收入的影响并没有非常大的改变。这表明我们的结果是比较稳健的。

3. *教育的劳动力转移回报率*

根据以上结果,我们可以计算教育的劳动力转移回报率。

表 5 中 $\beta_0 g \gamma_0$ 表示教育水平增加一年,劳动者通过到工业部门工作而给家庭人均收入带来的增加量。而这个收益是由劳动者个人带来的。如果我们假设不存在收入共享[19],同时只关心教育对于劳动力个人的收益,我们还要将 $\beta_0 g \gamma_0$ 乘以家庭人口的数量。表 5 的第 4 列报告了家庭的平均规模。进一步地,我们可以得到教育通过增加人们到工业部门就业的机会而给人们带来的回报。1991 年和 1993 年,这一类教育回报分别为 5.4%和 6.8%。虽然,我们做这样的计算是包含了非常强的假设,但是从中我们也不难看出教育在上世纪 90 年代实际上得到了一定的回报。

表 5　教育通过提高到工业部门就业机会带来的回报率

年份	β_0(1)	γ_0(2)	$\beta_0 g \gamma_0$(3)	平均家庭规模(4)	教育回报率(5)
1991	0.55899	0.02226	0.012443117	4.34693	0.05408936
1993	0.470868	0.03197	0.01505365	4.507167	0.06784931

六、关于估计结果的讨论

(一) 计时工资与计件工资——工资的测度与工业部门内部的工资机制

这里我们讨论工资的测度问题,同时考虑第五部分第一节结尾中尚未回答的问题。在 1989 年的数据中包含了计时工资和计件工资的数据,考虑到计件工资更好地反映了劳动力的生产率,我们用这部分数据来讨论工资的测度问题。我们采用如下模型:

$$\ln(wage) = \alpha + \beta_1 sch + \beta_2 sch \times time_d + \beta_3 time_d + X\gamma + u \tag{11}$$

其中 $time_d$ 是表示计时工资的虚拟变量(计时工资=1/计件工资=0)。因此 β_1 反映了计件工资回报率,而 $\beta_1 + \beta_2$ 则反映了计时工资回报率。

表 6 的第 1—3 列报告了我们回归的结果。在第 1 列中,教育的系数在 0.0324 左右;第 3 列的结果表明,教育显著地提高了计件工资水平,增加一年的教育可以使得工资水平提高7.5%。由于计件工资较好地反映了劳动生产率,我们有理由相信教育提高了人们的知识和技能,进而提高了人们的收入;但是对于计时工资而言,增加一年的教育,工资水平只提高 3.1%左右。第 3 列的结果还表明,计时工资的基本工资水平要比计件工资高 22.2%,但是这一结果并不显著。而第 4 列的结果表明,教育水平增加一年,人们拥有计时工资的概率增加 3.6%,表明计时工资的工作性质对于劳动者来说是一种好处。

表 6　工业部门内部的工资机制

因变量＝ln(小时工资)/计时工资虚拟变量	1989 年			
	(1)	(2)	(3)	(4)
教育年限	0.032423*** (0.013457)	0.051112** (0.022005)	0.075198* (0.043687)	0.036177*** (0.006804)
教育年限×计时工资		−0.01806 (0.016830)	−0.04398 (0.043948)	
计时工资			0.222111 (0.347912)	
Adj. (Psudo)R^2 [样本量]	0.1486[334]	0.149[334]	0.1475[334]	0.226[345]

注:回归(1)—(3)的因变量为小时工资的自然对数,方法是 OLS,均控制了经验、性别、婚姻状况、工作单位性质和省份的变量。常数项没有报告。回归(4)采用的是 Probit 模型,因变量为表示计时/计件工资的虚拟变量,除教育和经验外,控制变量还包括省份和婚姻状况。

这里的研究结果也为我们回答工资方程估计问题提供了一定的信息。首先,计件工资的回报率高于计时工资以及计件工资劳动者受教育水平比较低这个事实可以说明,我们在第五部分得到比较低的教育回报率不是农村产业结构的问题。其次,农村的工资机制可能是导致教育工资回报率低的主要原因。但这并不表明教育没有得到回报。

(二) 教育的其他形式回报

教育的其他形式的回报可能体现在使人们有更加体面的工作。他们有足够的闲暇,同时很少受到失业的威胁。我们在文章的最后简单讨论这个问题。

数据表明,1991 年至 1997 年,工资收入者中有约 30%的人一年工作不满 12 个月。[20]表 7 中 1991 年、1993 年和 1997 年列(1)中的结果表明,教育水平增加一年,劳动者工作月数分别增加 0.13、0.04 和 0.09 个月,占每年平均工作月数的 1.3%、

0.4%和将近1.0%。列(2)和列(3)分别报告了教育水平与每周工作天数以及每天工作小时数的关系。除1991年每周工作的天数与教育水平显著正相关之外,其余的回归中教育水平的系数均为负值[1997列(3)除外],表明那些教育水平低的人倾向于有比较长的工作日,没有周末。

表7　工业劳动力的工作时间与教育水平的关系

因变量=工作时间	1991年		
	(1)	(2)	(3)
教育年限	0.13151***	0.03072**	−0.00409
	(0.035925)	(0.015173)	(0.023515)
Adj. R^2	0.2109	0.0646	0.03
[样本量]	[728]	[731]	[730]
因变量=工作时间	1993年		
	(1)	(2)	(3)
教育年限	0.044686	−0.01031	−0.02828
	(0.042671)	(0.015887)	(0.044227)
Adj. R^2	0.2067	0.0455	0.0318
[样本量]	[742]	[732]	[731]
因变量=工作时间	1997年		
	(1)	(2)	(3)
教育年限	0.091078***	−0.0366**	0.0037805
	(0.03070)	(0.01726)	(0.0420047)
Adj. R^2	0.1091	0.1131	0.0260
[样本量]	[680]	[683]	[681]

注:(1)、(2)和(3)分别为一年中工作的月数、每周工作的天数和每天工作的小时数与受教育年限回归。在上述所有回归中,均控制了经验(平方)、省份变量和工作单位的类型。常数项没有报告。

表7还表明,教育对于一年中工作月数的影响在1991年和1997年是显著的,而在1993年是不显著的。可能是整体的经济形式导致了这种差异。1991年到1997年,中国经济经历了比较大的变化。1990年和1996年的经济形势比1992年要差(1990年、1992年和1996年全国的经济增长率分别为4.2%、14.1%和9.8%)。因此,我们猜想在经济形势相对差的时候,教育水平对于提高人们的劳动参与率有着显著的作用,教育在帮助人们摆脱失业威胁方面可能起到了一定的作用。

七、结　论

人力资本是决定经济发展的重要因素。我们通过考察人力资本(尤其是教育)在农村工业部门中的回报以及教育在农村劳动力转移过程中的作用来分析中国农村的劳动力市场和农村的工业化过程。1990年到1996年教育年限对于农村工业部门内部的工资水平没有显著的影响。即使在考虑了样本选择问题后,估计的结果也没有显著的改善。但这并不表明教育在农村的劳动力市场中没有得到回报。

教育的另外一种形式的回报体现在教育提高了劳动力到工业部门工作的机会。考虑到农村地区部门之间的工资差异,教育确实给农村的劳动力带来了收益。本文利用农村地区家庭人均年收入等数据进行分析,结果表明在工业部门工作可以使家庭人均年收入在1990年和1992年分别增加56%和47%。而相应的教育增加一年,人们到工业部门工作的机会增加2.2%和3.2%左右,这意味着使得家庭人均年收入增加1.2%和1.5%,也相当于给个人带来5%—7%的回报。

利用1989年的数据,本文还分析了农村工业部门内部的工资机制问题。教育水平低的人接受计件工资的比较多。计件工资者教育的工资回报率在 7.5%左右,而计时工资者的教育回报率仅为 3%左右。但是计时工资的整体水平高于计件工资。这反映了教育的工资回报率低并不是农村工业部门产业结构的问题,而是工资机制的问题。工业部门内部的工资安排可能很好地激励了人力资本的积累,但是没有足够的激励使得这些人力资本得到发挥。

此外,教育使得劳动者的工作方式得以改变。教育水平高的人,工作时间的分配更加有利于人的发展。这应该被看作是教育回报的重要组成部分。

注　释

① 1996—2001 年,城镇居民收入年均增长 6.7%,而农村居民收入年均增长仅为 3.8%。与此同时工资收入占农民人均纯收入的比重从 1995 年的 22.5%上升到 2001 年的 32.6%。数据来自中国统计年鉴或根据年鉴数据进行的计算。

② DeBrauw, Huang, Rozelle, Zhang 和 Zhang(2002)的研究表明,以往对于中国农村教育回报率的估计在 0—6%之间。而且相当一部分研究(Meng, 1996; Parish et al., 1995)的研究表明,教育没有得到明显的回报。

③ 同时我们也看到,中国是一个人力资本积累迅速的国家。1965 年中国中等教育的毛入学率仅为 24%,而美国已经是 90%(World Bank, 2000)。

④ 统计年鉴中对应的数据为"文教娱乐用品及服务"一项。

⑤ 即便是工资水平本身也可能受到工资测度问题的影响,即工资水平不能够反映劳动生产率。

⑥ 宏观层面,Barro(1991)以及后来的一些研究表明,教育和人均 GDP 增长率之间存在着正相关关系,最近的研究结果表明,在世界范围内,教育对于消除贫困发挥了重要的作用(Besley and Burgess,

2003)。关于人力资本与经济增长之间关系的论述较早的有 Schultz(1961)。

⑦ 大量的实证结果表明，控制家庭背景或者采用孪生子女(兄弟姐妹)的数据降低了教育的回报率，而利用教育系统的制度因素作为工具变量反而使教育回报率增加(David Card, 1999)，本文的研究采取控制家庭背景的途径。

⑧ 感兴趣的读者可以参看 Lewis(1954)、Harris 和 Todaro(1970)、Stiglitz(1974)以及 Leibenstein(1957)。

⑨ 经验是另外一种人力资本，我们用毕业年龄来表示。毕业年龄=年龄-受教育年限-6。

⑩ 在其他一些农村劳动力转移模型的估计过程中[如 Zhang 等(2002)]，自变量还包括了家庭中需要照看的儿童数量和老人的数量。这些变量可能是影响人们时间分配的重要因素。但是考虑到这些因素可能主要对女性劳动力产生影响，而我们的分析主要考虑男性劳动力，所以没有这方面的变量。

⑪ 我们也采用了线性概率模型(LPM)进行估计，估计的结果与 Probit 模型的结果非常接近。LPM 的结果在本文中没有报告。

⑫ 其中收入方面的数据分别为上年数据，但本文仍然沿用调查数据获取的年份。1989 年的数据由于相关变量的样本较小，没有放在我们的主要分析中。但是，1989 年的数据提供了计件工资、计时工资以及小时工资等宝贵的信息。

⑬ 在估计工资方程的过程中，我们没有限制年龄。但是 1991 年、1993 年和 1997 年挣取工资的人中年龄小于 16 周岁大于 65 周岁的分别为 10 人、5 人和 13 人。在区分子女和户主的数据集中，只有 1991 年的子女样本中 3 个人的年龄小于 16 周岁。

⑭ 根据本套数据计算的平均受教育年限与 Zhang 等(2002)的结果略有不同，在 Zhang 等(2002)中，农村人口的平均受教育年限在 1988 年、1992 年和 1996 年分别为 5.33 年、6.10 年和 5.20 年。

⑮ 整个国民经济在 20 世纪 90 年代经历了大的波动，1990 年、1992 年和 1996 年，我国的经济增长率分别为 4.2%、14.1%和 9.8%。

⑯ 本文的研究结果表明,户主与子女的教育水平高度相关。利用1991年、1993年和1997年的数据,户主的教育增加一年,子女的教育增加0.228(0.028456)、0.226(0.027808)和0.190(0.02457)年左右(陈玉宇、邢春冰,2004),这与David Card(1999)第1823页的结果非常接近。

⑰ Zhang等(2002)的研究结果表明,教育的工资回报率在1988年以及1992年都不显著,只有到了1996年才变得非常显著。

⑱ 分别利用Probit和线性概率模型(LPM)进行回归。鉴于LPM和Probit模型的结论基本一致,这里我们只报告了Probit模型的结果。

⑲ Kochar(2000)对于巴基斯坦的研究表明,子女工资收入增加会减少户主工作的时间,这主要是通过子女提供更多的关于公共物品的支出而导致的,并没有证据表明子女和户主之间共享收入。

⑳ 当然,这并不完全意味着没有工作。农业劳动的需要也可能使得农村劳动力不能全年在工业部门工作。

参考文献

陈玉宇、邢春冰,2004:《农村工业化以及人力资本在农村劳动力市场中的角色》,北京大学光华管理学院工作论文。

马歇尔,A.,1965:《经济学原理》(中译本),商务印书馆。

魏众,2004:《健康对非农就业及其工资决定的影响》,《经济研究》第2期。

Barro, Robert J., 1991, "Economic Growth in a Cross Section of Countries", *Q. J. E.*, May, 106(2), pp. 407—408.

Becker, G. S., 1993, *Human Capital: A Theoretical and Empirical Analysis With special Reference to Education* (3e), Chicago and London: The University of Chicago Press.

Besley, Timothy and Burgess, Robin, 2003, "Halving Global Poverty", Working Paper, March.

Card, David, 1999, "Causal Effects of Education on Earnings", Orley Ashenfelter and David Card (eds.), *Handbook of Labor Economics*,

Elsevier.

DeBrauw, A., Huang, J., Rozelle, S., Zhang, L. and Zhang, Y., 2002, "The Evolution of China's Rural Labor Markets During the Reforms: Rapid, Accelerating, Transforming", *Journal of Comparative Economics*, June 30(2), pp. 329—53.

Duflo, Esther, 2000, "Schooling and Labor Market Consequences of School Construction in Indonesia: Evidence from an Unusual Policy Experiment", *A. E. R*, 91(4): pp. 795—813.

Harris, J. R. and Todaro, M. P., 1970, "Migration, Unemployment and Development: A Two-sector Analysis", *A. E. R.* 60: pp. 126—42.

Heckman, J. J., 1979, "Sample Selection Bias as a Specification Error", *Econometrica*, 47: pp. 153—161.

Kochar, Anjini, 2002, "Parental Benefits from Intergenerational Coresidence: empirical Evidence from Rural Pakistan", *J. P. E.* December, 108(6): pp. 1184—1209.

Leibenstein, H., 1957, "Underemployment in Backward Economies", *J. P. E.*, 65, pp. 91—103.

Lewis, W. A., 1954, "Economic Development with Unlimited Supplies of labor", *Manchester School*, 28, pp. 139—91.

Meng, Xin, 1996, "An Examination of Wage Determination in China's Rural Industrial Sector", *Applied Economics*, 28(1), pp. 715—24.

Meng, Xin, 2000, *Labor Market Reform in China*, Cambridge University Press.

Parish, W. L., Zhe, X., and Li, F., 1995, "Nonfarm Work and Marketization of the Chinese Countryside", *China Quarterly*, September, 143: pp. 697—730.

Psacharopoulos, G., 1994, "Returns to Investment in Education: A Global Up-date", *World Development*, 22, pp. 1325—1343.

Romer, Paul, 1990, "Endogenous Technological Change", *J. P. E.*,

October, Pt. 2, 99(5), pp. S71—S102.

Schultz, T. W., 1961, "Investment in human capital", *A. E. R.*, March, pp. 1—17.

Stiglitz, J. E., 1974, "Alternative Theories of Wage Determination and Unemployment in LDCs: The Labor Turnover Model", *Q. J. E*, 88: 194—227.

The World Bank, 2000, *Higher Education in Developing Countries: Peril and Promise*, Washington D. C.

Wooldridge, J. M., 2001, *Econometric Analysis of Cross Section and Panel Data*, Cambridge, Massachusetts, The MIT Press.

Zhang Linxiu, Jikun Huang and Scott Rozelle, 2002, "Employment, Emerging Labor Market, and the Role of Education in Rural China", *China Economic Review*, 13, pp. 313—328.

（原载《经济研究》2004 年第 8 期）

健康对非农就业及其工资决定的影响*

魏　众

（中国社会科学院经济研究所）

一、健康与收入关系研究的简要综述

在中国，健康被视为个人的事情，只有全国性的公共卫生事业才是政府的责任。而在城镇就业者中实行的健康保障制度长期以来更被视为社会福利事业的一部分。正因为如此，健康对就业乃至收入的作用长期以来被人们所忽视。

与公共卫生管理专家以及健康社会学家不同，经济学家对健康的认识来自人力资本学派的理论。在该理论中，健康与教育、培训、迁徙一起构成人力资本的四大部件。基于这样的认识，国外关于健康与就业和收入的实证研究在劳动经济学和健康经济学中一直占据着重要的地位。

随着计量经济学的发展，研究健康与收入关系的方法也在不断进步，从早期简单的 OLS 分析（Luft，1975；Bartel and Taubman，1979；Benham and Benham，1982）发展到后来的联

* 本文系作者博士论文的一部分，在论文的写作过程中，得到朱玲教授、高梦滔博士、周黎安博士和陈玉宇博士的帮助；在论文的答辩过程中，得到唐宗焜研究员和赵人伟研究员及各位答辩委员和论文评阅人的有益指点，在此一并表示感谢。

立方程估计(Lee，1982；Ettner et al.，1997)以及 Heckman 两阶段估计模型(Chiricos and Nestal，1985；Baldwin and Johnson，1994；Stern，1996)等，得到的结论大多有力地支持了健康对就业或收入的影响。但他们所使用的健康指标随研究内容的差异而有所不同，而且即便是同样类型的研究，所使用的指标仍然或多或少地存在这样或那样的差异，因此，尽管此类实证研究很多，但还无法清晰地给出健康对就业以及收入影响的全貌。换言之，这是一个正有待于研究者进行不断探索的领域。

与其他经济学分析一样，健康与收入关系的研究最初大多集中在工业化国家，相对而言，对于发展中国家和转型国家健康和就业以及收入间关系的研究还比较少。针对发展中国家和转型国家进行的研究又存在两种研究思路。一种以家庭农业和种植业作为研究对象，使用家庭生产函数进行分析(Strauss，1986)。国内第一篇、也是此前国内惟一一篇研究健康与收入关系的文章(张车伟，2003)就沿袭了这样的研究思路。该文章采用多种健康指标，利用家庭生产函数对贫困地区的种植业进行分析，得出健康对种植业生产具有显著影响的结论。另一种研究思路则着重于工资(收入)函数的研究，主要对工资性就业及其收入进行研究。上述对工业化国家进行的研究大多采用了这样的分析手段。当然，它同样适用于发展中国家和转型国家的研究，如 Schultz 和 Tansel(1997)对科特迪瓦和加纳的研究，以及 Ivaschenko(2003)对乌克兰的研究等，但在对中国的相关研究中，尚没有出现此类分析。

与张车伟(2003)的研究不同，本文以我国农村居民非农就业参与和工资决定作为研究对象，很自然地，将采用工资函数的分析方法。考虑到可能出现的选择性偏误，本文使用 Heckman 模型而不是联立方程模型。本文的结构如下：第二部分对本文所使用的数据及其实证分析方法进行介绍;第三部分是本文的主体部分,对健康变量的生成、健康对非农就业参与的影响以及对工资决定的影响进行实证分析,并在此基础上进行一些讨论;最后是一些强力检验和本文的总结。

二、数 据 及 方 法

(一) 数据简介和研究对象的选择

本研究所使用的数据来自中国预防科学研究院营养与食品卫生研究所进行的“中国经济、人口、营养与健康调查”(以下简称“营养调查”)。该调查始于 1989 年,以后又分别在 1991 年、1993 年、1997 年各进行了一次。该调查尽可能选取同样的样本户,覆盖了全国 8 个省区的城市和农村地区。我们从中选取 1993 年的农村数据作为本研究的基本数据。

该调查的抽样方法始于 1989 年的第一次调查,其最初的抽样方法如下:在全国抽取 8 个省区——辽宁、江苏、山东、河南、湖北、湖南、广西和贵州,覆盖了东中西三类地区的农村;在每个省区选择 4 个县——1 个高收入县,2 个中等收入县,1 个低收入县;在每个县抽选 1 个县城镇和 3 个非县城镇的村落,3 个村落又分别代表了该县的高中低三种收入情况,调查共覆盖 32 个县城镇和 96 个村庄;在每个村庄抽取 20 户作为调查对象。1989—1997 年农村调查的全部样本户大体保持在 2560 户左右。其中 1993 年的调查样本包括了 9978 条个人数据,其中 16 岁以上的人口为 7241 条,占全部样本的 72.6%;16—65 岁的人口为6683条,约占全部样本的 67%。根据以上描述,我们认为该调查基本上代表了全国农村的情况。

由于中国的农业生产具有以一家一户为单位的特征,并且没有清晰的退休年限,因此有一些60岁以上的农村居民仍然从事农业或其他生产活动,也有极少数未成年的儿童参与了农业生产,一些残疾人口也同样参与劳动。根据中国农村的义务教育情况,我们初步设定以16—65岁年龄段的人口作为考察对象,而将所有汇报了非农就业收入的个人作为工资方程的考察对象。样本描述性统计见表1。

表1 样本描述性统计

	全部样本	农业人口
样本数	6683	5054
非农劳动参与人数	1461	588
非农就业人员月工资(元)	241.22	218.19
生理因子	0.077	0.087
心理因子	0.013	0.017
男性	0.506	0.501
非农户口	0.241	
少数民族	0.152	0.166
年龄	35.97	35.44
在婚人口	0.704	0.701
教育年限	5.984	5.549

(二)实证分析方法

在本文的实证分析中,健康被视为一个复合的概念,无法通过观测直接获得。根据本文研究的需要,健康状况通过对一系列指标进行因子分析获得,从而本文所使用的健康测度为多维的连续变量。在国外的同类研究中,使用因子分析提取健康指标的方法也被广泛使用(Baldwin and Johnson, 1994; Van de Ven and Hooijmans, 1991)。

由于非农就业很可能存在选择性偏误(selection-bias)问

题，本文采用了 Heckman 两阶段估计模型进行分析，具体方法表述如下。

当对劳动供给、工资及收入等进行估计时，最为直接的方法是普通最小二乘法(OLS)，设

$$Y_i = X_i\beta + \varepsilon_i$$

其中 Y_i 为观测到的劳动供给、工资和收入等①，X_i 为解释变量，如教育、经验和健康等。但由于所观测到的参与者并非样本总体的随机选择，因此这种选择可能导致有偏的系数估计，即出现选择性偏误。Heckman 注意到在 OLS 估计中样本选择问题可能导致系数估计值存在偏差，在一篇影响很大的论文(Heckman, 1979)中他提出了自己的解决方案。这种新的模型估计被称为 Heckman 备择模型(Heckman selection model)，该模型的估计分为两个阶段进行。

首先以"是否参与非农个人劳动"作为第一阶段估计的被解释变量，使用全部参数对 16—65 岁全部人口进行 Probit 估计，以确定参与非农劳动的决定因素。

$$P_i^* = Z_i\gamma + u_i,\ P_i = 1 \text{ 如果 } Z_i\gamma + u_i > 0$$

其中，P_i^* 为某事件发生的概率，它可以由一系列因素解释，Z_i 为解释变量，γ 为待估参数，u_i 为随机扰动项。

其次，考虑到在 OLS 估计中可能存在选择性偏误，所以需要从 Probit 估计式中得到转换比率(Inverse Mills Ratio)λ，作为第二阶段的修正参数。λ 由以下公式获得：

$$\lambda = \frac{\phi(z_i\gamma/\sigma_0)}{\Phi(z_i\gamma/\sigma_0)}$$

其中 $\phi(\cdot)$为标准正态分布的密度函数，$\Phi(\cdot)$为相应的累积分

布函数。

最后，利用 OLS 方法对方程进行估计，使用 λ 作为方程估计的一个额外的变量以纠正选择性偏误，即

$$Y_i = X_i\beta + \lambda\alpha + \eta_i$$

其中 α 为待估系数。如果该系数是显著的，则证明选择性偏误是存在的；反之，则表明选择性偏误不存在，在这种情况下，就可以认为 OLS 估计是有效的。[②]

基于人力资本模型出发，本研究使用年龄作为经验的代表，以受教育年限作为人力资本的一个变量，以获得的健康因子作为人力资本的另一个变量，即在经典的 Mincer 方程中加入健康变量。由于中国劳动力市场的情况千差万别，本研究加入了其他一些控制变量以获得对劳动工资决定更为准确的估计，这些控制变量包括性别、户籍身份[③] 及所在地区等。而在劳动参与估计方程中，我们进一步加入民族、婚姻、家庭中儿童数量以及家庭经营占用时间作为解释变量。

最后需要说明的是，本研究的统计分析使用了 STATA 软件。

三、实证分析及其解释

（一）健康的测度

由于缺乏直接可用的测度标准，健康指标的客观性始终困扰着健康经济学家们。如同能力评价的偏差一样，在健康经济学研究中，健康测度的偏差最终会导致研究结果的偏差。因而在所有的健康经济学研究中，首先要解决的问题是健康的测度问题。

由于健康测度的复杂性，所有健康经济学研究不可避免地要

对所使用的健康指标进行说明，本文也不例外。正如前文提到的，健康经济学研究中使用的健康指标林林总总，归纳起来大体包括这样一些指标：死亡率和儿童死亡率、寿命和预期寿命、健康自评（SRHS或SRH、SSH）、健康（赋权）得分、因病损失的工作时间、工作受限、残疾、疾病种类以及本文使用的健康因子等。

运用因子分析的方法进行多维健康指数的构造有这样一些优势：比起所谓的客观指标，如因病离开等，它较为综合，也更接近健康的内涵；同健康评价等主观指标相比，它又是一个连续变量；同时，它避免了赋权的主观性，从而更加客观。但它也具有自身无法克服的问题：首先，由于因子提取来自数据本身，因而同样的健康因子在不同的研究之间不具有可比性；其次，该研究的成功与否首先取决于能否提取合理的、尽可能少的健康因子；另外，对健康因子的估计系数不够直观，而且缺乏量化的实际意义，从而在政策研究方面缺乏优势。

为比较不同健康指标的敏感性，本文根据问卷调查的指标体系，采用了多种健康指标：健康自评、健康因子测度、健康测度打分以及健康受限天数等。本文将以健康因子作为主要的分析变量，而将基于其他健康指标的估计结果用于强力检验。

1993年的营养调查设计了有关个人健康状况的6个问题，这6个问题又分别涉及了生理和心理方面的功能，具体为："心肺和腹部功能"、"上肢、肩部、后背和颈部功能"、"下肢和脊髓功能"、"听说和视力功能"、"大小便失禁情况"、"精神和心理问题"等。答案分为4级，从1至4分别为："正常"、"偶尔失能（无需他人帮助）"、"经常失能（需要他人帮助）"、"功能完全丧失"。

根据上面的测度可知，所有变量的变化都是同方向的，但这些变量数值越大，则健康状况就越差。为了符合多数人的习惯，更好地代表健康状况，使健康因子与健康状况同方向变化，本文对所有答案重新进行了标准化，即1—4按顺序分别为“功能完全丧失”、“经常失能”、“偶尔失能”、“正常”。本文在此基础上进行了因子分析工作，根据因子提取的一般原则，提取两个特征值超过1的因子作为健康因子。为更好地分离并强化各因子的作用，本文又使用了Varimax旋转方法对因子矩阵进行正交化旋转，进而得到旋转后的因子矩阵（见表2）。

表2 旋转后的因子矩阵

	Health 1	Health 2
心肺和腹部	0.5710	0.0055
上肢、肩部、后背和颈部	0.7820	0.0080
下肢和脊髓	0.7660	0.0284
听说和视力	0.5360	0.3160
大小便失禁情况	0.0237	0.7280
精神和心理问题	0.0594	0.6960

从表2中可以发现，在6个构筑健康测度指标体系的变量中，5个变量的系数明显地两极分化了，这为两个健康指数的解释提供了方便。其中“心肺和腹部功能”、“上肢、肩部、后背和颈部功能”、“下肢和脊髓功能”3个变量对于Health 1的影响比较大，并且方向一致，可以合理地将Health 1解释为与行动有关的健康指数，本文称之为“生理因子”。“大小便失禁情况”和“精神和心理问题”这2个变量对Health 2的解释力较强，并且方向一致，可以合理地将Health 2解释为与精神和神经系统有关的因子，本文称之为“心理因子”。而“听说和视力功能”这个指标既可能对行动产生影响又大多由神经系统的问题导致，因而本身就与两者都存在关系。由于进行了重新标准化的工作，所以因子得分越高，表明健康状况越好。

(二) 非农就业参与率的研究

基于 Heckman 模型第一阶段估计的方法，我们使用 Probit 模型分别对全体样本以及农业户籍人口的非农就业参与进行估计。所使用的解释变量为：1＝参与非农就业，0＝不参与非农就业。所得结果见表 3。

表 3　非农就业参与方程的系数估计

	全体样本		农业户籍人口	
	系数	t 值	系数	t 值
生理因子	0.164	4.43	0.197	3.36
心理因子	0.030	1.07	0.030	0.59
男性	0.262	5.58	0.201	3.35
非农户口	0.870	16.93		
少数民族	−0.374	−4.53	−0.372	−3.56
年龄	0.181	12.33	0.105	5.56
在婚	0.093	1.15	0.089	0.87
受教育年限	0.097	11.71	0.102	9.40
年龄平方	−0.002	−12.90	−0.001	−5.52
15 岁以下儿童数量	−0.092	−3.32	−0.079	−2.40
家庭经营时间	−0.032	−21.47	−0.030	−18.09
省虚拟变量(略)				
常数项	−4.357	−17.67	−3.124	−10.23
样本量	6006		4478	
χ^2 检验值	2500		947	
χ^2 显著性	0.000		0.000	
最大似然率	−2332		−1625	
虚拟 R^2	0.3489		0.2257	

从表 3 中可以看出，在各解释变量中，只有婚姻和心理因子两项不显著。在婚状态对于非农就业参与的影响并不显著，这在很大程度上与非农就业者相对年轻有关。另外，心理因子的

系数不显著也是比较合理的，因为在一个劳动力市场上，生理因子是比较容易识别的，如是否残疾、是否身体单薄甚至身体高度等，但心理因素就不那么容易识别，除一些明显的精神类疾病外，即便那些间歇性的精神类疾病也是很难被识别的。

在各主要的解释变量中，教育对非农就业起到了明显的正向作用，即在劳动力市场需求中，教育对就业的影响变得显著，较高的教育年限意味着较多的非农就业机会。同时，生理因子的作用变得更强，系数也增大了。综合这两个因素，笔者认为在非农就业问题上，人力资本确实起到了重要的作用。

另一个发生明显变化的是制度变量——户籍身份。我们看到，在方程中，非农户口的系数为正，不仅系数很大而且相当显著。这表明，在广义的农村[④]中，在非农就业市场上，二元结构依然清晰可见，拥有城镇户口的居民比没有城镇户口的居民有更多的机会参与非农就业。

在传统的农业社会中，性别对于劳动参与的影响一般是比较显著的，即男性作为主要的劳动力参与农业生产，而社会分工决定了女性较多地负担无经济收入的家务劳动，从而较少参与农业生产活动。在非农就业问题上，性别依旧是一个显著的因素，这是由劳动力市场需求决定的。1993 年，服务业还不是很发达，非农的劳动力市场对农村劳动力的需求主要集中在一些重体力劳动领域，如制造业和建筑业，这些对身体素质要求较高的行业决定了男性在劳动力市场上的重要地位，男性因此具有了比女性更多的就业机会。当时的非农就业的行业特征也有助于解释生理因子在劳动参与方程估计中的显著性。

民族因素在非农就业中呈现出显著的负相关关系，即少数民族在非农劳动力市场中处于弱势地位，这和少数民族的居住地以及文化差异有关。少数民族居住的地区大多远离中心城市，这些地区本身很少有非农就业的机会，而交通因素对外出打工的影响是比较显著的。另外，对于一个试图外出寻找工作的少数民族个体而言，语言差异可能使他们望而却步。这与我们的观察结果相一致。

作为个人经验变量的年龄因素，与其他一些参与模型的结果基本一致，即非农就业机会随年龄增长先增加后减少。

作为家庭因素的家庭未成年子女数，与非农就业机会成负相关关系，即家庭中未成年子女越多，打工的机会越少，该结论也同样比较显著。而考虑非农就业与家庭经营之间替代效应，家庭经营时间同样与非农就业机会呈负相关关系，即打工和家庭经营之间的替代效应是存在的。

除心理因素外，另一个在方程中不显著的变量为婚姻状态，在劳动经济学中这是一个典型的劳动供给的决定因素。

现在，让我们再重新审视一下非农就业参与估计方程。我们发现所有对劳动力需求起作用的限制条件大多是显著的，如个人的年龄、文化程度、健康状况以及代表制度因素的户籍身份等等。而那些不显著的变量，有些本身在劳动力市场中就是隐性的，如生理因素；有些则是劳动力供给方的因素。这一发现使我们更加相信，农村的非农就业劳动力市场在当时（当然现在也很可能一样）主要是一个“买方市场”。

在以农业户籍身份人口为研究对象的参与方程中，我们发现除系数大小略有差异外，所有待估系数的符号完全一致；而在系数估计的显著性方面，同样表现出惊人的一致性。

作为与非农就业的对照，笔者选取了家庭经营中最具代表性、参与人数最多的种植业来进行劳动参与率研究（见表 4）。该估计方程与非农就业参与估计方程相比，最大的差异表现在代表人力资本的健康和教育变量，所有健康因子的系数都变得

表 4　种植业劳动参与的决定因素分析

	方程(1)		方程(2)		方程(3)		方程(4)	
	系数	t 值	系数	t 值	系数	t 值	系数	t 值
常数项	−1.622	−8.63	−0.554	−2.54	−1.725	−8.80	−1.623	−8.63
生理因子	0.034	1.37	−0.007	−0.23	0.030	1.13		
心理因子	0.006	0.28	−0.026	−0.92	0.023	0.93		
男性	0.163	4.05	0.064	1.43	0.088	2.12	0.164	4.08
非农户口	−2.040	−32.11	−1.967	−26.50			−2.042	−32.15
少数民族	0.215	3.47	0.196	2.85	0.176	2.69	0.218	3.52
年龄	0.150	13.36	0.095	7.20	0.160	13.63	0.151	13.40
在婚	0.210	3.28	0.116	1.60	0.242	3.68	0.211	3.30
受教育年限	−0.047	−6.56	−0.040	−5.00	−0.061	−8.16	−0.046	−6.51
年龄平方	−0.002	−13.90	−0.001	−7.05	−0.002	−14.04	−0.002	−14.01
15 岁以下儿童数量	−0.027	−1.23	−0.015	−0.61	−0.022	−1.01	−0.027	−1.24
上周种植业以外的就业时间	−0.016	−15.99	−0.019	−18.19	−0.009	−10.27	−0.016	−15.95
样本量	6427		5405		4930		6427	
χ^2 检验值	3272.36		2702.99		791.72		3270.37	
χ^2 显著性	0.0000		0.0000		0.0000		0.0000	
最大似然率	−2792.92		−2237.33		−2623.29		−2793.91	
虚拟 R^2	0.3694		0.3766		0.1311		0.3692	

不显著，而教育的系数则变为显著的负值。这表明健康并非参与种植业的决定因素，而受教育程度越高的人越倾向于从事种植业以外的工作。

（三）对工资决定方程的估计

和非农劳动参与估计方程一样，对工资决定方程的估计也分别针对全体人群以及农业户籍人口进行。该方程基于著名的Mincer方程构建，增加了健康变量以扩大人力资本的维度，并适当增加性别、户籍身份以及省区虚拟变量作为控制变量。方程中的被解释变量为工资的对数。其中的工资由调查中询问的月工资与月津贴及奖金加总而来。结果见表5。

表5　对全体劳动力和农业人口分别进行的 Heckman 方程估计

	全体样本		农业人口	
	系数	*t* 值	系数	*t* 值
生理因子	0.001	0.03	0.056	0.83
心理因子	0.022	1.16	0.104	1.72
男性	0.143	3.82	0.234	3.87
非农户口	−0.151	−2.92		
年龄	0.042	3.94	0.044	3.10
受教育年限	−0.002	−0.30	−0.020	−1.68
年龄平方	−0.000	−3.34	−0.001	−3.08
省区虚拟变量(略)				
常数项	4.440	16.86	4.560	14.56
逆米尔斯比率	−0.164	−2.94	−0.186	−2.78
样本数	6006		4478	
删失样本数	4599		3919	
未删失样本数	1407		559	
χ^2 值	966.880		312.52	
χ^2 检验	0.000		0.000	

首先看一下全体人群的估计方程。我们看到多数的估计系数与其他类似的研究是一致的,最大的不同在于教育变量的待估系数出现了不显著的很小的负值,这意味着教育对工资的决定作用基本不存在,或者可以认为,教育对工资的回报率可能仅仅在0附近。

另外一个与一般印象不一致的系数估计来自户籍身份变量,非农人口身份对工资的作用为负值而且显著。根据Heckman备择模型,这种情况的发生主要有这样两种可能:第一,那些当前未就业的非农人口如果进入非农就业市场将得到较低的工资;第二,那些未能进入非农就业的个人如果进入劳动力市场将得到较高的工资。我们认为前者的作用是存在的,由于制度性因素,非农户籍人口中一些已就业的个人得到了比其实际能力更高的工资,而那些还可能就业的个人的加入将导致这一群体的收入下降;而农业户籍人口受到制度的限制较多,一些合格的劳动力未能进入劳动力市场,这些劳动力的加入将至少不降低其工资水平。

估计系数比较显著的变量还包括年龄和性别,其系数与一般的估计方程类似,只是这里是考虑选择过程以后得到的结果。

但在工资决定方程中,代表健康资本的生理因子和心理因子都变得不显著,比较一下前面的非农劳动参与估计方程,这样的结果多少有点令人吃惊。

农业人口工资率决定方程的估计系数与全体人口方向基本一致,但显著性有所不同,坏消息是教育的系数仍为负值但变得很显著,好消息则在于健康因子中心理因子的系数变得比较显著,且比全体人口的估计系数大得多。生理因子的系数为不显著的正值。同全部人口的工资方程相比,生理因子和心理因子的作用增强了。我们注意到,在第一阶段的估计中,心理因子的系数不显著，这意味着在挑选非农就业参与者的过程中，心理因子并没有起到明显的作用，而在加入就业者行列后，心理因子的影响开始显现。受教育年限较为显著的负系数可能与一些合格的劳动力未进入非农就业市场有关。我们看到，农业人口中未参与非农就业的群体与参与非农就业的群体在教育程度方面不存在显著的差异。

农业人口工资决定方程中的其他估计系数与全体人群的 Heckman 模型的估计结果基本相同，如性别因素的系数为正数而且显著。但值得一提的是，在对农业人口的估计中，性别的作用进一步增强了。另外，工资随年龄增加而边际递减的趋势依然显著存在，而且两个方程的估计系数没有显著性差异。

最后还有两点需要做进一步说明。首先，显著的逆米尔斯比率(inverse Mills ratio)说明，中国农村的非农就业中存在选择性偏误问题，也表明在本研究中使用 Heckman 备择模型是合适的；而负的逆米尔斯比率表明，那些未进入非农就业市场的劳动力其保留工资高于他们进入非农就业市场可能获得的工资，这就验证了保留工资理论在中国农村非农就业市场上的有效性。

另外，在非农劳动参与方程估计中，生理因子的系数都在1%水平上显著；在工资决定方程中，所有健康因子的估计系数都不显著或不够显著，这说明健康对非农劳动就业参与的影响大于其对工资决定的影响。

(四) 对实证分析结果的一些讨论

通过上述对工资率的 Heckman 最大似然估计，我们得到以下一些主要发现。

(1) 尽管大多数情况下健康因子的系数并不显著，但综合两个健康因子，我们可以初步认为健康因子与工资存在一定的正相关关系。但必须承认，健康对工资的影响并不显著，这意味着对于劳动年龄人口而言，当他们进入非农就业市场后，健康对工资并不发生影响，我们认为这很可能是由于进入时严格的筛选机制所致。

在工资决定方面本文得到的结果比较接近于 Schultz 和 Tansel(1997)的研究。在他们的研究中，只有对科特迪瓦男性工资收入者进行分析时，健康的估计系数才显著为正；而对加纳男性、两国男性和女性的研究中都没有得到显著的估计系数。但我们的研究与樊明(2002)的研究具有较大的差异，在樊明的研究中，几乎所有的估计方程均得到了显著的负系数。⑤但他的估计方程中，唯一不显著的恰好是在劳动力市场上一般被认为备受歧视的黑人，樊明援引 Luft(1975)的解释认为"白人由于受过较好的教育，从而较高的收入能够使他们更换到适合他们健康状况的工作。而黑人就没有这么灵活，在选择新工作时发现可供他们选择的工作较少"。这就是说，黑人在进入劳动力市场时需要经历一个较为严格的筛选机制，这一点与中国农村的情况比较相似。应当注意到，获得工资的行为是经过选择的过程，健康(特别是生理因子)在第一阶段中的作用依然表现为显著的正系数。而对于农民而言，进入工资较高的就业领域似乎更重要。

(2) 教育对非农就业者工资的回报率比较低，甚至为负值。特别是在农业人口中，教育的估计系数为较显著(10%水平)的负值。这是一个与传统人力资本理论发生冲突的结论。因为在 Schultz 和 Tansel(1997)的研究中，几乎所有教育变量的估计系数都显著为正，只有两国女性的估计方程得到了不很显著(10%水平)的负数；在樊明(2002)的研究中，所有对教育回报的估计方程无一例外地得到了显著的正估计系数。然而在国内的一些研究中，常见的结果是教育回报的系数较低乃至为负值，如张车伟(2003)对贫困地区种植业劳动的研究中,教育的系数为非常不显著的正数;而使用同样的数据,都阳(2001)在对非农就业的研究中同样使用 Heckman 两阶段估计方程,对于教育变量也得到了和我们一样的显著的负系数。对此,他的解释为:第一,非农活动对教育水平的要求不显著,而教育所要付出的成本对收益有负的影响;第二,教育的作用在于发现和识别劳动力市场的信息,在教育水平比较低的情况下,教育对提高劳动生产率没有什么影响;第三,教育可能培养人的各种不同能力,但对于贫困地区的劳动力市场而言,并非所有的能力都对提高劳动的边际生产率有帮助。但我们认为,都阳(2001)的三个理由只能解释不显著的教育估计系数,而不能保证得到显著的负系数。教育的负系数可能来自另外的原因:它很可能是过分强调经验的结果,以经验解释了一些应当由教育解释的问题;另外,与发达国家甚至一些发展中国家不同,中国正处于一个快速发展的阶段,受到较多教育的人群是比较年轻的人群,他们的工资通常会低于他们的长辈,从而得到了教育回报率较低、甚至为负的估计系数。

(3) 经验的作用非常强,而且在估计方程中是仅有的两个显著变量之一。这与都阳(2001)的研究比较相似,在他对非农就业工资的研究中,只有经验和技能对工资产生显著的影响。当然在其他人的研究中,经验大多也是非常显著的,如樊明(2002)与 Schultz 和 Tansel(1997)。对于中国这样一个处在转型与发展过程中的国家而言,这一估计结果应当是比较合理的。

(4) 在进行选择性过程矫正以后,制度变量户籍身份对工资具有负面影响,这个结论与一般的研究结果不同。这是因为,在现有的参与者中,制度因素是十分重要的正向因素,但经过选择性过程矫正后,制度因素已经被充分考虑,于是非农户籍身份对工资的贡献为负值。而在同时进行的 OLS 估计中，这一变量的系数估计值为显著的正数。另外，这也可能是使用横截面数据所致。

(5) 工资决定的性别歧视明显存在。在我们所有的估计方程中，性别始终是除经验以外唯一显著的变量，无论是对样本总体还是农业或非农居民，得到的结果是一致的。而且无论是否控制了其他变量，不同性别之间的工资差别都显著地存在。这意味着，即便在劳动力进行非农就业参与选择后，性别仍然是工资决定的重要因素。[⑥]这个结论与都阳(2001)的研究略有差异，在他的研究中性别变量并不显著。

四、强力检验及主要结论

(一) 关于健康测度选择的重新考察

由于健康测度的困难，所以有必要对健康测度指标的选择进行重新考察，通常的做法是，选择其他一些健康测度指标进行同样的分析，以检验分析结果的准确性，这种检验通常称作强力检验。

本文进行的强力检验选择了这样一些指标：健康自评、健康简单算术得分、健康的加权得分、健康受限天数。其中，除健康自评为离散变量外，其余三个健康指标都是连续变量。健康自评来自问卷中对一般健康状况的询问"你如何评价你的健康状况?"，答案为"很好、好、一般、差、很差"五级[⑦]，而健康的得分和加权得分基于与本研究同样的问题。樊明(2002)的研究中就采用了类似的打分法，即根据不同问题的不同回答规定不同的分数。由于此前中国没有相关的研究，我们只能凭借主观印象进行评判。为此我们粗略地构建了这两种健康指数：简单算术得分——将每项功能正常定义为0,存在轻微问题定义为1,严重问题为2,完全失能为3,然后对每项得分进行加总得到最终的总得分;健康的加权得分——将每项功能正常定义为0,存在轻微问题定义为2,严重问题为5,完全失能为10,再加总各项得分得到最终的总得分。健康受限天数直接取自调查前3个月的健康受限天数指标。

使用这些健康指数,我们对健康与劳动力市场的关系进行重新估计,估计结果与使用生理和心理因子分析的结果基本一致。其中健康自评、平均得分和加权得分与生理因子的估计结果更为相似,即在劳动参与估计中表现为非常显著的负数,在对工资决定进行的二阶段估计中为不显著的负数。⑧而在使用健康受限天数进行的估计中,无论在一阶段还是在二阶段健康的估计系数都不显著。值得一提的是,在以上所有的研究中,逆米尔斯比率都是显著的。

总结以上的结果我们发现,即便选择不同的健康测度指标,得到的结论也基本是一致的:健康的身体倾向于容易获得非农就业机会,而健康对劳动工资决定缺乏显著的影响,而且在非农就业市场中,选择性偏误明显存在。

(二)本研究的主要结论

作为国内非农就业与健康间关系研究的首次尝试,本研究的主要贡献表现在以下几个方面。

首先,通过加入健康变量,本文在一个更多维的人力资本概念下,对非农就业参与和工资决定的影响因素进行探讨。另外,本文使用因子分析方法成功提取了生理和心理因子,也扩大了对健康考察的维度。

其次,本文发现,健康对劳动参与和非农就业参与具有显著的作用,但它对于种植业参与并没有什么显著的作用,甚至可以说没有一点作用。我们的研究还发现，在 1993 年，面向农村的劳动力市场基本上是一个买方市场。而在分别对全体人口和农业人口的估计中，我们同样发现健康资本对劳动参与产生明显的影响。

然而，即便在一个广义的农村概念下，农业户籍人口和非农户籍人口在非农就业的劳动参与率方面仍然存在巨大的差距，因而二元结构在这里还是存在的。但我们的研究发现，提高健康资本存量对于农民获得非农就业机会具有重要的作用。我们知道，非农收入既有助于提高农民的经济生活水平，又有利于缩小城乡二元经济的差距，因而健康还具有更为重要和深远的意义。

再次，在工资决定方面，健康并没有表现出显著的影响。由于存在强的选择过程，不仅仅是健康，而且所有的人力资本变量在我们的估计方程中对非农就业劳动力市场表现的影响基本消失。

最后，无论是在非农劳动参与还是在劳动工资决定方面，在广大农村地区，性别歧视明显存在；经验在劳动力市场表现方面的作用异常显著。与健康一样，教育对于非农劳动参与的作用强于其对工资决定的作用。另外，仅仅从横截面分析的角度，户籍身份并不是受歧视的原因，但如果从更深层次探究原因，则不同户籍身份人口之间非农就业机会的明显差异已经说明了一切。

由于中国的发展速度很快，很多情况发生了巨大的变化，因而本研究仅仅适用于 20 世纪 90 年代初期的情况。当时，城市地区对外来劳动力务工的限制仍相对严格。随着这种限制的放松，农民拥有了更多的非农就业机会，因而在新的条件下，健康对非农就业和工资决定的影响这一课题还有待于基于更新的数据进行的更深广的研究。

注　释

① 本文采用了它们的对数形式。

② 根据笔者初步检索的资料，国内使用 Heckman 模型进行估计的文献不算很多，较早的应用见于朱玲和蒋中一(1994)，近期的研究如都阳(2001)。

③ 本研究数据包括了部分县城的居民，所以存在一部分非农户籍人口。

④ 广义的农村指县及县以下的地区，其居民既包括农业户口的人口也包括非农户口的人口。

⑤ 樊明的健康测度标准是，数值越大，健康状况越差。所以其负估计系数相当于我们的正估计系数。

⑥ 因为性别在参与率决定方程中就具有显著的正系数。

⑦ 新的趋势是，健康自评同样被认为是一个不可观察的连续潜变量，需要通过方程估计获得。但作为一种检验手段，我们认为直接使用离散变量是可以接受的。

⑧ 由于所使用的指标为健康的负指数，即得分越高健康状况越差，因此估计方程中打分法得到的正估计系数对应着因子法得到的负估计系数，反之亦然。

参考文献

都阳，2001：《中国贫困地区劳动供给研究》，华文出版社。

樊明，2002：《健康经济学——健康对劳动力市场表现的影响》，中国社科文献出版社。

约翰·G. 库里斯、皮特·A. 威斯特，1979：《卫生经济学概论》(中译本，1983)，中国展望出版社。

张车伟，2003：《营养、健康与效率》，《经济研究》第 1 期。

朱玲、蒋中一，1994：《以工代赈与缓解贫困》，上海三联书店、上海人民出版社。

Baldwin, Marjorie and William G. Johnson, 1994, "Labor Market Discrimination against Men with Disabilities", *The Journal of Human Resources*, Vol. 29, No. 1, pp. 1—19.

Bartel, Ann and Paul Taubman, 1979, "Health and Labor Market Success: The Role of Various Disease", *The Review of Economics and Statistics*, Vol. 61, No. 1, pp. 1—8.

Bartel, Ann and Paul Taubman, 1986, "Some Economic and Demographic Consequences of Mental Illness", *Journal of Labor Economics*, Vol. 4, No. 2, pp. 243—256.

Bazzoli, Gloria J., 1985, "The Early Retirement Decision: New Empirical Evidence On The Influence of Health", *Journal of Human Resources*, Vol. 20, pp. 214—234.

Benham, L. and A. Benham, 1982, "Employment, Earnings and Psychiatric Diagnosis", In V. Fuchs eds., *Economic Aspects of Health*, University of Chicago Press, pp. 203—220.

Chiricos, Thomas N. and Gilbert Nestel, 1985, "Further Evidence on the Economic Effects of Poor Health", *The Review of Economics and Statistics*, Vol. 67, No. 1, pp. 61—69.

Doorslaer, Von, 1987, *Health, Knowleage and the Demand for Medical Care: An Econometric Analysis*, Van Gorcum, Netherland, pp. 47—63.

Ettner, Susan L., Frank Richard G. and Ronald C. Kessler, 1997, "The Impact of Psychiatric Disorders on Labor Market Outcomes", NBER Working Paper no. 5989.

Heckman, J., 1979, "Sample Selection Bias as a Specification Error", *Econometrica*, Vol. 47, No. 1, pp. 153—162.

Ivaschenko, Oleksiy, 2003, "Adult Health and Earnings in the Ukrainian Labor Market", in Ivaschenko (eds), *Essays on Poverity, Income Inequality and Health in Transition Economics*, *Economic Study* 122, Department of Economics, Goteborg University PhD dissertation.

Lee, Lung-Fei, 1982, "Health and Wage: A Simultaneous Equation Model with Multiple Descrete Indicators", *International Economic Review*, Vol. 23, No. 1, pp. 199—221.

Luft, 1975, "The Impact of Poor Health on Earnings", *The Review of Economics and Statistics*, Vol. 57, No. 1, pp. 42—57.

Schultz, T. Paul and Tansel, Aysit, 1997, "Measurement of Returns to Adult Health", *Living Standards Measurement Study*, The World Bank Working Paper no. 95.

Stern, 1996, "Semiparametric Estimates of the Supply and Demands Effccts of the Disability on Labor Force Participation", *Journal of Econometrics*, Vol. 71, pp. 49—70.

Strauss, John, 1986, "Does Better Nutrition Raise Farm Productivity?", *The Journal of Political Economy*, Vol. 94, No. 2, pp. 297—320.

Van De Ven, W. P. M. M. and E. M. Hooijmans, 1991, "The MIMIC Health Status Index", In G. Duru and J. H. P. Paelinck eds., *Econometrics of Health Care*, Kluwer, Amsterdam.

Van Doorslaer, Eddy, 1987, *Health, Knowleage and The Demand for Medical Care: An Econometric Analysis*, Van Gorcum, Netherland, pp. 47—63.

(原载《经济研究》2004 年第 2 期)

性别、生命周期与家庭内部健康投资*

——中国农户就诊的经验证据

高梦滔　姚　洋

(北京大学中国经济研究中心)

一、绪　言

在研究家庭内部人力资本投资性别差异方面，已有的文献大多是从家庭成员市场活动收益(或者预期收益)导向的角度进行分析。例如 Rosenzweig 和 Schultz(1982)对于印度儿童死亡率的经济解释：在生存经济条件下，假定父母对于不同性别子女的投资决定不同性别子女的死亡率，则预期将来有更大经济生产能力的子女会获得更多的经济资源投入，此类性别儿童死亡率也就更低。他们使用不同性别儿童死亡率作为家庭投资的一种指数，并使用家庭数据与地区数据证明了这一点。Ram (1984)使用国别数据，并且将预期寿命差距作为家庭资源投资于男女的指数，对于男女整个生命周期的家庭资源分配进行分

* 本文系北京大学 211 项目阶段性成果；本文的研究获得美国中华医学会和福特基金会资助，并且在数据搜集方面得到农业部农研中心的合作与支持，在此表示感谢。本文在写作过程中，得到林毅夫、John Strauss、赵耀辉以及参加中国经济研究中心教师午餐研讨会参与者的宝贵意见，在此表示感谢。

析。他使用了108个国家的横截面数据和1947—1978年的州时间序列数据，结果显示，女性经济机会的增加拉大了男女预期寿命的差距，证明了家庭内部资源分配优先给予创收能力更强的成员；Pitt等(1990)使用印度Bangladesh的数据对于男女食物与营养的家庭内部分配进行了分析，发现家庭倾向于将更多的营养和食物分配给经济机会较强的家庭成员。[①]尤其是对于成年男女而言，用于创收的健康禀赋高的成员获得的食品与热量更多。但是就热量消耗而言，成年男子的这种禀赋强化投资的弹性比成年女子要小，正是在这个意义上，经验模型的结果拒绝了家庭收入最大化的假设。Alderman和Gertler(1997)使用一个两阶段的模型对巴基斯坦农户的就医行为进行了经验分析[②]，结果发现，在较低的收入组中，男孩比女孩更有可能去较好的医疗机构就诊，女孩就诊的收入弹性高于男孩，但是在非贫困的组别这种弹性差距消失了。

以上研究存在两个问题：(1)忽略了不同家庭成员在非市场活动中的专业分工比较优势，特别是在非市场活动中不同性别家庭成员的优势，例如妇女在孩子抚养方面的效率；(2)这些研究的模型框架暗含了一个假定，就是在一致性(consensus)效用函数中假定了可分性条件，使得家庭效用函数最大化简化为收入最大化。这些问题被一些研究者所注意，例如对于Rosenzweig和Schultz(1982)的研究，Folbre(1984)提出了质疑，主要集中于两点：(1)理论框架上，他们的研究假定了家庭一致性偏好行为；(2)家庭中，因为女孩对于母亲的工作分担较多，因此母亲偏好于对女孩进行更多投资。在这两个假设之下，Folbre认为非一致性模型同样可以解释Rosenzweig和Schultz的经验结论。Duncan(1998)使用博弈框架的经验研究结论部分支持了Folbre的质疑，他使用巴西的数据对儿童死亡率进行分析，经验结果拒绝了新古典模型的结论，母亲更倾向于对女儿的健康进行投资，而父亲更倾向于对儿子的健康投资。Behram 和 Deolatikar(1990)使用博弈模型的简约需求函数根据印度南部的农村数据对家庭内部营养分配进行经验估计，结果发现无论在平均营养摄取水平还是在方差意义上都不存在性别差异，但是女性营养摄取对于食品的价格弹性(绝对值)要高于男性成员，就是在饥荒和干旱时节，食品价格上升之际，女性面临饥荒的风险大于家庭中的男性成员。

这些研究部分考虑到家庭内部的性别分工对于人力资本投资的影响，但是未能从生命周期的角度对这些影响进行系统分析，尤其是妇女的不同的年龄段具有不同的家庭内部生产比较优势，妇女在生育与孩子幼年期抚育方面具有明显的效率。Rosenzweig 和 Schultz 的经典模型及其拓展，仅仅假设市场的收入机会是导致不同性别投资的关键因素，这是远远不够的。换言之，妇女的家庭生产效率往往体现在非市场的活动中。对于此，Gronau(1973)的论文对于家庭主妇的非市场活动“工资率”给予了估计，他证明非白人的家庭主妇有幼年后代者比没有幼年后代者的家务劳动“工资率”要高一些。Pitt 等的论文考虑了不同年龄段男女之间营养分配的差异，但是这种年龄段的划分仅仅是基于男女参与不同强度劳动的考虑，而非对于家庭内部分工的相对效率的考虑。

基于上述分析，本文主要提出的问题是，家庭内人力资本投资的性别差异主要是由于成员的市场经济活动或者创收能力所致，还是由于男女对于家庭内部分工不同的“生产”效率所致。换言之，本文检验的是在女性不同的生命周期中，尤其是在妇女怀孕以及家庭后代幼年时，对于女性的人力资本投资是否得到优先的考虑。本文主要分为两部分考察就诊与治疗花费在男女生命周期上的差异:(1)对于数据以及差异的描述统计分析;(2)对于男女两周患病及其治疗支出的分析。

二、理论与计量框架

女性在怀孕以及子女幼年期间对于较为繁重的劳动参与是有限的,也就是说在农业为主的经济中,女性在怀孕期以及孩子幼年的抚育期对于家庭收入的贡献要小一些;但是按照 Becker 的家庭内部分工理论(Becker, 1991)妇女在抚育后代方面具有比男性更高的效率,前述 Reuben 的论文在一定程度上也证明了这一点。本文需要检验的就是家庭人力资本投资的性别差异性主要决定于女性家庭成员创收能力还是女性家庭成员对于抚育后代的比较优势。也就是分析家庭收入最大化和家庭整体效用函数最大化的经验证据。

基于博弈论框架的理论模型必须做出两个重要假定:(1)妇女讨价还价能力取决于其收入获取的机会与能力;(2)父母对于子女的投资具有性别偏向(Rosenzweig and Schultz, 1984)。这两个假设显得太苛刻,其中之一也正是本文需要检验的。由于受数据的限制,本文主要考虑的还是采用 Rosenzweig 和Schultz的新古典思路。

Rosenzweig 和 Schultz 的经典模型主要考虑死亡率差异,Ram 对此模型的拓展考虑预期寿命差异,这种解释不免受到生物和人体功能函数的影响。他们的主要处理办法是通过比较不同收入水平与教育程度对于死亡率的影响来剔除生物决定函数的影响,但是这种处理毕竟要经过人体生物作用的黑箱。其他营养摄取与男女体质差异的有关研究也有类似不足。基于这些考虑与数据因素,本文主要对于男女健康投资的另一个部分，即患病治疗的投资花费进行分析，实际上患病的治疗花费主要是减轻疾病带来的负效用。本文主要采用的理论模型是 Grossman(1972)的框架，即认为健康投资是人力资本投资的一个重要组成部分，其投资水平决定于家庭联合效用函数在收入约束条件下的最优水平。主要考虑如下的需求函数简约形式：

$$D = D(AGE_M,\ AGE_F,\ I,\ \Omega) \tag{1}$$

其中，D 表示健康投资需求函数，AGE_M 和 AGE_F 分别表示男女所处的不同年龄段变量，I 表示家庭收入以及财富等变量，Ω 表示有关环境以及医疗服务可及性等的变量。

通过估计下式，利用家庭和个人数据对理论模型进行经验检验：

$$D = \beta_0 + \beta_M AGE_M + \beta_F AGE_F + \beta_i I + \beta_\Omega \Omega + \varepsilon \tag{2}$$

β 表示诸待估系数向量；ε 表示误差项。

在(2)式中，本文待检验的假设主要就是检验系数 β_F 在不同生命周期段的符号和显著性，并和相应的 β_M 对比。这里先验地认为妇女在孩子生育与抚育期 β_F 的系数显著为正。

本文使用的数据来自于中国农业部在中国 8 个省③的家庭调查数据集，包含了 1428 个农户(8414 个个人)的收入、支出、财富、家庭结构等广泛信息，跨度为 1987—2002 年。治疗行为以及治疗花费等数据来自于北京大学中国经济研究中心对于这些农户的问卷调查，包含了广泛的“大病”治疗、两周患病治疗、卫生服务等丰富信息，并且按照中国卫生部对于疾病的分类方法对病种进行划分(中国卫生部，1998)。

(一) 两周患病与治疗的总体性别差异

在样本中(见表 1)，男女两周内患病与受伤的百分比分别是4.5%和6.0%。两周患病但是未到医疗机构就诊的比例分别为男性18.6%，女性16.3%。对于治疗的花费情况和就诊情况分别进行t检验和χ^2检验，总体上看，无论是两周患病就诊的比例还是治疗的花费，男女都有显著的差异（5%的置信水平上）。男性两周患病到医疗机构就诊的比例低于女性，而就诊的平均花费却高于女性。在未就诊的首要原因中，男性自我治疗的比例为42.8%，女性为35.4%；而“认为病轻”的比例男女分别为40.5%和39.6%，差异不大。

表1　男女两周患病就诊情况与治疗花费

性别	是否两周内患病受伤未就诊		治疗花费	
	未就诊	就诊	均值(元)	标准差
男	18.60%	81.40%	818.20	2207.04
女	16.30%	83.70%	538.61	1635.94
检验结果	$\chi^2=4.322$	$p=0.0376$	$t=2.314$	$p=0.0478$

（二）划分性别与年龄组的两周患病与就诊

样本的女性结婚年龄众数为20.4岁，结束生育的年龄众数集中在26—27岁之间，据此推算家中有10岁以下儿童的母亲年龄大多数集中在20—37岁之间。根据这些信息，将样本人群划分为7个年龄组进行两周患病与治疗费用的分析。不同年龄性别分组的就诊比例和就诊费用如图1、图2所示。从图1、2中可以看出，女性在未结婚以前两周患病就诊的比例低于男性，在生育期和孩子幼年期的就诊比例反而大大高于同一年龄段的男性；到了中年和老年时期，男女之间的未就诊情况又有趋同的倾向。这种不同生命周期的健康投资模式显示了家庭对女性在生育及孩子幼年期健康投资的一种偏向。

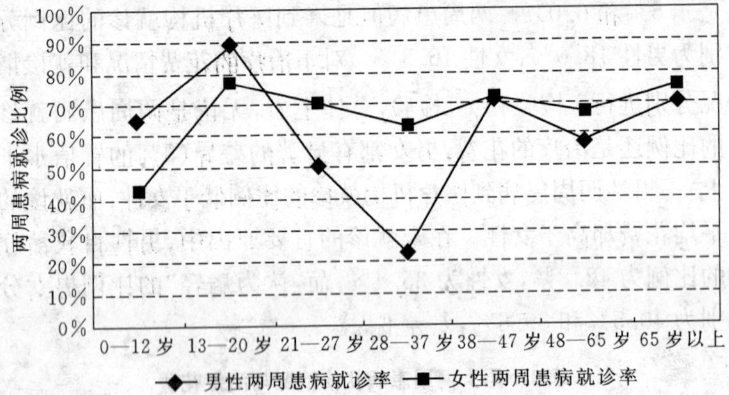

图1　年龄、性别分组两周患病就诊率

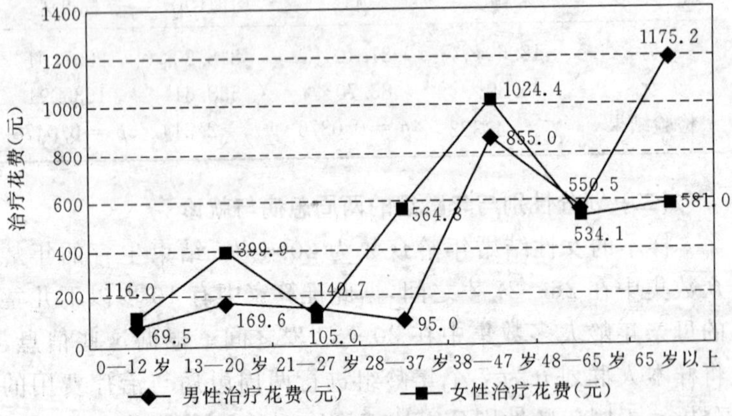

图2　年龄性别分组两周患病治疗花费

从两周患病治疗花费来看，女性在28—37岁之间的治疗花费是男性的594.5%，这是差距最大的年龄段，在中年以后差距减小。

使用t检验对于不同年龄组治疗支出均值进行分析，结果发现在0—12岁、20—27岁、28—37岁3个组别上，两者的差异是统计上显著的(Levene's Test 不拒绝方差齐性的假设)。3 个年龄段中仅有 20—27 岁组男性治疗支出显著高于女性。但是问题在于男性在 20—27 岁、28—37 岁 2 个年龄段就诊的比例都比女性低很多,综合的考虑需要后面使用两阶段模型正式计算完全效应。

(三) 收入分组的两周患病就诊比例及治疗支出

家庭的收入水平对于就诊行为有直接的影响,在此使用全部样本人均纯收入 3 等分组观察不同收入组农户男女在几个年龄段上的就诊比例和治疗支出(见表 2)。

表 2　人均纯收入 3 等分组治疗支出对比(单位:元)

年龄分组	低收入组			中等收入组			高收入组		
	男性	女性	t Sig.	男性	女性	t Sig.	男性	女性	t Sig.
13—20 岁	16.0	674.0	0.23	190.0	202.6	0.32	71.7	39.5	0.32
20—27 岁	276.7	372.1	0.20	80.0	150.0	0.21	25.0	139.0	0.41
28—37 岁	315.2	402.3	0.07	76.6	140.0	0.32	72.3	15.0	0.42
38—47 岁	682.5	296.1	0.09	223.3	595.0	0.09	1350.6	1510.3	0.53
48—65 岁	535.5	499.3	0.87	1072.4	210.8	0.04	334.6	583.6	0.56
65 岁以上	1324.5	296.0	0.05	1078.8	1473.6	0.12	932.6	304.0	0.15

对于低收入组来说,女性在生育及抚育期两周患病就诊的比例最高,中等收入组女性在抚育期就诊的比例高于男性,但是高收入组显出的特征恰恰相反,女性在抚育期就诊的比例低于男性。

从治疗支出来看,低收入组和中等收入组生育与抚育期女性的治疗开支高于同年龄组男性,到了高收入组,这种治疗开支上的差异就变得微乎其微了。考虑到中等收入以下的家庭其卫生资源的内部分配上比高收入家庭的竞争性要强烈,因为家庭资源较为有限。这种家庭健康投资的分配在中低收入家庭的倾向性较高收入家庭更为明显。图 1、2 显示出了对于不同性别、不同生命周期家庭成员的分配差异，换言之，就是在有限资源条件下，优先分配给家庭内部生产效率较高的成员——生育与抚育期的女性。这也正是 Strauss 和 Duncan(1998)提到的“生存经济”条件下健康和营养对家庭成员生产率的影响，基于性别差异的这种健康资源分配的不平等随着收入的提高而减小。

但是，对这种均值的差异使用 t 检验，统计上几乎不显著。低收入家庭 20—27 岁、28—37 岁两个年龄段的治疗支出差异勉强在 10%的置信水平上显著。

三、两周患病就诊概率与就诊费用的模型结果

上面所述的家庭内部对于男女分年龄段成员的健康投资，基于的是简单描述统计结果和 t 检验的初步结论。因为就诊概率与就诊的花费还受到其他因素的影响，诸如家庭成员的教育程度、卫生服务可及性等方面，病种对于就诊的影响也非常重要，男女所患疾病严重程度的不同也会使就诊概率与费用极为不一致(见表 3)。因此，我们需要使用多元回归的技术控制这些因素来进行计量分析。

表 3　两周患病就诊概率与就诊费用选择模型解释变量描述

解释变量	均值	标准差
户主受教育年限	5.75	2.79
2002 年人均纯收入(千元)	4.36	7.46
人均家庭财富(千元)	22.54	57.59
2002 年非农收入比重	0.10	0.24
人均土地面积(亩)	0.95	1.88
家庭负担系数	0.25	0.19
2002 年家庭规模	5.66	2.44

（续表）

解释变量	均值	标准差
本人治疗需自费百分数	98.77	9.53
平均千人拥有卫生人员数	3.26	3.33
村集体发给村医平均工资(千元/年)	0.69	2.08
乡距离(公里)[a]	2.88	3.35
县距离(公里)[a]	16.17	12.18
是否独生子女(虚拟变量)	0.17	0.38
年龄与性别分组虚拟变量(对照:男性(0—12岁))		
(13—20岁)	0.06	0.24
(20—27岁)	0.04	0.19
(28—37岁)	0.06	0.24
(38—47岁)	0.14	0.35
(48—65岁)	0.37	0.48
(65岁以上)	0.18	0.38
女性(0—12岁)	0.05	0.22
女性(13—20岁)	0.04	0.19
女性(20—27岁)	0.02	0.15
女性(28—37岁)	0.04	0.20
女性(38—47岁)	0.09	0.29
女性(48—65岁)	0.23	0.42
女性(65岁以上)	0.09	0.28
省虚拟变量(对照组:山西)		
吉林	0.03	0.17
浙江	0.16	0.37
河南	0.04	0.19
湖南	0.09	0.28
广东	0.34	0.47
四川	0.12	0.32
甘肃	0.12	0.33
病种虚拟变量(对照组:感冒)		
消化系统病	0.09	0.29
肌肉骨骼系统病	0.09	0.29

（续表）

解 释 变 量	均值	标准差
循环系统病	0.11	0.32
神经系统病	0.08	0.27
其他急性疾病	0.07	0.25
地势虚拟变量(对照:平原)		
丘陵[a]	0.37	0.48
山区[a]	0.29	0.46

注:a. 仅仅出现在 x 中,不在 v 中出现,即这 4 个解释变量仅仅影响就诊概率,对于就诊费用不产生影响。

计量方程分别使用两周患病就诊概率和两周患病治疗花费的估计来分析不同年龄段男女健康投资差异。在估计方法上存在下面两个问题:(1)在对就诊的估计上,考虑测量偏误问题。Strauss J. 等(1993)使用“自评健康”和广泛的物理指标分析了 4 个国家的成人在不同生命周期的健康状况,发现在控制了大量社会经济协变量以后,妇女在年轻时期比男子报告更多的健康问题。为了克服这种可能存在的偏误,本文使用一个“sample selection bivariate probit model”来描述“两周内患病报告与否”和“两周内患病就诊与否”这样一种有两个决策阶段构成的过程。具体而言,由于两个过程是序贯决定的,因此使用 Abowd 和 Farber(1982)的模型进行估计,以克服可能的测量偏误。(2)在就诊费用的估计上,还存在一个样本选择的问题,因为就诊人员对于医疗费用的报告较为完整。未就诊的人群中,“自我治疗”和“认为病轻”的占了很大比例,治疗费用的估计存在一个样本选择的问题,因此估计就诊费用的时候必须考虑这种选择因素。使用 Heckman 两阶段过程对此进行处理,首先对于“两周是否患病”和“两周患病是否就诊”进行 bivariate probit 的 AF 模型估计，然后对就诊费用的影响因素使用 OLS 估计：

$$\exp = \nu\beta + \rho\lambda(x\gamma) + \mu \tag{3}$$

$$P(y=1) = P(y1=1) \quad P(y2=1) = \Phi(\beta1'x1)\Phi(\beta2'x2) \tag{4}$$

$$P(y=0) = 1 - P(y=1) \tag{5}$$

(3)式中 λ 表示逆米尔斯比率(inverse Mills ratio)，ν 表示就诊费用方程中的解释变量(向量)，x 表示选择方程中的解释变量(向量)；(4)式中的 $y1$、$y2$ 分别表示“是否就诊”与“是否患病”两值因变量，在 AF 估计中，因变量实际上是 $y = y1 \times y2$；$x1$、$x2$ 分别表示 $y1$ 与 $y2$ 的解释变量向量(部分重合)。

文中同时给出一般二值 Probit 和 Heckman 两阶段的结果，以便和 AF 模型结果比较。

对于上述三式的解释变量含义和描述如下表所示：

使用户主教育年限而非患者本人教育年限作为解释变量，主要是因为部分患者是儿童，尚未进入学校或者年幼，对于治疗决定由家长代为做出的缘故。家庭的收入、财富、负担系数等皆是 2002 年的数据，健康问卷调查时间是在 2003 年 4 月中旬。总负担系数采用《中国统计年鉴(2002)》的定义：被抚养人口(0—14 岁和 65 岁以上人口)与 15—64 岁人口的比值。计算公式为：总负担系数 = 100×被抚养人口 /15—64 岁人口(中国国家统计局，2003)。在样本中占了 55.3%的两周患病病种是“感冒”，将其作为病种虚拟变量的对照组，“其他疾病”是除了列出的疾病以外的病种，没有包括分娩在内，主要是“中毒、车祸、受伤”等一些较为紧急和严重的情况。就诊概率模型估计结果见表 4。

表 4　两周患病与就诊概率影响因素分析(Abowd/Farber models VS Probit)

(因变量:两周患病就诊=1)	Abowd Farber models (N = 7048)		Probit (N = 723)	
自变量	Coeff.	t-ratio	Coeff.	t-ratio
Constant	3.917**	3.606	3.082**	4.431
户主受教育年限	0.016	0.937	−0.021*	−2.104
2002 年人均纯收入(千元)	0.018	0.465	0.029	1.505
人均家庭财富(千元)	0.000	0.457	0.001*	2.117
非农收入比重	−0.188	−0.831	−0.282*	−2.158
人均土地面积	0.053	0.902	0.016	1.035
家庭负担系数	0.711	1.985	0.302	1.517
2002 年家庭规模	0.010	0.364	0.003	0.193
平均千人有村医数	0.054	1.832	0.013	1.609
村集体发给村医平均工资(千元/年)	0.005	1.711	0.001**	3.888
本人门诊治疗自费比例	−0.037**	−3.872	−0.032**	−6.234
乡距离(公里)	0.030	1.467	0.005	0.418
县距离(公里)	−0.050**	−7.505	−0.024**	−7.523
是否独生子女(独生子女=1)	0.462**	3.191	0.369**	4.381

（续表）

（因变量：两周患病就诊＝1）	Abowd Farber models（N = 7048）		Probit（N = 723）	
自变量	Coeff.	t-ratio	Coeff.	t-ratio
年龄与性别分组虚拟变量（对照：男性（0—12 岁））				
（13—20 岁）	0.222**	4.121	0.608**	3.981
（20—27 岁）	−0.728**	−3.567	−0.708**	−4.191
（28—37 岁）	−0.904**	−5.112	−0.146**	−6.713
（38—47 岁）	0.205**	3.002	0.242	1.880
（48—65 岁）	−0.165**	−3.574	−0.143	−1.237
（65 岁以上）	−0.323**	−3.131	−0.287*	−2.017
女性（0—12 岁）	−0.238**	−2.995	−0.484**	−3.143
女性（13—20 岁）	−0.380**	−3.676	−0.343**	−2.182
女性（20—27 岁）	0.286	1.710	0.188	1.052
女性（28—37 岁）	0.290	1.865	0.426**	2.401
女性（38—47 岁）	−0.321**	−4.789	−0.222	−1.777
女性（48—65 岁）	−0.399**	−8.156	−0.251**	−2.648
女性（65 岁以上）	−0.016	−0.166	−0.034	−0.211
省虚拟变量（对照组：山西）				
吉林	−1.186*	−2.290	−1.078**	−3.643
浙江	−1.867*	−2.360	−0.560	−1.748
河南	−1.007	−0.712	−0.650*	−2.186

（续表）

（因变量：两周患病就诊=1）	Abowd Farber models（$N=7048$）		Probit（$N=723$）	
自变量	Coeff.	t-ratio	Coeff.	t-ratio
湖南	−0.494	−1.015	−0.692*	−2.385
广东	−0.790	−1.526	−0.160	−0.544
四川	−0.014	−0.027	−0.394	−1.329
甘肃	−1.021*	−2.025	−0.574	−1.936
病种虚拟变量（对照组：感冒）				
消化系统病	−0.297	−1.399	−0.236	−1.799
肌肉骨骼系统病	0.441*	2.086	0.327*	2.410
循环系统病	0.461	1.828	0.470**	3.000
神经系统病	0.568*	2.191	0.587**	3.543
其他急性疾病	0.300**	4.928	0.255**	2.196
地势虚拟变量（对照：平原）				
丘陵	−1.107**	−5.741	−0.326**	−3.719
山区	−0.153	−1.044	−0.106	−1.348
	$\chi^2=438.99$**	$\log L=-721.60$	$\chi^2=254.597$**	$\log L=-629.41$
	McFadd $R^2=0.149$	回代准确率 = 71.49%	McFadd $R^2=0.239$	回代准确率 = 74.64%

注：** 表示 1%水平上显著；* 表示 5%水平上显著。

从AF模型的结果上看，家庭的收入和财富变量对于两周患病的就诊决定没有显著的影响，可能是因为两周患病的报告绝大部分都是较为轻微的疾病，这些疾病的治疗对于家庭而言不会成为太大的负担。“人均土地面积”对于治疗可能性的一种正的影响，或许说明了，劳动相对于土地的边际效用较高，从而提高对于人力的健康投入水平。

从社区变量的情况看来，距离对于卫生服务的获取会造成不便，因此降低了就诊的可能性。而“平均千人有村医数”对于就诊概率有显著正向影响，体现提高基础农村卫生服务的可得性对于农户就诊的重要意义。实际上我国农村地区现阶段村级医疗卫生服务提供者主要是私人医生，根据中国卫生部1998年第二次全国卫生服务调查的结果，中国农村平均私人医疗点比例为42.7%。看来基础卫生服务的所有制形式并非关键，重要的是通过竞争来提高基层卫生服务的可得性。中国农村的医疗保障制度自从开始了市场化进程以后就几乎是空缺的，从描述统计中可以看出样本的自费医疗百分数均值是98.77%，标准差较小，但是从回归的结果来看，拥有健康保障对于农户患病的及时就诊是有显著作用的。同样地，在中国村集体给村医发放工资往往要求村医疗人员对村民的治疗减免一定的挂号费或者处理费用，一些村集体还对村医的用药价格给予一定的控制，这种具备一定公共性质的村级医疗设施对于农户就诊概率有显著的正面影响。

和非独生子女相比，独生子女由于没有兄弟姐妹的竞争(sibling rivaling)，治疗的就诊概率得到显著的提高。这一点也为Garg A.和Morduch J.(1998)对加纳孩子的教育与健康投资的研究所证实。

和普通的感冒相比，消化系统疾病的就诊概率要显著地低，主要的原因是，这种消化系统疾病大多是"腹泻"，农户自我治疗的比例往往较大，而急性的其他疾病就诊的可能性要显著地高。

对比 AF 模型和普通 Probit 模型的估计结果发现，"非农收入比重"和"人均财富"对就诊概率的影响在 AF 模型中变得不显著了，并且系数变小。户主受教育程度在 Probit 估计中为显著的负数，在 AF 模型中变为正的符号，但是统计上不显著。使用 AF 模型的显著功效还体现在诸生命周期的虚拟变量虽然显著性增加，但是系数普遍都有增大，凸现了不同性别、生命周期的家庭成员在就诊概率上的重要性。

通过对于 AF 模型年龄性别虚拟变量的边际效果计算④，男女不同生命周期两周就诊概率的预测如图 3 所示。

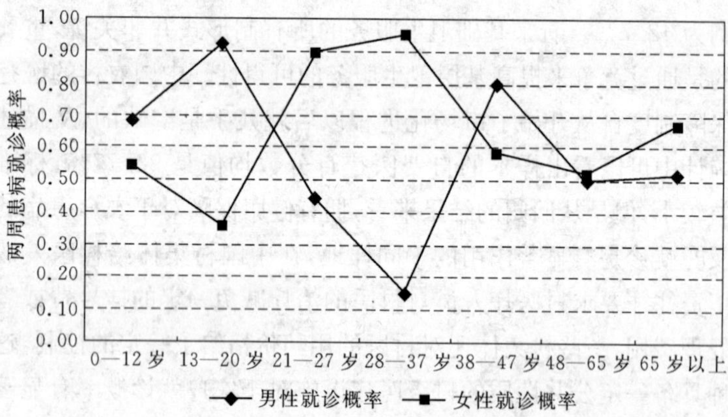

图 3 年龄与性别两周就诊概率预测(Abowd/Farber model)

在控制了收入、财富、教育特征以及社区的变量以后，处于不同生命周期男女的就诊可能性和女性抚育功能的假说较为吻合。女性在 20—37 岁这段生育期以及家庭幼年后代的抚育期间两周患病就诊的可能性大大高于同一年龄段的男性家庭成员，并且在统计上显著。这一段时期，正是女性对于市场性的创收活动参与较少的时期。在这段时期以后，男女之间的两周患病就诊概率逐渐趋同。

使用样本选择模型对于第二阶段就诊费用的估计结果见表5。

逆米尔斯比率在统计上不显著，显示了模型不存在选择偏误的情形。与就诊概率不同的情形是人均收入对于就诊概率没有影响，但是对于就诊花费有统计上显著的正影响。主要可以考虑两种情形下富裕家庭需求医疗服务质量较高治疗方案的情形：(1)相对富裕家庭可能使用较贵的药品；(2)相对富裕家庭可能到更高级别医疗机构就诊的比例较高，花费比到低级医疗机构要昂贵。相对于代表家庭财富的永久性收入来说，现期收入边际上的影响较大。平均水平上拥有的村医数量对于治疗花费的负的影响可能体现出一种竞争对于压低医疗服务价格的作用。从病种来看，循环系统疾病和急性病的花费显著高于感冒发烧就诊花费。

从男女不同生命周期虚拟变量来看，女性从21—47岁，就诊费用始终高于同年龄段男性。与就诊概率不同的是，男性在47岁以后年龄段就诊费用高于女性。这可能是因为这一年龄段的男性等到病情严重才去就诊。对于不同生命周期男女治疗花费的预测使用两阶段方程的边际效用计算完成⑤，结果如图4所示。

估计的结果显示，男女不同生命周期的就诊花费和就诊概率不完全一致。主要是20—27岁年龄组的女性预测的就诊费用虽然高于男性，但是差距不如就诊概率的区别明显。但是从图2可以看出，综合考虑了就诊概率对于就诊花费的影响以后，对于处于生育与抚育期的女性健康投资在统计意义上极为显著。这种男女健康投资的总体差异在女性处于家庭专业分工效

表 5　两周内就诊费用样本选择模型(基于 Abowd/Farber model 和 Probit model)

因变量:两周就诊费用对数	Abowd/Farber ($N=267$)		Probit ($N=267$)	
自变量	Coeff.	t-ratio	Coeff.	t-ratio
Constant	5. 730	1. 481	7. 615**	4. 731
户主受教育年限	0. 230	1. 294	0. 017	0. 526
2002 年人均纯收入(千元)	2. 573**	3. 553	0. 264**	3. 901
人均家庭财富(千元)	0. 032	1. 675	0. 023	1. 346
非农收入比重	0. 010	0. 844	0. 001	0. 820
人均土地面积	−0. 157	−0. 092	−0. 140	−0. 310
家庭负担系数	−0. 611**	−3. 735	−0. 691	−1. 016
2002 年家庭规模	−0. 035	−1. 469	−0. 034	−0. 687
平均千人有村医数	−0. 334**	−4. 780	−0. 303**	−5. 059
村集体发给村医平均工资(千元/年)	−0. 001	−0. 612	−0. 001	−1. 793
本人门诊治疗自费百分数	−0. 020**	−52. 364	−0. 021**	−54. 364
是否独生子女	0. 621	0. 422	0. 781	1. 268
年龄与性别分组虚拟变量(对照:男性(0—12 岁))				
(13—20 岁)	0. 627	0. 743	0. 769	1. 574

（续表）

因变量:两周就诊费用对数	Abowd/Farber（$N=267$）		Probit（$N=267$）	
自变量	Coeff.	*t*-ratio	Coeff.	*t*-ratio
(21—27 岁)	−0.649	−0.744	−0.474	−0.690
(28—37 岁)	−0.890	−0.312	−0.686	−1.124
(38—47 岁)	0.220	0.180	0.122	0.402
(48—65 岁)	0.468	0.572	0.469*	2.048
(65 岁以上)	0.955	1.139	1.001**	3.534
女性(0—12 岁)	0.210	1.664	0.058*	2.965
女性(13—20 岁)	0.121**	2.103	0.113*	2.080
女性(21—27 岁)	0.336	0.895	0.418	0.882
女性(28—37 岁)	0.448**	9.062	0.690**	4.646
女性(38—47 岁)	0.591**	5.620	0.545*	2.929
女性(48—65 岁)	−0.302*	−2.750	−0.428**	−3.330
女性(65 岁以上)	−0.380*	−2.848	−0.449*	−2.221
省虚拟变量(对照组:山西)				
吉林	0.165	0.062	0.311	0.400

（续表）

因变量：两周就诊费用对数	Abowd/Farber（$N=267$）		Probit（$N=267$）	
自变量	Coeff.	t-ratio	Coeff.	t-ratio
浙江	−1.063	−0.226	−1.180	−1.330
河南	−2.784	−0.381	−2.674	−3.267
湖南	−1.000	−0.535	−1.273	−1.593
广东	−1.047	−0.522	−1.471	−1.811
四川	−1.575	−0.608	−1.656*	−2.078
甘肃	−2.238	−0.918	−2.321*	−2.789
病种虚拟变量（对照组：感冒）				
消化系统病	0.207	0.676	0.206	0.590
肌肉骨骼系统病	0.214	1.122	0.113	0.318
循环系统病	1.075**	7.748	0.924*	2.274
神经系统病	−1.299	−0.441	−0.311	−0.713
其他疾病	0.640**	3.215	0.664	1.981
LAMBDA	−0.164	−0.774	−0.425	−0.543
	Adj $R^2=0.319$	$F=3.02$	Adj $R^2=0.317$	$F=3.00$
	S. E corrected for selection 1.25		S. E corrected for selection 1.28	

注：** 表示在1%水平上显著；* 表示在5%水平上显著。

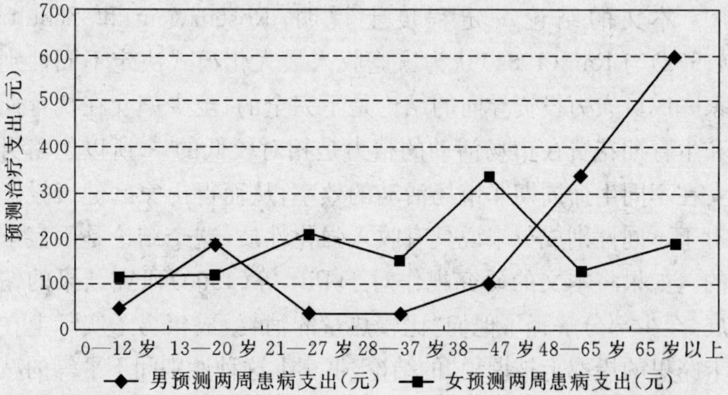

图 4　性别年龄分组的两周患病治疗支出预测(基于 AF 的选择模型)

率较高的时期获得优先的地位。

无论是从就诊概率还是从就诊费用观察，女性在生育与养育后代的时期得到较为有限的家庭健康资源分配这一结论是一致并且强健的。

四、总 结 与 评 论

本文的研究在人力资本的分析框架内拓展了 Rosenzweig 和 Schultz(1982)与 Pitt 等(1990)的研究。从家庭内不同性别成员健康投资的取向上看，单单考虑市场化的经济机会是远远不够的。追溯 Becker(1991)的家庭分工理论，可以发现家庭的组织很大程度上源于家庭内部相对生产效率不一致而导致的专业化分工。即使按照新古典模型的框架，不考虑家庭内部博弈，本文的结论也证实了家庭健康资源的分配是由家庭内部男女成员全部家庭生产比较优势所决定，并非仅仅由市场收入能力所决定。

本文的结论一定程度上说明，Rosenzweig 和 Schultz (1982)与 Ram(1984)认为家庭收入最大化模式决定不同性别家庭成员人力投资导向的结论是不完全的，至少妇女在抚育期和生育期花费在市场活动的精力是相对较低的⑥，所以忽略男女在不同生命周期非市场活动的效率，从而得出家庭健康投资对于不同性别成员来说具有收入强化性质，这个结论是不完全的。如果将本文的研究视作对于 Pitt 等(1990)研究结果的拓展，至少部分解释了他们“比较热量的消耗，成年男子实际上在卡路里的摄取上被课税”的结论，事实上这种性别间不平等的减小在本文看来，一个主要的原因是女性在生育与抚育家庭后代方面具有比较优势。

在中国实行计划生育以后，农村家庭一般可以生育两个孩子，而城市家庭仅仅能生育一个孩子，但相比较而言，城市家庭女性在市场活动中的相对效率较农村女性高(和男性相比)，对于本文进一步的检验可以对照城市家庭健康投资在两性之间的差异。当然，必须考虑生命周期所隐含的非市场活动比较优势的因素，而非仅仅是市场活动中的“工资率”。

注　释

① 该研究强调了生存经济条件下家庭营养分配的竞争性，并且使用残差的方法来估计家庭成员禀赋。

② 分析结果拒绝了一致性模型。

③ 8 个省包括东部的浙江和广东，中部的山西、吉林、河南、湖南，西部的四川及甘肃。样本具有较好的代表性。

④ bivariate probit model 基于条件均值函数 $E(y1 \mid x1, x2, y2 = 1) = P(y1 = 1 \mid x1, x2, y2 = 1)$。

⑤ 对于就诊费用边际效率的估计这里使用的是完全的效用。诸性别年龄虚拟变量都同时出现在 v 和 x 中，这种就诊费用的边际效果就包

含两个部分：(1)直接对于费用回归方程的影响；(2)通过选择方程中 λ 的影响。这种完全的边际效果表述如：$\partial E[y_i \mid x_i, z_i = 1]/\partial x_i = \beta + \rho(-\lambda_i \gamma' x_i - \lambda_i^2)\gamma$。

⑥ Becker(1991)曾提到："生育率的下降明显地增加了已婚妇女每小时的收入，因为她们有较多的能力和较灵活的时间投入市场工作，而不是照料孩子。"

参考文献

国家统计局，2003：《人口部分指标解释》，载于《中国统计年鉴(2002)》(电子版)，中国统计出版社。

卫生部，1998：《国家卫生服务研究——1998 年第二次国家卫生服务调查分析报告》(内部资料)。

Abowd J. and H. Farber, 1982, "Job Queues and Union Status of Workers", *Industrial and Labor Relations Review*, 35, pp. 354—367.

Alderman H. and Gertler P., 1997, "Family Resources and Gender Differences in Human Capital Investment: The Demand for Children in Pakistan", Edited by Haddad. L et al., *Intrahousehold Resources Allocation in Developing Countries*, International Food Policy Research Institute, The Johns Hopkins University Press, pp. 231—248, U. S. A.

Behram, J. and Deolatikar A., 1990, "The Intrahousehold Demand for Nutrients in Rural South India: Individual Estimates ,Fixed Effects, and Permanents Income", *The Journal of Human Resources*, 25, pp. 665—696.

Folbre N., 1984, "Market Opportunities, Genetic Endowments, and Intrafamily Resources Distribution: Comment", *American Economic Review*, Jun. 74, pp. 18—520.

G. S. Becker, 1991, *A Treatise on The Family*, Harvard University Press, U. S. A, pp. 60—65.

Garg A. and Morduch J., 1998, "Sibling Rivalry", *Development Discussion Paper*, No. 630, HIID Development Discussion Paper, U. S. A.

Grosman M. , 1972, "On the Concept of Health Capital and the Demand for Health", *The Journal of Political Econimics*, 80, pp. 223—255.

Mark. M. Pitt et al. , 1990, "Productivity, Health, and Inequality in the Intrahousehold Distribution of Food in Low-income Countries", *American Economic Review*, 72, pp. 1139—1156.

PRC MOH, 1998, *Research on National Health Services-An Analysis Report of the Second National Health Services Survey in 1998*, Unpublished documents ,Beijing, China.

Rati Ram, 1984, "Market Opportunities, Intrafamily Resource Allocation, and Sex-Specific Survival Rats: An Intercountry Extension", *American Economic Review*, 74, pp. 1080—1086.

Reuben Gronau, 1973, "The Intrafamily Allocation of Time: The Value of the Housewives' Time", *American Economic Review*, 63, pp. 634—651.

Rosenzweig M. and Schultz T. P. , 1982, "Market Opportunities, Genetic Endowments, and Intrafamily Resources Distribution: Child Survival in Rural India", *American Economic Review*, 72, pp. 803—815.

Rosenzweig. M and Schultz T. P. , 1984, "Market Opportunities, Genetic Endowments, and Intrafamily Resources Distribution: Reply", *American Economic Review*, 74, pp. 521—522.

Strauss J. and Duncan Thomas, 1998, "Health, Nutrition, and Economic Development", *Journal of Economic Literature*, 36, pp. 766—817.

Strauss J. et al. , 1993, "Gender and Life-Cycle Differentials in the Patterns and Determinants of Adult Health", *Journal of Human Resources*, Special Issue: Symposium on Investments in Women's Human Capital and Development, 28, pp. 791—837.

（原载《经济研究》2004 年第 7 期）

政策性负担、道德风险与预算软约束*

林毅夫　李志赟

（北京大学中国经济研究中心）

“预算软约束”是 Kornai(1980)在分析社会主义经济时所提出的一个概念，它描述的是社会主义经济中一个普遍存在的现象，即政府不能承诺不去解救亏损的国有企业，这些解救措施包括财政补贴、贷款支持等等。预算软约束会带来经济中很多的问题，比如企业经理的道德风险、银行的呆坏账、财政风险等。人们也越来越深刻地意识到，硬化企业的预算约束，已经成为解决社会主义和转轨经济中一系列问题的先决条件。

要想真正解决企业预算软约束问题，就必须对预算软约束形成的原因有正确的认识。对预算软约束形成的原因，曾经有一种流行观点，认为企业的公有制性质是形成预算软约束的原因。然而，很多转型国家的国有企业在进行了大规模私有化之后，这些企业的预算软约束问题并没有消失，有些甚至变得更严重了。可见，企业的预算软约束同企业的公有产权之间并没有必然的联系。

林毅夫等(1994，1997，1999)在一系列文章中，对转轨经济中国有企业的预算软约束问题进行了系统分析，认为国有企

---

* 作者感谢李永军、张鹏飞、盛柳刚、邢兆鹏同学在经济中心发展战略研究组的讨论会上对本文提出的意见，也感谢与会的其他同学对本文的讨论。

业所承担的“政策性负担”是形成企业预算软约束的根本原因，而剥离政策性负担则是硬化企业预算约束的关键条件。本文就是力图通过一个规范的模型来阐述这些思想。

文章的结构如下：第一部分文献综述；第二部分简要阐述了文章将要论证的关于预算软约束问题的主要思想；第三部分和第四部分是文章的理论模型部分，我们分别考察了政策性负担对国有企业和私有企业在预算软约束问题上的影响，并得到了一些具体结论；第五部分是对现实经济问题的解释和政策建议；第六部分是结论。

一、文 献 综 述

虽然关于“预算软约束”已经有很多的文献，并在一些问题上达成了共识，但是，到目前为止，理论界对产生预算软约束的原因和制度环境仍然存在着争论。对于预算软约束的文献，我们可以按照如下的逻辑链条来归纳：(1)形成预算软约束的制度因素→(2)政府或银行进行救助的动机→(3)预算软约束的后果(Kornai et al., 2002)。现有的文献都集中于分析从(2)到(3)的逻辑关系，并且对预算软约束的后果，已经形成了共识；但是，对于(1)预算软约束所产生的制度环境，实际也就是预算软约束产生的根本原因，文献中系统论述却非常少，并且对预算软约束产生的原因(1)及政府(银行)进行救助的具体动机(2)，仍然存在许多争论。

Kornai(1980)将预算软约束的起因归结为社会主义政府的“父爱主义”(paternalism)，这种解释现在看来是缺乏说服力的，因为在社会主义经济中并非每一个企业都存在预算软约束，而且资本主义市场经济中也存在预算软约束的情形，因此社会主义的父爱主义并不是产生预算软约束现象的充分条件，也不是必要条件。

另外一种曾经非常有影响的观点认为，公有产权是产生预算软约束的原因。李稻葵(Li，1992)认为，公有制可能是社会主义比资本主义更容易受预算软约束影响的原因。在他的模型中，公有制就意味着再融资的决策是政府(银行)和企业共同做出的，这会导致预算软约束。但是，在东欧和俄罗斯大规模私有化之后，预算软约束现象并没有消失，有不少企业从政府得到的补贴不减反增(World Bank，1996，2002)，这些事实都说明公有产权并不是造成预算软约束的根本原因。

Dewatripond 和 Maskin(1995)认为，社会主义经济之所以比资本主义经济更容易出现预算软约束现象，是因为前者是一个高度集中的计划经济，而后者则是一个高度分权的经济，在企业进行再融资时，后者的交易成本会更高，使得再融资变成"事后无效"的，从而能够硬化企业的预算约束。[1] 钱颖一和 Roland (Qian and Roland，1998)的文章也持类似观点：他们认为中国的经济改革之所以比东欧和原苏联要成功，一个重要原因是中国的行政结构相当于联邦制，由于各个地区之间投资于基础设施以吸引外资的竞争具有外部性，所以地区竞争会提高地方政府补贴亏损企业的机会成本，这就有利于硬化企业的预算约束。虽然分权化的确有可能硬化企业的预算软约束，但是，从我们下文的分析中可以看到，分权化在一定情况下同样可能恶化企业的预算软约束问题。

Segal(1998)对俄罗斯大规模私有化后出现的严重的预算软约束现象提供了一个解释。他认为垄断是造成预算软约束的原因：由于垄断企业不能实现完全的差别定价，所以垄断企业的利润带来的社会剩余少，政府为了实现这部分社会剩余，便对垄断企业进行补贴。他的分析显得非常牵强,因为他的结论只在局部均衡的情况下成立,从整个经济来讲,垄断会带来巨大的效率损失。

Boycko、Sheleifer 和 Vishny(1996)在解释俄罗斯的私有化问题时提出了一个解释预算软约束的思路。他们认为,政府官员往往倾向于让企业雇用冗员,因为企业雇用更多的工人对政府是有利的,为了让企业雇用更多的工人,政府就向企业提供补贴,这就形成了预算软约束。但是,他们在分析预算软约束问题时也存在局限:首先,雇用更多的工人并非预算软约束存在的唯一原因,不少新设立的高科技企业雇用的人员不多,但是也存在预算软约束的情形;其次,在他们的静态模型下,也难以得到更多有意义的推论。

二、主 要 思 想

现有的文献在预算软约束的制度原因上还存在许多争论。虽然任何一个单一的理论都不可能解释预算软约束所有方面的现象,但是,对于前社会主义经济和转型经济来讲,预算软约束的形成却有一些共同的原因。

林毅夫等(1994, 1997, 1999)系统阐述了转型经济中企业的预算软约束问题的观点,认为"政策性负担"是形成企业预算软约束问题的根本原因,企业的所有权性质与企业的预算软约束之间并不存在必然的因果关系。进一步,林毅夫等在一个更大的框架下分析了为什么转型经济中企业的"政策性负担"会普遍存在:这些国家都不同程度地推行着违背经济比较优势的赶超战略。下面我们以中国的经济现实为例,对上述思想进行简要的归纳。

中国的国有企业普遍承担着两方面的政策性负担:战略性政策负担和社会性政策负担。战略性政策负担,是指在传统的赶超战略的影响下,投资于我国不具备比较优势的资本密集型产业或产业区段所形成的负担;社会性政策负担,则是指由于国有企业承担过多的冗员和工人福利等社会性职能而形成的负担。这两方面的政策性负担,都是中国推行重工业优先发展战略的内生产物。

中国从20世纪50年代开始推行重工业优先发展的战略,而中国是一个资本非常稀缺、劳动力相对富余的经济,政府想要优先发展的资本密集型的重工业是同中国经济的比较优势相背离的,所以这些企业在开放、竞争的市场环境中缺乏自生能力(Lin, 2003)。为了实施重工业优先发展的战略,就必然会对经济进行扭曲,人为压低利率、汇率、原材料价格等以降低重工业企业的成本,并且给予市场垄断地位以提高产品价格;但是,当市场化改革开始后,经济中的要素和产品价格逐渐由市场竞争决定,失去了这些补贴和保护以后,重工业企业缺乏自生能力,在开放竞争的市场中无法盈利的问题就由隐性变为显性,这便形成了国有企业的战略性政策负担。另一方面,由于重工业是资本密集型的产业,它能够吸收的就业人口非常少,而中国却是一个劳动力富余的国家,为了解决社会就业问题,政府就会要求国有企业雇用过多的冗员②,并承担起一些企业所不应当承担的社会职能,这就形成了国有企业的社会性负担,它无疑也将增加国有企业经营的成本。③

政府对企业的政策性负担所造成的亏损负有责无旁贷的责任,政府为了让这些承担着政策性负担的国有企业继续生存,就必然对国有企业进行事前的保护或者补贴,但是由于信息不对称,政府无法确知政策性负担给企业带来的亏损是多少,也很难分清楚一个企业的亏损是政策性负担造成的还是由于企业自身管理不当或是企业经理人员的道德风险造成的，在激励不相容的情况下，企业经理人员会将各种亏损，包括政策性负担形成的亏损和道德风险、管理不当等造成的亏损都归咎于政策性负担，在政府无法分清楚这两种亏损的差别，而又不能推托对政策性负担所造成的亏损的责任时，就只好把企业的所有亏损的责任都负担起来，在企业的亏损形成后又给予事后的补贴，因此形成了企业的预算软约束。由于事后的保护或者补贴的可能性的存在，更加重了企业经理事前的道德风险问题。这样，在信息不对称和激励不相容的情况下，这种由于政策性负担带来的企业的预算软约束，会严重影响国有企业的经营效率和激励机制。

只要企业承担着政策性负担，就会引发企业的预算软约束。而企业是否背负政策性负担实际上同企业的所有制形式没有关系，所以在预算软约束与企业的所有制性质之间并不存在必然的联系。东欧与俄罗斯等国家的国有企业在大规模私有化之后，它们的政策性负担并没有剥离，而且私有化还会增加企业的讨价还价能力，所以预算软约束问题不但没有解决，政府补贴反而增加了，这些事实都可以由上面的理论来解释。

三、政策性负担与国有企业的预算软约束

（一）国有企业不承担政策性负担的基准模型

我们首先考虑国有企业不承担政策性负担的情况，目的是将这种基准情形同国有企业承担政策性负担的情况做比较。我们假定经济中有 N 家国有企业，这些企业都生产同一种产品，该产品的市场反需求函数为 $P(Q)$，Q 为产品的总供给量，反需求函数满足对任意的 $Q \geqslant 0$ 都有 $P'(Q) < 0$；假定每家企业的

成本函数都相同，成本函数为$C(q)=K+e(q)$，K为企业进行生产的固定成本，q为企业的产量，而$e(q)$代表国有企业经理付出努力的成本，对于任意的$q\geqslant 0$，我们有$e'(q)>0$，$e''(q)>0$，$e(0)=0$，$\bar{N}$为纳什-古诺市场自由进入均衡下，市场所能容纳的最大企业数量，为简化起见，假设$N\leqslant\bar{N}$；国有企业的利润为$\pi(q_i)=P(Q)\cdot q_i-e(q_i)-K$，其中$Q=Q_{-i}+q^i$，$Q_{-i}$为除企业$i$外其他$N-1$家企业的产量。我们假设，当国有企业不承担政策性负担时，政府与国有企业经理间的信息是对称的。④

在如上的模型设定下，我们可以得到当市场达到纳什-古诺均衡时，应该满足如下条件：

(1) 企业的利润最大化条件，即$q_i\in\arg\max p(Q_{-i}+q_i)\cdot q_i-K-e(q_i)$；

(2) 市场均衡条件，即$p(Q)=p(Q_{-i}+q_i)$；

(3) 个人参与条件，即$w-e(q_i)=0$，$i=1, 2, \cdots, N$。其中w表示政府付给国有企业经理的工资。根据Novshek (1980)的结果，上述问题的解一定存在，我们假设上述问题的均衡解为$\{q^*(N), w^*(N)\}$，政府获得的企业利润为$\pi^*(N)$，国有企业经理获得工资$w^*(N)=e[q^*(N)]$。⑤一般情况下，企业的边际收益曲线斜率总是比需求曲线要陡，那么就有条件$p'+p''\cdot q<0$成立，由此我们可以得到如下引理：

引理一：如果$N^*<N^{**}\leqslant\bar{N}$，那么在纳什-古诺市场均衡下就有$\pi^*>\pi^{**}$和$q^*>q^{**}$。即如果市场中的企业数量增加，那么市场中企业的均衡利润和均衡产出都会下降。也就是说，市场竞争程度的增加会使企业的利润水平降低。⑥后面我们将分析，市场竞争程度增加对企业预算软约束问题的影响。

(二) 政策性负担与国有企业的预算软约束

上面的基准模型是一种理想情况，现实中我们看到更多的是，国有企业承担着各种各样的政策性负担。下面我们将引入政策性负担，在一个动态博弈的框架下分析政策性负担所带来的国有企业的预算软约束问题。

我们用 L 表示国有企业承担的政策性负担，用 π 表示没有政策性负担时国有企业的利润，则企业承担政策性负担后的利润为 $\Pi=\pi-L$。我们用 $B(L)$ 表示企业承担政策性负担 L 给政府带来的好处，假设一般情况下有 $B(L)>L$，也就是说除了经济上的利益，政策性负担还带给政府其他的一些好处，比如建立了政府官员可以炫耀政绩的资金密集的先进产业，或是增加就业促进了社会的稳定等。假设政府向国有企业的经理支付一个固定的报酬 w^*，国有企业经理的支付函数为 $U_S=w^*-e(q)$，在没有补贴情况下政府的支付函数为 $U_G=B(L)+\Pi=B(L)+\pi(q)-L$。

下面我们来考虑当国有企业承担政策性负担时，政府与企业之间的如下博弈：

博弈一：

时期一，在国有企业生产之前，政府选择是否让国有企业承担政策性负担 L；

时期二，国有企业经理观察到企业是否承担政策性负担 L，然后选择自己的努力程度 $e(q)$进行生产；

时期三，生产完成，政府观察到国有企业的利润情况，然后决定是否补贴及补贴多少。

对于上述博弈需要进行几点说明。首先是政府的补贴策略，假设政府只有在企业生产亏损的情况下才会考虑是否补贴；并且，如果政府决定对企业进行补贴，则补贴额正好等于企业的亏损额，也就是说补贴额 $S=|\pi(q)-L|$；此外，政府所承担的补贴成本为 $\theta\cdot S$，其中 $\theta\in(0,1]$，也就是说，有可能政府只承

担部分的补贴成本。[7]其次是企业经理的报酬问题，我们假设只有在生产完成之后，并对生产的启动资金 K 和企业的政策性负担 L 进行支付后，才支付企业经理的报酬 w^*；也就是说，如果在时期三企业亏损并且政府不提供补贴，经理便拿不到报酬，在这种情况下企业倒闭，政府获得的支付为 0。第三是模型的信息结构，如果存在政策性负担，企业生产增加了一些不确定因素，这会带来信息不对称问题，假设在企业的生产过程中（时期二），政府观察不到、从而无法控制企业家的努力程度。最后，就是政府和企业经理的保留支付问题，如果政府不让企业承担政策性负担，则政府的保留支付为 π^*，国有企业经理的保留支付为 0。我们假设在相同的支付水平下，政府总是倾向于让企业承担政策性负担，而企业经理则总是倾向于尽量少地付出努力。我们采用逆推法求解上面的博弈，可得到如下的命题：

命题一，上述博弈的子博弈精练均衡为：

(1) 如果 $\pi^* < B(L)$，则国有企业经理选择生产产量 $q_L = \left\{q \middle| \pi(q) = L - \frac{1}{\theta}[B(L) - \pi^*]\right\}$，企业亏损，政府选择让国有企业承担政策性负担 L，并对国有企业补贴 $\frac{1}{\theta}[B(L) - \pi^*]$；

(2) 如果 $\pi^* \geqslant B(L)$，则国企经理选择生产产量 $q_H = \{q \mid \pi(q) = L + [\pi^* - B(L)]\}$，企业不亏损，政府选择让国有企业承担政策性负担 L，并且不补贴国有企业。

从命题一我们可以看到，π^* 与 $B(L)$ 的相对大小决定了承担政策性负担的国有企业是否盈利，进而决定了政府是否对国有企业进行补贴。我们将上述命题的(1)部分描述为国有企业的“预算软约束”结果，因为在这种情况下企业亏损，并且政府在事后对国有企业进行了补贴。从命题一我们可以清楚地看到，政策性负担是如何影响国有企业的生产行为，以及承担着政策性负担的企业是如何获得生存条件的。

首先,政策性负担会影响国有企业的生产效率,这从命题一中国有企业经理所选择的产量就可以看到。很多实证研究都发现,国有企业的生产效率比私有企业要低,文献中往往将其归结于国有企业的公有性质,但是从这里的分析可以看到一点,国有企业承担政策性负担也是导致国有企业缺乏效率的一个重要原因。

其次,由于承担政策性负担 L 必然增加国有企业的成本,所以这些企业在竞争性的市场环境中没有"自生能力"。命题一告诉我们,承担政策性负担的国有企业要获得生存的条件,可以依赖两条途径:一是依靠政府补贴来救助亏损的国有企业,这就是命题一的(1)部分描述的情形;二是维护国有企业的垄断地位,限制市场进入以获取垄断利润,这就是命题一的(2)部分描述的情形。实际上,从一种更广义的概念来讲,维护国企的垄断地位实际也是一种补贴,这是以损失社会效率为代价向国有企业提供的一种隐性补贴。

对命题一进行进一步分析,我们可以得到如下的一些推论:

推论一,当国有企业承担政策性负担时,国企经理选择生产的产量 q 总是小于最优产量 q^*。

推论一实际上说明了在信息不对称情况下,政策性负担必然会带来企业经理的道德风险问题,企业经理会降低自己的努力程度,从而降低国有企业的生产效率,增加社会的生产者和消费者剩余损失(如图 1 所示)。在我们的模型中,政策性负担是导致国有企业低效率的原因,因为它引发了国有企业经理的道德风险问题。实质上,从命题一的临界值为 $B(L)$ 而非 L 这点,我们就已经看到了政策性负担对国有企业效率的影响,因为当 $L < \pi^* < B(L)$ 时,即使国有企业承担政策性负担,但只要国企经理选择最优产量,国有企业是能够实现盈利的;但是,由于

承担政策性负担，国有企业经理却没有动机去实现企业盈利，因为他从政府事后的补贴中能够获得更高的支付水平。

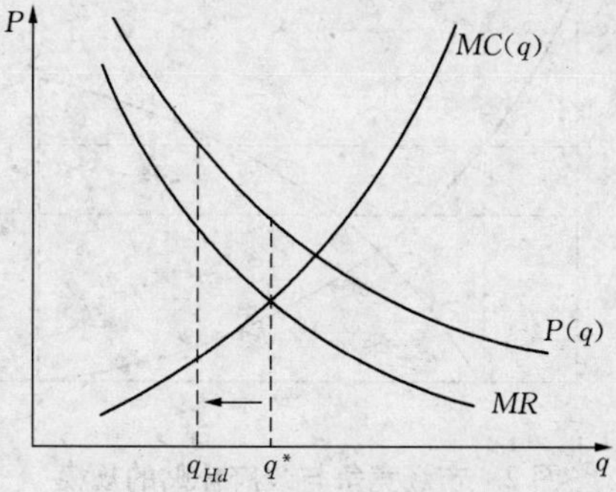

图 1　政策性负担与道德风险

推论二，当国有企业承担政策性负担时，市场竞争程度的增加会使国有企业更容易出现亏损，并使政府补贴的成本增加。

推论二实际上说明了，市场竞争程度的增加会使国有企业的预算软约束问题显性化，并增加政府补贴的成本（如图 2 所示）。中国经济改革的历程能够很好地反映推论二的结论：改革开放以前，国有企业普遍盈利，改革开放以来，中小型国有企业的亏损面越来越大，很大程度上就是因为它们所处的行业市场进入门槛低，大量非公有制经济进入加剧了竞争程度。由于承担着政策性负担，并由此而带来国有企业的低效率（推论一），所以中小型国企的亏损也就在所难免，并且亏损面越来越大，政府对这些企业的补贴也不断增加，这就带来了财政和金融体系的风险。由推论二，我们同样可以理解为什么中央政府对国有企业改革会采取“抓大放小”的战略，因为全国国有企业几乎所有的利润都是由处于垄断行业的大型国有企业创造的⑧，中小国企普遍亏损，政府便有动机甩掉中小国有企业这个包袱。⑨

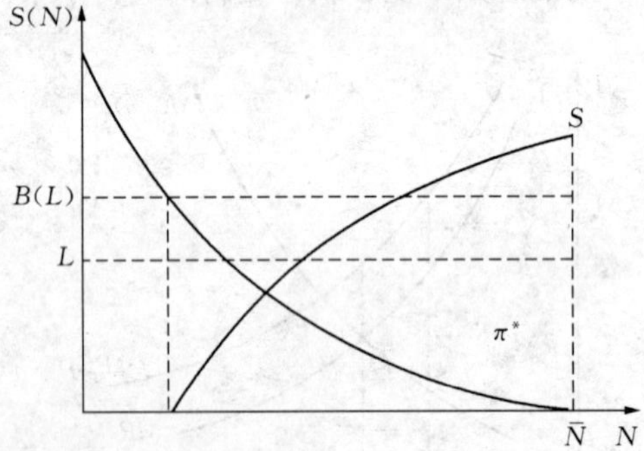

图 2　市场竞争与政府补贴的规模

推论三，当国有企业承担政策性负担并亏损时，θ 越低则政府补贴越多，国有企业的产量偏离（偏低）最优产量 q^* 的幅度也越大。

推论三告诉我们，如果政府承担的补贴成本的比率越低，那么它能够承担的补贴规模就越大。国有企业经理就有动机扩大企业的亏损额，以使得企业能够从政府那里得到更多的补贴。推论三的结论反映了中国经济的特点：地方政府都有很强的动机去干预金融机构，要求这些金融机构向地方性的国有企业提供贷款，而一旦这些贷款形成呆坏账，则这种贷款损失的成本却大多是由中央政府来承担；中国国有商业银行的经营者也反映，自从 1994 年银行商业化改革以来，国有商业银行受到中央政府的干预已经越来越少，而他们所受到的干预主要来自地方政府。从推论三我们可以推断，当市场竞争程度足够高时，如果实行严厉的金融财政政策，地方政府的财政或金融约束越硬（θ 越高），那么地方国有企业的预算约束也越硬（得到的补贴越少），国有企业的效率也越高。

推论四，当国有企业承担政策性负担时，如果 $B(L)$ 越大，则国有企业的产量偏离（偏低）最优产量 q^* 的幅度就越大。

推论四和推论三道理相似，只不过它适用的范围更广（并不要求国有企业亏损）。如果政府从企业承担政策性负担中得到的好处越多，则政府愿意支付的补贴额也就越大，那么国有企业经理就有动机更少地付出努力，以分享政府从政策性负担中得到的好处。

（三）国有企业的政策性负担与生产自主权的限制

从上面的模型我们看到，如果国有企业经理具有完全的生产自主权（Autonomy），则在国有企业承担政策性负担并存在信息不对称问题的条件下，国有企业经理会出现严重的道德风险问题，在上面的模型中表现为产量 q 低于企业利润最大化的产量 q^*，经理的努力程度不足。但在转型前高度计划的社会主义经济中，我们常常看到国有企业经理并不拥有生产自主权，政府往往通过计划或者行政手段去干预企业生产，剥夺企业经理在人、财、物、产、供、销上的自主权，这当中产量配额就是一个常见的干预手段。一种制度的存在往往都有它的合理性，下面我们就将对博弈一进行调整，以考察产量配额是如何影响模型的均衡结果的。我们将会发现在社会主义或转型经济中剥夺企业的生产自主权，往往是一种次优的制度安排，具有存在的合理性。

我们对博弈一进行调整，我们假设在时期一政府规定国有企业经理必须完成生产配额 $\underline{q}$，为简化起见，我们假设 $\underline{q}$ 在国有企业经理能够承受的范围内 $[e(\underline{q}) \leqslant w^*]$；在时期三生产完成，如果企业经理没有完成生产配额 $(q < \underline{q})$，则国有企业经理被政府撤职，国有企业经理的支付为 $U_S = -e(q)$。模型的其他设定不变，求解这个博弈我们可以得到如下的命题：

命题二,在政府规定国企的生产配额$\underline{q}$的情况下,调整后的博弈一的子博弈精练均衡为:

(1) 如果 $\pi^* \geqslant B(L)$,则国企经理选择生产产量 $q = \max\{Q_H, \underline{q}\}$;如果 $\pi^* < B(L)$,则国有企业经理选择生产产量 $q = \max\{q_L, \underline{q}\}$;

(2) 政府选择让国有企业承担政策性负担 L,如果国有企业亏损,则对企业进行补贴。

由命题二的结果我们看到,在任何一种情况下,国有企业生产的产量都不会比博弈一的结果低,政府得到的支付也不会比博弈一更少。当 $\underline{q} > q_H, q_L$ 时,国有企业的均衡产量将高于博弈一的水平,企业效率的损失将减小,而政府得到的支付将增加。所以,当国有企业承担政策性负担时,政府通过规定一个合理的生产配额,剥夺国有企业经理部分的生产自主权,能够有效地缓解国有企业经理的道德风险问题,减小国有企业的效率损失,增加社会福利水平,并提高政府所获得的支付。

从前面的分析我们知道,当国有企业承担政策性负担时,单纯的"放权"会引起国有企业经理严重的道德风险问题,但当我们回顾中国国有企业的改革历程时,我们会发现国企改革的"放权"是与"让利"联系在一起的。下面我们将在上面的模型框架下对"放权让利"这种改革方式进行一个简单的解释,以说明这种改革方式作为一种次优安排存在的合理性。当政府决定让利时,比如国有企业经理可以获得企业利润的一个份额,比如,这时国有企业经理的支付就变为$U_S = w^* + \alpha \cdot \pi(q) - e(q)$,这就给企业经理提供了一个付出努力的激励。如图 3 所示,在单纯只"放权"的情况下,国有企业经理会选择 q_H 或 q_L,而在放权让利的情况下,如果$U_S(q') > U(q_{H/L})$,则国有企业经理会选择 q',在这种情况下国有企业的效率提高,社会福利的损失减小了。

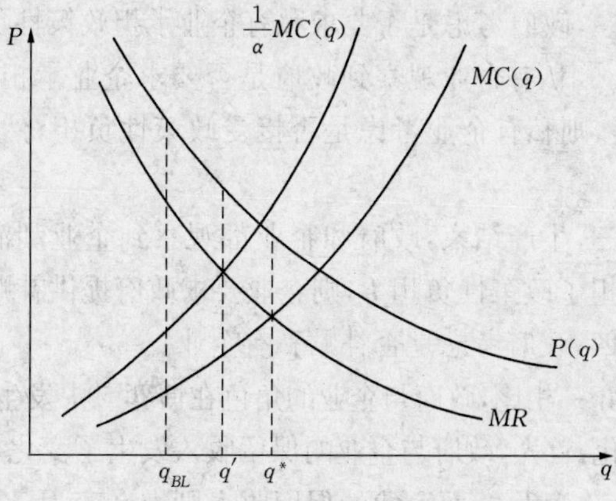

图 3　政策性负担与“放权让利”

四、私有化、政策性负担与预算软约束

人们曾经普遍认为，社会主义和转型经济中企业的预算软约束问题主要归结于这些企业的公有制性质，然而转型国家的经验却告诉我们这个命题并不成立。在这里，我们将考虑私有化后，政策性负担与私有企业预算软约束的关系。根据 Grossman 和 Hart(1986)，企业所有权的差别就在于企业控制权的差别，比如对民营企业来讲，企业的所有者就拥有企业的剩余索取权和企业的生产控制权。所以，国有企业一旦私有化，企业的这些控制权也就从政府转移到私人手中，政府不再拥有企业的控制权，企业利润不归政府所有，如果政府想继续让私有化后的企业承担政策性负担，就必然要同企业的所有者进行谈判，以决定事后补贴的规模。伴随着企业产权的转移，博弈双方在博弈中的地位也发生了变化，对博弈一进行部分的调整，我们来考察私有化后政府与企业间的如下博弈：

博弈二：

时期一，政府考虑是否要求私有企业承担政策性负担 L；

时期二，私有企业观察到政府是否要求企业承担政策性负担 L，如是，则私有企业考虑是否接受政策性负担，然后企业进行生产；

时期三，生产结束，政府和企业都观察到企业利润；如果私有企业承担了政策性负担 L，则企业要求政府提供补贴 S；

时期四，政府考虑是否补贴私有企业。

同博弈一相比，政府与企业的角色在博弈二中发生了以下几方面的变化：首先，政府与企业的保留收入发生了变化，政府的保留收入由 π^* 变为 0，而企业的保留收入则由 0 变为 π^*；其次，私有企业的所有者对企业拥有控制权，企业可以选择生产多少，也可以选择是否承担政策性负担 L；第三，补贴额不再是亏多少补多少，而是企业向政府要求一个补贴额 S，政府考虑是否接受。模型的其他设定同博弈一，求解博弈二可以得到如下的命题：

命题三，博弈二的子博弈精练均衡为：

(1) 如果 $\pi^* < \frac{1}{\theta}B(L)$，则政府选择要求私有企业承担政策性负担 L，私有企业选择接受政策性负担 L，并选择生产产量 $q=\{q \mid \pi(q) = \min(L, \pi^*)\}$，政府对私有企业补贴 $S = \frac{1}{\theta}B(L)$；

(2) 如果 $\pi^* \geqslant \frac{1}{\theta}B(L)$，则政府选择要求私有企业承担政策性负担 L，私有企业选择不接受政策性负担 L，并选择生产产量 $q=q^*$。

从命题三我们看到，如果私有企业承担政策性负担，那么必然有政府对企业事后的补贴，也就是存在企业的预算软约束问题。我们将命题一与命题三的预算软约束结果列于表 1，从中可以看到承担政策性负担的情况下，国有企业与私有企业的预算软约束问题的不同。

表1　承担政策性负担的国有企业和私有企业的预算软约束

	命题一(国有企业)	命题三(私有企业)
预算软约束的产生条件	$\pi^* < B(L)$	$\pi^* < \frac{1}{\theta}B(L)$
政府的补贴额	$\frac{1}{\theta}[B(L)-\pi^*]$	$\frac{1}{\theta}B(L)$
企业选择的产量	$q_L = \left\{q \middle\vert \pi(q) = L-\frac{1}{\theta}[B(L)-\pi^*]\right\}$	$q=\{q \mid \pi(q) = \min(L,\ \pi^*)\}$

从表1的比较我们可以得到如下一些结论：(1)如果都承担政策性负担L，并且$\theta \in (0,\ 1)$，那么在其他条件都相同的情况下，私有企业比国有企业更容易产生预算软约束问题，比如当条件$B(L) < \pi^* < \frac{1}{\theta}B(L)$成立时，国有企业不会产生预算软约束，而私有企业则会产生预算软约束问题；(2)当$\pi^* > 0$，并且国有企业和私有企业都有预算软约束问题时，政府需要向私有企业提供更多的补贴，这是因为产权转移后企业经理的保留收入发生了变化的缘故，这一点实际上可以解释为什么俄罗斯的国有企业在私有化之后，从政府得到的补贴反而增加了；(3)当国有企业和私有企业都有预算软约束问题时，在其他条件都相同的情况下，国有企业的产量比私有企业更低，也就是说国有企业的效率损失比私有企业更大。

五、对现实问题的解释及政策建议

前面两部分对林毅夫等(1994, 1997, 1999)提出的关于政策性负担与预算软约束关系的理论进行了模型化，并在一些方面进行了扩展，模型的结果有助于加深我们对社会主义和转轨经济现实问题的理解。下面我们将对模型的构造和关键假设做进一步的说明，对现实经济问题做出解释，并提出相应的政策建议。

首先，模型关于政策性负担和预算软约束的结果来自于两个关键的假设。一是政府能够从企业的政策性负担中获得额外的好处，或者说如果企业不承担政策性负担政府将蒙受更大的损失，在模型设定中也就表现为 $B(L)-L>0$，这样一来政府就会有动机让企业承担政策性负担。二是政府可能只承担企业补贴的部分成本，在模型假设中就表现为 $\theta\in(0,1)$，在这种情况下，即使前面的假设 $B(L)-L>0$ 不成立，政府也有动机让企业承担政策性负担，因为政策性负担给政府带来的好处有可能大于政府补贴的成本。在这两个假设下，政府就一直有动机让企业承担政策性负担，而政策性负担则会带来企业的道德风险和预算软约束问题，这便会损失经济的效率(命题一、三)。政策性负担与预算软约束问题在国有企业与私有企业所表现出来的不同，主要来自于产权转移改变了政府与企业在博弈中的相对地位，私有企业具有更高的保留支付水平，也具有更大的企业生产的控制权，这都使得政府让私有企业承担政策性负担时处于更不利的地位(命题三)。

下面我们就利用模型的结果来对社会主义和转轨经济中的一些现实问题进行分析。首先，为什么在计划经济时代，企业基本上没有任何生产的自主权？从命题一和命题二的结论我们可以知道，当企业承担着政策性负担时，企业经理完全的自主权会带来严重的道德风险问题，而剥夺企业的自主权，比如采用产量配额手段，则是一种次优的制度安排，它在一定的条件下能够减少企业的效率损失，保证企业经理最低的努力程度。其次，为什么在中国国有企业的改革过程中，政府对国有企业的补贴经历了从财政补贴到银行贷款再到股市融资的一个过程？实际上对于政府而言，这是因为财政对政府的财务约束是最硬的，银行贷款次之，股市融资的财务约束最软（即 θ 最低），财政是政府拿自己的钱去补贴，而银行贷款则是拿别人的钱去补贴，而股市融资亦然，并且股权融资的约束比债权融资更软。第三，为什么俄罗斯在对国有企业大规模私有化之后，政府向企业提供的补贴反而更多了？从命题三的结论我们看到，如果私有企业承担政策性负担，则私有企业从政府获得的补贴要比国有企业多，这可以解释俄罗斯经济的现象。那为什么俄罗斯政府不剥离私有化后企业的政策性负担呢？这是因为在“大爆炸”式的改革措施下，企业的政策性负担并未被剥离，或者不具备剥离企业政策性负担的条件，即 $B(L)-L>0$ 的条件仍然成立。[10]

最后，我们对上述模型结果的政策含义进行讨论。实际上从对转轨经济的研究中，理论界对“硬化企业的预算约束”的必要性已经形成了共识，但是，如何硬化企业的预算约束大家还存在很多的争论，因为大家对预算软约束的原因各执一词。在经济由计划经济向市场经济转轨的过程中，市场的竞争程度必然越来越激烈，而从命题一的结论我们可以知道，在这种情况下，企业的政策性负担必然带来企业的预算软约束问题，所以，要硬化企业的预算软约束问题就必须剥离企业的政策性负担。但是，如何剥离企业的政策性负担？从前面的分析可以看到，关键要从两个方面入手：

一是要降低企业承担政策性负担给政府带来的好处 $B(L)$，或者增加政府让企业承担政策性负担的成本。$B(L)$ 在我们的模型中是外生的，但显而易见的是，$B(L)$ 的大小也受外部经济制度因素的影响，比如，如果社会充分就业或者具有完善的社会保障系统，那么，政府让企业保持大量冗员的必要性就降低，$B(L)$就会比较小，同时如果全社会都清楚地知道赶超的代价，政府放弃了赶超的思想，那么$B(L)$也会减小。

二是要硬化政府的财务约束，对政府行为实施比较紧的金融和财政政策，目的在于让政府承担它补贴企业的全部成本($\theta = 1$)，比如，减少政府对金融体系的干预，实现金融机构独立的商业化经营，以免后者成为政府补贴国有企业的工具。另外，加入WTO给金融体系带来的竞争压力也有助于金融体系的商业化改革。

当如上两方面的条件具备时，政府就会有积极性去消除企业的政策性负担，而一旦政策性负担消除，政府就不再对企业的亏损负有责任，企业的预算约束也就能够硬化，经济效率可以提高。从上面的分析我们可以看到，为什么俄罗斯的私有化改革没有硬化企业的预算约束，因为它没有剥离企业政策性负担，私有化只会使政府的补贴增加，财政金融压力增大，进而导致严重的通货膨胀和金融风险。

政策性负担是转型国家中企业预算软约束存在的根本原因，起因于政府的赶超思想，所以，我国若要取消现有的企业的预算软约束，并且避免造成新企业的预算软约束问题，首先必须放弃赶超的思想。其次，要对症下药剥离国有企业现在承担的政策性负担。从近期来看，就是要加快健全社会保障系统，加快发展劳动密集型的中小企业，以减轻剥离企业的社会性政策型负担给政府和社会带来的压力；另一方面，就是要减少政府对金融机构和金融体系的干预，硬化政府的财务约束，降低金融体系的风险，同时要创造条件让资本过度密集的企业利用国际资本或是转产到劳动力比较密集的产业以解决国有企业的自生能力问题，消除国有企业的战略性政策负担。

六、结　　论

本文在一个动态博弈的框架下，对林毅夫等(1994，1997，1999)所提出的关于政策性负担与企业预算软约束的理论进行了模型化。文章的主要结论包括：在信息不对称、激励不相容的情况下，政策性负担必然会带来企业的道德风险问题，降低企业的效率；进一步，如果市场竞争程度足够充分，则政策性负担必然带来企业的预算软约束问题，也就是说，在这样的情况下前者是后者的充分条件；预算软约束问题与企业的公有制性质无关，相反在企业承担政策性负担的情况下，私有企业会比国有企业更容易产生预算软约束问题，并且有激励向政府要更多的补贴；当国有企业承担政策性负担时，剥夺国有企业经理的生产自主权，比如产量配额规定，往往是一种次优的制度安排，这解释了改革前为何国有企业厂长、经理的人、财、物、产、供、销的自主权都被剥夺的原因。进一步，在本文的逻辑框架下我们提出了相应的政策建议：在经济转轨过程中，市场化程度不断加深的情况下，要想硬化国有企业的预算软约束，就必须剥离国有企业的政策性负担，而要剥离国有企业的政策性负担，就必须放弃赶超思想，降低政府从让国有企业承担政策性负担中获得的好处，并硬化政府本身的财务约束。

注　释

① Dewatripond 和 Maskin(1995)最重要的贡献并不在于他们对预算软约束原因的解释，而在于他们从动态承诺不一致的角度为分析预算软约束问题提供了一个一般性的分析框架。

② 比如，河南民营的钢铁企业海鑫集团年产钢 200 多万吨，企业职工 4000多人，而国有钢铁企业包钢年产钢 500 多万吨，企业职工却高达

12 万(《财经》2003 年第 15 期,第 104 页)。

③ 许多大型的国有企业同时承担了战略性政策负担和社会性政策负担,但是许多劳动密集型产业的国有企业只承担了社会性政策负担。

④ 做这个假定只具有相对含义,因为同后面将要讨论的企业承担政策性负担,从而造成扭曲的情况相比,这种情况下信息不对称的程度应该更低,所以在基准模型中,我们假设信息是对称的。

⑤ 如无特殊说明,我们在下文中都将 N 省略,而简单地表示为 q^{*}, w^{*} 等等。

⑥ 需要本文各推论和命题的具体证明过程的读者可以同作者联系,Email:zhiyunlee@china.com.cn。实质上,这一部分的模型设定与结论同样适用于私有企业的情况,只需要对假设做一点调整即可。

⑦ 这一假设尤其反映中国的情况,地方政府往往会强迫金融机构对本地国有企业提供优惠贷款,而一旦这些成本形成呆坏账,所带来的成本却往往由中央政府和整个经济来承担。

⑧ 2001 年,我国0.9万户国有大型和特大型企业的资产总额为109643.8亿元,户均资产规模 12.2 亿元,占全部国有企业资产总额的 65.8%,实现利润 2731 亿元,占全部国有企业利润总额的97.1%。2001 年,国有大型企业前 50 家的资产总额、利润总额、销售收入和上缴税金占全部国有企业的比重分别为 37%、73.6%、34.4%和 44.7%(张卓元、路遥,2003)。

⑨ 在我们的模型中,"政府"实质上更相当于地方政府,因为它们不承担补贴的全部成本。我们并没有将补贴成本的最终承担者——中央政府或财政部——的行为纳入分析,所以仅仅从现有的模型,我们得不出政府想"甩包袱"的结论。

⑩ 例如,由于重型军工产业的存在才使俄罗斯继续成为世界军事强国,而许多私有化后的企业继续雇用大量冗员是保持社会稳定所必需的。

参考文献

林毅夫、蔡昉、李周,1994(1999):《中国的奇迹:发展战略与经济改革》,上海三联书店、上海人民出版社(1999 年增订版)。

林毅夫、蔡昉、李周,1997:《充分信息与国有企业改革》,上海三联书店、上海人民出版社。

林毅夫,刘培林,2003:《何以加速增长,唯解自生难题》,北京大学中国经济研究中心工作论文。

张卓元、路遥,2003:《积极推进国有企业改革》,《财经论丛》第 1 期。

Boycko, Maxim, Sheleifer, Andrei and Vishny, Robert, 1996, "A Theory of Privatization", *The Economic Journal*, 106, pp. 309—319.

Dewatripont, Mathias and Eric Maskin, 1995, "Credit and Efficiency in Centralized and Decentralized Economies", *Review of Economic Studies*, 62(4), pp. 541—55.

Grossman, Sanford and Hart, Oliver, 1986, "The Costs and Benefits of Ownership: A Theory of Vertical and Lateral Integration", *Journal of Political Economy*, 94(4), pp. 691—719.

Kornai, Janos, 1980, *Economics of Shortage*, Amsterdam: North-Holland.

Kornai, Janos, Maskin, Eric and Roland, Gerard, 2002, "Understanding the Soft Budget Constraint", Working Paper, UC Berkeley.

Li, Daokui, 1992, "Public Ownership as the Cause of a Soft Budget Constraint", Mimeo, Harvard University.

Lin, Justin Yifu; Cai, Fang and Li, Zhou. 1998, "Competition, Policy Burdens, and State-Owned Enterprise Reform", *American Economic Review*, 88(2), pp. 422—27.

Lin, Justin Yifu and Tan, Guofu, 1999, "Policy Burdens, Accountability and Soft Budget Constraint", *American Economic Review*, 89(2), pp. 426—31.

Lin, Justin Yifu, 2003, "Development Strategy and Economic Convergence", *Economic Development and Cultural Change*, 51(2), pp. 277—308.

Novshek, William, 1980, "Cournot Equilibrium with Free Entry",

Review of Economic Studies, XLVII, pp. 473—486.

Qian, Yingyi and Gerard Roland. 1998. "Federalism and Soft Budget Constraint", *American Economic Review*, 88(5), pp. 1143—1162.

Roland, Gerard, 2000, *Transition and Economics*, (Ch. 9), MIT Press.

Segal ,Ilya R. , 1998, "Monopoly and Soft Budget Constraint", *Rand Journal of Economics*, 29(3), pp. 596—609.

World Bank, 1996, *World Development Report 1996*, *From Plan to Market*, Oxford: Oxford University Press.

World Bank, 2002, *Transition: The First Ten Years*, *Analysis and Lessons for Eastern Europe and the Former Soviet Union*, Washington, DC: World Bank.

（原载《经济研究》2004 年第 2 期）

注资与国有银行改革：一个金融政治经济学的视角*

张　杰

（中国人民大学中国财政金融政策研究中心）

一、引　言

中国国有银行的改革又面临着一个重要而敏感的时刻。2003 年末，国家悄然为四大国有银行中据说是绩效较好的两家（中国银行和中国建设银行）注入了 450 亿美元（约合 3800 亿元人民币）的资本，这是继 1998 年国家向四大国有银行注入 2700亿元人民币（约合 326 亿美元）资本金之后的又一次注资行动。和上一次注资相比，此次注资行动使用了罕见的外汇储备方式（上一次是发行特别国债）并用美元直接注资，而且专门成立了一家国有金融投资公司（中央汇金投资有限责任公司）代表国务院行使出资人权利。毫无疑问，这是自 1979

* 本文完稿后，其主要内容曾先后在中国社会科学院金融研究所和山东大学经济学院举办的学术论坛上做过介绍，感谢李扬教授颇具启发性和建设性的评论以及其他许多学者的有益讨论，但文责自负。此项研究得到国家教育部“高等学校优秀青年教师教学科研奖励计划（TRAPOYT）”以及教育部人文社会科学研究重大项目（02JAZD790009）专项资金的资助。

年中国经济体制改革以来国家在金融领域推行的最为“昂贵”的一次改革行动。

平心而论，对于资本金长期严重亏欠的国有银行而言，国家的此次注资行动实属寻常，从某种意义上讲，更是天经地义。从银行业的演进过程看，政府通过注资（还有其他方式）对有问题的银行实施救助也属常态。虽然近十余年来各国政府（包括成熟市场经济国家的政府）不同程度地经受着一些银行“大而不倒”现象的困扰，采取救助行动的频率和成本有增加趋势，但迄今对于一些主要国家的银行体系，救助并没有演变成为银行经营者的普遍心理依赖。既然如此，我们显然没有必要过于关注此次注资行动，它只不过是中国长期制度变迁过程已经经历和正在经历着的众多改革故事中的一个故事而已。

问题在于，中国的国有银行与其他国家特别是成熟市场经济国家的银行相比有着太多的不同。它有着独特的演进逻辑与效用函数，尤其是其资本结构已被证明是相当特殊的（张杰，2003a）。它处在一个频繁变动与调整的社会经济环境中，与政府的利害关系牵扯极深且表现得相当复杂。由此决定了国家对于国有银行的注资就不是一种简单的救助和资本结构的修复，而具有更深层次的政治经济学含义。

本文的结构安排如下：第二部分讨论国有银行注资的背景并回顾相关文献；第三部分考察国有银行存在的经济、法律与金融需求基础；第四部分阐发一种银行制度弱相关观点并对国有银行与一般商业银行出资人获取红利的方式进行比较分析；第五部分揭示无形资产这个被巴塞尔协议和一些国家金融监管当局剔除的核心资本要素对于中国国有银行的重要性；最后，在第六部分给出全文的结论。

二、背景与文献

在市场经济体制中,银行资本的数量和资本账户的构成大致由监督规则与市场力量共同决定(Rose, 1996, p. 527)。近年来的大多数研究结果表明,从长期看,市场力量在决定银行所必须持有的资本数量与类型方面可能比政府监管更为重要。但自 20 世纪 80 年代以来,随着以巴塞尔协议为代表的最低资本金要求的提出与多数市场经济国家银行业的逐步遵从,政府监管对一国银行资本金要求的重要性几乎与市场力量等量齐观。而在此之前,政府监管者只能以道义劝告的方式让银行增加资本以满足事先设定的标准(Gart, 1994, p. 118)。各国政府之所以普遍倾向于对银行资本施以更为严格的监管,其理由则如标准的银行理论告诉我们的那样,银行的较高资本水平可以抑制其道德风险,同时降低破产倒闭的可能性(Diamond, 1984; Mishkin, 2001, p. 225)。[①] 尽管如此,在市场经济国家,政府对银行资本问题的直接介入仍是相当谨慎的。世界银行(2001)的研究结果揭示出,政府之所以采取谨慎态度,是因为许多国家的经验表明,政府对银行重组的注资几乎都错失了建立有效激励机制以鼓励银行审慎其未来行为的重要机会。

在转型经济国家的银行业重组过程中,针对国有银行的注资行动十分普遍。经验研究结果表明,尽管快速步入市场经济轨道和实现银行的市场化转型是绝大多数发展中国家特别是转型经济国家的一种长期期望,但剧变式的银行私有化和市场化很难行得通。可是,通过政府的注资与刻意推动来使国内银行业特别是政府银行业达到巴塞尔协议标准的要求,从而得到国际社会的普遍认可(如更高档次的评级)已经成为这些国家政府和银行业界竞相追逐的改革时尚，并在很大程度上左右着银行改革决策者的思维倾向。这种所谓的“巴塞尔协议约束效应”已被证明在许多国家的后果是灾难性的。银行账面指标的短期和静态达标固然诱人且往往可以短期见效，但由此造成的成本则会严重影响长期的银行改革过程以及社会经济对整体改革的信心。正是在这种意义上，世界银行才反复提醒，保留部分银行的国有制在经济转型进程中可以起到“缓冲垫”的作用（World Bank，2001）。

中国银行业特别是国有银行的改革一开始关注的并不是银行的资本金问题，政府对资本金问题（还有不良债权问题）的真正关注是1997年东南亚金融危机以后的事情。在此之前银行改革基本上着眼于内部结构与组织体系的调整，且围绕着政府对银行实施更加有效的控制从而服务于整体经济的转型与增长。1997年以前的国有银行改革虽然也不时有模仿市场经济国家银行体制的成分，但从总体上讲是独立行事的，从而形成了中国特有的国有银行制度。1997年以后，国有银行的改革开始凸显出“他人诱导”的色彩。虽然巴塞尔协议对于中国银行业界和决策层来说已不陌生，但1998年的政府注资主要不是为国有银行的市场化改革所准备，而是一种防范金融危机的本能反应。即便如此，我们已经越来越清晰地观察到政府逐步赋予国有银行改革行动以强烈的寻求与国际银行业接轨的意愿。可以说，一旦这种意愿左右了改革决策者的思维，则更为大胆的改革计划就会被迅速拟出并付诸实施。正是在此过程中，与加入世界贸易组织同步形成的对银行改革进程的时间约束效应就开始发挥作用。这样，此后国有银行改革过程出现的一系列举措便被置于一个十分明确的过渡期时间表中。随着某些重要时刻的临近，许多银行改革行动便在政府的推动下开始实施。[②] 这就是我们前面已经提及的“巴塞尔协议约束效应”。显然，最近一次政府对国有银行的巨额注资行动是这种效应在国有银行改革过程中的一种具体体现。

我们注意到，早在1994年，围绕当时国有经济的债务重组，理论界开始关注国有银行的重新注资问题，其中刘遵义和钱颖一、周小川、吴晓灵等都设计了具体方案与实施路径[③]。现在看来，这些方案尽管有这样那样的问题，尤其是过于强调其技术性，但对当时及此后政府的国有银行注资思路产生了不同程度的影响。1997年和2003年的两次注资就或多或少地带有当年他们思路的影子。不过，虽然本文不打算具体评价这些方案的具体细节，但有一点是明确的，那就是这些方案所考虑的银行与企业联动注资的一揽子思路并没有在随后的改革过程中得到完整的贯彻。尽管当时钱颖一(1995)曾坚持认为一个向银行重新注资的好方法应是为银行提供重组企业的激励，而不是单独就银行进行注资。可是，针对国有银行的两次注资行动都是单独进行的。1998年的第一次注资之所以没有达到预想的效果，说到底就是源于注资行动的单方面性质。由此不难进一步推断，此次注资行动很有可能成为“纳税人向银行所有者进行的一次转移支付”，如果没有其他配套改革措施跟上，注入的资本也极有可能被银行代理人的轻率金融行为很快挥霍掉(World Bank, 2001, p. 158; Clarke and Cull, 1999)。当然，如果和前面的讨论相联系，则不难理解，政府之所以最终偏好于银行层面的单独行动，则显然是因为相对于银行与企业的联合行动，单独注资行动更易操作且收效更快，而巴塞尔协议约束效应也从外部赋予这种短期见效的行动以某种合理性。

很显然，如果政府对国有银行的注资只是出于实现某种短期目的，则极有可能诱致随后的一系列重复注资行动。仅从理论上讲,判断是否为最后一次注资的一个重要尺度是看注资与银行的资产重组行动是否同步进行。如果依然是上述单方面行动,就注定了只是在负债一方作些技术性处理,从而为下一次更加昂贵与痛苦的注资埋下伏笔。而理论界的担忧大都集中于此。

实际上,理论界的这种担忧由来已久。早在20世纪90年代初,刘遵义和钱颖一(1994)就已提醒,对于企业呆账的注销和银行的重新注资只能做一次,由此形成一种可信的政府承诺,以防止流量再次变成存量;在注资之后,紧随其后的应当是改革制度。张春霖(1996)觉察到,国有资本实际上是被当作一种免费资本来筹集和分配的,而国有企业的经营者作为资本的使用者大都存在免费资本幻觉。同样的道理,国有银行对于由国家注入的国有资本也存在这种幻觉。可以想象,既然是免费资本,就意味着不承担低效使用的成本与风险。

笔者曾对1998年那次注资行动提出质疑:注资能否改善国有银行的资本结构,并给出了否定的回答。认为在国家作为最后风险承担者的情况下,单方面通过注资追求资本充足率是没有任何意义的(张杰,1998, p. 280)。后来,笔者给出了一个国有银行资本金的特殊等式,认为国有银行资本结构是国家声誉与居民存款的一种联盟,由于国家声誉具有不可分性,因此,如果国有银行资本结构的重组意味着国家声誉的退出,必将引发居民存款的流失,从而危及银行稳定。因此,政府单方面向国有银行注入真实资本,从而换取国有银行走向商业化经营,是在求证一个无解的方程(张杰,2003a)。无疑地,以上分析对于解读此次注资行动的绩效依然适用。

尽管理论界对于政府向国有银行注资等改革行动一直表示担忧或提出质疑,但从总体上讲,人们并未怀疑国有银行商业化改革方向的正确性。也就是说,最主要的分歧在于改革的方式而不是改革的目标。值得注意的是，此种情形实际上隐含着这样一种价值判断，即国有银行制度本身就是低效率的，而这种低效率主要来自国有银行的内部结构（如产权结构与治理结构）。既然如此，问题的要害就在于改变这种内部结构，而改变内部结构的参照系则是在欧美国家运转良好并经巴塞尔协议加以规范的那种商业银行样式。在这种情况下，近年来讨论国有银行改革条件的文献自然就少了，因为事实证明这些条件（经济的、政治的以及社会的等）只有在一个相当长的时期内才能逐步具备，而国有银行与国际接轨的迫切性已容不得这些条件是否具备。相比之下，议论如何对国有银行进行技术性处理的文字则明显多了起来。完全可以说，政府近年来对国有银行进行的几次技术性改革行动与理论界的上述政策倾向密切相关。

可是，与国内理论界形成鲜明对照的是，近年来国外学术界讨论和论证国有银行存在合理性与存在条件的文献却多了起来。[4]这方面的讨论一般认为是由 Gerschenkron(1962)开创的，在后来的争论中，许多主流经济学家都被卷入其中，如 Shleifer 等(1998)、La Porta (2001)以及 La Porta 等(2000)，世界银行(2001)曾经一度也对此问题进行了跟踪研究。随着讨论的不断深入，不少经济学家的视角已经超越标准的经济学界限而扩展到法律、文化、制度等层面，从而形成一种崭新的金融政治经济学范式(Political Economy of Finance)。

三、国有银行存在的理由：换一角度看问题

让许多人困惑不解的是，经过多年的改革，国有银行的外部框架以及技术参数越来越接近于国际标准的商业银行，但其内部结构以及行动绩效却似乎依然故我。为什么国家的改革努力

与国有银行的实际表现竟会如此大相径庭？其中的原因肯定是多方面的，但值得特别注意的是，由政府自上而下推动的改革一般都存在外部变化与内部变化不相协调的情形。因为政府作为改革的推动者，总会倾向于追求某种短期效果，而国有银行行为的变化与内部结构的制度性调整则需要一个长时期的演进过程。

以上改革情形或许包含着这样一种可能性，那就是，既然政府推动下的强有力的改革都只是触及国有银行的皮毛，这是否意味着并非改革策略有误，而是社会经济本身依然对国有银行制度存在某种内在需求。或者说，经济中所蕴藏着的金融需求并不希望国有银行体制像政府所企盼的那样改变得过快。更进一步地，这是否同时意味着要想改革国有银行体制就得首先改变人们原有的金融需求，而金融需求的改变则不是一个简单的问题，它是收入、习惯以及风险偏好等因素的函数。

不过，实质经济的变化以及对国有银行的经济需求固然重要，但也未必是决定国有银行存在与否的唯一重要的因素。如果不是这样，则当中国的人均收入达到美国的标准时，银行体系也必然会趋同于美国。La Porta 等(2000)的研究表明，从全球范围看，政府对银行的所有权相当普遍，甚至在许多国家的银行完成私有化之后的 1995 年，世界平均的政府对银行的所有权比重仍为 41.6%，即便排除前社会主义国家，也达 38.5%。尽管自 1970 年以来，这个比例在逐步下降(1970 年该比例为 58.9%，排除前社会主义国家则为 52.7%)，但下降的幅度还是比主流经济学家所预想的要慢得多。如此看来，像许多人所预期的，在中国，即便政府不去推动国有银行的商业化改革，但随着人均收入的大幅增加，经济中也会产生一种内生的力量使国有银行自动走向商业化道路，这种观点显然是把问题简单化了。事实表明，经济对国有银行的需求并不简单取决于收入等经济总量，而在很大程度上受人们对待和处置其收入的行为的影响。重要的是，决定人们上述行为的因素也十分复杂。

既有的文献已经就不同类型的法律体系会导致不同国家存在不同的金融结构进行了广泛的讨论，人们倾向于认同，有习惯法传统的国家拥有市场主导型的金融体系，而具有大陆法传统的国家则一般存在银行主导型的金融系统（Asli Demirgul-Kunt and R. Levine, 1999）。虽然从总体上看，人们趋于承认市场主导型的金融体系具有比较优势，但由于这两种金融体系都分别存在于市场经济成熟的发达国家（如市场主导型的英美和银行主导型的德日），因此，或许存在这样一种可能性，即实行何种金融体系关系不大（Allen and Gale, 1997; Levine, 1997）。La Porta 等（2000）的研究也表明，与普通法国家相比，在法律渊源为民法系的国家，政府对银行的所有权更为普遍。这也同时预示着，一国国有银行与私人银行的比例是一种制度演进过程的结果，而无法从别国模仿与移植。政府以及其他外生因素的推动固然可以暂时改变这种比例，但却要付出高昂的代价，经济和制度的内生因素会通过各种方式（如银行挤兑、金融市场无序等）将该比例拉回到与其经济发展与制度结构相适应的水平。世界银行（2001）的经验考察结果表明，在曾经迅速推行银行改革和金融自由化（可理解为追求上述标准比例）的国家（如泰国、韩国和印度尼西亚），在付出了巨额代价的同时，银行部门的国有比例在危机期间迅速上升。如韩国由危机前的不足20%上升到危机期间（1998—2000年）的40%以上，而印度尼西亚1999年甚至接近80%（危机前为40%左右）。

在大多数情况下，传统和法律等因素对国有银行制度重要性的影响是间接的，或者是通过作用于一些具体的经济因素和变量而影响到银行体系。储蓄率便是这样一个值得单独考察的因素。在标准的经济学分析中，储蓄率受一国传统习俗和社会保障制度等因素的影响。可以说，具有更高储蓄率的经济更需要和倚重银行体系，日本的例子经常被经济学家所引用，这似乎是一个无须再强调的命题。但有意思的是，如果一种经济具有更高的储蓄率且银行的储蓄存单在居民手持的金融工具中占比越大，则这种经济中的国有银行所占的比例就会越高。与成熟市场经济国家中银行的存单不同，在中国，对绝大多数居民而言，他们在国有银行的储蓄存款几乎等于把全部的鸡蛋放到一只篮子里，风险十分集中。而在大多数市场经济国家，居民在银行的存款只是其手持的众多金融工具中的一种，风险是分散的。仅从这种意义上讲，市场经济中的银行业可以有较多的市场竞争，而对于中国的银行业而言，则只能将竞争限制在一定的限度之内。原因很简单，对于大多数储户而言，他们更加关心存款的安全，而不是存款的收益。实际上，中国居民金融资产过多地集中于储蓄存单为国有银行的市场化改革规定了一条短期难以逾越的边界。

不仅如此，国有银行的存在还被认为是在市场不成熟经济中项目选择的有效安排。Dewatripont 和 Maskin(1989)的一个软预算约束模型揭示出，具有不同预算约束的银行制度会做出不同的项目选择。如果经济中存在三种项目，即长短期都无效的坏项目、长期见效的最优项目和短期见效的次优项目，那么，在成熟的市场经济条件下，一个标准的商业银行会更多地选择短期见效的次优项目，而在市场不太成熟的经济中，坏项目与长期有效项目更容易得到银行的资金支持。给这些项目提供资金的金融机构往往是政府控制下的银行，因为这种银行在促使借款人选择具有社会效益的项目方面更有效率(Boot and Thakor, 1996)。在中国改革过程中，有利于经济增长的许多项目都是长期见效的，它们不会进入标准商业银行的筛选机制，而这些项目被改革实践证明是国有银行的主要支持对象。虽然在实际项目筛选过程中，不少坏项目也时常被选中，但那可以视做国有银行体制选择最优项目所付出的一种必要代价（张杰，2003b）。国有银行在中国改革过程存在的必要性不是依赖于它是否与国际标准的银行尺寸相吻合，而是取决于经济中项目的分布状况与筛选绩效。

四、重要的是资产：一个银行制度弱相关观点

经济中存在对国有银行信贷的巨大需求，这一点在前文中曾被我们用做论证国有银行存在的一个基本理由。这里，更为重要的是，它同时表明国有银行问题的真正根源在于对国有银行产生信贷需求的经济而不是其他。有什么样的经济，就会有什么样的信贷需求，有什么样的信贷需求，就会有什么样的银行制度来满足。这显然是一个再浅显不过的道理。

或许，国家急于改变国有银行体制本身，而不是首先触动更为基本的经济层面，除了后者难度更大、见效更慢之外，从理论上讲，可能还有其他方面的考虑。比如，银行制度的率先改革可以诱导经济中的信贷需求，从而改变整个经济的金融需求结构。理论界已经有人注意到，金融系统的设计能够影响实际的经济行为和经济发展（Thakor，1996）。金融的先期发展可以提高储蓄转化为投资的比例，并提高资本的社会边际生产率，进而影响私人储蓄率（Pagano，1993）。若果真如此，则国家着眼于改造国有银行体制，企图由此产生诱导效应进而改变经济中的金融期望与偏好，最终推动金融需求的转型，这一切就是合理的改革安排。可是，以上命题迄今却只在成熟市场经济国家得到过较

好的验证。其原因大致在于,这些国家的市场是如此之成熟,从而能够为金融体系的事先设计所产生的诱导效应提供传递与扩散的渠道与空间。而中国的市场体系远未成熟,银行体系即便可以独立行事,也未必存在足够大且完善的行为空间,其信贷行为与金融服务仍在很大程度上是事后的和被动的。在这种情况下,国有银行体制先行改革的理由就难言充分。

更有趣的问题在于,如果基本的经济状况有了改变,其信贷需求也随之发生变化,那么,国有银行制度是否还能够继续给这种已经变化了的经济(如市场经济)提供金融服务呢?或者说,一个市场取向的经济就一定得要求私人银行业来提供相应的信贷支持吗?这显然不是一个简单的问题。尽管如前文所述,大部分经济发达国家的国有银行所占比例低于经济相对落后的国家,但在一些市场经济十分成熟的国家,国有银行的比例并不算低。这种状况促使我们倾向于相信世界银行(2001)和 La Porta 等(2000)的研究结论,即国有制并非总是不利于经济增长。他们的研究进一步证明,银行国有制的负面效应会随着人均收入的提高而递减。德国的银行业被这些研究文献经常提及。作为一个具有长期国有制传统的国家,1988 年,德国的国有银行资产占全部银行总资产的比例高达 42%,法国与意大利也有近似的纪录。当然,我们所关注的不只是德国较高的国有银行资产占比,还有与这种较高的国有银行资产占比相对应的微观经济(企业部门)状况。在德国,与其高比例的国有银行资产相对应的是低比例的企业部门的国有成分。由此提示我们,国有银行制度之所以能够在德国长期存在,固然可以用银行内部的治理结构和政府良好的监管来解释,但更为充分的理由则在于,德国企业部门的低国有化为国有银行提供了一个有效运作的微观经济基础。事实表明,企业部门的低国有化在客观上使得政府官员避免了把信贷资金配置给关联企业以便从中获利的诱惑。

以上例证的普遍意义尚待进一步地观察与讨论，但它至少已经初步表明，一个经济中金融资源配置效率的高低，与采用何种银行制度弱相关，而与企业制度强相关。实际上，由此也就部分地证伪了前述的金融系统设计和金融企业家观点。更直观地看，决定一种银行体制是否有效率的关键是其资产状况，而银行的资产状况又直接取决于微观经济部门对待银行贷款的态度与行为。人们经常引用的温州案例可以直接佐证这一观点。在温州经济中，由于国有成分很低，即便是那里的国有银行也获得了良好的经营绩效。可以设想，当这个地方的政府面对一个低国有化的经济时，一定较少有胁迫国有银行“干这干那”的激励。从理论上讲，不管谁出资设立的银行都会追求较好的投资回报，作为出资人(哪怕是政府)一般不会执意让银行将资金投向没有多少回报的项目而甘愿忍受资产的损失。经济的市场化与非国有化是割断政府与国有银行资产部分的血肉联系从而避免其左右国有银行信贷行为的最佳手段。一旦在银行的资产部分没有了国家或政府的既得利益，政府就会仅以普通出资人的身份获取正常红利。也只有在这种情况下，政府才会根据实际需要选择应在国有银行持有多少资本(所有权)份额。

与一般商业银行相比，中国国有银行出资人的红利获取方式十分特殊。一般商业银行的出资人红利主要体现在银行的负债方，红利分配取决于银行代理人在分红(以吸引出资人)与留利(以扩充资本)之间所做的权衡。从某种意义上讲，巴塞尔协议所规定的8%的资本充足率标准是商业银行股东(出资人)追求红利最大化行为与银行代理人追求经营安全最大化行为之间达成的一种妥协。中国国有银行的出资人(国家)也从银行的负债部分获取“红利”(比如税收),但更多的回报则是从银行的资产部分拿走的。更直接地讲,国有银行的资产扩张本身就是出资人以及相关利益各方获取红利的过程。不难想象,当同样是国家作为出资人的国有企业得到一笔国有银行的贷款时,这对国家意味着什么呢?如果这笔贷款正好可以缓解这家国有企业的经营困境从而节约了国家财政的救助成本以及其他社会成本,那么,这笔贷款尽管可能会成为国有银行资产部分的一笔呆账,但却显然不能一概算作出资人的当期损失。原因很简单,这种损失并不需要在当期由国家财政拿钱冲销,而居民储蓄借助国家声誉大量地进入并留存于国有银行存款账户则为国家财政的延期冲销提供着财务支持。显而易见,正如前面已经指出的那样,国有银行之所以成为问题,从根本上讲是因为经济中企业部门的高国有成分使得国家这个出资人一直存在把信贷资金配置给政府企业并从中获取红利的诱惑,而与国家是否作为出资人无关。

总的来说,企业部门的国有化一定是低效率的,而银行的国有制则不一定低效率。企业部门的效率需要通过更多的市场竞争来保持,但对于银行来说,则并不意味着竞争越多越好。相比之下,后者需要更多的信息披露、更为严格的市场准入以及更加良好的监管,而不是更多的竞争。仅从这种意义上讲,在任何一种经济中,都不同程度地存在更具竞争性的企业部门和不太具有竞争性的银行部门相互搭配的制度格局。毋庸置疑,在中国,金融改革的当务之急应当是使经济中的企业部门(尤其是国有企业)更具竞争性,而不是使国有银行更加市场化。[⑤]当国有银行与更多具有竞争性的非国有企业(或经过改造的国有企业)建立金融联系从而重建其资产结构时,国有银行的问题也就不再成为问题了。

五、国家声誉、核心存款与无形资产

更明确一点讲，以上有关银行制度弱相关的观点实际上隐含着这样一个重要命题，那就是国有银行的低效率与其资产结构强相关，与其资本（负债）结构弱相关。这一命题也可视做“MM 定理”在国有银行问题上的一种具体应用。如果以上命题最终被证明是成立的，那么我们已经采取的针对国有银行资本结构的注资行动就极有可能无功而返。不仅如此，在资产结构未得到有效改善的情况下，这种旨在修补资本结构从而促使国有银行走向市场的努力与良好愿望反而会产生进一步动摇本来尚属稳定的资本结构的后果。

我们需要从国有银行资本金的特殊性说起。笔者一项专门针对国有银行资本金问题的研究（张杰，2003a）表明，国有银行的资本金是国家声誉与居民储蓄之间达成的一种奇特的资本联盟。在这个资本联盟中，国家作为一方出资人是以其声誉入股的，而居民作为另一方出资人，则通过持有国有银行存单的形式入股。多年的改革实践证明，这种资本联盟具有相当强的稳定性。既然被改革过程证明是十分稳定的资本结构，为何非要通过所谓的“单独行动”对其进行改造呢？我们不妨设想，如果国有银行的资本结构在通过国家的注资并经上市后形成了某种合乎现代商业银行要求的标准样式，但在资产状况依然如故的情况下，它会比原来的资本结构更加稳定吗？

更直观地看，中国国有银行既有的资本结构与巴塞尔协议标准样式的最大区别在于对所谓“无形资产”的确认。根据巴塞尔协议的有关条款，银行核心资本的标准内容除普通股和溢价、未分配利润（留存收益）、合法非积累性永久优先股以及附属机构的少数股东权益外，还可包括一些可确认的无形资产。这些无形资产最常见的有两种，一种是购买抵押服务权（purchased mortgage servicing rights，PMSRs），即银行通过一系列服务如托收分配贷款支付、监督借款人遵守由贷款自身产生或其他借款人授予的贷款条款取得收入，从而为以银行所提供服务的抵押贷款留存本金为基础的预期未来收费创造条件；另一种是购买信用卡关系（purchased credit card relationships，PCCRs），即由银行提供信用卡服务而可能带来的潜在客户群，他们购买信用卡的关系可视为银行获取未来收入的一项承诺。[6]其他一些无形资产则从资本中剔除，而这些被剔除的无形资产则恰好是国有银行资本结构中必须考虑和得到确认的内容。

在巴塞尔协议标准所剔除的无形资产中有两种类型的资产值得关注。第一种是所谓的商誉（reputation）。按照标准教科书的解释，对于商业银行而言，商誉是通过为客户提供良好的金融服务而取得的。在商誉存在的场合，银行的市场价值会超出账面价值。由于在市场竞争过程中，任何一家银行的商誉都会随时出现波动，而它又没有相应的物质担保，因此许多国家的监管机构不允许将其作为银行的资本。我们已知，在中国国有银行的资本结构中，存在国家声誉入股从而充当资本的情形。如果按照上述解释，则人们很有可能把国家声誉作为一般商誉而从国有银行的资本中剔除。国家之所以数次给国有银行注资，实际上也就是在无形中把国家声誉视为一般商誉而低估了国有银行的核心资本水平。在这里，我们并不是认为巴塞尔协议标准或许多国家监管当局把商誉从银行核心资本中剔除有什么不妥，而是觉得国家声誉之于国有银行与商誉之于一般商业银行有很大的不同。与一般商誉相比，国家声誉具有可预见性、稳定性与内在的可担保性，因此完全可以作为一种可确认的无形资产计入国有银行的核心资本。[7]根据既有的讨论，国家声誉实际上在国有银行资本结构中长期充当着核心资本的角色，而国际评级机构在对国有银行的评级中也都充分考虑到国家声誉如政府支持力度的因素。

另一种被剔除的无形资产是所谓的核心存款无形资产(core deposit intangibles, CDIs)。根据教科书的标准定义，核心存款是指那些对市场利率变化反应不敏感，一直会保留在银行中的稳定的存款，这种存款往往在银行账户里呆上数年，因此是银行拥有的最忠实和成本最低的存款(Rose, 1996, p. 379, p. 500)。仅从这种意义上讲，这种核心存款完全可以视作银行的核心资本。这里，我们姑且不去讨论巴塞尔协议标准为什么不把核心存款作为可确认的无形资产计入核心资本，而是看看在国有银行的资本结构中核心存款无形资产到底是一种什么样的情形？

实际上，在国有银行的存款账户中，存在着大量忠实而低成本的居民储蓄存款，这些存款无疑符合核心存款的条件。事实表明，这笔核心存款长期以来一直充当着国有银行的核心资本。根据已有的讨论，这种核心存款无形资产与国家声誉互为表里，共同支撑着国有银行的特殊资本结构。与一般商业银行的核心存款相比，国有银行的核心存款对市场利率的变化更不敏感，而对国家声誉的依赖性更强。因此，如果我们假定国家声誉在未来一段较长的时期内会有良好表现，则这笔核心存款就会继续充当国有银行的核心资本。既然如此，国有银行的实际资本状况就比我们想象的或从一般视角衡量的要好许多。在这种情况下，国家注资行动的紧迫性与合理性也就值得斟酌了。

如果我们可以确认国家声誉与核心存款充当国有银行核心资本的合理性，那么，在企业部门的市场化进程较为迟缓，无法在短期内改善国有银行资产状况的情况下，单方面推进国有银行的市场化改革极有可能伤及上述核心资本，从而增强国有银行的不稳定性和诱发严重的银行危机。如果是那样的话，国家花费了巨额的注资成本，却发觉，不但没有换取国有银行资本结构的有效改善，反而会使原先隐性的资本缺口显性化。以上担忧并非杞人忧天。从理论上讲，国家注入真实资本的一个直接目的是替换原先入股的国家声誉，这显然是符合巴塞尔协议标准的举动。但问题在于，随着国有银行步入市场化(如上市)进程以及国家声誉无形资产的逐步退出，人们尤其是国有银行储蓄存单的忠实持有者对国家声誉的稳定预期会发生微妙变化，从而影响其存单持有的心理与行为。当这种心理与行为恰好遭受利率变化与物价波动时，则这些存款就会逐渐退出核心存款行列而转变为一般存款(倾向于追逐短期收益)。道理很简单，当核心存款持有者原有的稳定预期被打破之后，其持有核心存款的机会成本就会随之上升。[8]或许有人会问，注资本身并不必然意味着国家声誉的退出，于是也就不会出现核心存款的转化与消散。若果真如此，则国家向已经有国家声誉和核心存款作为核心资本的国有银行注入如此巨额的真实资本就更属多余之举了。

六、结　论

长期以来，人们似乎已经习惯于用所谓的一般视角和国际商业银行的通行安排来思考中国国有银行的改革取向问题。如今，可能很少有人怀疑国有银行制度只有仿效国外商业银行的做法才能最终获得理想的经营绩效这一推断的合理性，而这种推断在近年来越来越紧地与国家的有关国有银行迅速与国际接轨的改革偏好走到一起并达成一致，从而使与这种推断相关的研究及其政策建议取得了“主流”或“正统”的地位。毫无疑问，2003年年底的450亿美元的国家注资便是上述所谓主流观点与国家政策偏好取得一致的一种实际结果。

就以往的经验看，国有银行寻求与国际接轨的改革努力所取得的实际绩效是相当有限的。每经过一轮改革，国有银行的外观与技术参数越来越接近于国际通行水平，但其内部的核心制度结构与金融行为却似乎变化不大。让不少人迷惑不解的是，国有银行的改革目标已经明确无误，而国家与国有银行自身也在朝着这个目标努力，可最终除了付出巨额的改革成本、重组和派生出一些在概念上符合改革要求的机构之外⑨，为什么我们总是感到离那个目标不是更近，而是更远了呢?!

从总体上讲，既往的国有银行改革寻求的是短期见效的结果。与此相联系，改革倡导者一定偏好于对国外商业银行制度要素的模仿、移植与重组。由于在商业银行制度的全部要素中，能够被模仿与移植的只有那些技术性要素和有形的外部框架，因此，经过改革的国有银行与标准的商业银行相比，总是显得“貌合神离”；许多被国外商业银行制度证明是十分有效的做法也大都“逾淮而枳”。显然，眼下十分流行且长期左右政策取向的“主流”观点无法就上述现象给出令人信服的解释。

本文所提供的金融政治经济学的新视角便旨在回应与诘问“主流”观点的基本主张，并在此过程中，寻求我们对于国有银行改革过程与绩效的新的理解。本文除继续坚持中国国有银行体制是一个长期制度变迁的结晶这一既有的观点之外，尝试性地引入了一些新因素以丰富问题讨论的维度。其中最值得关注的一个考虑是，从世界范围看，国有银行并不是处在改革过程的经济或者发展中经济的专利，而在各国普遍存在。因此，银行的国有或政府所有并非低效率或高风险的代名词。至于在一国银行业的市场结构中，国有银行应占有多大比例才算适度，则没有一个既定的标准，而在很大程度上取决于这个国家的经济结构、收入水平以及文化法律传统等众多因素的交互影响。由此意味着，当一个国家决定国有银行存在的一些深层次因素未发生变化时，如果人为地和单方面地寻求国有银行制度的改变，则结果往往会适得其反。中国以往针对国有银行制度改革之所以未能取得预期的效果，其原因大致就在于此。

如果以上判断最终被证明是正确的，那么，我们在以往的改革过程中，极有可能把造成金融资源低效率配置的许多原本不属于国有银行制度的问题算在了国有银行制度身上；由此产生误导效应，使得国家几度对国有银行大动干戈，而又几度无功而返。针对于此，本文提出了一个银行制度弱相关的观点，认为在中国，国有银行制度的低效率表现源自其出资人（国家）获取红利的方式，而这种方式又内生于中国经济改革与制度变迁的长期过程。与一般商业银行相比，国家（出资人）在很大程度上依赖于国有银行的资产扩张来获取红利。之所以会形成这种情形，则是因为经济中企业部门的高国有成分使得同为出资人的国家时常存在把国有银行的信贷资金配置给国有企业的激励。无疑地，中国国有银行的问题出在作为其主要服务对象的高比例的国有经济身上，而与国家是否充当其出资人无关。因此，增进国有银行效率的根本出路就不在于通过注资等技术手段修补其资本结构以达到国际通行标准，而在于借助国有企业的市场化改革降低经济的国有化成分，由此疏远国家与经济部门之间过于紧密的金融联系。如果经济的国有成分下降到一定水平，国家作为国有银行的出资人开始寻求获取正常的投资回报时，则国有银行的改革将会呈现出另一番景象。

本文在强调国有银行资本结构的修复须以改善其资产状况

为前提的同时，还对国有银行的资本结构进行了重新解读。这种解读既是对人们一直奉为清规戒律的巴塞尔协议资本标准的中国式扩展，也是对笔者那个曾经引起人们广泛争议的国有银行资本金等式(张杰，2003a)的进一步引申。我们关注的核心问题是，一些被巴塞尔协议和许多国家银行监管当局从银行核心资本中剔除的无形资产能否计入中国国有银行的资本结构？本文讨论的结果表明，国家声誉(近似于巴塞尔协议中的商誉)和核心存款在特定的改革背景下实际上长期承担着国有银行核心资本的角色，并保持着足够的持续性与稳定性，由此形成中国国有银行的资本特征。因此，我们没有理由非要机械地依据巴塞尔协议将它们从国有银行的核心资本中剔除。确认这两项无形资产的实际政策涵义不容忽视。一方面，若考虑到无形资产的存在，人们特别是改革决策层对国有银行整体资本状况的估价会发生某种程度的转变，从而缓释巴塞尔协议约束效应对国有银行改革决策的刺激与压力，使得改革者会更加从容地从中国长期制度变迁的角度重新审视和对待国有银行的改革；另一方面，无形资产对于国有银行的重要性也同时提醒我们，旨在追求短期绩效的国有银行改革方式(如上市)极有可能导致无形资产的迅速流失，从而危及整个金融体系的稳定。

注 释

① 当然，另有一些观点认为，政府对银行资本水平的要求实际上助长了银行的高风险倾向，同时会使银行陷入被公众挤兑的被动境地。更为严重的是，那些经营状况良好但资本金水平却未达标的银行将面临人为设定的困境(Gart, 1994, p. 90; Rose, 1996, p. 498)。

② 2004 年 3 月 11 日中国银监会主席刘明康明确表示，向中国银行和中国建设银行注资是为了在 2006 年加入世界贸易组织过渡期届满之前把两行改造成股份制商业银行。

③ 具体内容请读者参阅吴敬琏、周小川等著《公司治理结构、债务重组和破产程序:重温 1994 年京伦会议》,中央编译出版社,1999 年。

④ 国内研究国有银行存在合理性的文献并不是没有,如张杰(1998;2003b)。

⑤ 世界银行 2003 年的一份专门的研究报告指出,中国金融部门的腐败在很大程度上损害着企业的表现。那些效率高,经营活跃的公司得不到银行的信贷支持。被调查的公司中有 10%—15%表示,必须给银行回扣才能获得贷款。从总体上讲,中国的银行系统对非国有企业提供的金融服务十分贫乏,并且银行是否给某个企业贷款与该企业的效益并无直接关系(引自《新财富》2004 年第 2 期)。不过,种种迹象也表明,在过去几年里,银行之间争夺所谓优质客户的竞争也十分激烈。

⑥ 有关可确认无形资产的详尽讨论可参见 P. S. Rose(1996, p. 500)。

⑦ 实际上,尽管巴塞尔协议提供了一个统一的资本定义,但各国监管者在实践中和在资本的项目选择上却有一定的自主权。一个人们通常提到的差别是,美国银行不将持有证券的潜在收益计入资本,但日本却把证券持有潜在收益的 45%计入二级资本(Dowatripont, M. and Tirole, J., 1993, *The Prudential Regulation of Banks*, MIT Press, p. 44.)。各国之间的类似差异还有许多,参见 Hall(1993)。

⑧ 格林斯潘最近在致美国参议院银行委员会主席 Richard Shelby 的信中提醒,中国银行系统能够在不良贷款率为 50%的情况下运行的唯一前提就是存款人不提款(引自《新京报》2004 年 3 月 4 日 B42 版)。而保证存款人不提款的一个主要前提又是国家声誉的继续存在。

⑨ 自 1994 年以来,围绕国有银行改革所派生的主要金融机构有三大政策性银行、四大金融资产管理公司以及新近成立的中央汇金投资有限责任公司。

参考文献

刘遵义、钱颖一,1994:《关于中国的银行与企业财务重组的建议》,《改革》第 6 期。

钱颖一,1995:《中国的公司治理结构改革和融资改革》,《经济研究》第3期。

世界银行(World Bank),2001:《金融与增长——动荡条件下的政策选择》,中译本,经济科学出版社。

吴敬琏、周小川等,1999:《公司治理结构、债务重组和破产程序:重温1994年京伦会议》,中央编译出版社。

张春霖,1996:《论国有企业的债务问题》,《改革》第1期。

张杰,1995:《中国金融改革的检讨与进一步改革的途径》,《经济研究》第5期。

张杰,1997:《国有银行的不良债权与清债博弈》,《经济学家》第6期。

张杰,1998:《中国金融制度的结构与变迁》,山西经济出版社。

张杰,2003a:《中国国有银行的资本金谜团》,《经济研究》第1期。

张杰,2003b:《经济变迁中的金融中介与国有银行》,中国人民大学出版社。

Allen, Franklin and Gale Douglas, 1997, "Financial Markets, Intermediaries and Inter-temporal Smoothing", *Journal of Political Economy* (105), pp. 523—546.

Boot, A. W. and Thakor, A. V., 1996, *Financial System Architecture*, Working Paper, Indiana University.

Clarke, Geroge R. G., and Cull, Robert, 1999, *Getting to Yes*, World Bank, Development Research Group, Washington, D. C.

Demirg-Kunt, Asli and Levine, Ross, 1999, *Bank-Based and Market-Based Financial Systems: Cross-Country Comparisons*, World Bank, Working Paper.

Dewatripont, M. and Maskin, E., 1989, *Credit and Efficiency in Centralized and Decentralized Economies*, Mimeograph, Harvard University, Aug.

Diamond, D., 1984, "Financial Intermediation and Delegated Monitoring", *Review of Economic Studies* (59): pp. 393—414.

Dewatripont, M. and Tirole, J., 1993, *The Prudential Regulation of Banks*, MIT Press, p. 44.

Gart, Alan, 1994, *Regulation, Deregulation, Reregulation: the Future of the Banking, Insurance, and Securities Industries*, John Wiley & Sons, Inc.

Gerschenkron, Alexander, 1962, *Economic Backwardness in Historical Perspective: A Book of Essays*, Cambridge, Mass: Belknap Press of Harvard University Press.

Hall, M., 1993, *Banking Regulation and Supervision: A Comparative Study of the UK, USA and Japan*, Edward Elgar Publishing.

La Porta, Refael; Lopez-de-Silanes, Florencio; Shleifer, Andrei and Vishny, Robert., 1999,《投资者保护:起源、影响及改革》,中译文载《奥尔多投资评论》第1卷第1辑《风险、不确定性与秩序》,中国财政经济出版社2001年版。

La Porta, Refael, Lopez-de-Silanes, Florencio, Shleifer, Andrei, 2000, *Government Ownership of Banks*, Harvard University, August.

Levine, R., 1997, "Financial Development and Economic Growth, Views and Agenda", *Journal of Economic Literature*(35), pp. 688—726.

Mishkin, F. S., 2001, *The Economics of Money, Banking, and Financial Markets*, Harper Collins College Publishers.

Pagano, M., 1993, "Financial Markets and Growth: An Overview", *European Economic Review*(37), pp. 613—622.

Rose, Peter. S., 1996, *Commercial Bank Management*, McGraw-Hill Companies, Inc.

Shleifer, A. and Vishny, R., 1998, *The Crabbing Hand: Government Pathologies and their Cures*, Cambridge: Harvard University press.

Thakor, A. V., 1996,《金融系统设计:一个概览》,中译文载《奥尔多投资评论》第1卷第2辑,《金融系统演变考》,中国财政经济出版社2002年版。

(原载《经济研究》2004年第6期)

中国银行业效率的实证分析

姚树洁

（英国米德萨斯大学）

冯根福　姜春霞

（西安交通大学经济与金融学院）

一、引　　言

尽管在过去的几十年中发生了重大的改革和变化，但中国的银行业体系仍然以其效益低下和大量不良贷款而著称，并使进一步的改革越来越困难且富有挑战性。在中国于 2001 年 12 月加入 WTO 后，国内银行业市场必须逐步对国外银行和其他海外金融机构等竞争对手全面开放。激烈的竞争很快就会到来，如何使国内银行可以同国外银行进行有效竞争，无疑是中国政府目前面临的一个棘手的和富有挑战性的课题。

为了回应即将到来的更为激烈的挑战，中国政府已加快银行业改革的步伐。除了解决四大国有银行巨大的不良贷款外，国务院还决定从 4030 亿美元的外汇储备中拿出 450 亿美元支持中国银行和中国建设银行进行改革。这是到目前为止中国政府为了把大型国有银行改变为真正的商业机构而采取的最果断的一项行动。这意味着这两家银行将变成股份制公司，不久将在股票交易所公开上市。如果上述改革成功的话，对中国工商银行和中国农业银行也将采取类似的改革举措。

最近中国银行业改革的主要经济理论基础之一是委托—代理理论。过去，不论国有银行做什么，委托人(国家)总是在银行陷入困境时把它们解救出来。代理人(银行)知道国家是其最后的求助对象，因而源源不断地向它们认为值得信任的客户贷款，结果大量的不良贷款无法收回。把国有银行变为股份制公司，是希望国家在未来不再解救它们。在短期内，国家有责任帮助国有银行清理全部或大量不良贷款，以便让它们具有类似于真正的商业银行那样的资本结构，从而使它们同正在进入的国外银行在一个平台上开展竞争。从长期看，国有银行必须自负盈亏，且不受任何政治和行政的干预。银行改革的另一个理论基础是预算约束理论。过去，由于国家用其信用作担保，因而国有银行实际上把一部分居民储蓄存款视作国有资本来使用，所以，软预算约束实际上包括国家直接注入国有银行的资本和在国家信用担保下部分被国有银行视作资本金的居民储蓄存款。在未来，一旦它们公开上市，则必须越来越多地依靠股东筹集资本，必须主要为股东的利益而不是国家或地方政府的利益负责。这些银行的竞争力将取决于它们的盈利能力和向股东支付股息的能力。

不论改革的动机是基于委托—代理问题，还是预算约束的影响，最终的目标是提高国内银行的效率和竞争力。上述目标能否实现，将主要取决于对以下两个问题的解答：第一，所有制改革和硬预算约束能帮助银行提高效率吗？第二，在如此短的一段时间内，即在国外银行纷纷涌入中国开展竞争之前，中国能够完成银行体系的所有制结构改革，让所有的国有银行实行硬预算约束吗？

在本文，我们的目的是根据可获得的资料和信息回答第一个问题。我们难以对第二个问题做出回答，这是因为我们还不清楚国务院将会以多快的速度推进四大国有银行的资本重组。

本文的其他部分安排如下：第二部分介绍中国银行体系的背景情况；第三部分评述有关效率研究特别是银行效率问题研究的文献；第四部分讨论研究方法问题，包括模型和数据的说明；第五部分评价回归结果；第六部分是本文的结论。

二、银行改革和入世后的挑战

（一）银行体系改革

改革前很长一个时期内，中国的银行体系完全为中国人民银行所控制。中国人民银行既是中央银行，又是中国唯一的商业银行。1978 年经济改革以来，中国的银行体系发生了重大变化。第一个变化是把中国人民银行一分为二：中央银行和专业银行。中央银行仍然使用中国人民银行的名称，原中国人民银行承担的商业业务分给了陆续组建的四大国有专业银行（本文以下简称“四大国有银行”）。直到 20 世纪 90 年代中期，一些非国有银行和股份制银行方被允许在中国开展业务，在此之前，整个银行体系完全被中国人民银行和四大国有银行所控制（Wong and Wong，2001）。

四大国有银行以效率低下、亏损和大量不良贷款而著称。四大国有银行目前的困境主要由以下两个因素所导致。其一，四大国有银行主要向指定部门的国有企业提供服务。四大国有银行作为受政府严格控制的垄断机构开展业务，没有义务与动力跨地区和部门开拓市场与进行竞争。四大国有银行的每一家都有省级和地县级分支行，每一家分支行在各自地方政府的行政控制和指导下开展业务。其结果是,所有的银行和它们的分支行都有自己的服务地域,不可能开展任何自由的竞争。其二,四大国有银行作为计划经济中的政府机构开展活动。它们是政府当局执行国家和地方计委制定的生产计划的左膀右臂。为了完成国家和地方生产计划,不管是否盈利,四大国有银行都必须向国有企业发放贷款,结果导致了巨大的不良贷款和损失。

从上个世纪 80 年代初开始,中国的银行体系发生了一些变革,其目的是促使国有银行由政策驱动转换为由利润和竞争驱动。在转轨过程中,政府为了创造一个富有竞争和有效的银行体系而采取了一系列的改革步骤。第一步是在 1985 年取消了对专业银行只能服务于指定部门国有企业的限制,以建立一个竞争性的以市场为基础的金融体系。然而,由于经常受到中央和地方政府的干预,因而竞争是有限的。地方分支行仍被地方政府所控制,主要业务仍然为政策制定者的需要所驱动。第二步是在 1994 年建立了 3 家政策性银行,接管四大国有银行提供政策性贷款的职能。然而国有商业银行在政策性贷款中仍然发挥着重要作用。由于指定的政策性银行的服务和贷款能力缺少足够的分支行网络和资本作支撑,因而不能满足以前由四大国有银行提供的政策性贷款的需要。而且,国有商业银行经常面临来自中央和地方政府要求向其偏爱的部门和企业发放贷款的压力。第三步是在 1998 年底,为了避免地方政府的干预重构了中央银行组织。中国人民银行把全国所有的省、市级分行合并成 9 家大型地方分行。地方政府不再像以前一样有权任命中国人民银行地方分支机构的高级官员。第四步是在 1999 年成立了 4 家资产管理公司,即信达资产管理公司、长城资产管理公司、东方资产管理公司和华融资产管理公司,目的是解决四大国有银行的不良贷款。这 4 家资产管理公司的任务和使命是分别负责帮助四大国有银行清理资产负债表和增强它们的竞争力。另外，为了控制新贷款的不良贷款率，所有的国内银行都使用了5类贷款标准方案。

除了改革四大国有银行外，国家还开始允许成立地方银行，甚至允许成立非国有银行同四大国有银行开展竞争。股份制商业银行的建立形成了新的竞争源，从而为中国的银行业注入了活力。另外，以前地方的城市信用社合并成立了90家城市商业银行。城市商业银行都采用股份制所有权结构，并被限制在本地区内开展业务。这些股份制银行的经营以纯商业活动为基础，目标是利润最大化和扩大市场份额。

基于上述改革措施，强化银行体系的竞争力和提高银行效率等方面取得了很大的进展。目前，一个开放的竞争性的银行体系已初步建立起来，它以中国人民银行为中央银行，以四大国有商业银行为支柱，以股份制商业银行为增长引擎，以地方商业银行和外资开放式银行为补充。

然而，尽管非国有银行迅速发展，四大国有银行仍然主导着中国的银行业。在1998年，四大国有银行的总资产、贷款和存款的集中率分别是84.93%、84.26%和88.51%，而四大国有银行的利润集中率只有55.33%(Wong and Wong, 2001)。这些粗略的指标表明，四大国有银行总资产规模虽然很大，但它们的获利能力比其他类型的银行低得多。这也正是本文所要探讨的问题。

(二) 入世后面临的挑战

虽然中国在改革银行体系方面取得了很大进展，但是四大国有银行仍然面临着许多来自内部或外部的挑战。内部的困境主要是由于向亏损的国有企业发放政策性贷款所造成的大量不良贷款。外部的困境是由于四大国有银行长期服务于国有企业，所以在以市场为基础的金融体系中缺少国际经营经验。目前中国银行业的竞争环境还不足以让中国的商业银行同资金雄厚并具有娴熟国际经营经验的外资银行竞争。在过去,对外资银行来说有许许多多的准入壁垒和业务限制,包括地域限制和进入规定。中国加入 WTO 意味着所有的壁垒和限制将会逐步取消。从 2006 年开始,外资银行可以享受国民待遇。入世后的挑战迫在眉睫,它在许多方面威胁着国内的商业银行——不论是国有银行还是非国有银行。如何改革国内银行尤其是四大国有银行,如何提高它们的效率,已成为一个紧迫而重要的令人关注的问题。事实上,对四大国有银行进行根本性改革,不仅是迫于国内外的竞争压力,而且是自我发展的内在要求。中国经济体制改革的不断深化和中国经济的快速发展给中国带来了前所未有的发展机遇,中国银行业在国际金融体系中的影响越来越大。深化银行业改革是抓住这一难得机遇的唯一有效途径。

三、有关银行效率研究的文献

在过去 50 多年中,银行效率问题研究一直受到关注。有关银行业效率低下的根源,早期的研究倾向于强调规模经济的影响,即考察单位成本能否随着产量的增加而降低;也倾向于强调范围经济的影响,即考察单位成本能否通过联合生产而降低。规模经济和范围经济的经验研究表明,在 20 世纪 80 年代,资产为 1 亿—50 亿美元的中型银行具有显著的规模经济。然而,最近的研究表明,规模经济所要求的银行资产规模大幅度增长。在 20 世纪 90 年代,规模经济显著的资产规模为 100 亿—250 亿美元。关于范围经济,经验研究显示较小的范围无成本效率(Saunders, 1999)。

近来,有关效率的研究转到了生产效率问题上。生产效率由两部分组成:技术效率和配置效率。技术效率指的是现有资源最优利用的能力，即在一定的投入水平下产出最大化或在给定的产出水平下投入最小化。配置效率指的是在一定的价格水平下实现投入和产出最优组合的能力（Lovell，1993）。在有关生产效率的研究方面，Leibenstein（1996）首先把X效率引入全面客观的因素分析中，如管理的改进和技术的应用，而不考虑大小（规模经济）和产品组合（范围经济）。在一组资料数据中，可以估计最佳业务边界或最差业务边界，最佳业务边界和某个公司实践之间的差幅反映了其X效率低下的程度。

在金融机构效率研究的文献中，有两个有争议的问题：一是怎样定义和计量银行的投入和产出；二是怎样确定最佳业务边界来评价它们的业绩。

由于银行的特征不同于一般意义上的公司，因而如何计量银行的投入和产出是最困难的问题之一。不像生产有形商品的制造业，银行不仅生产无法识别的产品——中间服务，而且也提供一系列产品——复合型产品。早期的银行效率研究使用了许多计量银行产出的方法，如存贷款账户的数目和每个账户中的美元金额。

由于强调银行生产过程的基本性质而不是存量变动，向客户提供的服务流量可以被认为是银行产出。计量服务流量主要有两种方法：生产方法和中介方法。生产方法认为银行是生产不同存贷款账户的公司。交易和凭证的数量和类型被认为是银行产出的最佳计量。然而，一般情况下难以获得上述的特定数据，因此，在实践中，存贷款账户的数量通常被用来计量银行的产出。中介方法认为银行是在存款人和贷款人之间融通资金的金融中介。在生产过程中，银行贷款和投资的金额代表产出，而劳动力和存款表示投入。这种方法是把存款作为投入，同时考虑了经营成本和利息成本，这也是它不同于生产方法之处

(Goddard et al.，2001)。生产方法和中介方法都不是完美的，它们可以相互补充(Berger and Humphrey，1997)。上述方法强调了银行某一方面的功能，可用于分析不同层次的效率研究。在考虑银行经营成本的情况下，生产方法适合于研究银行的成本效率。在控制银行全面成本的情况下，中介方法适合于分析银行的经济差异性(Ferrier and Lovell，1990)。这种方法考虑了利息费用，对检验银行效率和边界分析都是有用的。

在银行效率的研究中，运用哪种估计方法来确定最佳业务边界颇有争议。Berger 和 Humphrey(1997)对 130 多篇有关金融机构效率的研究论文进行了很有价值的综述，从中总结出了 5 种主要的估计方法。这些方法可划分成两大类——参数方法和非参数方法。在这些论文中，参数方法和非参数方法做出了相似的效率估计。平均来说，美国的金融机构中成本无效率的达 20%，利润无效率的达 50%。与使用参数方法的研究相比，使用非参数方法的研究获得较低的平均效率估计和较大的离散趋势。尽管两种方法估计的平均效率相似，但对各个公司的无效率排名并不完全一致。

参数方法可被进一步划分成 3 种主要方法来确定最佳业务边界。第一种方法是随机边界方法(SFA)，它由 Aigner、Lovell、Schmidt(1977)，Meeuser、Van den Broeck(1977)分别独立发展而成。随机边界方法界定了成本、利润或生产函数的函数形式，并且允许误差项中包括无效率因素。为区分两种成分而对误差项分布所做的两个假设是：(1)无效率用 μ 表示，服从非对称半正态分布，这一假设的逻辑是无效率只能使成本增加而超出最佳边界水平；(2)随机误差项用 V 表示，由于随机波动可增加或减少成本，所以随机误差项服从对称标准正态分布(Bauer et al.，1993)。随机边界方法应用的相关文献可参见

Ferrier 和 Lovell(1990)、Bauer 等(1993)、Kwan 和 Eisenbeis(1995)以及 Clark 和 Siems(2002)等人的成果。在中国,中国银行业的研究中至今还未发现有人使用过上述研究方法。其他两种确定最佳业务边界的方法是自由分布方法(DFA)和厚边界方法(TFA)。DFA 假定在所有时间内效率差别是稳定的,对每家公司估计的效率是其平均剩余和在边界线上的行业平均剩余之间的差额。Clark 和 Siems(2002)在他们的研究中曾经运用过 TFA。在他们的研究中,TFA 被用于考察银行业中表外业务的 X 效率。TFA 为单个公司提供了总体效率水平估计而不是点效率估计。这种方法曾被 Berger 和 Humphrey(1997)、Bauer 等(1993)使用过。

与界定生产效率函数形式的参数方法不同,非参数方法对生产边界的限制较少。非参数方法可进一步划分成两类:数据包络分析(DEA)和自由可置壳(FDH)。DEA 是一个线性的程序化方法,被用来估计决策单位的效率。DEA 是直接基于一组特定的公司数据而不是一种特定的函数形式界定生产边界的。与最优业务边界的差幅反映了一家公司的无效率(Cooper and Rhodes, 1978)。在金融机构效率研究中,使用过 DEA 分析技术的有 Ferrier 和 Lovell(1990)和 Aly 等(1990)。在中国,最近 Zheng Liu 和 Bigsten(2003)在评价国有企业绩效时曾经使用过 DEA 技术。FDH 是 DEA 的一种特例,它只是放松了凸性假定而已(Berger and Humphrey, 1997)。

用于确定效率最佳边界的方法各有利弊。非参数方法允许效率在一定时期内发生变动,不要求对所有研究样本数据的无效率分布做先定假设。然而,它的一大缺陷是假设没有随机误差影响银行业绩。由于忽略潜在的偏误,随机误差的影响可能会包括到效率项的估计中(Berger and Humphrey, 1997)。非参数方法的另一个缺陷是忽略了价格对效率——配置效率的影响，只是说明了技术效率(Berger and Mester, 1997)。至于参数方法，一个主要缺陷是为最佳效率边界先定了函数形式，因而可能导致效率计量出现偏差(Berger and Humphrey, 1997)。我们的研究使用22家银行6年期间的一组数据，不同时期不同类型的银行的效率会有显著的区别。换言之，随机误差项的影响是很大的。因此，参数方法，尤其是随机前沿生产函数方法更适合于本文的研究需要。

四、随机前沿生产函数模型

(一) 理论模型

由于笔者关注的是验证效率的主要决定因素，所以本文采用中介方法计量银行投入和产出。银行的产出可定义为税前利润的账面价值或贷款的账面价值，这是因为特定的前沿生产函数模型不考虑复合产出。贷款量包括扣除贷款损失准备金后的短期、中期、长期和其他贷款。税前利润是资产负债表中的会计利润。在利润和贷款模型中，银行投入被定义为固定资产、存款、权益和劳动力，其中劳动力成本包括在营业费用中。然而，多次的估计模型结果表明这个变量是不显著的，所以在最终确定的模型中剔除了营业成本这一变量。

有人批评随机前沿生产函数方法使用了先定函数形式以及假设随机误差项和无效率的分布。然而，恰恰是随机误差项和无效率的分离，才使被估技术效率有效且一致。

以前的研究多采用两阶段估计程序，但它有缺点，即它在两估计阶段中关于无效率影响的独立性的假定是不一致的。本文采用 Battese 和 Coelli(1995)提出的单阶段估计方法，同时假定非负技术无效率的影响是特定公司变量和时间的函数，而且假定技术无效率的影响服从常方差、期望是可观测变量的线性函数的截尾正态分布。下面的模型考虑了随机边界中的技术变化和不同时间的技术无效率的估计问题。

$$Y_{it} = \beta_0 + \beta_t t + \beta x_{it} + (V_{it} - U_{it}),\ i = 1, \cdots, N;\ t = 1, \cdots, T \tag{1}$$

其中 i 和 t 分别表示公司和时间，x_{it} 表示解释变量向量，设 $V_{it} \sim N(0, \sigma_v^2)$，$\beta$ 表示待估参数向量，U_{it} 表示非负随机变量，该变量与生产的技术无效率相关联，设其服从截尾（在 0 点处截断）正态分布 $N(m_{it}, \sigma_u^2)$。等式(2)说明了 U_{it} 即技术无效率影响的界定：

$$U_{it} = \delta_0 + \delta_t t + \delta z_{it} + W_{it} \tag{2}$$

其中 z_{it} 表示与生产期间的技术无效率相关联的解释变量向量，δ 表示待估系数向量，设 W_{it} 服从截尾正态分布 $N(0, \sigma^2)$。第 i 家银行在 t 时间的生产技术效率被定义为

$$TE_{it} = E(-U_{it}) = E(-z_{it}\delta - w_{it}) \tag{3}$$

随机生产函数(1)式中的时间趋势变量 t 解释的是不变速率的中性技术进步，无效率函数(2)式中的 t 则是为了捕捉无效率的短暂变化，相对于以不变速率移动的最佳边界效率。于是，生产率的变化可被分解为边界的移动和对边界的趋近或远离两部分（Yao and Liu，1998）。

（二）经验模型

由于银行产出可用利润或贷款量予以计量，所以同样的生产函数可以用两种不同的形式进行估计。一种是把税前利润作为产出，另一种是把贷款量作为产出。方程(4)式和(5)式说明的是利润模型。贷款模型与利润模型一样，具有相同的结构和

解释变量。

$$
\begin{aligned}
\ln(profit_{it}) = \beta_0 + \beta_1 t + \beta_2 \ln(Fixedasset_{it}) \\
+ \beta_3 \ln(Deposit_{it}) \\
+ \beta_4 \ln(Equity_{it}) + V_{it} - U_{it}
\end{aligned} \tag{4}
$$

$$
| U_{it} | = \delta_0 + \delta_1 \ln(E/Aratio) + \delta_2 Ownership \tag{5}
$$

其中下标 i 和 t 分别表示银行和时间,ln 表示自然对数。在这个模型中,用税前利润计量产出,用固定资产、存款和权益测量投入。

在无效率函数中,两个解释变量是银行特定变量——权益/资产比率和所有权特征,这两个变量被假设为对无效率有显著影响。其中第一项是对风险—权益/资产比率的会计学计量,用 E/A 表示,它计量的是银行账面资产的资本化程度,这个因素被用来分析无效率与行为尤其是银行承担风险行为之间的联系。Kwan 和 Eisenbeis(1996)主张并证明效率越高的银行越倾向于承担更多的风险。本文特别关注资本化程度,并用权益/资产比率作为计量银行承担风险的指标。E/A 比率低的银行愿意承担更多的风险,由于风险金更高的缘故,其效率可能更高。因此,E/A 比率对效率有负影响。另一个因素是所有权特征。为了对银行的进一步改革提供有价值的信息,本文详细考察了所有制对银行效率的影响。这是因为国有银行的私有化是改革的一个重要政策问题。在估计时,所有制形式使用虚拟变量表示,非国有银行被赋值为 1,国有银行被赋值为 0。

(三) 数据

本文采用的数据是从 Bankscope 中 22 家商业银行的资产负债表和损益表中取得的。Bankscope 提供了世界上许多国家大量的银行资料。在 22 家银行中,2 家银行的数据是 1996—2001 年的数据,7 家银行的数据是 1995—2000 年的数据,其余的是1995—2001年的数据,上述数据形成了一个非平衡性的数据表。非平衡性的数据可在计算机程序——Frontier 4.1中运算。就所有制而言,样本银行包括四大国有银行、11家股份制银行和7家其他所有制形式的银行(Bankscope)。表1描述了银行投入和产出概况。

表1　1995—2001年22家银行的基本指标和均值概况

单位:10亿元

变　量	1995年	1996年	1997年	1998年	1999年	2000年	2001年
税前利润	6.81	8.26	9.19	8.49	8.50	8.77	7.81
贷　款	745.5	903.3	1004.6	1142.2	1214.7	1210.7	1359.9
固定资产	13.52	19.22	20.15	22.46	29.80	36.41	32.97
存　款	334.27	406.07	512.72	604.70	716.04	820.51	920.97
权　益	48.28	49.12	50.75	94.42	93.25	96.24	97.31
E/A比率	6.67	6.115	6.955	8.25	8.135	8.165	8.172

资料来源:作者根据从Bankscope中得到的样本资料数据计算而得。

五、结果和解释

(一)利润模型

在利润模型中,运用计算机程序Frontier 4.1(Coelli,1996),可获得极大似然比参数估计值(ML)。表2列出了这些估计值和标准差。

表2　回归结果[因变量=ln(税前利润)]

变　量	ML估计	t值
A. 生产函数		
截距	0.9469	6.5502
时间	−0.1240	−6.6178

（续表）

变　量	ML 估计	t 值
固定资产	0.1111	2.4673
存款	0.3303	5.6373
权益	0.3044	3.60000
B. 无效函数		
截距	−12.9033	−7.2360
E/A 比率	4.7702	16.6217
所有制	−2.5344	−4.4537
C. 方差参数		
δ^2	3.5463	4.1056
R	0.9941	237.0926
D. 诊断和其他信息		
LR 检验	146.4644	
自然对数(可能性)	−95.5927	
样本数	154	
年份	7	
横截面数量	22	
平均技术效率	0.6300	

注：(1) 所有的变量是自然对数形式。

(2) 无效率函数中的负号表示变量对生产效率有正影响，反之亦然。

被估系数的符号与预期一致，而且所有的系数在 5%或低于 5%的临界值水平上是统计显著的。固定资产、存款和权益的被估计系数分别是它们对利润的弹性。存款和权益几乎有相同的弹性，它们分别是 0.3303 和 0.3044。固定资产的弹性相对较小，为 0.1111，但统计上也是显著的。其中单侧偏误成分由似然比(LR)检验来鉴定，且最终似然比(LR)是高度显著的。变差率的估计值$[\gamma=\sigma_u^2/(\sigma_u^2+\sigma_v^2)]$为 0.9941，表明无效率因素 U_{it} 是随机的。

在样本期间，技术效率的平均水平为 63%，同最大可能水平 100%差 37%。图 1 描述的是 22 家银行的平均估计效率。效率最高的是中国招商银行，其平均技术效率为 91.23%；效率最低的是中国农业银行，平均技术效率为 40.95%。各银行间效率的很大差别说明提高中国商业银行整体效率的潜力巨大。

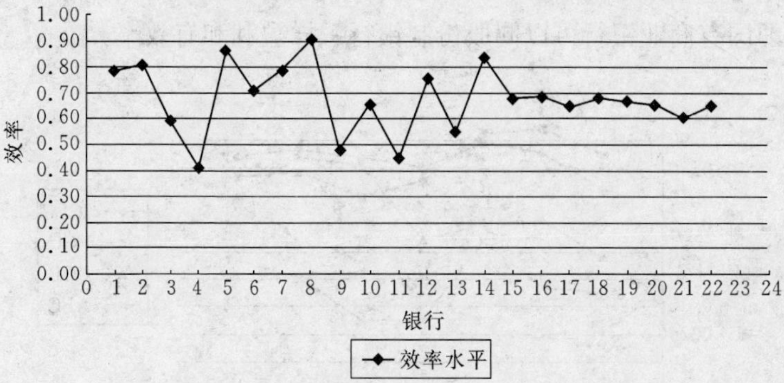

图 1　中国的银行平均效率(利润)(1995—2001 年)

由于四大国有银行在银行业中处于主导地位，是改革的焦点，因而它们的效率水平值得进一步详细地考察。图 2 描述了样本期四大国有银行的平均效率。利润模型表明，中国农业银行的效率最低，而且它的效率在样本期间波动最剧烈。另一方面，从 1995 年起，同中国工商银行与中国银行一样，中国农业银行的效率也略有提高。1998 年，在遭受亚洲金融危机的系统冲击后，中国建设银行的效率提高了许多。然而，在 2000 年和 2001 年，中国建设银行的效率急剧下降，与此同时，中国工商银行和中国银行的效率略有下降，而中国农业银行的效率却有所提高。中国工商银行和中国银行的效率呈现出类似且稳定的特征。这两家银行在 1995 年之后的两年间效率都得以提高，但从

1997 年起都出现了下降,这显示了亚洲金融危机的冲击。1998 年,中国工商银行的效率有所提高,而且尔后持续提高。中国银行效率水平的恶化一直延续到 1999 年,尔后两年有所改善。中国工商银行和中国银行的平均技术效率分别为78.28%和80.55%,都比行业平均水平高很多,也比股份制银行77.84%的平均水平高。这个结果表明了一个国有商业银行的例外情况,即国有商业银行可以同股份制银行一样盈利和有效率。

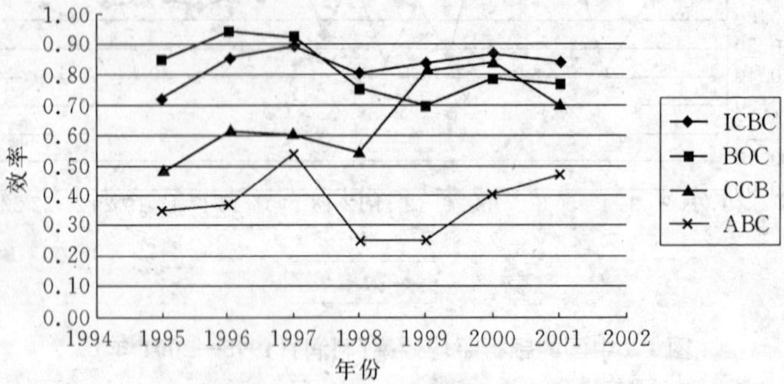

注:ICBC 为中国工商银行;BOC 为中国银行;CCB 为中国建设银行;ABC 为中国农业银行。

图 2　四大国有银行平均效率(利润)(1995—2001 年)

无效率模型中的被估系数是本文研究的兴趣所在。在技术的无效率回归分析中,包括了两个解释变量:E/A 比率和所有制特征。研究发现 E/A 比率对无效率有正的影响,E/A 比例较低的银行更有效率。换句话说,高度资本化的银行效率是比较低的,这证实了我们关于预算约束的假设。另一个解释变量是所有权特征。正如表 2 的第二部分所显示,所有制对技术效率有显著的影响,其估计系数为−2.53。负号表明股份制银行更有效率。图 3 描述了所有制特征对银行效率的影响。研究发现,数据期内的股份制银行的效率比国有银行大约高18个百分点。国有银行的平均技术效率为59.67%,而股份制银行为77.48%。结果表明所有权结构是解释总的无效率差异的一个重要因素。而且,图3表明国有银行和非国有银行的技术效率有相似的趋势。国有银行和非国有银行的平均效率从1995年开始提高,分别于1996年和1997年达到最高点。在亚洲金融危机时期,效率水平下降,并在1998年下降到了最低点。尔后,在数据期的后4年里,国有银行和非国有银行的平均技术效率都稳步提高。这些相似的趋势既反映了外部的冲击,也反映了内部的冲击。外部冲击主要是由亚洲金融危机触发的,而内部冲击则反映了在危机后政府在提高银行效率方面所做的努力。我们的分析结果表明,亚洲金融危机后中国的紧缩银行政策得到了丰厚的回报。

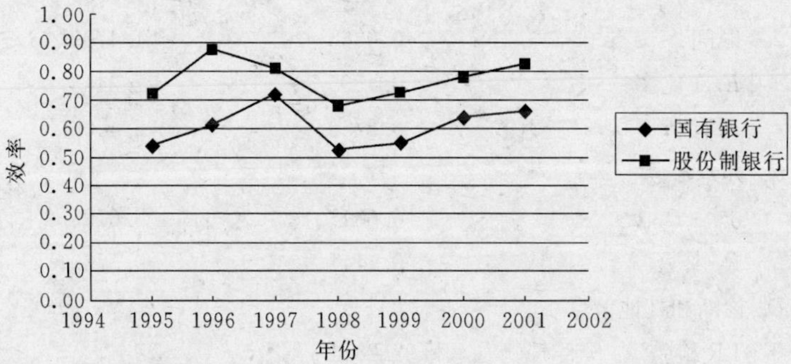

图3　四大国有银行和股份制银行的平均效率(利润)(1995—2001年)

(二) 贷款模型

如表3所示,来自于贷款模型的结果与利润模型相似。系数的符号与利润模型的系数符号相同,且所有的系数都是统计上显著的。固定资产、存款和权益的被估系数分别是8.41%、46.06%和62.32%。与利润模型相比,存款和权益似乎在贷款模型中有更大的影响。负的时间系数(年)表明在样本期内,产出水平每年下降1.09%。LR检验和变差率估计值再一次证实了单侧偏误成分的存在,该偏误代表了随机无效率。

表3 回归结果[因变量=ln(贷款)]

变 量	ML估计	t值
A. 生产函数		
截距	0.1909	1.6207
时间	−0.0109	−0.6404
固定资产	0.0841	2.4651
存款	0.4606	11.5178
权益	0.6232	9.5670
B. 无效函数		
截距	−0.2683	−1.9051
时间	0.0268	1.4709
E/A比率	0.4525	7.3413
所有制	−0.2756	−6.4406
C. 方差参数		
δ^2	0.0347	8.6795
R	0.1141	0.5730
D. 诊断和其他信息		
LR检验	92.2811	
自然对数(可能性)	40.7622	
样本数	154	
年份	7	
横截面数量	22	
平均技术效率	0.6392	

注:(1) 所有的变量是自然对数形式。

(2) 无效率函数中的负号表示变量对生产效率有正影响,反之亦然。

被估计的平均技术效率是 63.19%。它稍高于利润模型的结果。图 4 描述了 22 家银行的平均估计效率。效率最高的银行是中国民生银行,它的平均技术效率是 89%。而效率最低的是中国银行,其平均技术效率只有 58.03%。

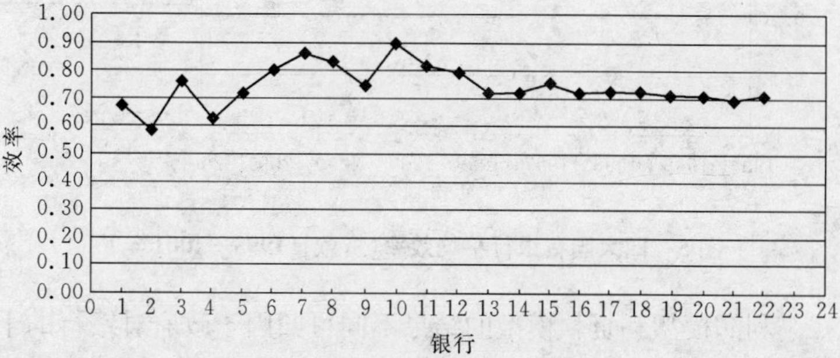

图 4　中国的银行平均效率(贷款)(1995—2001 年)

尽管在前沿生产函数模型中对时间趋势变量的系数的估计在统计上并不显著,但它也揭示了一定时期内的下降趋势。前沿生产函数模型中的时间趋势变量的负系数表明,生产前沿每年以 1.09%的水平下滑。在无效率函数中时间趋势变量的负系数揭示出,生产的无效率倾向于以每年 2.68%的水平上升。这意味着数据期内的效率和生产前沿都在下滑。

图 5 说明的是四大国有银行的效率,它与利润模型图是不同的。四大国有银行的平均估计效率有相似的趋势和水平。在样本期的前 3 年,四大国有银行的效率是稳定的,但在 1997 年出现下滑。这与亚洲金融危机的发生相一致。后来,除中国银行的效率水平下滑外,四大国有银行的效率水平大致不变。这个结果证实了政府对银行贷款决策的干预。在亚洲金融危机期间及其之后,国务院曾命令四大国有银行每年发放 1000 亿元的特别贷款来刺激国内经济。

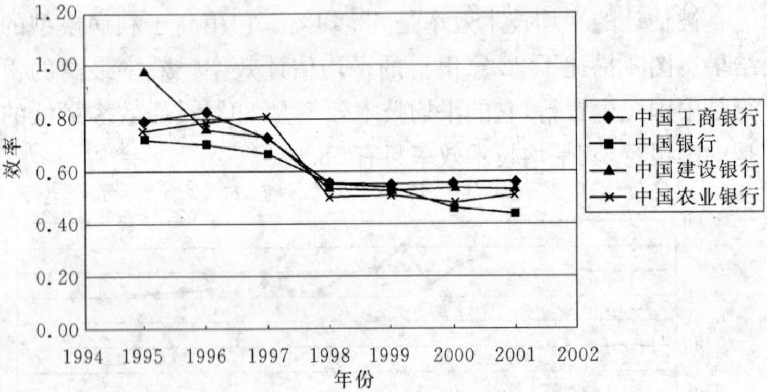

图 5　四大国有银行平均效率(贷款)(1995—2001 年)

利润模型和贷款模型的结果不同可归因于政府对银行的干预程度不同。在贷款模型中,政府的直接干预导致四大国有银行具有相似的效率趋势和水平。尽管我国为减少干预和政策性贷款而进行了多年改革,但四大国有银行仍然作为政府的左膀右臂在发挥作用。

对于无效率而言,它们同样受 E/A 比率和所有制特征的影响。其中,E/A 比率的弹性是 0.4525,且统计上是显著的,这表明它对无效率有正影响。这一结果与利润模型的结果是一致的。所有制对无效率的影响的估计系数为−0.2756,它尽管小但统计上是显著的。同利润模型相比,贷款模型中的所有制特征对银行无效率的影响较小,这证明国有银行和股份制银行都受到了政府对贷款的干预。图 6 描述的是 1995—2001 年期间所有制特征对银行效率的影响。在前 3 年,四大国有银行比股份制银行的效率高出 10 个百分点。在 1998 年,四大国有银行的效率急剧下降,从 76.90%下降到 52.68%;而与此同时,股份制银行的效率却保持不变。在最后 3 年,股份制银行比国有银行变得更有效率。在样本期内,股份制银行的效率平均比国有银行高出8个百分点。这个结果与利润模型的结果略有不同，这是由于政府对银行贷款的干预程度不同造成的。虽然政府可以影响国有银行和非国有银行的主要决策，但是，对后者的干预程度显然比前者小。

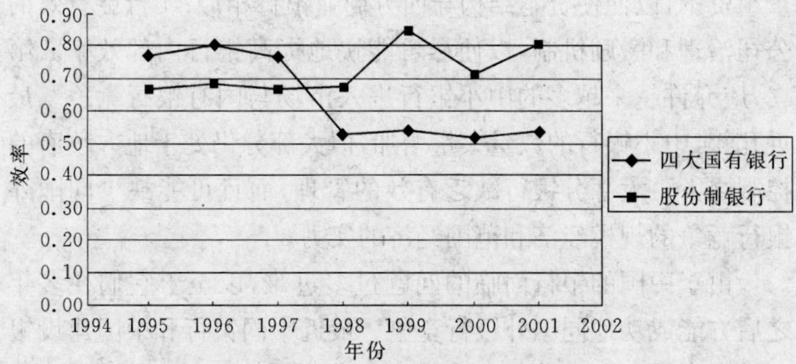

图6　四大国有银行和股份制银行的平均效率（贷款）（1995—2001年）

六、讨论和结论

在利润模型和贷款模型中，对样本银行估计的平均效率非常低，大约为63%，但同其他国家的研究结果没有本质区别。在相关文献中，美国银行的平均效率大约是80%（Berger and Humphrey, 1997）。与欧美国家相比，较低效率的估计值符合中国的客观实际情况，即尽管进行了多年的改革，中国的商业银行仍然在很大程度上受到政府的干预和控制。

四大国有银行在银行业中仍居于主导地位。虽然经过多年的改革，四大国有银行的效率水平至今仍然很低，没有明显的改进。它一方面表明政府对银行的主要决策的干预仍然存在；另一方面，它也反映出提高银行效率的巨大潜力和空间。

本文的经验结果说明所有制改革和预算约束的变化能有效

提高竞争水平和效率，这个结果对于迎接更为激烈的来自入世挑战的中国银行业来说具有重要的政策含义。

中国必须进行以下两项根本性改革：第一，享有主导地位的国有银行，必须真正实现商业化，完全摆脱政府的控制和干预，重组资本，以便使资本结构与西方商业银行相似；实行更有效的公司治理和激励机制，以便尽可能快地提高银行内部效率。第二，应允许越来越多的中小银行进入市场与国有银行竞争。最近几年，中小银行的数量大量增加，但大部分仍处于地方政府的控制之下。大部分银行缺乏有效的管理，而且可能缺少同国外银行竞争的规模经济和范围经济的实力。

由于中国的银行面临的问题过多过难，以至于它们在多年之后方能成功地同国外银行竞争。最近中国银行和中国建设银行的资本重组标志着朝这个方向迈出了重要一步。然而，改革能否成功将取决于四大国有银行对新的改革方法作何反应。我们没有过于关注不良贷款问题。如果银行仍然有巨额不良贷款，如果公司治理仍然在很大程度上受政治影响，改革成功的可能性将很小。我们的结论是，在不远的将来，当国外大银行进入国内市场同四大国有银行进行竞争时，中国将不得不面临许多痛苦。真正的战斗即将开始，所以，中国必须采取根本性的改革措施。这些措施不仅包括银行的资本重组，而且包括银行治理方式和高级管理人员任命方法的改革等。

参考文献

Aigner, D., Lovell, C. A. K. and Schmidt, P., 1977, "Formulation and Estimation of Stochastic frontier Production Models", *Journal of Econometrics*, Vol. 6, pp. 21—37.

Aly, Hassan Y., Grabowski, Richard, Pasurka, Carl, Rangan, Nanda, 1990, "Technical, Scale, and Allocative Efficiencies in U. S. Banking: an Empirical Investigation", *Review of Economics and Statistics*, Vol. 72, Issue 2: pp. 211—218.

Battese, G. E. and Coelli, T. J., 1995, "A Model for Technical Inefficiency Effects in a Stochastic Frontier Production Function for Panel Date", *Empirical Economics*, Vol. 120, pp. 325—332.

Bauer, P. W., Berger, A. N. and Humphrey, D. B., 1993, "Efficiency and Productive Growth in US Banking", in Fried, H. O., Lovell, C. A. K. and Schmidt, S. S. (eds), *The Measurement of Productive Efficiency: Techniques and Applications*, Oxford University Press, New York.

Berger A. N. and Humphrey, D. B., 1997. "Efficiency of Financial Institutions: International Survey and Directions for Future Research", Finance and Economics Discussion Series, Federal Reserve Board, No. 11. Available from: http://netec. mcc. ac. uk/WoPEc/data/Papers/fipfedgfe 1997—11. html.

Berger A. N. and Mester L. J., 1997, "Inside the Black Box: What Explains Differences in the Efficiencies of Financial Institutions?", Finance and Economics Discussion Series, Federal Reserve Board, No. 10. Available from: http://netec. mcc. ac. uk/WoPEc/data/Papers/fipfedpwp97—1. html.

Chang, G., 2001, *The Coming Collapse of China*, New York: Random House.

Charnes, A., Cooper, W. W. and Rhodes, E., 1978, "Measuring the Efficiency of Decision Making Units", *European Journal of Operational Research*, Vol. 6, pp. 429—444.

Clark, Jeffrey A., Siems, Thomas F., 2002, "X-Efficiency in Banking: Looking Beyond the Balance Sheet", *Journal of Money, Credit and Banking*, Nov, 2002, Vol. 34, Issue 4: pp. 987—1013.

Coelli, T., 1992, "A Computer Program for Frontier Production Function Estimation": Frontier, Version 2. 0. Economics Letters, Vol. 39, pp. 29—32.

Coelli, T., 1996, "A Guide to Frontier Version 4.1: A computer Program for Stochastic Frontier Production and Cost Function Estimation", University of New England: Centre for Efficiency and Productivity Analysis Working Paper.

Dai, X., 2003, "Developing China's Capital Market and Speeding Up Banking Reform", *Journal of Chinese Economic and Business Studies*, Vol. 1, pp. 131—135.

Ferrier, G. D. and Lovell, C. A. K., 1990, "Measuring Cost Efficiency in Banking: Econometric and Linear Programming Evidence", *Journal of Econometrics*, Vol. 46, pp. 229—245.

Goddard, J., Molyneux, P. and Wilson, J., 2001, *European Banking*, John Wiley & Sons.

Huang M. and Zhang Q., 2002, "Changes in Asian Banking Industry", Göteborg, Graduate Business School. Available from: http://www.handels.gu.se/epc/archive/00002088.

Ikeya, M., 2001, "Chinese NPLs-A Struggle Against Chaos", *R&I Asian Focus*, October 24, 2001. Available from: http://www.r-i.co.jp/eng/release/nr_asia/asia011024.pdf.

Koch T. W. and MacDonald S. S., 2000, *Bank Management*, 4th ed., Dryden Press.

Kwan S. H. and Eisenbeis, R. A., 1996, "An Analysis of Inefficiency in Banking: A Stochastic Cost Frontier Approach", Working paper, Working Papers in Applied Economics, Federal Reserve Bank of San Francisco. Online available from: http://www.sf.frb.org/econrsrch/econrev/96—2/kwan.pdf.

Leibenstein, Harvey, 1996, "Allocative Efficiency versus 'X-Efficiency'", *American Economic Review*, Vol. 56, pp. 392—415.

Liu T., 2001, "The Entry of Foreign Banks into the Chinese Banking Sector", in *The Banking Industry in the Emerging Market Economies: Competition, Consolidation and Systemic Stability*, BIS papers, NO. 4

pp. 54—55. Online available from: http://www.bis.org/publ/bispap04.pdf.

Lovell, C. A. K., 1993, "Production Frontiers and Productive Efficiency", in Fried, H. O., Lovell, C. A. K. and Schmidt, S. S. (eds), *The Measurement of Productive Efficiency: Techniques and Applications*, Oxford University Press, New York.

Meeusen, W. and J. van den Broeck, 1977, "Efficiency Estimation from Cobb-Douglas Production Functions with Composed Error", *International Economic Review*, Vol. 18, pp. 435—444.

Molyneux, P., Altunbas, Y. and Gardener, E., 1996, *Efficiency in European Banking*, John Wiley & Sons.

Reifschneider, D. and Stevenson, R., 1991, "Systematic Departures from the Frontier: A Framework for the Analysis of Firm Inefficiency", *International Economics Review*, Vol. 32, pp. 715—723.

Saunders A., 1999, *Financial Institutions Management*, McGraw-Hill HE.

Wong Y. C. R. and Wong M. L. S., 2001, "Competition in China's Domestic Banking Industry", *Cato Journal*, Vol. 21, 1.

Yao, S. and Liu, Z., 1998, "Determinants of Grain Production and Technical Efficiency in China", *Journal of Agricultural Economics*, Vol. 49, pp. 171—184.

Zheng, Jinghai, Liu Xiaoxuan, Bigsten, Arne, 2003, "Efficiency, Technical Progress, and Best Practice in Chinese State Enterprises(1980—1994)", *Journal of Comparative Economics*, Vol. 31, Issue 1: pp. 134—152.

(原载《经济研究》2004 年第 8 期)

正式契约的第三方实施与权力最优化

——对农民工工资纠纷的契约论解释

杨瑞龙　卢周来

（中国人民大学经济学院）

一、引　言

农民工工资被严重拖欠已成为社会不稳定的重要因素，为了保护农民工的利益，从 2003 年底，中央政府发动了一场全国范围的清理拖欠农民工工资的"运动"。本文将运用契约理论分析农民工工资纠纷背后的深层次问题，因为从经济学以及法学的角度看，农民工与用人单位之间，无论是否签订了正式用工合同，都构成了事实上的契约关系。

工资纠纷与其他合同纠纷一样，都涉及到契约履行。而制度的实施特征（enforcement character）就是解决契约的实施问题。一个契约被有效地实施无非有三种方式，即自我实施（self enforcement）、相互实施以及第三方实施（the third-party enforcement）。其中，第三方实施又主要是国家（政府）作为强制实施者，即国家"作为契约的第三方和最终强制根源"（诺斯，1995）。不同的契约类型对应于不同的契约环境，但在发达市场经济体中占统治地位的是国家作为强制实施者的第三方实施契约(Claude Ménard, 2000)。如果国家作为强制实施者出现的第三方实施契约未得到履行。其原因则在于国家强制实施能力不足(巴泽尔,1997)。而一旦国家作为第三方失败后,将出现其他可替代的第三方,或者导致由第三方实施退回到某种私人方式实施(R. Sherwood, 1994; A. Shleifer, 1998)。此时,对那些因采取私人方式实施所导致行为非法的主体追究责任时,应该区分开是适应"产权法则"(property rule)还是"责任法则"(liability rule)(Lars Werin, 2001)。而要彻底解决问题,则要努力寻找实施国家作为第三方权力的最优化途径。

本文依据上述分析框架,首先试图回答农民工工资纠纷的根源何在;然后分析是什么原因导致应该由国家作为强制执行第三方的正式合同得不到履行,进而分析正式合同得不到履行可能导致的后果,最后给出若干简短的结论。

二、"自我实施"还是"第三方实施":农民工工资纠纷的根源

目前,对农民工工资纠纷的解释之一是农民工与用人单位之间并没有签订正式用工合同,大多是口头协议,导致法律介入困难。在2003年年底"清欠运动"之前,有关劳动仲裁机构也的确以农民工与用人单位之间未签订正式合同为由拒绝调解。在进一步分析为何农民工不与用工单位之间签订正式用工合同时,目前流行的解释有两条:一是农民工维权意识淡漠;二是由于农民工供大于求,使得在谈判能力上处于弱势的农民工无法提出要求与用人单位签订正式契约。

上述解释从现象看似乎有道理,尤其是关于谈判地位与谈判能力之间的不对等的解释。但透过现象我们发现,我国农民

工工资纠纷绝大部分发生在建筑行业，而此行业农民工供大于求的矛盾并不突出。相反，随着房地产热以及国家基本建设不断升温，对农民工的需求非常旺盛。

重要的是上述解释与主流契约理论之间存在矛盾。不同的契约性质取决于不同的签约环境。“自我实施”契约是交易成本最低的一种契约。然而，随着社会交易范围扩大，“自我实施所需要的前提条件，即共同知识、博弈的稳定性和无限重复这些假定不仅很强，而且根本不可能在现实世界中观察到”（诺斯，1995），正因为“自我实施”的交易成本随着社会交易面的扩大越来越高，因此，这种方式逐渐减少，目前仅存在于核心家庭内部、很亲密的邻里或朋友之间。

相比较而言，在现代社会交易面非常大、人员流动性极强的情况下，国家作为“第三方实施契约”能降低交易成本。一个法治国家，首先对于交易者的“准入”有严格的规范，大大降低了“逆向选择”成本；其次，对于交易过程也有严格的规范，对契约履行情况有足够能力进行监督，因为它拥有工商行政管理部门、劳动执法部门、劳动保护部门、财务审计部门等等，从而大大降低了“道德风险”成本；最后，国家还拥有军队、警察、法庭等暴力机器，与任何其他性质的交易主体相比，都处于强势地位，有足够的能力对毁约者进行事后的惩罚。正是不断降低交易成本的制度变迁方式使得现代社会更多地选择国家作为第三方实施的契约（Barzel，1998a）。

从以上理论框架，很容易得出结论：在任何一个劳动力流动性很大的市场经济体中，劳动合同应该是国家需要规范与管理的合同。再具体到我国农民工用工契约，农民工更不可能选择与用人单位之间口头非正式自我实施契约。这是因为，与一般已经有集体合约的城市企业雇工面临的签约环境不同，农民工进城后，面对的签约环境不确定性因素更大：流动性强、“共同知识”缺少、反复交易不可能，使得农民工更需要国家来保护其权益。也就是说，进城务工的农民作为谈判过程中弱势的一方，面对完全陌生、可能存心想通过不签订正式合同规避约束的一次性交易的雇主，农民工更愿意也更应该选择由国家作为第三方强制实施的正式合同。

但现实中情况相反，即农民工用工契约更多地是“自我实施”契约。因而也就需要有更深入的观察以及更合理的解释来说明。为此我们对北京6个工地320名农民工进行了一项随机调查。① 在320名农民工中，通过亲戚、老乡与朋友介绍进入工地的为273名，占被调查对象的85.3%。其中236名农民工并不知道工程的建设方与发包方是谁，他们仅与工程的某个环节的最后分承包方认识，而这个最后分承包商正是带这些民工进城的老乡、亲戚或朋友。

由此，我们发现，农民工用工契约其实并不仅仅涉及到两方即农民工与用工单位，而且还涉及到另外一个经济主体即农民工的直接雇主。农民工更多地是与他们的直接雇主签约，而直接雇主才与更上层承包商发生关系。

农民工与其直接雇主一般具有“关系人”(relationship)性质。North(诺斯，1995)曾将这种关系构成的世界称之为一个“人际交换”的世界。在这个世界中，由于有一个紧密的社会相互作用系统，交易的衡量成本非常低，所有这些组织中的机会主义问题很有限或根本不存在。更具体地说，“人际交换的世界”中之所以具备自我实施契约的基本前提是：首先，老乡、亲戚与朋友，相互比较熟悉，拥有“共同知识”；其次，这种地缘或血缘关系使得直接雇主不仅仅追求利润最大化动机，同时还有追求声誉最大化。这种动机增加了直接雇主自我实施契约的刺激；再次，地缘与血缘关系，使得农民工与直接雇主之间博弈的稳定性与可重复性有保障；最后，并非不重要的一点，尽管存在农民工在总量上的供过于求，但正是因为不确定性与不信任程度很高的农民工用工市场的整体环境，使得由“关系人”交易的相互依赖程度很高，这也提高了契约自我实施的可能性。以上原因使农民工用工契约更多地是一种“关系人契约”，在不确定性的环境中，它具备了某种自我实施的性质，因而不需要国家作为第三方介入。

因此，农民工工资被拖欠，原因就不能归咎于农民工与其直接雇主之间自我实施的契约未被履行，而是其直接雇主与承包商或建设方之间的正式契约没有被实施，所以就有必要分析作为农民工直接雇主的分包商与总承包商的关系，以及总承包商与建设方（发包方）的关系。这些契约关系发生在一个典型的“非人际交换世界”。在这样的世界中，交换是在两个毫无人际关系的经济人之间进行，没有重复交易关系。“在一个财富最大化世界的逻辑下，衡量成本可能很高，从欺骗和违约中获取的收益可能大于从合作行为中获取的收益”，因而，“由政治团体来充当第三方并使用强制方法来实施合约，这在监察与实施合约时会具有巨大的规模经济”（诺斯，1995，第75—79页）。所以，作为农民工直接雇主的分包商与上层承包商以及建设方应该签订正式契约。②

我们将从建设方到农民工之间的各层次契约关系以下图表示：

建设方 —正式契约→ 总承包商 —正式契约→ 分包商（包工头，农民工直接雇主）—自我实施契约→ 农民工

农民工与其直接雇主之间的自我实施契约未被执行的重要根源可追溯到建设方（发包方）以及总承包商与农民工的直接雇

主的契约未被有效实施。在当前建筑市场竞争异常激烈的情况下,工程的承包商往往不惜采用先期垫付建设资金的手段以期在竞标中胜出,这就为建设方或总承包商拖欠工程款留下了余地。但即便如此,因为建设方与总承包商的契约,以及总承包商与大的分承包商之间的契约是通过国家作为第三方强制实施的正式契约,分包商(农民工的直接雇主)仍然预期建设方或总承包商不敢不履行契约。而现实往往与他们预期的相反。正是这种本来通过国家作为第三方实施的契约没有被有效地执行,最后的分包商往往无法及时拿到工程款,因而也就无法及时给农民工发放工钱,导致了后继的自我实施契约没有办法执行。

综上所述,一旦契约具备了自我实施的基础,应该可以被自我实施。而最后没有被自我实施,就应该寻找其他原因。农民工工资纠纷不在于其与直接雇主的自我实施合约失效,而在于其上层正式契约没有被执行。[3]而由国家作为第三方实施的正式契约都无法执行,体现的是政府作为强制实施者的失败。因此,追根溯源,农民工工资被拖欠现象的发生,其实是国家(政府)作为强制实施者的第三方的失败[4]导致的。

三、绝对权力与相对权力:国家(政府)作为第三方失败的原因

为什么国家(政府)作为正式契约实施的第三方会出现失败?我们可以运用诺斯的国家悖论来解释。North(1981)认为,为了促使一个社会走上经济增长路径,国家的功能远不是仅仅推行自由放任的原则,它还应该减少市场运作中的交易费用并使得个人企业家从交易中受益成为可能。为此,一个国家必须演化为一个有效、公正的契约第三方执行者。第三方强制实施意味

着国家应该强大到能有效监督产权、强制实施契约。但他紧接着却悲叹道，在现阶段，以我们现有的知识，还无人知晓如何创建这样一个实体。其原因是，如果一个国家一旦具有了这样强制的力量，那么，那些管理该国家的人便会利用这种力量来谋取自身的收益最大化，而以牺牲社会其他人的利益为代价。

Barzel(1998a)也认为，国家作为第三方强制，也不得不同时考虑强制实施行动的现值最大化。而同时，"国家作为强制实施者(与一般的第三方实施者的区别在于)并不因长期关系而受其个人客户的约束。如果没有限制，他可能从没收其强制实施所带来的收益中获益"。Barzel 还认为，任何一级政府作为第三方，"为了使强制实施行动的现值最大化，强制实施者必须考虑他们目前的行为会怎样影响其从随后行为中所得的净收益"，"而由于罚金是在长时期内产生的，它也就依赖于强制方与被强制方的持续关系"。

我们知道，农民工流动性很强，所在地政府从某一个(群)民工那里只能收取有限次数的租金；而农民工所服务的单位或企业则将与所在地政府长期打交道，并能长期与反复抽取租金。因此，在处理农民工与用工单位的契约纠纷时，政府作为第三方，一旦将租金最大化作为自身的目标，将不可避免导致产权界定中"歧视"(discriminate)问题的出现，从而有可能不去强制实施不利于自身租金最大化的契约。

尤其值得注意的是，在中国特定的税收体系下，面临竞争压力的地方政府为了通过追求本地经济的更快增长来获取更多的财政分成及更好的政绩，会争相出台吸引投资的超国民待遇政策(杨瑞龙，1998)。而一旦这些投资者与农民工发生经济纠纷时，为了能留住投资者，即使投资者不履行正式契约，政府作为第三方，其行为选择也可能会偏向投资者一边。

我们将丁际刚等(2002)关于司法公正的模型加以改造和简化,建立起一个简单的模型,分析当作为第三方工具的地方政府,将租金最大化作为目标时,在管理与执行正式契约中的行为选择。

假设某企业 E 应向民工 P 支付工资额为 Q,企业有财产 L,某地政府 G 督查工资支付的努力水平为 $e(e \geqslant 0)$。设督查企业支付额为 $T(e)$,且 $T(e)=ke(k>0)$,即督查的努力与督查的结果成正比;督查的成本为 $C(e)$,且 $C(e)=me^2(m>0)$,显然,$C'>0$, $C''>0$,督查的边际成本递增,m 为政府督查成本系数,k、m 与政府的督查能力以及制度环境有关。再假定该地政府正常的收入为 w,督查后从农民工处可能获得的租金系数为 r。假设企业为拖欠或不付工资,有向政府寻租和不寻租两种策略,通过寻租使政府放弃督查或部分执行督查的结果,而同政府共享剩余的财产,寻租的成本为 b(也可以是政府向企业索取的租金)。政府有接受租金(或向企业索取租金)伙同企业"合谋"和拒绝租金(不向企业索取租金)两种选择。为简单起见,我们再假定企业寻租被拒绝时政府要求企业支付 $T(e)$,但对企业无其他惩罚,可知寻租是企业的占优策略。政府 G 若接受租金则为 G 与企业 E 合谋,企业 E 与 G 共同分享合作的"剩余"(分配系数记为 β, $\beta \in [0, 1]$,实际支付的工资为 $\delta T(e)$ $(\delta \in [0, 1])$。由于局外人对督查工作和合谋行为很难监督,也就是说存在信息不完全,因而合谋行为只有部分事后被发现且得到查处,设发现的概率记为 θ, θ 也可作为政策控制变量,它与监督检查的力度、各方的检举揭发及其他偶然情况有关;合谋后不被发现的概率为 $(1-\theta)$。发现后对政府的惩罚包括基本收入和接受的租金额(如合谋被发现,公众对政府的信用度将降低,由此引起投资水平和消费水平的降低,进而影响政府的财税收入;同时,政府接受的租金额度越高，上级政府施加惩罚的力度越大)，而对企业 E 的惩罚则针对政府要求支付但没有支付的工资额，拖欠的工资额越大则受罚越重。政府 G 和企业 E 的惩罚强度系数分别记为 P_G，P_E。下面讨论政府的行为选择。

政府接受企业租金，双方合谋被发现时，政府与企业各自的收益为：

$$U_{G1} = W + b + r\delta T(e) - C(e) - P_G(b + w) \tag{1}$$

$$U_{E1} = L - b - \delta T(e) - P_E(1 - \delta) T(e) \tag{2}$$

政府接受企业租金，双方合谋未被发现时，政府与企业各自收益为：

$$U_{G2} = w + b + r\delta T(e) - C(e) \tag{3}$$

$$U_{E2} = L - b - \delta T(e) \tag{4}$$

政府与企业必须符合激励相容，即只有当政府、企业合谋的收益大于不合谋的收益时，政府才有合谋而执行部分财产的可能。设企业寻租且被政府接受后的(期望)收益记为 U_{EXPE1}，其寻租被拒绝或不寻租时的收益记为 U_{EXPE2}，则当寻租的期望收益增量 $\Delta E = U_{\text{EXPE1}} - U_{\text{EXPE2}} \geqslant 0$ 时 E 才有寻租的动力。即：

$$\begin{aligned} U_{\text{EXPE1}} &= \theta U_{E1} + (1-\theta) U_{E2} \\ &= \theta[L - b - \delta T(e) - P_E(1-\delta) T(e)] \\ &\quad + (1-\theta)[L - b - \delta T(e)] \end{aligned} \tag{5}$$

$$U_{\text{EXPE2}} = L - T(e) \tag{6}$$

$$\begin{aligned} \Delta E &= U_{\text{EXPE1}} - U_{\text{EXPE2}} \\ &= (1-\delta)(1-\theta P_E) T(e) - b \geqslant 0 \end{aligned} \tag{7}$$

同理，对政府来说，合谋的收益 U_{EXPG1} 大于不合谋的收益

U_{EXPG2}时才有放弃督查或放松督查工资支付额 $T(e)$的动力。即：

$$\begin{aligned} U_{EXPG1} &= \theta U_{G1} + (1-\theta)U_{G2} \\ &= \theta[W + b + r\delta T(e) - C(e) - P_G(b+w)] \\ &\quad + (1-\theta)[w + b + r\delta T(e) - C(e)] \end{aligned} \tag{8}$$

$$U_{EXPG2} = w + rT(e) - C(e) \tag{9}$$

$$\begin{aligned} \Delta G &= U_{EXPG1} - U_{EXPG2} \\ &= (1-\theta P_G)b - \theta P_G w - r(1-\delta)T(e) \geqslant 0 \end{aligned} \tag{10}$$

因此，合谋的必要条件是(7)式、(10)式同时成立。若令 $B_1 \equiv [\theta P_G w + r(1-\delta)T(e)]/(1-\theta PG)$，$B_2 \equiv (1-\delta)(1-\theta P_E)T(e)$，则有：$B_1 \leqslant b \leqslant B_2$。(11)

B_1、B_2 分别为 b 的下限和上限。可见，当租金处于某一区域内，政府将与企业勾结在一起，即政府选择不督查或主动督查不力，而企业将向政府寻租。而实际上，当政府从农民工工资处索取的租金系数 r 很小，政府与企业合谋被发现的概率 θ 很小，或者政府与企业被惩罚的系数 $P_G P_E$ 也很低的情况下，(11)式很容易成立。而正如前文所述，政府从流动性很强、分摊后平均收入很低的农民工那里，得到的租金比率的确很低。在现有的农民工远远供大于求的背景以及现有的制度环境下，政府与企业合谋，农民工工资被拖欠，政府的损失很低。因此，$U_{EXPG1} \geqslant U_{EXPG2}$ 成立，政府会“站”在企业的一方。而从企业的角度看，只要(7)式中$(1-\delta)(1-\theta P_E) \geqslant 0$，企业 E 就有寻租的动力。企业宁可拿出部分利润向政府寻租，也不愿(足额)支付农民工工资。

我们特别考虑当(11)式成立时，将有

$$\max U_G = \max U_{EXPG2} \tag{12}$$

$$\max U_E = \max U_{EXPE1} \tag{13}$$

因为企业 E 与政府 G“合作剩余”的分摊系数 β，($\beta \in [0, 1]$)，$b^* = (1-\beta)B_1 + \beta B_2$，故有：

$$b^* = \{\beta(1-\delta)(1-\theta P_E)(1-\theta P_G)T(e) + (1-\beta)[\theta P_G w + r(1-\delta)T(e)]\} \quad (14)$$

由于 $\Delta G = U_{EXPG1} - U_{EXPG2} \geqslant 0$，故合谋是政府 G 的占优策略，同时寻租也是企业 E 的占优策略，故：

$$\max U_G = \max U_{EXPG1} = \max[(1-\theta P_G)(b+w) + r\delta T(e) - C(e)] \quad (15)$$

由(11)式可推知 $r-(1-\theta P_E)(1-\theta P_G) \leqslant 0$，而 $e \geqslant 0$，将 $C(e) = \mathrm{m}e^2$，$T = ke$，以及(14)式代入(15)式，可求得 e 的极值点：

$$e^* = [\beta(1-\theta P_E)(1-\theta P_G) + r(1-\beta)]k/2m \quad (16)$$

当 U_G 取最大值时(U_{EXPG1} 的二阶条件满足 $U''_{EXPG2} = -2m$，最大值存在)，$e = e^*$ 而 δ 取最小值 0 [因 δ 的系数 $r-(1-\theta P_E)(1-\theta P_G) \leqslant 0$]，$G$ 与 E 共同瓜分督查额 $T(e)[T(e) = ke^*]$，而农民工 P 获得的工资 Q^* 为 0。也就是说，此时政府所负有的督查任务将完全得不到执行，《劳动法》成一纸空文，原因是政府和企业都没有要求支付工人工资的动力。另外我们还可以看出，只要租金额 b 满足条件(11)式，则政府和企业之间“合作剩余”的分配系数 β 对实际的执行财产没有影响。

根据以上分析，我们可以给出具体的博弈结构和收益矩阵，如下图：

		企业：寻租	企业：不寻租
政府	接受	(U_{EXPG1}, U_{EXPE1})	(U_{EXPG2}, U_{EXPE2})
政府	拒绝	(U_{EXPG2}, U_{EXPE2})	(U_{EXPG2}, U_{EXPE2})

由此可知,(接受,寻租)可能是一个符合激励相容条件的均衡结果,在租金最大化目标的驱使下,作为第三方的政府有可能会选择与其承诺作为强制实施的第三方或先期政策不一致的行为,从而导致承诺和政策不具有动态一致性(dynamic consistency,或 time consistency)。

Barzel 将由于第三方追求租金最大化而导致的正式契约无法执行称为"权力的滥用"。而究其原因,则是因为"事前没有形成一个能够控制第三方的集体行动机制",使得第三方拥有了某种"绝对权力"。然而,Barzel 又指出,"第三方的强制实施能力却不是用它的绝对权力来评价的,而是用相对于其他人抵制或抵消它的能力评价的"。更具体地说,遵从强制实施者的裁决不仅依赖于他相对于被强制实施者权力而言的真实的权力,也依赖于双方对彼此拥有的权力所了解的信息,是否遵从依赖于各方对相对权力的评估。如果各方可以准确地评价对方的权力,那么权力将不会被使用。当被强制者认识到他将失利时就会让步,然后仅是简单地服从第三方裁定。当强制实施者认识到他将失利时,他也会让步。那么,被强制实施者将会选择不服从(Barzel, 1998b)。

从上述模型可以看出,政府作为强制实施的第三方,之所以无法有效实施正式契约,一方面在于追求租金最大化使其滥用了权力,另一方面在于追求租金最大化使其相对权力受到各种利益关系约束,使得租金提供者对其相对权力的评价很低,进而导致不执行契约或者不执行第三方的裁决。例如,当某企业认识到它是政府的纳税大户,政府不敢轻易得罪,它就可能选择违约。当然,现实中还有更深层次原因导致第三方相对权力被削弱,即当前中国司法独立性不够。司法机构作为第三方强制实施的力量,受到行政部门的干预。因而当正式契约的执行与裁决涉及到行政部门的利益时，司法机构往往显得无能为力，甚至与行政部门成为“利益相关者”(stockholder)。

除了政府作为第三方未能正确使用权力，导致强制实施失败之外，农民工借助国家(政府)作为强制实施契约的第三方的成本过高，也是第三方失败的一个重要原因。这种过高的成本来源于三方面的原因：一是农民工现有的素质无法适应繁琐、细密的司法程序要求。从信息经济学角度看，农民工一旦与用人单位或“城里人”通过司法程序解决工资拖欠，农民工首先因为不拥有“相应知识”而处于信息劣势的一方。而现行司法要求农民工负有举证的责任则更是抬高了农民的司法求助门槛。二是农民工现有的收入无力支付司法程序中的各种费用，甚至有一些农民工为了追讨几百元，花费了更多的用于司法过程的费用，最后还讨不回一分钱。三是由于司法歧视或腐败，加之司法系统本身的低效率，进一步抬高了农民工试图通过国家作为第三方讨回公道的成本。这种成本甚至是无形的，无法用货币计算的。

综上所述，在追求租金最大化的动机下，国家(政府)有可能滥用绝对权力，偏向更强大的租金直接提供者；而租金直接提供者也因此倾向于低估国家(政府)作为第三方的强制实施能力，加之作为第三方强制实施的直接力量的司法机构的独立性差，导致第三方相对权力更被低估。同时，农民工借助于国家作为第三方强制的交易成本过高。这些都构成国家作为第三方失败的深层次原因。

四、可替代的实施方式与权力最优化：国家作为第三方失败的后果及解决之道

在管理与规范农民工用工契约方面，国家作为强制实施的

第三方的失败,其后果必然是正式契约的履行从公共性强制退回到私人秩序,即"国家作为第三方弱执行将导致私人执行方式的出现"(R. Sherwood, 1994),这种现象叫做"公法的私人实施"(private enforcement of public laws; Andre Shleifer, 1998)。其原因在于,"第三方实施"与"相互实施"同作为强制实施方式,本身存在可替代性,同时,在"第三方实施"中,还存在国家之外的其他形式的第三方,而且多种形式的第三方之间存在相互竞争。"当人们意识到国家强制实施者从事敲诈勒索时,他们将减少使用他的服务并可能完全不使用他的服务。个人成为第三方竞争性服务的提供者的机会越多,他们通过用脚投票方式降低敲诈勒索损失的速度就越快。"(Barzel, 1998a)

反观当下中国农民工在处理工资纠纷中的行为选择,正是在国家作为强制实施的第三方失败情况下,大多数农民工对求助于司法体系讨回公道失去了信心,被迫更多地使用了私人性质的手段。⑤一种手段是许多求告无门的农民工总会以各种"相互实施"的方式索要血汗钱。甚至有些农民工最后只能以各种暴力相要挟。另一种手段是求助于私人性质的第三方,甚至也求助于当地黑社会,索要工钱。这往往发生在"相互实施"达不到目的的情况下。因为农民工本身相对于雇主处于绝对弱势,没有办法对对方造成成本,根本不符合"相互实施"的条件,甚至反过来被对方造成进一步的成本,因而,最后被迫采取非法手段讨要工钱。第三种手段,是各种私人性质的手段都无法解决问题时,一些农民工被迫选择通过冲击公共秩序来达到迫使国家作为强制实施的第三方出面讨回公道的目的。还有一些农民工可能选择报复社会,最终后果是危及社会稳定。

那么,应如何对待农民工选择"非法"的私人手段索要工钱的行为? Lars Werin(2001)区分了法律实施的两种法则。其中，产权法则指的是，如果在达成自愿协议的交易成本很低的情况下，A不是购买而是侵犯了B的产权，那么A应受到惩罚。责任法则是指，如果达成自愿协议的交易成本太高，A不得已侵犯了B的产权，那么A应该对B进行赔偿，赔偿的额度由法官决定，但A不应该受到惩罚。而区分应该适用哪种法则，关键在于交易成本高低。如果以此分析农民工在索要欠薪过程中"非法"的私人手段，我们完全可以说，正是达到自愿协议（国家作为第三方，能使雇工还工钱）的交易成本太高，农民工才被迫选择了侵犯雇主甚至国家的权利。因而，对农民工这样的"非法手段"，应该适用责任法则而非产权法则。当然，如果以私人手段索要工钱的行为导致法律后果，则当事人需承担法律责任。

Barzel(1998b)认为，当强制实施者的相对权力被削弱时，其效用迅速下降，权力被实际使用的次数将会被迫增加。这可以解释为什么2003年年底中央政府只能通过发动全国范围内的运动，来解决拖欠农民工工资的问题。

理论上讲，我国已经有完备的《劳动法》，其中对于拖欠工资有明确的规定；同时，有劳动执法部门，有完备的司法系统，这足以对雇主形成威慑，从而达到第三方"通过改变交易双方的预期而最终不需要实际使用权力"的目的，但正是由于各级政府作为强制实施者的权力被各种利益关系以及体制的弊端而受到削弱，使雇主对《劳动法》以及执法部门的权威置若罔闻，导致劳资矛盾越积越深，最终达到影响社会稳定的程度，国家只能被迫通过实际使用中央的权力，通过中央政府的推动，在《劳动法》之外又由劳动和社会保障部、建设部联合下发行政性文件，要求切实解决建筑企业存在的拖欠和克扣农民工工资问题，保护农民工合法权益，维护社会稳定。也就是说，是在法治系统作为国家第三方强制的直接工具无法解决后，中央政府被迫以行政性"运动”的方式解决这一问题，这就是2003年年底“清欠运动”的真正背景。

但Barzel(2000)又指出，当强制实施者频繁地实际使用权力时，权力的边际效用将逐渐下降。这意味着，通过中央政府用“运动”的方式来解决问题，不能一而再、再而三，否则只会进一步降低中央政府的相对权力。因而，在通过“清欠运动”部分解决了农民工工资问题的基础上，重新树立国家作为第三方强制实施者的权威，通过法律程序正常解决问题就成为下一步所要考虑的要务。

为了避免国家作为强制实施的第三方的失败，针对绝对权力过大而相对权力过弱的事实，Barzel又提出“使第三方权力最优化”的命题。所谓“第三方权力最优化”，是指国家作为第三方，其相对权力要强大到能保证第三方实施契约的确被有效履行，但另一方面其绝对权力又被限制在无法被滥用的范围之内。在Barzel看来，国家作为强制实施的第三方，与个人作为第三方的不同之处在于，“客户不能避免国家权力的事后的滥用，但他们可以防止事前的滥用。因而他们可以与他人合作，形成一个能够控制第三方的集体行动机制”。而这个“第三方的集体行动机制”，使得作为第三方的国家既是强有力的、同时权力又是被有效地限定了的。

五、结　　论

本文运用契约理论框架分析当下中国农民工经济纠纷涉及的深层次问题，得出了以下主要结论：

(1) 农民工工资被拖欠，其主要原因并非农民工与直接“关系”雇主之间的非正式口头契约无法有效实施，而恰是受国家明文保护的应该由国家作为第三方强制实施的正式契约无法有效实施。相反，农民工与直接雇主之间的非正式契约的确带有自我实施契约的性质。

(2) 国家作为强制实施的第三方，在实施正式契约方面的失败，农民工的合法权益得不到国家的保护，其原因在于一方面国家存在部分的绝对权力，而这种绝对权力在追求租金最大化的动机下被滥用；而另一方面，作为国家强制实施的直接工具的司法体系的相对权力又被强势利益群体所削弱，因而无法有效进行强制。

(3) 国家作为第三方在保护农民工合法权益方面的失败，必然导致农民工选择契约的其他执行方法，使得契约的实施由“公共强制”倒退回“私人秩序”，进而可能导致暴力的无序使用，危及社会稳定，反过来又迫使政府选择更大力度地实际使用权力，这是中央政府2003年年底以行政力量发起全国范围的“清欠运动”的真正原因。

(4) 国家要重新建立国家作为强制实施第三方在保护农民工权益中的权威，就必须考虑“第三方权力的最优化”问题。而要做到使“第三方权力最优化”，就必须在事前建立起能有效制衡第三方的集体选择机制。

注 释

① 此调查有详细资料备案。

② 《中华人民共和国合同法》第二百七十条规定：“建设工程合同应当采用书面形式。”《中华人民共和国建筑法》第十五条更是明确规定：“建筑工程的发包单位与承包单位应当依法订立书面合同，明确双方的权利和义务。发包单位和承包单位应当全面履行合同约定的义务。不按照合同约定履行义务的，依法承担违约责任。”同时，《合同法》与《建筑法》都还规定了违约的责任惩罚及执行惩罚的国家相关机构。

③ 新华社2003年11月10日的报道《工程"连环债"引发民工欠薪，专家提醒留神陷阱》称，因为工程被层层转包，因而存在一个"工资链"，但断裂之处往往不是小包工头与农民工之间，而在于总发包商与大转包商之间，以及中间大转包商与小包工头之间，而他们之间的合同是正式合同。也就是说，民工权益被侵害并非因为与直接雇主只有非正式合同，而在于正式合同没有得到执行。

④ "国家失败(state failed)"的概念，起始于国际关系领域(参见：Michael Stohl，George Lopez，1998，"Failed States and International Security：Causes，Prospects，and Consequences"，Purdue University，Working Paper)，指国家无法有效地履行治理的职能。此处应用此概念，系指国家在保证契约被实施方面的低效率或无效率。

⑤ 在新华社记者进行的一项粗略调查(央视国际转新华社北京2004年1月13日电《一项关于拖欠民工工资现象的调查》)中，在工资被拖欠的情况下，有60%的民工选择反复寻找老板、直至把老板找烦的方式来讨要钱款；有10%的受访民工表示，只能用吓唬等手段对老板形成压力；仅有30%的人表示将求助于劳动管理部门。

参考文献

〔美〕巴泽尔，1997：《产权的经济分析》，中译本，上海人民出版社。

〔美〕道格拉斯·C.诺斯，1995：《制度、制度变迁与经济绩效》，中译本，上海三联书店。

〔美〕道格拉斯·C.诺斯，1994a：《制度》，《经济译文》第3期。

〔美〕道格拉斯·C.诺斯，1994b：《历时经济绩效》，《经济译文》第6期。

丁际刚、张建华，2002：《第三方利益的相关性与司法执行障碍》，《中国经济评论》第1期。

〔美〕理查德·A.波斯纳，1997：《法律的经济分析》，中译本，中国大百科全书出版社。

〔美〕罗伯特·考特、托马斯·尤伦，1994：《法和经济学》，中译本，上海三联书店。

钱颖一，2000：《市场与法治》，《经济与社会体制比较》第3期。

杨瑞龙,1998:《我国制度变迁方式转换的三阶段论》,《经济研究》第1期。

张维迎,2003:《信息、信任与法律》,三联书店。

Alberto, J. and Garibaldi-Fernandez, 2000, "The Lens Through Which We See: The Impact of Ideas on Institutional Enforcement", in Claude Ménard, *Institutions, Contracts and Organizations*, Edward Elgar.

Barzel, Yoram, 1998a, "A Theory of the State: Economic Rights, Legal Rights and the Scope of the State", mimeo, Department of Economics, University of Washington.

Barzel, Yoram, 1998b, "The State and the Diversity of Third Party Enforcement", paper presented at the Inaugural Conference of the International Society for New Institutional Economics, Washington University, St. Louis.

Barzel, Yoram, 2000, "Property Right and the Evolution of the State", *Economics of Governance*, Ⅰ(1), February.

Drobak, John N., 2000, "A Cognative Science Perspective on Legal Incentives", in Claude Ménard, *Institutions, Contracts and Organizations*, Edward Elgar.

Garibaldi, Jose A., 1998, "Legal Traditions, Contract Enforcement and Institutional Reform", paper presented at the Conference of the International Society for New Institutional Economics, Washington University, St. Louis.

Ménard, Claude, 2000, "Enforcement Procedures and Governance Structure: What Relationships", in Claude Ménard, *Institutions, contracts and Organizations*, Edward Elgar.

North, Douglass C. and Robert P. Thomas, 1973, *The Rise of Western World*, Cambridge: Cambridge University Press.

North, Douglass C., 1981, *Structure and Change in Economic History*, New York: W. W. Norton.

Sherwood, R., G. Shepherd and C. M. De Souza, 1994, "Judicial Systems and Economic Performance", *Quarterly Review of Economics and Finance*, 34, pp. 101—12.

Shleifer, A. and J. Hay, 1998, "Private Enforcement of Public Laws: a Theory of Legal Reform", *American Economic Review Paper and Proceedings*, May, 1998.

Werin, Lars, 2001, *Economic Behavior and Legal Institutions: An Introductory Survey*, London: World Scientific Publishing Co. Pte. Ltd.

（原载《经济研究》2004 年第 5 期）

政府管制、法律软约束与农村基层民主*

章　奇

（中国社会科学院世界经济与政治研究所）

刘明兴

（北京大学政府管理学院）

单　伟

（美国得克萨斯大学政治系）

一、引　　言

近年来中国农村有两个现象值得注意，一是包括农村税费负担问题在内的农村社会、经济等问题变得更加严重，另一个是中国农村基层民主建设工作以由上至下的方式在农村中开始全面展开。然而，这两个看起来存在明显矛盾冲突的现象却并行不悖，从而为我们提供了一个很好的研究对象。由于中央政府自20世纪80年代以来的确投入大量资源以推动农村基层民主建设，1998年更通过了《村委会组织法》，从而以法律的形式确定了农村基层民主的框架和基本内容。因此，对上述矛盾现象的一个直接解释就是因为地方基层政府① 的消极对待，农村基

* 作者感谢姚洋、李连江的讨论及所提出的一些建议。

层民主建设并没有得到真正的贯彻和实施。但这样的回答过于简单，因为在中国这样一个中央政府高度集权的国家，即使中央政府和地方政府存在利益冲突，中央政府可以通过各种方式使地方政府执行某些政策。同样，得到中央政府的大力支持，农村基层民主建设步伐将大大加快。不过，如果由于某种原因，并且这种原因和中央政府的政策直接相关，使得地方政府有法(《村委会组织法》)不依，而中央政府对地方政府的某些行为表示默认，则出现前文所说的看似矛盾的现象也就不足为怪了。我们把中央政府出于政策原因而默许地方政府消极对待农村基层民主、导致相关法律无法落实的现象称作"法律软约束"。

这里借鉴了"预算软约束"(soft budget constraint, SBC)概念，后者已经在经济学界中得到了极为热烈的讨论。Kornai(1980)首创性地利用这一概念来分析传统计划经济体制下政府不得不追认企业亏损的事实，并继续对绩效差的企业提供资金支持。经过时间的检验，对预算软约束的分析和应用已经超出了传统计划经济的范围，在转型经济中私有化后的企业仍然存在着预算软约束的现象并不新鲜，即使是在成熟的市场经济国家，预算软约束现象也可能处处存在(Kornai, Maskin and Roland 2003)。例如已经被广泛引用的克莱斯勒汽车公司破产事件、亚洲金融危机期间的长期资本管理公司(LTCM)破产事件等等，政府都出面对陷入财务困境的企业进行了援助。而韩国大型企业集团、日本的大银行财团长期处于预算软约束状态之下，也是众所周知的事实。越来越多的研究者承认，只要一个组织(例如企业、银行)的赤字可以部分甚至全部地由其他组织(政府或其他银行、企业)——可以称之为支持组织(Supporting Organization)——所支付，从而不会因为财务问题而破产，预算软约束现象就会存在(Kornai, Maskin and Roland 2003)。早期的研究一般把预算软约束的形成看作是外生变量(Kornai, 1980; Goldfeld and Quandt, 1988; Schleifer and Vishny, 1994),近年来的研究则将预算软约束看作是内生变量(Qian, 1994; Dewatripont and Maskin, 1995; Li Daokui, 1992; Qian and Roland, 1998; Kornai, Maskin and Roland, 2003),从而使问题的关键不再是人们是否想获得软预算约束,而是形成硬的或软的预算约束的条件或环境是什么。其中值得一提的是Dewatripont和Maskin(1995)所建立的一个动态承诺机制模型,在这个模型里,预算软约束被看作是内生于特定体制,即当事人由于知道他必然会得到追加资金而不采取有效行为,或从事无效行为。其含义也很明显,除非使硬化预算约束的承诺真实可信的制度已经确立,硬化预算约束的承诺就不会是真实可信的。

林毅夫及其合作者的工作将预算软约束的研究向前推进了一步,他们指出,如果政府要求企业承担某种政策性的任务,从而使得企业的技术选择不符合经济中的比较优势,那么就向企业施加了所谓的"政策性负担",政府因而需要对企业的经营绩效负责,而企业也会估计到这一结果而必然会对企业的行为和绩效产生影响,从而必然产生预算软约束现象。即使在经济转型后甚至在成熟市场经济国家,只要政策性负担仍然存在,预算软约束的现象也就一定会存在(Lin and Tan, 1999;林毅夫、李志赟,2004)。

法律软约束A和预算软约束B概念显然有很大的相似之处,即某一行为主体(在A中是地方基层政府,在B中是企业)因为某种原因,使得自身的行为后果不受规则(在A中是《村委会组织法》的相关规定,在B中是企业破产)的约束。两者的区别在于在法律软约束概念中,地方政府并不会因为陷入(财务)困境而寻求中央政府的支持,它必须面对中央政府的行政约束,需要中央政府对自己的行为予以默认。因此，对经济中预算软约束的分析逻辑同样适用于法律软约束，尤其是中央政府事前承诺的可置信度必然影响地方政府的行为，这和动态承诺机制在预算软约束中的作用机理是一致的。

更具体地说，中央政府在颁布《村委会组织法》的同时，也对地方政府下达了各种政策性任务——我们称之为管制任务，对中央政府来说，它需要地方政府来执行自己所下达的各项任务，但又不向地方政府提供相应的资金，这样地方政府有理由自行收费以弥补成本。并且由于信息不对称，地方政府收取的费用，可能会大大超过实施中央政府管制政策所要求的水平。如果完全实现村级民主自治，地方政府搭车收费的行为会导致很高的成本，这样，地方政府很有可能出于自身利益的考虑而消极对待村级民主自治。与此同时，如果中央政府更看重保证政策性任务的完成，其为使地方政府完成管制任务，也可能默许地方政府的行为，从而出现所谓的"法律软约束"问题。

本文分析中央和地方政府在管制、搭车收费以及推行农村基层民主中的行为。我们发现由于存在法律软约束，地方政府收取的费用会超过仅仅为贯彻中央政府管制任务所需要的费用水平，并消极对待农村基层民主，从而导致村级民主供给不足。

二、中国农村基层民主实践与政府管制

20 世纪 70 年代末 80 年代初，随着中国农村中家庭联产承包责任制的推行以及人民公社的解体，一方面农民成为具有独立经济利益的市场主体，其经济权利需要得到制度保证；另一方面乡镇政府取代公社成为一级基层政权，原有的农村基层管理体制被打破，从而出现了体制转换期里"某种公共权力和基层组

织的真空”(徐勇,1997)。如何重建农村基层管理体制,重新将农民组织起来,就成为当时亟待解决的重大问题。由广西一些农村自发组建的“村民委员会”组织作为一种替代形式得到了中央政府的迅速认可,并在1982年的宪法中首次确认了村民委员会的法律地位。随后中共中央在[1982]36号文件中要求各地要“有计划地进行建立村民(乡民)委员会的试点”。1985年春全国5.6万多个人民公社、镇改建为9.2万多个乡、镇人民政府。同时按照宪法规定,取消了原有的生产大队和生产小队,建立了82万多个村民委员会。不过,由于1982年的宪法并没有对村委会的组织及其运作方式进行详细的规范,不少地方的村民委员会不过是将原来的生产大队或生产队换了块牌子。

直到1987年,全国人大常委会通过《村民委员会组织法》(试行),对村民委员会组织、功能和选举方式首次进行了比较明确和全面的规定。该法案的试行,标志着包括村级直选在内的农村民主自治开始启动,不过直到十年以后,随着1998年11月九届全国人大第五次会议修订并通过了《村委会组织法》,农村民主自治才算是完成了从试行到正式法制化的历史转变。②

根据《村委会组织法》,在新的村民自治制度下,由民主选举的方式(包括直选、公开选举等方式)产生的村委会,“是村民自我管理、自我教育、自我服务的基层群众性自治组织,实行民主选举、民主决策、民主管理、民主监督”。应该说,这一规定正确反映了农民民主意识和民主要求的提高,反映了经济改革以来农民经济利益的提高对制度保证的诉求。

特别值得注意的是,法律规定村委会不再是国家基层政权组织——乡镇政府的下级组织机构,和乡镇政府不再存在行政上的隶属关系,而乡镇政府可以“对村民委员会的工作进行指导、支持和帮助,但是不得干预依法属于村民自治范围内的事项”。如果这些法律条文规定能够得到地方基层政府——这里主要指乡镇政府[3]——的大力配合的话，那么不但农村基层民主建设的过程将会相对更加顺利，而且由于杜绝了来自政府权力部门的行政干预，农村中原有的各种社会、经济矛盾将更有可能根据各地区的实际情况，在村庄内部尝试解决。

不过实际情况远远要比法律条文所规定的更为复杂。虽然从法律上讲由村民选举产生的村委会不再是任何政府行政组织的下属机构，但在现实中地方政府仍然对乡村政治生活——包括农村基层民主选举——保持着影响力，起着主导性的作用。这一直觉上的判断也得到了初步的实证研究的支持。例如，肖唐镖等(2001)对江西省 40 个村委会选举的一项综合调查表明，“(村委会)选举中县乡政府除了不亲自投票、不作候选人外，几乎无所不在。具体地说，政府承担了规则制定与解释、信息传输与发布、组织与操作、仲裁、秩序监督与维持等功能，扮演者几近于‘全能’角色：既是‘立法者’，又是‘执法者’，还是‘监督者’”。张静(1998)对吉林省梨树村的村委会选举的调查也得出了相似的结论。即使对村民自治持乐观态度的学者，也承认地方政府对村委会具有相当大的影响力(胡荣，1998)。

地方政府影响农村基层民主建设的渠道和途径，除了通过行政手段直接干涉村级事务、任免村干部外，由于在现有政治体制下，地方政府相对于村庄拥有政治、经济以及社会方面的资源优势，因此地方政府可以利用手中所掌握的资源，通过利益诱导和激励，使村委会自愿服从其“支配”。正如上文所提到的那样，有的学者也注意到地方政府在某种程度上也垄断了对《村委会组织法》的解释权。例如通过对规则解释权的掌控，地方政府对村委会选举施加影响也就有了合法性的基础。当然这种立法、法理解释和执法标准的“上移”，在客观上增强了国家法律规范基层秩序的准则作用(张静,1998),但是这同样会使得农村基层民主的建设有可能更依赖于地方政府的态度。

令人担忧的是,大多数地方政府并没有完全遵循《村委会组织法》的规定,无视村民自治发展和村民的合理、合法要求,仍然采用传统的行政支配、强制命令的工作方法,对村委会的日常工作进行干预,甚至直接干预、阻挠乃至拒绝村委会的选举。地方政府对基层民主的消极甚至反对态度,在许多学者的调查和研究中都有所强调。柯丹青(1997)、O'Brien 与 Lianjiang Li (2000)对地方政府在推进村民自治中的某些行为作了描述。肖唐镖等(2001)对乡镇干部的问卷调查发现,乡镇干部对村民自治怀有深深的疑虑和恐惧心态。张静(1998)在调查中也发现,省级以上政府的确对基层民主选举予以肯定和支持,但同时基层民主选举的阻力,"理所当然地主要来自于乡村两级班子"。我们会在下文对地方政府的这种普遍态度继续进行分析。

由于地方政府对农村基层民主事务的干预和介入在很大程度上忽视了农民的合法权益和要求,因此必然激化村民、村委会与地方政府间的矛盾,甚至引起激烈的冲突。④一旦发生冲突,"农民为了自己的权益,通过信访、个人上访、集体上访等形式……甚至通过法庭来争取自己的权益。近些年来……农民越来越利用法律手段维护自己的民主权益"(李凡,2002)。

在这种情况下,中央政府的态度就显得特别重要。由于中国中央政府高度集权的政治结构,中央政府完全可以通过各种方式要求地方政府的行为符合自己的政策要求,在农村基层民主问题上也不会例外。⑤如果地方基层政府和农民发生冲突时,能够按照《村委会组织法》的精神进行处理,那么农村基层民主建设就会顺利许多。但实际上,地方政府往往得到偏袒,而对农民的民主化要求的支持并不那么坚决。《村委会组织法》在实施过程中步履维艰。⑥与此性质类似的另一个极具代表性的例子是中国农村税费问题，进入 90 年代以来中国农民税费负担变得更加严重，为此中央政府至少下发了 37 份文件专门强调减轻农民税费负担，但直至今日农民税费负担问题并没有很大的好转。由于中国农村基层民主建设和农民税费负担的上升几乎是同步发生，这多少令人感到尴尬。

我们认为，产生以上问题根源在于中央政府对农村社会、经济生活的各项管制政策。就其实施力度和影响而言，目前国家对农村的经济和社会管制措施主要有以下几项：强制性粮棉收购政策（无论以低于市场价还是高于市场价收购）、户籍制度以及计划生育等等。

中国的粮食政策和发达国家的农业保护政策有着根本性的区别，中国现行的粮食政策是一种管制性政策，即对农业的生产资料投入、农产品的生产决策、农产品的销售过程进行全方面的干预，农民作为一个市场经济个体完全处于被动地位。而西方的粮食保护政策是出于国家粮食安全的考虑，对国内粮食价格进行的一种财政补贴。至于农场主愿意生产什么、生产多少，政府无权干预。⑦应当说，改革开放以来，这种格局已经有了较大的变化，但是传统体制的惯性很大，且在 20 世纪 90 年代中期有被加强的趋势。

户籍制度的作用在于政府可以很方便地控制劳动力的流动。但是，单靠户籍制度并不能有效解决闲置劳动力问题，因此，中央从 20 世纪 70 年代初开始推行计划生育政策，以便抑制闲置劳动力的进一步增加。考虑到农村地区极不发达的社会保障体系、较低的教育水平、传统观念以及农村妇女较低的就业率，现行计划生育的政策要求与农民对生育的预期理想水平有很大的差异。因此农村计划生育工作难度很大，相应所需的人手和经费也日趋庞大。

当政府为了贯彻管制政策时，除了去控制市场、企业和农民以外，还要控制政府本身，因为中央政府任何管制政策的实施实际上均有赖于基层政府的配合。这里需要引入的一个重要假定是信息不对称，即给定一个中央政府的政策措施，其在基层的具体执行成本是无法观测的。即由于监督成本巨大，上级政府无法确切知道下级政府完成这些任务需要多少人手、多少预算，更不知道下级政府在执行过程中使用什么方法来完成任务。更重要的是，国家在向农村下达了各项管制任务的同时，又不提供足额的资金（实际上由于信息不对称，上级政府也无法为管制政策的实施提供足额的资金），这就为基层政府大肆收取超额费用直接提供了条件和借口。⑧而下级政府正可以以此为理由同上级政府讨价还价——扩充编制、增加预算。由于固有的政治体制和信息优势，下级政府往往在谈判中占有主动地位。而中央的政策本身又具有一定的合法性，结果基层政府无论是对上级政府，还是对农民，就有充分的借口来扩大管制政策的实施范围和力度，并巧立名目、从中渔利，这就是说税费摊派具有所谓“搭班收费”的性质。

中央政府管制政策对地方基层政府的含义不仅仅在于后者可以借实施政策之名获得额外收益，而且它必然会影响地方政府和中央政府对待农村基层民主建设的态度。在目前的政治体制下，地方政府实施管制任务，必须依靠村委会等村级组织去完成，尤其是农村税费征缴、计划生育以及完成生产指标任务，如果离开村委会的配合和支持，地方政府无法完成。由于管制必然会对农民的经济利益造成损害⑨，尤其是各种税费的征收已经引发了一些矛盾，因此一旦在农村实现了民主自治，地方政府的某些无理要求必然遭到抵制。因此地方政府天然具有消极对待村级民主自治、控制并操纵村委会的激励和冲动(胡荣,1998)。当矛盾积累到一定程度,冲突就会变得显性化。因此,从某种角度说,正是中央政府一方面赋予村民民主自治的法律权力,另一方面又要通过地方基层政府在农村中推行管制政策,从而把地方政府推上了矛盾的前沿,并由地方政府去面对这两个矛盾目标所引发出的矛盾。[10]有些国外学者也注意到了来自于更高层政府的政策会影响地方基层政府对农村基层民主自治的态度(Ray Yep, 2002)。

问题不仅仅如此,我们有充足的理由判断,在中央政府的政策篮子里,达到管制政策的目标相对于实现农村基层民主被排在更优先的位置(至少目前仍然如此)。这样,为了保证地方政府能够完成中央政府所下达的管制任务,中央政府就必然默许地方政府的某些行为。这就是我们在文章开始所提出的"法律软约束"的主要逻辑和内容。

三、计量模型设定与数据

这里提出两个可检验的假说:

H1:政府管制任务越重,则地方政府收取的(各种合理以及不合理)费用也就越多;

H2:村级民主水平和政府管制任务之间呈现U形曲线关系,即在一般情况下,中央政府管制任务越重,就越依赖于地方基层政府贯彻执行,地方政府的讨价还价能力也就越高,从中获得的利益(例如"搭车收费")就越大。这样一来,地方政府就越反对实行村级民主,从而导致村级民主实现水平越低。但当管制任务超过一定水平,导致管制的成本大大超过了管制为政府所带来的收益(例如过高的管制力度导致农村经济无法维持一定的增长速度甚至简单再生产水平)，那么中央政府有可能支持推行村级民主以缓解社会压力。

在假说1和假说2的基础上，可以进一步得到假说3，即：

H3：村级民主水平和村级农民负担之间出现U形曲线关系。

第一个假说已经在陶然、刘明兴和章奇(2003)的研究中进行了证明。因此这里仅仅对假说2和假说3进行证明。对H2和H3进行检验的计量模型的设定形式分别为：

$$\begin{aligned} DEMO_{it} = &\alpha \cdot REGU_{it} + \beta \cdot REGU_{it}^2 + \phi \cdot VINC \\ &+ \varphi \cdot VINC^2 + \rho \cdot t + \gamma \cdot X_{it} + \varepsilon \end{aligned} \quad (1)$$

$$\begin{aligned} DEMO_{it} = &\alpha \cdot VFEE_{it} + \beta \cdot VFEE_{it}^2 + \phi \cdot VINC \\ &+ \varphi \cdot VINC^2 + \rho \cdot t + \gamma \cdot X_{it} + \varepsilon \end{aligned} \quad (2)$$

在方程(1)中，下标i、t分别代表第i个村和第t年。DEMO是所实现的村级民主水平变量，REGU为代表来自中央政府的管制任务变量，$REGU^2$是REGU的二次项。VFEE和$VFEE^2$是村级农民负担水平及其二次项。VINC和$VINC^2$是按可比价格计算的村级农户家庭人均纯收入(对数化)及其二次项。t是1998年的时间虚拟变量(从1998年开始取值为1，否则为0)，加入t是因为在1998年颁布了《组织法》。X是其他可能会对村级民主水平产生影响的变量，包括省虚拟变量和年份虚拟变量。ε是服从标准正态分布的误差项。根据假说2，我们预期α和β分别为负号和正号并且在统计上应该显著地异于零。

找出能够反映DEMO和REGU、VFEE的合适变量并据此选择合适的计量模型是估计方程(1)的关键。首先，我们依然遵循陶然、刘明兴和章奇(2003)在证明假说1中所采用的方法，以对数化的村人均所负担的国家定购粮数量(VFOOD)作为表征国家管制政策的变量。这些数据来自农业部农村固定观察点办公室所提供的数据库（1987—2002）。这一变量值越大，表示国家管制力度越高。[11]另外，我们同时考察了两种不同定义下的村级农民负担对村级民主选举水平的影响。定义之一是用一个村农户家庭上缴国家税金和上缴乡、村、组集体的金额（包括集体提留和统筹、各种摊派以及罚款）之和占农户家庭纯收入比例的平均水平（VFEE1），定义之二是在VFEE1的基础上减去向国家缴纳税金的部分（VFEE2）。由于无论是VFOOD、VFEE1还是VFEE2均可视作是内生变量，因此我们利用工具变量法对方程（1）和（2）进行估计，由于在很大程度上上缴的粮食和税费负担与农户的耕地面积大小相关，因此我们选择村农户家庭平均耕地面积作为它们的工具变量，另外在工具变量估计中还同时控制住了省份虚拟变量和年份虚拟变量。

其次，农业部固定观察点办公室数据库于2002年补充了1987—2002年间有关村级民主选举的各种信息，其中有一个关于村级民主选举方式的变量（DEMO），反映了1987—2002年期间47个村选举村委会成员时所采纳的选举方式，包括：由上级指定产生、由村民推举和上级指定相结合产生、由村民代表推举产生、海选产生。我们根据经验，对这四种选举方式分别赋值为1、2、3、4，值越高表示选举方式的民主程度越高。需要指出的是，该数据库所有被调查的村所给出的信息均包括了第一次选举的时间，因此凡是在1987年之后才汇报了选举方式信息的村，在其第一次汇报之前至1987年间均可视作没有进行选举，对于这些年份我们对DEMO赋值为0，它表示相对最低的民主水平。另外，实际中一个村在两次选举年份之间会有一段间隔期，不同的村间隔期也不同。如果将这段期间的民主水平作为缺失值处理，将会遗漏掉很多信息。为此我们将两次选举间隔期的民主水平按照上一次选举方式的取值进行赋值。[12]显然,ORDER LOGIT(OLOGIT)模型是估计方程(1)的有效模型设定形式。[13]

样本中各村进行村委会选举的时序以及历年所采纳的选举方式变化均存在很大差异。在1987—2002年间,有的村最多进行了7次村委会选举,平均每2—3年选举一次,而有的村仅仅举行了1次选举。超过50%的样本村在样本期内至少进行了4次选举,平均每2—4年选举一次。且样本村近一半的选举发生在1998年《村委会组织法》颁布之后。

另外,按照我们对村委会候选人选举方式民主水平(DEMO)的赋值方法,1998年前后该变量的简单算术平均值分别为2.17和2.86,这说明1998年后样本村村委会选举形式的民主水平有所提高。

通过该数据库还可以发现很多有用的信息,一是村党组织在村委会中扮演了非常重要的角色。尽管1987—2002年村委会选举方式几经变化,但历年党员人数在入选村委会委员总数中所占比例的平均值从未低于62%。这意味着迄今党组织在基层政治生活中仍保持着相当大的影响力。

另外,所有样本村历年村民参选率的平均值也相当高,均达到了77%以上,这可能意味着村民对村委会选举一直维持着较高的热情。并且1998年后该比例均值接近90%,比1998年以前提高了近6个百分点。

四、实 证 结 果

表1在工具变量估计的基础上给出了对方程(1)的OLOGIT回归的最终结果。[14]在第一列中,VFOOD的一次项和二次项的估计系数分别显著地为负、正号,从而印证了我们的假

说，即在管制任务和村级民主水平之间的确存在着一个U形曲线关系。在第二列中，我们控制住了村级农户外出劳动力流动状况（VOUT，村劳动力总数中外出打工劳动力所占比例），因为如果一个村的大部分劳动力均在外打工，那么由于他们可以“用脚投票”，因此他们可能对村民主状况并不十分热心，从而减少了基层政府推行民主选举的压力。⑮不过在第二列中，该变量并不显著。在第三列中，我们控制住了村整体劳动力的受教育水平（VEDU，以村劳动力总数中具有初中文化以上人数所占比例代替）。许多人认为，一个村平均受教育水平越高，村民就越可能通过热衷于选举来维护自己的权益，从而给基层政府以压力以迫使他们尽快推行民主。但该变量同样也不显著。在第三列中，我们控制住了村集体工业化平均程度（VINCSTR，农户家庭全年总收入中来自于集体企业的收入所占比例）。如果集体工业化程度较高，那么由于地方基层政府能够从集体工业中获得利益，因此对民主选举的干预热情或许会降低。但与前两列类似，该变量同样并不显著。最后，我们控制住了村级收入的农业依赖程度（AGRSTR，农户家庭经营收入中来自于农业的收入所占比例）。该变量的估计系数显著为正，说明在控制住其他因素时，那些收入结构中更依赖于农业收入的村，选举的民主程度会更高。另外，虚拟变量 T 在大多数情况下不显著，说明《村委会组织法》的颁布对选举情况的影响是有限的。

表1　回归结果Ⅰ

解释变量	(1)	(2)	(3)	(4)	(5)
VFOOD	−2.988***	−2.919***	−4.409***	−4.613***	−3.619***
	0.884	0.885	1.169	1.060	0.925
$VFOOD^2$	0.260***	0.249***	0.334***	0.342***	0.280***
	0.068	0.067	0.099	0.074	0.069

（续表）

解释变量	(1)	(2)	(3)	(4)	(5)
T	−0.177	0.195	1.808***	−4.070	−1.459
	1.974	1.985	0.656	2.553	2.031
Pseudo R^2	0.20	0.21	0.21	0.21	0.21
Prob(>Chi²)	0.00	0.00	0.00	0.00	0.00
观测数	569	564	448	362	569

注：1. 在以上三个回归中，均以村人均耕地面积作为工具变量；2. *、** 和 *** 分别代表估计系数在 10%、5%和 1%的统计水平上显著异于 0。

表 2 各列的结果和表 1 基本上类似，即在税费负担和村级民主选举水平之间存在 U 形曲线关系。这和我们的理论预期是一致的。表 2 结果和表 1 的最大差异在于此时时间虚拟变量 T 在所有的回归中均是显著为正的。这说明，在方程(2)的设定中，村委会选举法颁布后会对选举方式产生明显的影响。但对待这一结论需要小心，因为和表 1 结果的对比说明 T 的统计性质对模型设定形式的变化是十分敏感的。其他控制变量的统计表现和表 1 则大同小异。

表 2　回归结果 Ⅱ

解释变量	(1)	(2)	(3)	(4)	(5)
VFEE1	−144.399***	−147.668***	−162.496***	−188.811**	−171.805**
	53.999	56.931	69.836	83.835	54.878
VFEE1²	554.534**	560.764**	483.704	507.831	613.719**
	255.929	272.419	343.535	475.480	257.687
T	4.902***	5.244***	6.203***	4.671***	5.075***
	0.567	0.565	1.101	0.725	0.576
Pseudo R^2	0.19	0.20	0.2	0.19	0.2
Prob(>Chi²)	0.00	0.00	0.00	0.00	0.00
观测数	569	564	448	362	569

在表2中，税费负担的定义包含了国家税收，表3中的税收负担定义则剔除了国家税收部分。有意思的是，当税费负担不包括国家税收时，农民负担和民主选举水平之间不再存在U形曲线关系，而是随着农民负担的上升，村民主选举水平呈单调递减状态。一个可能的解释是，当排除国家税收以后，农民负担总体水平低于中央政府所无法接受的上限，换言之，总体而言，扣除了国家税收部分后的农民负担还没有达到使中央政府转变它的政策优先序的水平，因而U形曲线的右半部分没有在数据中体现出来。当然也可能存在另一种解释，说明地方基层政府对待民主选举的基本态度，即当它们收取的税费收入越高时，它们的利益动机驱使自己更加消极对待农村基层民主选举。究竟哪一种解释更合理，只能等待当我们获得更大量和质量更高的数据后才能进行相应的判断。另外，和表2结果相同，T 在所有回归中均十分显著，说明《村委会组织法》颁布后对基层民主选举产生了显著的影响。在其他控制变量中，收入水平也显示在相对发达的地区，选举的民主水平也更高。

表3　回归结果Ⅲ

解释变量	(1)	(2)	(3)	(4)	(5)
VFEE^2	−17.460	−20.891	−42.235	−48.401	−29.137
	21.390	22.339	30.878	52.193	21.910
VFEE2^2	−122.134**	−106.338*	−114.380*	−236.095***	−125.240***
	56.778	57.915	71.037	70.897	57.489
T	6.489***	6.896***	8.584***	8.438***	7.239***
	1.061	1.106	2.500	2.747	1.094
Pseudo R^2	0.19	0.20	0.20	0.20	0.2
Prob(>Chi^2)	0.00	0.00	0.00	0.00	0.00
观测数	569	564	448	362	569

五、结　论

《村委会组织法》的颁布，使得农民有可能第一次通过行使民主权力来维护自己的经济和政治利益，由于这不可避免地会触及地方政府的既得利益，因此“对于村民自治态度的分歧更多地突出表现在地方、基层政府和干部上”(李凡，2002)。有学者更直接指出，尽管国家进行了村民自治的制度供给，但宏观体制与政策又使得基层政府成为实行村民自治的阻截者(肖唐镖等，2001)。由于地方政府掌握着组织、经费、制度资源，并且越到基层，这种村民与地方政府之间掌握资源和权力不对称的情况就越明显。这导致地方政府在是否实行村民自治及民主选举，以及在多大程度上实行自治及实行什么样的选举方面事实上拥有相当大的决定权，从而使得一个地方农村基层民主建设的实际情况在相当大的程度上依然取决于当地政府的态度。因此村民和地方政府之间必然存在一定的冲突。由于地方政府完成管制任务被置于比贯彻《村委会组织法》更优先的位置，因此一旦村民和地方政府间在村民民主自治问题上发生冲突，中央政府会默许地方政府的某些行为。地方政府由于预期到中央政府的这一态度，当然也继续扮演消极对待农村基层民主的角色，并在这一制度框架下收取超过仅为实施管制任务所需的更高费用，从而出现我们所说的“法律软约束”现象。

本文的一个政策含义是，如果农村基层民主建设要更加顺利的话，那么一个前提条件是改变中央政府政策篮子里的各项政策方案的优先序。考虑到减轻甚至放弃管制对农村经济的正面效应(陶然、刘明兴、章奇，2003)，中央政府实际上并不存在两难选择。

注 释

① 这里主要指地方乡镇政府。在下文中，如无特别说明，地方基层政府均指地方政府。

② 有关农村基层民主建设的详细历史进程介绍，可参见李凡(2002)。

③ 根据中国乡村政治的现状，在下文中，如果不作特殊说明，所说的地方政府指乡镇政府。

④ 例如2000年山东栖霞市4个镇57名村委会主任集体辞职以抗议当地乡镇政府的行政干涉。

⑤ 许多案例(包括中央政府对一些基本国策的执行效率，对SARS蔓延的成功控制，等等)均说明了这一点。

⑥ 按照李凡(2002)的研究，按照中国目前农村民主建设的实际情况来判断，至少90%的乡村还没有建立起新型的村民自治制度。如果把地方政府利用"软控制"方式对乡村进行操纵的情况也算在内，情况还会更悲观一些。

⑦ 对中国粮食购销政策变化的讨论可参见陶然、刘明兴和章奇(2003)中的相关分析。这里需要补充的是，国家对粮食购销的控制力度在20世纪90年代曾一度加大，但在2002年后重新开始松动。

⑧ 例如，国家规定每个孩子都应该享有9年义务教育的权利。但政府并没有为所有的政策提供预算，教育部也没有足够的资金为贫困乡村修建校舍、发放教师工资。这样一来，为了达到这些政策要求，就必须就地集资。

⑨ 在另一篇文章中，我们指出管制政策扭曲了农村各种生产要素和产出的相对价格，抑制了农村产品和要素市场的发育，阻碍了农村各种生产要素的合理流动和资源配置，使得农村资源的配置以及农户的生产、经营决策背离自身的比较优势，从而不利于农民收入的增加以及农村经济的长期增长(陶然、刘明兴、章奇，2003)。

⑩ 90年代以来，随着农村基层民主建设的深入，农村干群冲突呈有增无减之趋势的一个重要原因就在于中央政府在赋予农民民主权力的同时，却并不放弃管制任务，并且仍然依赖地方政府作为贯彻任务的骨干力量。

⑪ 在数据集的考察期内没有其他更好的反映 REGU 的指标，也是我们选取 VFOOD 的一个重要原因。

⑫ 例如某村在一段时期之间分别选举了两次，第一次和第二次分别取值为 2 和 3，则 DEMO 在这两次选举期间的间隔期均取值为 2。

⑬ 除了对残差分布的假设不同外，ORDER PROBIT 模型与 ORDER LOGIT 模型并无本质差异。因此 ORDER LOGIT 模型适用的估计，原则上也可以用 ORDER PROBIT 模型进行估计。实际上，就本文的研究而言，两个模型的估计结果极其相近。

⑭ 在本部分所有的表中，为了节约篇幅，我们只列出了方程(1)、(2)中有关 REGU、*T* 和 VINC 变量的估计结果，其他控制变量(*X*)的估计结果则略去，有兴趣的读者可以向作者索取。

⑮ SCOTT 等将外出打工严格定义为外出 3 个月以上，在我们的数据中缺乏如此严格的外出打工时间划分，这或许影响了外出打工变量的统计性质。

参考文献

胡荣，1998:《村民委员会的自治及其与乡镇政府之间的关系》，《二十一世纪》12 月号总第 50 期。

柯丹青(Daniel Kelliher)，1997，《中国国内关于村民自治的争论》，《中国学刊》(*The China Journal*)，No. 37，pp. 63—86。

李凡主编，2002:《中国基层民主发展报告:2000—2001》，东方出版社。

林毅夫、李志赟，2004:《政策性负担、道德风险与预算软约束》，《经济研究》第 2 期。

陶然、刘明兴、章奇，2003a，《农民负担、政府管制与财政体制改革》，《经济研究》第 4 期。

陶然、刘明兴、章奇，2003b，《中国农村税费改革:政治经济学的考察和分析》，《中国社会科学评论》第 2 卷第 1 期。

肖唐镖等，2001:《中国乡村社会中的选举——对江西省 40 个村委会选举的一项综合调查》，《战略与管理》第 5 期。

徐勇，1997:《中国农村村民自治》，华中师范大学出版社。

张静，1998：《梨树县村委会换届选举观察》，《二十一世纪》（香港中文大学中国文化研究所），冬季卷。

Dewatripont, Mathias and Eric Maskin, 1995, "Credit and Efficiency in Centralized and Decentralized Economies", *The Review of Economic Studies*, 62:4, pp. 541—55.

Goldfel, S., and R. Quandt, 1988, "Budget Constraints, Bailouts and the Firm Under Central Planning", *Journal of Comparative Economics*, 12(4): pp. 502—520.

Kornai, János, 1980, *Economics of Shortage*, Amsterdam: North-Holland.

Kornai, János, Eric Maskin and Gérard Roland, 2003, "Understanding the Soft Budget Constraint", *Journal of Economic Literature*, Vol. XLI(December): pp. 1095—1136.

Li, Daokui, 1992, "Public Ownership as the cause of a soft budget constraint", mimeo, Harvard University.

Li, Lianjiang, 2004, "Political Trust in Rural China", presentation at Midwestern Political Science Association Annual Meeting at Chicago, USA, April 18, 2004.

O'Brien, K. J. and Lianjiang Li, 2000, "Accommodating 'Democracy' in a One-Party State: Introducing Village Elections in China", *China Quarterly*, Vol. 162, June, pp. 465—89.

Qian, Y., 1994, "A Theory of Shortage in Socialist Economies Based on the Soft Budget Constraint", *American Economic Review*, 84: pp. 145—156.

Qian, Y. and G. Roland, 1998, "Federalism and The Soft Budget Constraint", *American Economic Review*, 88(5): pp. 1143—1162.

Ray Yep, 2002, "Maintaining Stability in Rural China: Challenges and Responses," unpublished paper.

Justin Yifu, Lin and Fuguo Tan, 1999, "Accountability, Viability, and Soft Budget Constraint", *American Economic Review*, Papers and

Proceedings, Volume 89, Number 2, pp. 426—431.

Schleifer A., Lakonishok J., Vishny R. W., 1994, "Contrarian Investment, Extrapolation and Risk", *Journal of Finance*, vol. 49, pp. 1541—1578.

(原载《经济研究》2004年第6期)

晋升博弈中政府官员的激励与合作*

——兼论我国地方保护主义和重复建设问题长期存在的原因

周黎安

(北京大学光华管理学院)

一、引 言

由于我国地方政府长期以来对地区经济增长和发展具有至关重要的影响力,地方官员的激励与行为一直备受学术界的关注,成为分析地区经济现象的一个重要的透视点。迄今对我国政府官员,尤其是地方政府官员激励与行为的研究主要强调行政性分权和财政包干改革以来地方官员的财政与经济激励。沈立人、戴园晨(1990)分析了行政性分权和财政包干对中国“诸侯经济”形成的影响;Oi(1992), Jin、Qian 和 Weingast(2000)强调了财政包干改革对地方政府推动地方经济发展,尤其是乡镇企业迅速发展的意义;Young(2000)提供了中国地区间贸易保护主义和产业同构化的经验证据,并强调地方财政激励和扭曲

* 作者感谢朱玲、魏众、刘小玄、剧锦文、汪森军、陈烨以及中国社科院经济研究所学术研讨会的参与者对本文提出的富有价值的意见。在形成本文想法的过程中,作者也得益于车嘉华的评论,特此致谢。

的价格体系对产业同构化的影响。

毫无疑问，财政和经济激励构成地方官员激励最重要的组成部分之一，但这些激励本身仍然无法满意地解释很多地方官员的行为，比如长期困惑我国经济发展的两大顽疾——地方保护主义和重复建设问题。主流文献关于这些问题的解释主要是基于市场和经济竞争的逻辑（沈立人、戴园晨，1990；银温泉、才婉如，2001；Young，2000）：20 世纪 80 年代以来的财政包干体制强化了地方政府的财政和经济激励，各个地区为保护本地的资源、市场和税基而各自为战，为寻求高额利润而过度进入某一行业。可是这种解释并不完全令人信服。如果说地方官员的财税激励是地方保护主义存在的根本原因，那么，为什么同样面临税收激励的国家之间却可以通过双边和多边贸易协定达成市场开放和自由贸易，而同在一国之内的各地区却一直不能达成类似的协定？在刚刚结束的“两会”上，一位东北的人大代表在谈及振兴大东北过程中出现的“诸侯经济”现象时尖锐地指出：当市场渴望连接在一起也应该连接在一起的时候，政府官员们却没有坐到一起研究彼此间的协调发展，这种现象不仅在东北存在，在全国也存在。[①] 为什么市场渴望协调与合作时政府官员却迟迟不愿意坐到一起？这是传统解释所无法回答的。

关于重复建设问题的传统解释也存在一些未解的疑问：如果地方重复投资只为了寻求高额利润和相应的税收利益，那为什么有些地区在注定要亏损的前景下仍然要过度投资？更关键的是，在我国长期存在的一浪接一浪的重复建设“大战”中，各地区带有明显的“相互攀比”和“相互较劲”的色彩，这又如何用市场和财税动机来理解？

本文试图从一个新的角度对地方官员经济合作失败的深层原因提供解释。我认为，地方官员合作困难的根源并不主要在于地方官员的财税激励及他们所处的经济竞争的性质，而是在于嵌入在经济竞争当中的政治晋升博弈的性质。同一行政级别的地方官员，无论是省、市、县还是乡镇一级，都处于一种政治晋升博弈，或者说政治锦标赛(political tournaments)。自上世纪80年代初以来地方官员的选拔和提升的标准由过去的纯政治指标变成经济绩效指标，尤其是地方GDP增长的绩效，系统的经验研究也证实了这一点(Li and Zhou, 2004)。不同地区的地方官员不仅在经济上为GDP和利税进行竞争，而且同时也在"官场"上为晋升而竞争。在政治晋升博弈中，给定只有有限数目的人可以获得提升，一个人获得提升将直接降低另一人提升的机会，一人所得构成另一人所失，因此参与人面临的是一个零和博弈。而在正常的经济竞争中，合作使得参与人实现"来自交易的收益"(gain from trade)，合作博弈所对应的是一个正和博弈。"官场"竞争的逻辑将深刻地改变由官员所主导的经济竞争的方式和内容，而这一点正是被以往的研究所忽略的。

本文建立了一个非常简单的模型说明政治晋升博弈下官员的激励与合作倾向。在地方官员的行为对邻近地区存有"溢出效应"的场合，政治晋升博弈的基本特征就是促使参与人只关心自己与竞争者的相对位次，在成本允许的情况下，参与人不仅有激励做有利于本地区经济发展的事情，而且也有同样的激励去做不利于其竞争对手所在地区的事情(如阻碍外地的产品进入本地市场)；对于那些利己不利人的事情激励最充分，而对于那些既利己又利人的"双赢"合作则激励不足。这就是为什么处于政治锦标赛博弈中的政府官员不愿意合作却愿意支持"恶性"竞争的基本原因。作为一个运用，我将从政治晋升博弈模型出发对我国长期存在的地方保护主义和重复建设问题提出一个系统的解释。

本文的主要贡献在于从政府官员晋升激励的角度研究了政治晋升竞争对政府主导型的区域竞争和合作的影响，在一个全新和系统的解释性框架下理解我国区域经济发展、竞争与互动过程。本文另一隐含的贡献在于提供了转型经济中国有企业软预算约束的政治竞争方面的根源。[②] 在本文的模型中，地方官员依赖于对地方经济尤其是国有企业的影响力，通过恶性的经济竞争达到政治竞争的目的，这正是在改革开放条件下我国国有企业存在软预算约束的一个新的根源。众所周知，Kornai 对国有企业软预算约束的经典的解释是政府对国有企业的“父爱主义”倾向(Kornai, 1979)，这在计划经济体制下是普遍存在的动机；但在我国经济转型过程中，地方政府官员出于对晋升的政治激励而不惜以地方产业和企业的经济预算为代价参与地区竞争，已不再是简单的“父爱主义”的行动了。

二、晋升博弈中的地方官员的激励与合作：一个简单模型

本部分将试图建立一个非常简单的模型，以揭示具有锦标赛特征的政治晋升博弈的基本结构、政府官员的激励及其对经济合作的影响。本模型是对 Lazear 和 Rosen(1981)锦标赛模型的一个扩展。我们设想有这样一个晋升博弈，其中上一级政府对两个地区的地方政府首脑 A 和 B 的地区经济绩效进行考核，绩效较高者将获得政治提拔。[③] 每个地区的经济绩效由 y_i 代表，地方官员的努力与其所在地区经济绩效的关系可以由下列式子代表：

$$y_i = a_i + ra_j + e_i \qquad (i = A,\ B;\ i \neq j)$$

其中 a_i 代表地方官员 i 的努力程度，a_j 代表地方官员 j 的努力

程度。上述假设说明我们的模型适用的条件是政府官员的决策和行为(如重大投资决策)对地方经济或某些产业的影响力必须非常大。我们假定上级政府能够观察到 y_i,但无法观察到 a_i,a_i 只有官员 i 自己知道。这样,上级政府所能采用的激励机制都只能基于可观察的经济业绩。系数 r 代表官员 j 的努力对地区 i 经济业绩直接产生的边际影响,如果 r 不为零,则表明地方官员 i 的行为对地区 j 有"溢出效应"。为简化问题起见,我们假定 $|r|<1$,即不论"溢出效应"为正抑或为负,任何一个官员的行为对自己业绩的影响要超过对别人业绩的影响。e_i 是一个随机扰动项,e_i 和 e_j 相互独立,我们假定 (e_j-e_i) 服从一个期望值为 0、独立和相同的对称分布 F。

假定政治锦标赛的规则是:如果地方 i 的经济业绩超过地区 j,即 $y_i>y_j$,那么官员 i 将得到提拔,获得 V 的效用,这时官员 j 则不被提拔,获得的效用为 $v(V>v)$。这个关于晋升标准的假设符合自从 20 世纪 80 年代初以来我国地方官员的考核和晋升的实际情况,即地方官员政绩考核的标准以地方 GDP 增长的绩效为主。由于 (e_j-e_i) 服从分布 F,官员 i 获得提拔的概率可通过下列运算得出,即对于 $i\neq j$,

$$\begin{aligned}\text{Prob}(y_i>y_j)&=\text{Prob}[a_i+ra_j+e_i-(a_j+ra_i+e_j)>0]\\&=\text{Prob}[e_j-e_i<(1-r)(a_i-a_j)]\\&=F[(1-r)(a_i-a_j)]\end{aligned}$$

这样我们就可以得到官员 i 的效用函数:

$$\begin{aligned}U_i(a_i,\ a_j)=&F[(1-r)(a_i-a_j)]V\\&+\{1-F[(1-r)(a_i-a_j)]\}v-C(a_i)\end{aligned}$$

由上式我们得到官员 i 实现效用最大化的一阶条件:④

$$(1-r)f[(1-r)(a_i-a_j)](V-v)=C'(a_i),\ i=A,\ B$$

其中 $f(\cdot)$是分布函数 F 的密度函数。在对称性纳什均衡下，上述一阶条件变成：

$$(1-r)f(0)(V-v)=C'(a_i),\ i=A,\ B$$

为了理解上式所隐含的福利含义，我们可以将上述条件与社会福利最大化的一阶条件相比较。在社会最优(first-best)的安排下，我们将选择 a_i 和 a_j 使得社会剩余的期望值最大化，即对于 $i\neq j$,

$$\max_{a_i,\ a_j}(1+r)(a_i+a_j)-C(a_i)-C(a_j)$$

其一阶条件为：

$$(1+r)=C'(a_i),\ i=A,\ B$$

比较这两个一阶条件不难发现，在社会最优的情况下，r 越大意味着地方官员激励应该越大，可是，在政治锦标赛下，r 越大却意味着地方官员的激励越小。换句话说，如果一个地区的官员的发展经济的努力对其他地区也有积极(消极)影响，那么这种影响的存在会削弱(加强)该官员努力工作的激励。

在政治锦标赛中，每个官员都将自己行为的"溢出效应"内在化了，把对竞争对手有利的"溢出效应"当作对自己不利的事情。有趣的是，这与微观经济学所讨论的外在性问题有很大的不同。在那种情况下，个人通常不考虑其行为的"溢出效应"，如果有某种机制使其内在化这些"溢出效应"(如征税或产权的重新界定)，那也是把利他之事当作利己之事，而不会反过来。然而，在存有"溢出效应"的场合，政治锦标赛的基本特征就是促使参与人只关心自己与竞争者的相对位次，在成本允许的情况下，参与人不仅有激励做有利于自己的事情，而且也有同样的激励去做不利于其竞争对手的事情;对于那些利己不利人的事情激励最充分,但是,对于那些"双赢"的合作则激励不足。

上述模型的结果可以系统地解释我国地区发展与互动的几个相互关联的现象:(1)地方官员出于晋升的考虑有充分的激励支持本地的企业和发展本地的经济,这解释了自80年代以来地方官员一直有非常强烈的动机推动本地经济的快速增长;(2)处于政治锦标赛博弈中的地方官员不愿意进行区域合作与分工,对于那些双赢的区域合作机会"反应冷淡";这有助于解释我国长期存在的地区封锁、地方保护主义和"大而全"的地区发展战略;(3)地方官员为了提高自己的政绩位次、同时降低其竞争对手的位次,会"不择手段"地进行"恶性竞争",这有助于解释我国自80年代中期以来地区间不断上演的形形色色的"大战",从各种各样的产业大战、开发区建设热到吸引外资的"让利竞赛"。

三、关于我国地方保护主义和重复建设问题长期存在的一个解释

地方保护主义和重复建设问题自改革开放以来一直是困扰我国经济健康发展的两大顽疾。如前所述,经济学界对于这些问题的解释主要强调行政分权下的财政激励。⑤这些因素固然非常重要,但它们并不足以解释一些非常困惑的现象。

比如说地区封锁和市场分割问题。经济学关于"来自交易的收益"的基本常识告诉我们,自由贸易可以扩大市场范围,提高各贸易地区的专业化水平,促进这些地区的经济发展。因此,更根本的一个问题是,当合作解对所有的参与方带来更好的经济收益的时候,为什么地方官员在经济上不合作?当然,在历史上,地区之间、尤其是国家之间的贸易战或税收壁垒经常出现,

有时还演变得非常激烈，但同时我们也可以看到，国家间关税同盟、双边及多边贸易协定自二战以来越来越普遍，成为促成国际贸易合作的主要力量，当今的世贸组织和它的前身关税总协定所发挥的巨大作用就是一个极好的例子。从这个角度看，我国地区间长期的地方保护主义就变得很难理解了：为什么国家之间可以通过双边和多边贸易协定达成市场开放和自由贸易，而同在一国之内的各地区却一直不能达成类似的协定？国家之间出现贸易纠纷只能诉诸效力有限的国际法或多边协调机制，而中国的地区贸易纠纷可以诉诸中国法律，也可以诉诸强有力的行政协调，那么同处于一个政党系统领导和协调的地方官员为什么不能坐在一起达成一个双边或多边贸易协定？虽然政策界和理论界关于杜绝地方保护主义的呼声自 80 年代中后期就一直不绝于耳，但迄今，我们尚未见到任何关于协商开放地区市场的任何正式努力。从财政激励解释地方保护主义的理论无法解释这一点，因为同是出于税收和经济发展的考虑，国家之间已达成各种形式、且行之有效的贸易合作协定，为什么中国的地区之间却不能这样做？况且中国的地方官员还同时处于一个行政系统，比国家之间的合作还多出一个监督和制约的渠道。

重复建设问题或产业同构化问题在最近温家宝总理的政府工作报告中再次被重点提及。温总理指出，今年宏观调控的一项重要任务就是坚决遏制部分行业和地区盲目投资、低水平重复建设。产业同构化问题在近年来人们讨论珠三角、长三角、京津冀以及东三省的区域合作问题时不断被涉及。各个地方竞相甚至过度进入同一行业或一拥而上从事每个国家重点项目，从 80 年代的轻纺热、90 年代的“开发区热”，到现在各地“造车大跃进”、“机场建设大战”等。对此的一个可能的解释是，政府管制导致市场价格严重扭曲，垄断利润高。这在改革初期可能是其中的原因，但现在随着市场进一步的完善，价格扭曲方面的因素的比重应该逐渐下降。关键在于，这些重复建设的背后都有政府主导或推动的影子，而这些一拥而上、一哄而起的过程中包含着明显的相互攀比和相互较劲的动机，无法简单地用利润或财税动机来解释，否则，我们无法解释为什么各地方在同一产业或建设项目的竞争中会经常无视经济亏损这一现实。⑥

从上述的这些例子不难看出，我国长期存在的产业同构化和地方保护主义问题不是简单的企业为谋求高额利润而过度进入某行业和保护本地市场的问题，而是政府官员实施地区发展战略和产业政策的一部分，它包含着明显的政治收益的计算。基于上一部分的模型，我提出一个基本解释是，与纯粹的经济竞争相比(如两个企业或两国之间的经济竞争)，我国地方官员同时处于两种竞争之中，既有为地区的经济产出和税收而竞争，同时又为各自的政治晋升而竞争。为简化术语起见，让我们称这种竞争为"混合竞争"。这就使得地方官员在考虑竞争利益时不仅需要计算经济收益，而且还要计算晋升博弈中的政治收益，两者的总和才真正构成对他们行为的激励。作为政府官员，政治收益的计算也许更为重要。从这个角度出发，在前面提出的模型基础上，我尝试提出以下两个推论：⑦

推论 1：经济合作的政治激励约束。在纯经济竞争中，合作的正收益可以激发贸易和合作的发生，但对于混合竞争来说，只有当合作的净结果不改变参与人的相对位次时，合作收益才可能实现，否则合作很难发生。

推论 2：市场进入的政治参与约束。在纯经济竞争中，投资的负利润前景足以阻止市场进入行为，但对于混合竞争来说，如果进入后的竞争结果会有利于参与人的相对位次，那么，投资的负利润前景也不足以阻止市场进入。

推论1说明混合竞争的合作空间比纯粹的经济竞争的合作空间要小得多，好比“刀刃上的增长”一样困难，而且经济实力越是接近的地区越不容易合作。该推论有助于说明当市场渴望连接的时候，地方官员为什么不愿意坐在一起研究区域合作和开发市场的问题。我国长期存在的地区封锁、地方保护主义和“大而全”的地区发展战略都可以看作是地方官员在政治晋升博弈中做出最优反应的必然后果。举一个例子，当振兴东北老工业基地的方案开始具体落实时，东三省都纷纷提出要发展石油化工，都把石油化工列为各自的支柱产业，而且自成体系、大而全地发展。这样一来，在“大东北”振兴战略之下，还有辽宁、吉林和黑龙江三个“小东北”振兴战略，三省互不相通，各自为战(转引自《北京娱乐信报》2004年3月11日)。在这种相互较劲和攀比的背后是地方官员那种争当龙头老大的心理和算计，是政治竞争导致的一种必然反应。另一个例子涉及到京津冀区域合作的问题。据区域经济专家樊杰透露，90年代初原国家计委曾制定一个环渤海经济圈的发展规划，在规划中，北京的主导产业被确定为高新技术产业和现代服务业，天津被作为重型制造业的中心。然而，因北京和天津围绕着谁是环渤海经济区的龙头一直有竞争，导致北京一度成为在中国特大型城市里仅次于沈阳的重工业城市(参见《南方周末》2003年12月5日报道《环渤海经济圈前世今生》)。有专家认为，就区域合作而言，京津冀目前还处于停滞对抗型，京津对抗的结果是“北京吃不了，天津吃不饱”(参见《21世纪经济报道》2003年11月12日报道《环渤海经济圈合作新契机》)。

推论1不仅可以解释我国区域合作的困难，还可以进一步解释不同经济带区域整合程度的差异。为什么长三角和珠三角区域整合的程度要高于京津地区？在长三角，上海与邻近的浙江和江苏的经济实力之差要大于北京和天津之间的差距，而在珠三角，香港和广州的龙头地位是比较明显的。如果一个经济区"群龙无首"，那么地方官员推动产业整合和区域合作的激励会相对较小，而相互较劲和争当老大的激励会相对较大。这意味着经济实力越是接近的地区将越难合作，而发达地区与欠发达地区的区域合作则相对更容易一些。所以，本文虽然强调地方官员经济合作的困难，但绝非主张所有地区的经济合作都不可能，关键在于经济合作是否会影响地方官员之间的相对位次。

推论2的一个基本经济含义就是，政治晋升激励的考虑可能使得官员主导型的投资过度进入某个行业或项目，甚至进行"恶性竞争"。虽然长期投资的利润前景并不乐观，但如果市场进入可以阻止其竞争地区同一行业的业绩上升，有时即便两败俱伤，也可能是值得的。该推论有助于解释长期以来各地区对许多项目的投资在明显面临亏损的情况下"一哄而上"的现象。沈立人、戴园晨(1990)在描述我国"诸侯经济"的特征时指出：各个地方热衷于不顾条件搞速度攀比，展开"速度大战"；而且，"地方搞攀比，一个动机是为地方谋利益，另一个动机是显示政绩。这也不算错，只是如果把后者凌驾于前者之上，往往会不择手段"。这是80年代的情况。然而，20多年后的今天，问题的性质并未发生实质性改变。据媒体报道⑧，长三角在新一轮经济发展的竞争中，各地正在上演新一轮的"机场建设大战"。有人做过统计，目前长三角地区每万平方公里的机场密度为0.8个，超过美国每万平方公里0.6个的水平。与如此高密度的机场布局相对应的是许多机场的资源闲置和大量亏损，但这仍然阻止不了一些地级市加入这场造机场运动的热情。其中苏州的一位政府官员在列举建机场的几大"利好"时特别提到，建机场有利于提高苏州的地位。也许机场数目多少本身不能完全说明重复建设的严重性，但有一点却是值得关注的，那就是，长三角不同地区的机场定位应该反映各地区的发展水平和地理位置的差异，如上海和无锡的机场定位就应该不一样。然而，许多地区在考虑机场发展规划时却都不愿意做“二级机场”，不愿意主动与上海机场进行分工协作。[9]有意思的是，珠三角在经济高速发展的过程中也曾出现过这种类似的现象。

近年来我国各地的外资引进中的“恶性竞争”也可以用地方官员的晋升激励来解释。自改革开放以来，我国沿海地区借助其优越的区位和经济优势，一直对吸引外资非常重视，各地为争夺外资项目也因此处于激烈竞争之中，最近几年尤为明显。新华社记者将之概括为“门槛一降再降，成本一减再减，空间一让再让”。[10]在许多地方，如上海、江苏、浙江等地纷纷以远远低于成本价的土地价格吸引外商，税收优惠也一再突破国家规定的外资优惠政策的底线。在这种“让利竞赛”的背后是各地政府级级下任务、层层压指标，招商引资被当作地方政府“一把手”工程，一些省市的主要媒体还定期公布下级政府和开发区招商引资的名次。在长三角和珠三角的许多城市活跃着一些来自全国各地的“招商游击队”，在东莞市，每年就有300多个招商团上门招商，有的还将招商办事处直接设在乡镇。更有甚者，一些地方政府还将机关干部的工资与引资数量挂钩，完不出任务指标的将被取消基础工资。引资竞争本身并不奇怪，但值得注意的是这种竞争所采取的形式和推进的程度。单单用地方政府财税激励是无法理解这种竞争所达到的“恶性”程度，而必须诉诸地方官员对政绩的强烈追求和对落后于竞争地区的巨大恐惧才能理解。

四、模型的其他一些应用

由于晋升竞争属于所有科层组织（包括官僚组织）的一个基

本特征，因此本文所提出的分析框架具有更为一般的意义。在官僚组织中普遍存在各部门之间相互封闭、相互扯皮的非合作现象，但人们通常将这一类现象笼统地归结为“官僚主义作风”或“官僚病”，而忽略了导致这种现象背后更深层的激励因素。

近年来我国电子政务发展迅速，但也一直存在着严重的“互联互通”问题，其中一个突出的现象是所谓的“纵强横弱”现象，即一个政府部门内部的信息共享和交换相对容易，而不同部门之间横向的互联互通则相对困难，存在一个个分散的所谓的“信息孤岛”（参见张维迎、刘鹤，2004，第107—115页）。需要注意的是，互联互通的主要障碍不在于信息技术，因为在很多情况下是“联而不通”，数据库相接，但信息不能交换和共享，而且如果纯粹是技术原因，就不应该有“纵强”与“横弱”共存的现象。这说明互联互通背后主要是一个激励问题。在本文模型的框架下，“纵强横弱”现象并不难以理解。首先，给定中央政府三令五申强调电子政务的重要性，各部门的电子政务的发展自然会进入到主管的政府官员的政绩当中；其次，为了在电子政务的锦标赛中引人注目，一些有条件的部门会有较强的激励发展本部门的信息化，所以，中国300亿电子政务投资绝大部分投在了纵向垂直部门；最后，部门之间的信息共享与合作属于利己又利人的事情，根据我们前面的模型，参与人的激励会很小，而且，“利人”成分越高，主管官员的激励就越小，这就是“横弱”的原因。

晋升竞争不仅仅只局限于政府部门，其激励后果也会反映在M型结构的公司中。M型公司的设计虽然赋予中层经理更多的权力，并便于设计带有同类竞争性质的（yardstick competition）激励合同（Maskin, Qian and Xu, 2000），但中层经理所处的晋升博弈也会阻碍他们之间的有效合作，这是为什么各个利润中心必须尽可能在技术、产品或者区域上相互独立，以减少晋升博弈的不利后果。因此本文的模型对于理解 M 型公司的组织和激励设计也会有一定的帮助。

五、结　论

从激励结构来说，我国地方官员具有双重特征：他们一方面是"经济参与人"，即像任何经济主体一样关注经济利益，上世纪 80 年代以来的行政性分权和财政包干强化了地方政府的经济动机；但另一方面，这些地方官员同时也是"政治参与人"，他们关注政治晋升和政治收益，各地的官员不仅在经济上为财税和利润而竞争，同时也在"官场"上为晋升而竞争。上世纪 80 年代初期实施的领导干部选拔和晋升标准的重大改革使地方官员的晋升与地方经济发展绩效挂钩。过去大量的研究从市场和经济竞争的逻辑出发强调行政性分权和地方官员的财政激励对区域间经济互动的影响。这种研究角度的一个缺陷是只注重于我国地方官员的第一种特征，而忽略了地方官员的第二种特征及其影响。本文建立了一个地方官员政治晋升博弈的简单模型，旨在强调地方官员的晋升激励及其对地区间经济竞争和互动的影响。

以 GDP 增长为基础的晋升激励在调动地方官员发展地区经济的积极性方面曾发挥过重要的历史作用，这在经济改革初期、计划体制的束缚还相当严重的时候尤为如此。但随着市场的发育和完善，区域分工与整合的需求日益增加，这种激励机制的消极后果也越来越明显。因此，我们有必要对地方官员的政绩考核制度进行反思。目前中央政府特别强调地方政府的科学发展观问题，如淡化 GDP 指标、强调绿色 GDP 概念等等，正是改革传统政绩考核体系的一种积极举措。本文的研究有助于我们更深入地理解设计一项政绩考核机制所必须注意的问题，比如，为了尽量降低晋升激励所带来的消极后果，我们应该将地方政府的注意力集中在服务本地公众的能力和满意度等方面；另外进一步减少地方政府对市场的干预能力也是一种治本之策。

注 释

① 据新华社电，转引自《北京娱乐信报》2004 年 3 月 11 日的报道《"大东北"下还有"小东北"："诸侯经济"抬头》。

② Shleifer 和 Vishny(1994)也提出了一个关于软预算约束的政治解释，所不同的是，他们考察在一个民主政体下，政治家如何通过补贴企业来获取企业雇员对他们的政治支持，以赢得连任。

③ 本模型也完全适用于两个同级的政府部门和一个部门的两个科室的情况，或者一个大型 M-型公司的两个分公司，我们所需要的只是这些参与人处于同一级的晋升竞争，晋升的标准是参与人的相对绩效。

④ 效用最大化的二阶条件要求 $\frac{\partial^2 U_i}{\partial a_i^2} = (1-r)^2 f'(\cdot)(V-v) - C''(a_i) < 0$，由于据我们的假定，$(e_j - e_i)$ 是对称分布，因此在对称的纳什均衡下，$a_i^* = a_j^*$，$f'(0) = 0$，又由于 $C'' > 0$，该条件将自动得到满足。

⑤ 有些经济地理学家提出"行政区经济"的概念，强调行政干预和行政区划对市场分割的影响(如舒庆、周克瑜，2003)。但是，这种观点并没有进一步说明行政区划或行政干预为什么一定会导致市场分割和重复建设。

⑥ 张维迎和马捷(1999)从产权制度和技术的角度解释了我国国有企业恶性竞争倾向，其中产权制度的影响主要体现在国有企业经理所面临的软预算约束问题。我们之间的区别主要在于，在我的解释中，产业过度进入或恶性竞争是政治竞争的锦标赛性质所致，企业面临的软预算约束是这种政治竞争的一个结果。

⑦ 虽然从理论直觉上不难理解，但从前面的模型到以下的两个推论仍然存在一定的跳跃。关于这两个推论更严格的模型基础，参见周黎安、汪森军(2004)。

⑧ 参见新华网北京 2003 年 12 月 11 日电文和《国际金融报》2004 年 3 月 8 日的报道“空中通道一掷‘亿’金,谁解长三角机场困局”。

⑨ 参见《中国青年报》2004 年 5 月 10 日的报道《长三角机场建设“多少”之争,谁愿做二级机场?》。

⑩ 参见新华社记者车晓慧、陈钢的报道《级级下任务层层压指标,招商引资成“让利竞赛”》,新华社 2003 年 11 月 11 日。

参考文献

沈立人、戴园晨,1990:《我国“诸侯经济”的形成及其弊端和根源》,《经济研究》第 3 期。

舒庆、周克瑜,2003:《从封闭走向开放:中国行政区经济透视》,华东师范大学出版社。

银温泉、才婉如,2001:《我国地方市场分割的成因和对策》,《经济研究》第 6 期。

张维迎、马捷,1999:《恶性竞争的产权基础》,《经济研究》第 6 期。

张维迎、刘鹤主编,2004:《我国地级市电子政务研究报告》,中国经济出版社。

周黎安、汪淼军,2004:《地方官员的晋升激励与地区专业化》,工作论文。

Lazear, E. and S. Rosen, 1981, “Rank-Ordered Tournaments as Optimal Labor Contracts”, *Journal of Political Economy*, 89:S, pp. 841—864.

Li, H. and L. Zhou, 2004, “Political Turnover and Economic Performance: The Incentive Role of China's Personnel Control”, memo.

Jin, H., Y. Qian and B. Weingast, 2000, “Regional Decentralization and Fiscal Incentives: Federalism, Chinese Style”, memo.

Kornai, J., 1979, “Resource-Constrained versus Demand-Constrained Systems”, *Econometrica*, 47: pp. 801—820.

Oi, J., 1992, “Fiscal Reform and the Economic Foundations of Local State Corporatism in China”, *World Politics*, 45: pp. 99—126.

Maskin, E., Y. Qian and C. Xu, 2000, "Incentives, Scale Economies, and Organization Forms", *Review of Economic Studies*, 67: pp. 359—378.

Shleifer, A. and R. Vishny, 1994, "Politicians and Firms", *Quarterly Journal of Economics* 109: pp. 995—1025.

Young, A., 2000, "The Razor's Edge: Distortions and Incremental Reform in the People's Republic of China", *Quarterly Journal of Economics* 115: pp. 1091—1135.

（原载《经济研究》2004年第6期）

农地产权与征地制度*

——中国城市化面临的重大选择

周其仁

（北京大学中国经济研究中心）

一、问 题 所 在

制度对经济绩效的决定性作用早已引起学者的注意（Coase，1937，1960；North，1990）。如果制度不能适当地反映资源稀缺性和经济机会，经济中就会出现行为的扭曲（North，1990）。对于任何一个社会而言，制度的基础总是一组关于产权的法律规定，它界定了社会成员运用特别资产权利的范围（Bazel，1989；Libecap，1989；Eggertsson，1990；North，1990；Alston，1996）。产权一般包括资源的排他性使用权，通过使用资源而获取租金的收益权，以及通过出售或其他办法转让资源给他人的转让权（Chueng，1973，中文著作见张五常《经济解释》

* 本文的基础是作者2003年9月至12月在耶鲁大学法学院访问期间完成的一篇工作论文，该文曾在耶鲁大学中国法律中心（China Law Center at Yale）于2003年11月25日举行的研讨会上作为专题讨论。作者感谢该讨论会的参加者，特别是Ellikcson、Rose、Gewirtz、陈志武、文贯中、陈洁和其他与会者的评论、批评和建议。作者尤其感谢Jamie Horsley和耶鲁大学中国法律中心对访问的安排和关照，以及耶鲁大学各图书馆提供的研究条件。

(三卷本),2002)。这样,产权不但提供了影响经济绩效的行为的激励,而且决定谁是经济活动的主角并因此决定着社会财富的分配。

在组成产权的三项权利当中,转让权起着更为关键的作用。理论上,得到清楚界定的转让权一定包含着清楚界定的使用权和收益权。但是反过来,清楚的使用权或收益权并不一定意味可以自由转让。在实践中,经济增长常常引起经济结构的改变,而经济结构的变化恰恰是大规模的资源转让的结果。如果转让权受到限制,潜在的资源转让连同经济增长就受到阻碍。

历史一定充满如下经验:急速的经济变化带来了要求改变现存法律关于转让权界定的压力。在需要的法律改变完成之前,违法行为可能大量发生,因为经济变化要求加快资源转让,而现存的法律制度并没有对转让权做出清楚的界定。这时,如果不制止违法行为,经济秩序就受到冲击。但是同时,依靠执行原有的产权制度来消除混乱则不得不以限制资源转让作为代价。解决这个矛盾的办法是适时改变法律关于转让权的界定。问题在于,合乎需要的法律变革究竟在什么样的条件下才易于发生?

中国近年城市化加速的经验为研究上述问题提供了一个难得的案例。在1978年到2000年间,中国城市从193个增加到663个,镇的数目从2173个增加到20312个,城镇人口从1.7亿增加到4.56亿。与此同时,论千万计的农民工从农村转入城镇,数千万亩的农地转为城镇的工商建设用地。基于改革开放和经济增长的累计效果,人们一般预计未来二十年中国的城市化还将加速。①

但是,近年城市化的加速,恰恰是在现存法律关于土地资源转让权的重新界定严重滞后的情况下发生的。中国现存土地法奠基于计划公有制时代，其主要特色是政府用行政命令代替市场交易来达成经济资源的转让。虽然二十多年市场取向的改革已经动摇了现存土地法律的基础，但是几经修订的土地法还是远不能满足经济实践的要求。结果，城市化加速伴随着利益冲突的加剧，提出了一个重大的两难性问题：不惜以土地转让中的利益冲突为代价来继续加速城市化，还是不得不抑制城市化来缓减土地转让中的利益冲突？

问题的根源是，加速的城市化——中国长期经济增长的一个重要源泉——发生在含糊不清的农地转让权的限制条件下。这就无法避免 Bazel(1989)指出过的困境：离开了清楚界定并得到良好执行的产权制度，人们必定争相攫取稀缺的经济资源和机会。这里所谓的“攫取”，就是人们竞争稀缺资源而不受法律限制。重要的是，攫取表明混乱与机会经常紧密地纠缠在一起。不能认识和分析攫取行为，难以重新在法律上界定权利。

沿着上述思想线索，本文探讨以下问题：在现存土地转让权的法律安排下，人们实际上怎样行为？如何理解这些行为的经济含义？然后，我们讨论将要修订的《宪法》和《土地法》面临的主要选择。本文的结构如下：第二部分调查现存农地转让权的法律制度；第三部分分析土地转让中的攫取行为；第四部分研究重新界定转让权的实践经验；第五部分提出关于转让权管制的经济分析；第六部分讨论相关政策建议，以及重修土地法面临的选择；最后是全文的结论和有待进一步研究的问题。②

二、现存法律对农地转让权的界定

现存法律涉及农地转让权的主要有两部，一部《中华人民共和国农村土地承包法》，另外一部是《中华人民共和国土地管理法》。[3]转让权问题是如此重大，以至于为了制定和修订上述两部法律，不得不修改《宪法》的相关条款。本部分简要评论这些法律，着眼点是它们内在的矛盾冲突及其对经济行为的影响。

(一) 承认转让权的法律

在20世纪70年代末80年代初农村改革中形成的农民家庭土地承包经营权，差不多经过了二十年时间，才得到第一个比较完备的法律表达。2002年8月29日全国人大常委会通过的《农村土地承包法》，不但确认并宣布保护农户的土地使用权和收益权，而且确认并宣布保护农户的土地转让权。至此，曾经在中国长期实行的农地集体所有制，全面改革为土地的农户私人承包经营制。

对农户私人土地转让权的全面承认和清楚界定，是《农村土地承包法》的基本内容。让我们简述其中最重要的几项规定：

(1) 土地转让权属于“承包方”(即“农户”)，而不属于“发包方”(即“集体”)[4]；

(2) 实施土地转让权的首要原则是平等协商、自愿、有偿，不受任何组织和个人的强迫和阻碍；

(3) 土地转让的形式可以包括转包、出租、互换等多种形式；

(4) 转让权的价格由当事人协商确定；

(5) 转让权的收益归承包方所有。

由于转让的是土地承包经营权，因此非常合乎逻辑，《农村土地承包法》必须综合改革以来关于土地承包经营的全部政策法规，以更清晰的法律语言全面界定土地的农户私人承包经营权。其要点是：农村集体所有的土地全部实行以农户家庭为基础的承包经营制，为此，法律规定了集体土地承包给农户私人经营的程序、期限、形式，以及在承包期内发包方与承包方的各自的权利和义务。

可以说,《农村土地承包法》全面完成了对我国土地集体所有制内容的正式更换。中国的农地依然可以说集体所有,但是当今的集体唯一可以作为的只是依法将土地发包给农户私人;在长达30年以上的法定承包期内,唯有私人承包方才有权使用和经营农地,获取相应的收益并可在市场上自主转让农地的经营权;集体发包方无权终止、收回、调整农户承包权,无权截流承包收益权,也无权干预承包方的转让权。很清楚,农户私人承包经营的集体土地所有制,再也不是人民公社时代集体经营的集体土地所有制。由法律清楚界定并加以保护的农户私人的土地使用权、收益权和转让权,为在经济结构快速变迁条件下有效利用农地资源,奠定了一个可以将稳定性与灵活性结合起来的制度基础。

《农村土地承包法》仍然存在一些瑕疵。去开枝节,一个重要的问题是承包农地的年期依然偏短。比较城镇住宅地50年到70年的批租期,30年的农地承包期是否就是完全合适的?与此相关,现行土地承包法没有交代土地承包到期后续约的准则。如果法律规定届时给予在位承包方某种优先续约权,那么承包年期的重要性也许就下降了。

另外一个缺陷,《农村土地承包法》关于农户私人土地承包权和转让权的清楚界定,全部以"土地的农业用途"为限。例如,《农村土地承包法》在总则中宣布,"未经批准不得将承包地用于非农建设"(第8条);在发包方的权利中,加入"制止承包方损害承包地和农业资源的行为"(第13条);在承包方的义务中,点明"维持土地的农业用途,不得用于非农建设"(第17条);更在土地承包经营权的流转原则中,规定"不得改变……土地的农业用途"(第33条)。很清楚,一旦土地用于非农业用途,这部法律对农户承包经营权的确认和保护，全部戛然中止。

（二）否认转让权的法律

农地转为非农建设用地，受《土地管理法》调节。这部法律，1986年6月25日经第六届全国人大常委会第16次会议通过，从1987年1月1日起执行。可是仅仅两年之后，1988年12月29日第七届全国人大常委会第5次会议就决定修改。这一改差不多就改了十年，到1998年8月29日才由第九届全国人大常委会第4次会议通过，从1999年1月1日起执行。《土地管理法》从制定到修订的时期，中国经济正在经历市场化改革的深化。可是，改来改去，这部法律还是没有在“转让权”的基础上处理农地转用这样重要的资源配置问题。

查阅修订后的1998年《土地管理法》，我们发现除了原则宣布“土地使用权可以依法转让”（第2条）之外，整部法律八章86条再没有一处提及“土地转让权”的内容、主体归属、转让程序、执行原则和定价方式。而一旦涉及农地资源转为非农业建设，该法明令“农民集体所有的土地的使用权不得出让、转让或者出租用于非农业建设”（第63条）。⑤当经济发展需要把一部分农地转为非农业建设的时候，现行《土地管理法》允许的唯一合法途径就是国家垄断，也就是举凡农业用地转为非农民自用的建设用地，必须完成从土地集体所有制向国有制的转变。

（三）城市土地国有化的来历

为什么本是集体所有、并已经长期承包给农户经营的农地，一旦转为城市建设用地，就一定要转变为国有？推究起来，这涉及到一个宪法准则。1982年宪法修正案宣布“城市的土地属于国家所有”（第10条）。这是第一次把过去宪法及其历次修正案确立土地国有范围，从“矿产、水流、国有森林、荒地”，扩大到全部城市土地。根据当时宪法修正案的说明，“草案第10条中原来是把镇的土地和农村、城市郊区一律看待”(就是作为集体土地看待——引者注)。⑥

但是,“城市土地全部属于国有”本身的来历,却不那么清楚。经查1975年宪法,第6条中尚有如下表达:“国家可以依照法律规定的条件,对城乡土地和其他生产资料实行征购、征用或者收归国有”。这个条款清楚地说明,至少在到“文化大革命”行将结束的时候,我国城市土地还没有全盘属于国家所有。否则,何须“国家对城乡土地可以征购、征用和宣布收归国有”?结束“文化大革命”后的1978年宪法,也并没有宣布全部城市土地国有化。此后我国进入改革开放新的历史时期,到1982年之前并没有关于国家如何“对全部城市土地完成实行征购、征用或者收归国有”的历史记载。难道“城市土地属于国有”这样一件大事,从来就没有经过政府的具体作为,直接就由1982年宪法宣布而成?

无论来历问题如何有待进一步的调查,“城市土地属于国有”构成现行土地法规的指导原则。这个原则的含义,正如我们将要详细讨论的,不但是“全部现存城市土地属于国家”,而且是“所有将成为城市的土地全部属于国家”。后者既包括现有城市向其郊区和周围农村的扩展,也包括从原农村、小城镇和郊区形成的新城市。很少有人注意到,1982年后的中国还经历过、经历着、并将继续经历规模浩大的土地资源国有化。

(四)征地悖论

现行土地法律规定了用于城市的农地必须全部转为国有制,同时也就把征地变成了农地转用的唯一合法形式。本来,即便在城、乡土地皆为私有的情况下,国家也可以依法拥有征地权。例如,1954年制定的我国第一部《宪法》宣布,“国家为了公共利益的需要,可以依照法律规定的条件,对城乡土地和其他生产资料实行征购、征用或者收归国有”(第13条)。众所周知,那时尽管已经宣布了向社会主义过渡的总路线，但城乡土地的大部分还是属于私有，并得到宪法的承认和保护。因此，国家征用农地，仅仅只是农地转为建设用地中的一种形式。为了界定国家征地与民间私人转让土地之间的界限，1954 年宪法对征地加了一个重要的限制条件，即必须是“为了公共利益”。这至少在法律上是清楚的：为了公共利益的农地转用，通过国家征地来完成；非公益性质的农地转用，通过受当时法律承认的私人转让权来完成。

随着城乡土地所有制改造的完成，特别是 1982 年宪法第一次宣布全部城市土地归国家所有之后，农地转为城市建设用地必须同时完成国有化，政府征地就成为农地转用的唯一合法的途径。但是颇为不协调的是，1982 年的宪法连同以后的土地管理法，仍然照搬 1954 年宪法对征地的限制条件——“为了公共利益”。悖论在于：非公共利益性质的农地转用怎么办？不经过征地是违宪，因为转为城市用的农地如果还是集体所有就违背了“全部城市土地为国有土地”的宪法准则；征地也违宪，因为不合“为了公共利益才可征地”的宪法准则。

（五）政府经营土地的牟利冲动

更严重的问题是，现存土地法律在禁止农民承包地转为非农用途的同时，却宣布国有的土地——包括从农民集体那里征用来的土地——“实行有偿使用制度”（第 2 条）。[⑦] 这就是说，政府可以把强制征得的土地——无论“为了公共利益”与否——按有偿原则向城市土地使用权市场出让。

应该看到，《土地管理法》宣布“国有土地有偿使用制度”，毕竟反映了逐步引入市场机制配置土地资源的改革现实。事实上，自 1987 年深圳、上海市政府分别试行向市场批租土地之后，我国城市建设用地市场发育很快，并形成一套法律法规。

问题是，土地市场化仅仅限于部分国有土地使用权的有偿转让和再转让。至于前述农地转为非农业建设用地，以及另外一部分由行政划拨的城市土地，仍然服从行政权力配置土地资源的准则。新的混合模式是这样的：政府凭对农地转用的行政垄断权获取城市建设用地，然后将部分国有土地批租给城市二级土地市场、部分留在政府手中划拨。这种行政配置和市场配置的特别混合，不能不激励各行政主体竞相成为经营城市土地的牟利组织。如果说征用农地成本与批租土地收益之间的差额意味政府经营土地的红利，那么“无偿划拨”与二级城市土地的市值之间的差额就显示了“划拨权”的租值。

现存法律甚至明文规定征地的补偿完全不同于批租土地的价格决定。一方面，《土地管理法》规定政府征用农地“按照被征用土地的原用途——当然就是农地的农业用途——给予补偿”(第 47 条)。另一方面，法律又允许政府按“土地的城市建设用途的市值”把征得的土地批租出去。这等于保证了政府经营土地的法定红利最大。因为在一个城市化严重不足、正在经历急速发展的经济里，一块土地从农业用途转为城市建设用途，市值的增加何止十倍、数十倍？土地市值越大，政府“无偿划拨”土地的权力租金越高。这实在是一门由法律保障政府独家垄断获取经营土地暴利的“新生意”。

(六) 三处例外、两点不明

并不是没有例外。根据现行法律，农地转为非农建设用地一般要同时完成土地被国家征用、成为国有土地的过程，在某些条件下可容例外，那就是没有经征用而转国有土地，农地也可合法转为建设用地。

前引《土地管理法》第 43 条所定准则(“任何单位和个人进行建设……必须依法申请使用国有土地”)，法律允许的例外如下：

“但是，兴办乡镇企业和村民建设住宅经依法批准使用本集体经济组织农民集体所有的土地的，或者乡（镇）村公共设施和公益事业建设经依法批准使用农民集体所有的土地的除外。”

就是说，农民自用于办企业、住宅、公共设施和公益事业的土地，虽然也是农地转为建设用地，但可以保留集体土地所有权。

第二处，农村集体经济组织“与其他单位、个人以土地使用权入股、联营等形式共同举办企业的”（第63条），也可以在符合土地利用规划、通过行政审批的条件下，合法将农地转为非农建设用地。

第三处，“符合土地利用总体规划并依法取得建设用地的企业，因破产、兼并等情形致使土地使用权发生转移的”，可以例外于“农民集体土地使用权不得出让、转让或者出租用于非农建设”的法条。直截了当地说，就是合乎上述要求的集体土地使用权可以出让、转让或者出租。

法律当然没有声明“城市土地必属国有”的原则也容例外。麻烦在于，在城市化急速扩张的经济现实中，当初农民自办企业或与人联办企业的农村，日后可能成为城市或城市的一部分！如我们将要看到的，一旦发生这种情况，现存法律中“例外”合法存在的转让权，又将引起很大的混淆。因为届时土地已是城市土地，原先的“例外”是否一定要再经征用转为国有土地，现存法律并没有清楚地交代。

另外，三处例外中只有第三处明确转让权的基础是“集体土地使用权”，也就是转让权归承包农户；前两处，有权“例外”合法转农地为建设用地的主体，都是“农村集体经济组织”。不明的地方是，在农地已经承包给农户经营的情况下，“集体”为了获得法定例外转用农地的好处，是否可以甚或一定要收回农户的土地承包权，然后再以集体的名义自办、联办企业和其他设施呢？

（七）现存转让权的一个概述

让我们概述我国农地转让权的法律表达。经过二十多年的改革，现存土地法律清楚界定并保护农地在农业用途范围内的转让权。作为农地转让权的权利主体，承包农户可以在平等协商、自愿、有偿，不受任何组织和个人的强迫和阻碍的条件下转包、出租、互换农地经营权，农地转让的价格由当事人协商确定，而转让收益归承包农户所得。这构成我国农业经济活动的一个重要制度基础。

但是，农地一旦转为非农建设用地，承包农户的农地转让权就不再得到现行法律的承认。农地转为建设用地，甚至也不是农村集体的权利。除开个别例外，法律要求农地转为城市建设用地必须以土地国有化为前提。国家征用农地就成了城市化利用农地资源的唯一合法途径。

现行法律在确认政府征用农地权利的同时，也确认政府可以向市场出售所征农地的使用权。一方面，政府征地补偿根据被征农地原用途——即农业用途——的收益来决定。另一方面，当政府出售土地使用权时，却可以根据市场原则来定价——根据土地未来用途的预期收益、由竞争各方中的出价高者得。这就是说，现行法律不但承认政府独家垄断的征地权，而且保证该项权利可获得最大的法定价值。这为政府经营土地内置了功率强大的发动机。

简言之，随着农地转为城市建设用地，农地转让权从承包农户那里转到了政府手中。现行法律为了约束政府的土地征用和经营权，一再重申“严格保护耕地”的立法意图，不断改进按行政等级分派土地审批权的程序，也始终坚持“为了公共利益才可征用农地”的宪法准则。下面我们开始调查:在现存法律的激励和约束下,政府主导非农业建设土地转让的实际行为。

三、农地转让权的经济分析

为了理解现行产权制度下农地转用行为,我们也许需要清楚相关学术传统,厘定关键概念,并建立能够解释复杂经济现象、可被验证的理论。在这件工作完成之前,我们不妨引用旧作,整理线索,做一些必要的准备。⑧

(一) 放弃农地的代价

农地一旦转成工业用地或城镇用地,其市值上升数倍甚至百倍。在工业化和城市化的过程中,农地的产权主人能够在多大程度上分享农地转为他用引起的增值,是由农地产权制度——特别是农地权利的转让制度——决定的。

差不多一百多年以来,有一个起源于美国空想社会主义者Henry George的理论流传甚广。这个理论说,土地从农业转为工业和城市用途而引起的市值上升,是社会因素使然,与土地的主人没有关系。因此,如果地主从地价增值中获利,是不公平的。当年孙中山先生受此学说的影响很深。作为中华民国的国父,孙中山不但以“平均地权”为革命纲领,而且认定必须禁止或限制地权的自由买卖,否则“富者田连阡陌,穷者无立锥之地”将卷土重来。在中华民国的政策传统上,“土地涨价要归公”一直是一个正面口号(做不做是另外一回事)。

但是,“土地涨价归公”的经济学却是错的。因为这种经济学认为,各种资源的市值是由其成本决定的。土地的“生产成本”为零或基本不变,为什么地价突然飙升?在现象上,一块农地对于工业、城市的意义不是其肥沃程度,而是“位置”。农地因

"位置"身价百倍,而农地之主对"位置的生产"显然没有贡献,也不因此耗费代价,为什么要由他们享受土地涨价的好处呢?

传统理论忽略的,是农地之主对土地增值有一项重要贡献,那就是"放弃"农地的使用权。倘若地主不放弃土地使用权,工业家、地产开发商、城市规划官员们看中的"位置",增值从何谈起?

放弃一项权利,要有代价。这个道理不难明白。农地之主本来可以通过使用农地而获得收入,现在要他放弃,就少了那笔收入。因此,"由自己使用农地的所得",就构成了放弃使用的一个机会成本。得不到一个合适的出价,他横竖不会放弃本来可以有所得的农地使用权的。

比较不容易明白的,是产权的主人只有在他认为"值"的条件下,才接受别人的出价而同意放弃使用权。在真实世界里,"值"还是"不值",不是小事情,不可以不讲清楚。这里先谈三点。第一,面对同一出价,张三说值,李四说不值,他们两个都对。这就是说,"值"还是"不值",是非常个体的、主观的判断。不明白这一点,经济学没法入门,诸如边际、比较优势这类概念,都以个体主观的判断为基础。第二,一根铅笔 5 毛钱,买者认为"值",是他认为得到的铅笔对他而言,高于他所付出的 5 毛。对卖者呢?"值"就是他所得的 5 毛,高于他为生产这根铅笔的全部所付。一笔生意成交,双方都认为"值"。这是市场经济令人着迷之处。第三,按照各方觉得"值"的原则成交,资源配置才有效率。这是因为,卖者放弃使用、换取收益对卖者更"值",而买者放弃收益、换取使用对买者更值。普遍照此办理,那就不论资源归谁所有,非落到更有效率的使用者手里不可。商业世界,熙熙攘攘,讲到底,就是不断在发现谁能够更有效地利用资源。

(二) 产权残缺与排除市场机能

所以,要证明农地被工业和城市使用更有效,最简单可靠的办法，就是占地者的出价，要高于农民自己种地的收益。唯有这样一条简单的准则，才能普遍有效利用土地。那么，“补偿”高到农地的主人认为“值”的程度，不会损害工业化城市化吗？看看历史吧。西欧、北美、日本的工业化和城市化领先全球，土地制度都是清楚的私人所有、自由买卖、按值成交。难道1700年的英国城镇人口占总人口的25%，是“普天之下，莫非王土”的结果？日本在明治维新以后，工业化城市化大有苗头，难道不正是法律保障土地自由交易的结果？

但是在我国现行土地制度下，农地一旦转为工业或城市用地，就由“民土(农民集体所有、家庭承包经营)”变为“国土”。这样一套土地制度，为解决工业化和城市化占用农地，混合了“土地不得买卖和涨价归公”(强制征地)，“国家工业化”(超低价补偿)，人民公社集体所有权(唯有“集体”成为农民合法代表)和“香港经验”(土地批租制)，实在自成一家。

这套组合起来的土地制度，特征如下：(1)决定工业和城市用地供给的，既不是农地的所有权，也不是农地的使用权。就是说，农地产权在法律上没有资格作为土地交易的一方，无权参加讨价还价。(2)政府对工业和城市用地的需求做出判断，运用行政权力(包括规划、审批、征地)决定土地的供给。(3)权力租金——而不是土地产权的权利租金——刺激农地转向工业、城市用地。最重要的是，市场价格机能因此被排除在城市化土地资源的配置之外。

(三)低价征地缘何易行

农地征用的补偿水平很低，但近年超低价补偿征走土地的数量大增。从农民方面看问题，这是违背需求定理的事情。在经济行为逻辑上，任何人要低价拿走资源的难度应该很大，为什么拿走农地的补偿金很少，却拿得相对容易？

可能的解释很多,我认为要害在“集体”。虽然农村改革20多年,人民公社制已经作古,但土地等最重要的生产资源,还是属于集体所有。若问“集体”与公社有何不同?可见的区别是,集体的土地由农户长期承包经营,而不再实行集体耕作制。

但是在法理上,集体还是土地所有者,是承包地的“发包方”。既然是所有者和发包人,集体当然有权决定承包期限和承包条件,也有权中止和收回承包权。现在靠中央政府的政策管制土地承包长期不变。但是,中央政府不可能替全国几十万个集体一一规定除期限以外的其他承包条件。于是,集体不能轻易“动”土地承包期,但其他条件经常在动,并且可以诉诸“如果农户不接受这些变化的条件,集体可以收回土地承包权”。近年农民负担严重,制度上的原因就是集体制。

至于农地转为非农用地,更是集体的职权。现行土地体制,规定国家征地面对集体,而不是农户——这是与城乡住户搬迁最不同的地方。《土地管理法》明文规定“征地补偿金归集体所有”。至于集体如何补偿失去土地承包权的农户,并没有法律规定,在实际中常常五花八门、可以便宜行事。

换句话说,集体以土地被征用的名义中止农户“长期不变”的土地承包权,完全合乎现行土地制度。在实际案例里,各级政府超越土地规划的“征地”,包括乡、镇、村卖地图利的事情,所在多有。横竖对农民来说,任何一级政府——甚至包括宪法规定自治的行政村——都是“国家”。

至于征地代价为什么如此之低,我的看法与农户不参与征地补偿谈判有关。有权去谈补偿条件的只是“集体”,而实际上的集体常常不过就是几个乡村权力人物。他们其实是在“卖”别人的地。以每亩几千元几万元的补偿就永久放弃农地的权利,不是“贱卖”了吗?但是这些微薄的补偿集中起来由几个人支配，则非常之“值”。何况，能不能完成征地任务，常常是乡村权力人物能不能掌权的条件。

更进一步分析，“集体制”可不是那个起源于欧洲的“合作制”——后者是基于成员私人拥有的产权的一种组织。在合作制下，个人入社的资源要界定得一清二楚，要有清楚的资产收益规定，资源的使用是合作的，但所有成员都参加决策——比较经典的合作社实行决策的一人一票制，这是合作制不同于股份制的地方。集体制消灭了成员的私人财产。因此，“集体财产”成为不可分解——现在流行的词汇是“量化”——为个人私有的财产。它永远归抽象的“劳动人民集体”所有，但实际控制权又总是落在集体代理人之手。当资源发生转让、定价的时候，信息成本比之于自用陡然上升，使得这些实际上没有委托人的代理人，更容易攫取成员的权益。

按照 Alchian，“所有定价问题都是产权问题”。反过来，所有产权残缺都影响价格机制发挥正常作用。我们的一个重要理论结论是，转让权管制与价格管制具有同样的行为逻辑。稍微不同的地方，转让权管制是“事先”执行的价格管制。我国现行征地制度通过管制农民土地转让权，将产权租金转变为行政权力租金，从而事先管制了农地转用的价格，妨碍运用市场机制配置土地资源。这套制度不但引发分配的不公正，而且导致生产和交易的低效率。

四、政策讨论和可能的选择

20 世纪 90 年代以来，中国发生了两次全国规模的农地转为非农业用地的浪潮。此期间，中央政府实施积极的财政政策、扩大基础设施建设规模，固然起了不可低估的带动作用，但工业化和城市化的加速，应该是农地大规模转用更为根本的经济动力。问题是，在现行土地制度下，相关利益主体的行为必不可免地扭曲。因此伴随城市化的加速，我国城乡协调发展的基础受到很大的冲击，农民土地权益遭到严重剥夺，成为制约农民收入增加的一个重要根源。同时，围绕土地的社会冲突呈上升趋势，特别是政府机构和官员个人违法、违规屡禁不止，土地腐败非常严重。

复杂性在于，城市化加速不但合乎国民经济发展的要求，而且也是包括农民在内的多方面经济利益实现的基本途径。我们的分析表明，问题的根源不是城市化、也不是市场关系的深化刺激的城市化加速，而是约束我国工业化城市化的制度条件的发展不平衡。中心的问题是，现行法律在开始允许政府按市场原则出让、出租、转让土地的同时，依旧坚持全部非农民自用建设土地国有化的准则，依旧维持政府独家征地的垄断权，依旧禁止和限制承包农户对非农建设用地的转让权。正由于对土地转让权的不当管制，使市场价格机制不能在工业化城市化的土地资源配置中发挥正常作用。

在城乡协调发展的总体思路的基础上，"按照保障农民权益、控制征地规模的原则，改革征地制度，完善征地程序"[⑨] 的任务已经提上日程。1999 年刚刚生效的《中华人民共和国土地管理法》，又面临重新修订的命运。因为仅仅强调严格执行现有土地法规，明显不能适应当前和今后城市化加速形势的需要。但是，究竟如何修改土地管理法和相关土地政策，人们还有不小的分歧。以下我们从一个特定的出发点——"清楚而有保障的农地转让权是运用价格机制配置城市化进程中土地资源的基础"——来讨论有关政策建议。

(一) 关于"最严格的耕地保护制度"

我们注意到，中共十六届三中全会通过的《中共中央关于完善社会主义市场经济体制若干问题的决定》，对农户土地承包经营权的流转给予了特别的关注：

“农户在承包期内可依法、自愿、有偿流转土地承包经营权，完善流转办法，逐步发展适度规模经营。”

与现行土地法规特别强调把土地转让权限制在“农业”和“农民自用的非农建设”范围内不同，这里关于农户土地转让权的界定，没有在农业/非农业用地之间设置绝对不能逾越的障碍。当然还是提到了“发展适度规模经营”，但农业与非农业、工业化以及城市化的经济活动，都有适度经营规模问题。至于“依法”之法，可以是现存法规，也可以是按照《决定》原则修改后的新法。我们认为，这一重要的新的政策原则——承认和保护不受农业/非农业建设用地限制的农户土地转让权——为在法律上打破农地转用的单一征地制度，提供了十分重要的依据。

这并不意味着农户的土地转让权就不受任何限制。在我们看来，这次征地制度改革的一个基本任务，就是在放宽“对农户非农用地转让权的绝对法律禁止”的同时，确立适应经济社会发展需要、又易于执行的约束。目前各方已经提出来的政策建议，基本可以看做是关于土地转让权的限制条件。那么，哪些限制条件，以及怎样理解和表达这些限制条件，将有利于最大限度发挥农地转让权的经济功能呢？

上引中共中央《决定》指出，“实行最严格的耕地保护制度，保证国家粮食安全”。这应该是农地转让权的一个边界条件。就是说，农地转让再自由，也不能自由到破坏最严格的耕地保护制度，以至于威胁国家粮食安全的程度。问题是，这个限制条件的内涵，还需要展开一些必要的讨论。首先，最严格的耕地保护制度，并不意味着任何耕地从此不得转为非耕地、任何粮田不得转为非种粮的其他用途。如果具有那样的极端含义，本项政策的执行就没有任何难度了。但是在经验上观察，全世界没有一个不减少一点耕地而又实现工业化城市化的经济。因此真正的问题，是如何做到“以较小的耕地减少为代价，得到包括粮食安全目标、城市化、农民收入等目标在内的较大收益”。

《决定》规定，减少耕地的最后底线是“确保国家粮食安全”。难点在于，“国家粮食安全”是一个随需求、技术和贸易条件变化而变化的目标，而在工业化城市化加速的国民经济环境里，达到上述目标的手段(成本)也在不断发生变化。究竟什么样的土地制度，可以大体准确反映相关经济条件的变化呢?

现行管制耕地转让权的基本办法就是行政审批，比如对农地转用、耕地占用、大面积耕地占用分别规定由不同级别的政府机构，按照不同的标准加以审批。问题是，行政审批制绝不能做到灵敏反映耕地转用的真实收益和机会成本。我国的经验已经显示，虽然严格保护耕地早已被定为国策，但经济制度一直没有提供恰当的机制来衡量“耕地减少的收益和代价”。从经济角度着眼，过犹不及:耕地减少过多过快、得不偿失甚至占而不用当然是祸害;但过度保护耕地，也就是完全放弃适当减少耕地去谋求城市化工业化的潜在收益，也并不是经济增长的福音。要灵敏地衡量耕地转用的得失，必须考虑增加耕地转用的经济性限制条件。

(二) 关于公益性与经营性的区分

目前已经提出的经济性限制条件包括，“区分公益性和经营性建设用地”，“大幅度提高法定征地补偿水平”，以及“以社保方式实现征地补偿”。以下分别讨论这些政策建议。首先，根据大量实际情况的调查和专家建议，针对各地政府把按公益性低价征得的土地高价向经营性项目出让的严重问题，中央《决定》提出“严格界定公益性和经营性建设用地”的原则。

要在征地制度改革和《土地管理法》修改中应用上述原则，还有必要考虑一系列相关问题。主要是：

(1) 公益性和经营性的含义。宪法对国家征地行为的限制是“为了公共利益”，现在又提出“公益性”，究竟是什么含义？在最严格的意义上，只有免费向全体国民提供的产品和服务才是“公益性”产品和服务，才称得上是为公益性项目。除国防、社会安全、公共卫生、公共教育等少之又少的品种之外，包括绝大部分国家重点工程在内的建设项目，都是只供部分国民消费、可以也应该按市价收费的项目。但是在概念上，那些五花八门的所谓具有“外部性”的活动、或者为了避税而选择的“非盈利”安排究竟是不是属于公益范围，并不是一个容易得到一致意见的问题。在纽约州，一位市长动用征用权将一个 5 人就业的牧场改成了一个可供 20 人就业的高尔夫球场，他是不是增加了社会就业？是不是改善了贫困，从而降低了潜在的犯罪率而减少了纳税人的公共治安开支？我们有没有把握说，这个项目完全没有公益性？

(2) 即使社会或立法机构就公益性和经营性的区别达成一致意见，那么公益性项目与经营性项目获得土地的代价是否要有法定的不同？如果没有什么不同，那么区别公益不公益还有什么意义？如果要设立法定差别——例如公益性项目得地的代价低于经营性项目的代价——那么选择什么标准来决定差别？是规定补偿数额的不同，还是规定不同的补偿机制——例如公益性项目经由政府征地，经营性项目经由土地市场交易？

(3) 从土地供应方的角度看，为什么轮到公益性项目，就只能获取法定低补偿，而向经营性项目供地，却可以得到市价水平的补偿？要害在于，向公益性项目供地的农民固然也是国民的一个组成部分，公益性项目使全体国民受益，也使这部分农民受益。但是另一方面，为什么单要这部分国民，做出其他国民无须承受的特别牺牲？不妨比照征兵制度来思考，“凡适龄合格的公民都要入伍”是普遍原则，“凡向公益性项目供地者交纳特别税”则是对部分国民的歧视。

(4) 公益性项目与非公益性项目之间任何方式形成的“差价”，终究要对资源在公益和非公益之间的配置发生影响。经济规律是:差价的倾斜程度越大，资源配置的歪曲程度就越严重。无须详细论证，在任何特定的收入水平，如果公益性项目因为法定代价过低而占用过多的资源，国民经济的增长总要承担一部分损失。这部分损失具有反公益性的性质。

(三) 关于“提高征地补偿的法定水平”

针对国家征地补偿的法定水平偏低，以及征地机构在执行中“尽可能靠近下限”的倾向，有关方面提出了提高征地的法定补偿的建议。要讨论的问题是，如果不同时考虑改革征地制度的独家行政垄断和单方面决定的根本性质，在现行补偿机制不变的基础上提高补偿倍数，究竟能不能反映被征土地的真实相对价格？过去的经验已经表明了这一点:从 1986 年到 1998 年，《土地管理法》把征地补偿的最高限制从土地原用途年平均产出的 20 倍，提高到了 30 倍以上。可是相对于国民经济的增长、特别是城市二级土地市场价格的更快增长，新的法定最高补偿不但没有上升，反而大幅度下降。

要使征地补偿反映土地的相对稀缺性，首先要考虑是否需要改变征地补偿的基准。现行基准是被征土地“原来用途产生的收益”，对于转用的农地而言，也就是土地的农业产出。这个基准导致征地需求脱离征地成本的制约，因为征地需求立足非农用地未来的收益，而征地成本仅仅代表农民放弃土地农业用途的代价。在这个基准下，土地的农用与非农用之间的市值差距越大，资源配置的效率损失越严重。从分配上看，农地主人被排除在城市化增加的土地市值的分享名单之外，抑制了农民增收的现实可能，恶化了国民收入的分配结构。

补偿倍数的选择，涉及资产收益的年期。土地是永久性资源，在现行土地制度下，政府征得的土地可以分期批租、永久收益；但政府给予农民的补偿却最高以30年为限。这也许反映了农户承包集体土地的年期，但也忽略了30年承包期后农村集体还可以继续把土地发包给农民经营的利益关系。如同补偿基准方面的制度歪曲效果一样，征地补偿在年期方面的歪曲，也对效率和公平同时产生不良影响。

法定征地补偿还有先天不够灵敏的缺点。非农土地的市值决定于各地经济水平和地块位置的相对稀缺性，受许多地方性复杂因素的支配。由一部全国性法律统一规定法定征地补偿水平，无论如何难以恰到好处。参照发达国家的经验，在征地改革和土地法修订中应该考虑"国家征地按市价补偿"的新原则。我们暂不阐释"市价补偿"的细节和众多的优越性。这里有必要提及，倘若考虑引入按市价补偿的新原则，就要连带考虑打破国家对一级土地市场的垄断。这里的道理很简单：没有一级土地市场的开放和竞争，社会无从知道土地的市价信号。

（四）关于"被征地农民纳入社保"

在改革现存征地补偿机制的实践中，浙江、上海、北京等地提出或试行为被征地农民群众建立社会保障、分期支付征地补偿的新办法。这些实践引起学者们的研究兴趣，也提出了"征地补偿社保模式"的政策建议。我们对此做非常粗略的讨论。

首先要明确，征地补偿的社保形式也是一种价格安排。因此，征地补偿水平的决定不但没有因社保模式的选择而被替代，而且构成社保模式的基础。很显然，征地社保基金来自征地补偿的强制储蓄，因此偏低的征地补偿额，只能向被征地农民提供偏低水平的征地社保。如果不改变征地补偿的数量形成机制，仅仅将一次性补偿改为分期补偿，被征地农民的利益没有、也不可能增加。

其次，征地社会保障就其本质来说，是一种承诺，也就是土地被一次性征用之后，被征地农民将分期得到征地补偿。如果征地社保是政府统一、强制建立的制度，那么就是一种国家信用，而不是任由投保人选择合约下形成的市场信用。征地社保未来的支付一旦发生问题，将由国家信用来负责。讲到底，就是由全体纳税人甚至全体国民来承担最终责任。

但是，负责管理征地社保的却是按期换届的政府。在此现实条件下，可能发生现在难以观察到的道德风险，那就是本届政府一次性得到征用土地的全部收益，却把分期支付的责任推给下届或下下届政府。即使征地补偿社保独立操作，并增加“个人账户”等最新社保制度安排，那也要依赖金融服务市场的成熟和金融监管的完善。目前除开国家信用，还看不清楚征地补偿社保模式可以多么普遍地可靠运转。局部的地区性实验可以继续，但全局的制度化、法制化则为时过早。

（五）关于“准许集体土地进入市场”

南海、昆山和上海等地的农村集体进入非农土地市场的实践，最重要的意义在于突破国家垄断农地转为非农用地市场，打破征地是农地转用的唯一合法途径，为形成与国家征地并行的市场化的农地转用机制，准备了条件。但是从目前的实践经验看，集体土地所有权进入市场的方向，有两个大问题需要研究。

一个问题是怎样明确界定集体与承包农户的产权权利。当集体为了开发非农土地资源、重新回收、集中农户的土地承包经营权的时候，二十年农村改革的基本制度成果，可能重新动摇。由于南海等地农民非农就业机会比较多，农户继续持有农地的成本上升，因此那里的集体回收集中农户的经营承包权，只要给予合理的补偿条件，一般不会遇到农户们的抵抗。但是，如果“集体进入非农土地市场”的政策被法规化、普遍化之后，刚刚被2002年通过的《农村土地承包法》作为“单纯的土地发包方”得到规范的“农村集体”，可能重新又变成容易侵犯农户产权的积极力量。如果法律不明确农户是土地承包经营权向非农业用途转让的权利主体，那么正如我们已经看到的，集体连同村庄权力人物同样参与攫取农地转用的租金，或者实际控制、支配农地转用的租金收入，而让农民担任基本不分红的股份组织的“股东”。

如果法律承认农户的承包土地转让权可以进入农地转用的领域，那么农户的利益可以有比较可靠的保障，也便于新的非农土地制度与《农村土地承包法》有更好的衔接，避免征地制度的改革动摇到农村家庭承包经营体制的根本。以农户完整的土地转让权为基础的体制，当然可能引起非农土地市场上较高的交易费用。为了解决这个问题，在理论上我们强调农户完整的转让权包含了自主的缔约权，他们可以缔结各种市场性合约来节约交易费用；在实践上，农户可以在自愿的基础上选择集体、新的合作组织或者其他合约组织，如昆山的农民投资合作社。

另外一个大问题是集体和农户进入非农土地市场的合约形式选择。目前无论南海、昆山还是上海郊区，我们可以看到的大体都是集体或农户向外来企业出租土地、厂房或设施。这类年度性出租合约，受到外来企业的欢迎，也得到研究者和权威人士的重视。因为比之于土地批租（卖地），出租方式由土地的供方按年收取租金，可以降低外来企业的进入门槛。

但是在把这些经验上升为政策和法律的时候，要研究年度性出租方式潜在的风险。在理论上，长期性的批租土地与年度性出租，都是市场合约的不同品种，代表经营风险的不同分布，各有适用的范围和对象。厂房、宿舍、居民住宅等固定建筑的建设和使用周期都比较长，投资量比较大，因此“能否被长期充分利用”是一个很大的风险。由外来投资方买地（批租土地）搞建设，土地和建筑物经营的长期风险和收益就归外来方；反过来，就归供地方也就是农村集体或农户。在理论上，这两种方式可以是等价的；但实际上取决于对付市场风险的信息优势和资本实力的分布，由此决定合约形式的选择。

因此，不宜由法律或政策替代供求双方在市场里自由缔约。目前农村供地方以年度性出租为主的模式，应该是农村集体和农户还没有明确的转让非农土地权利的结果。如果法律承认并保护集体和农户的全面的转让权，情况当有所不同。特别要考虑到，如果长期建筑物的投资只能与短期土地租用相结合，形成的合约隐含着极大的未来风险，而这类风险目前还不能完全观察清楚。我们仅可在理论上推断：法律和政策对合约形式的干预和限制越多，合约的执行成本就越高。这里的政策含义是，要明确完全的土地转让权和缔约权，可以批租（卖）、可以出租、可以入股，也可以用其他合约。重要的是自愿和自由协商。

（六）建议的政策组合和程序

根据以上讨论，我们认为可能寻找一组经济损失最小的政策，来处理农地转用必定要遭遇的种种复杂问题。我们建议的农地转用政策组合如下：

（1）修改“城市土地属于国家”的宪法准则，结束单一国家征地制度，发展农地转用市场。

（2）政府在法律严格规定的公益用地范围内，拥有最终依法征地的权力；完善政府征地程序，确立征地按市价向承包农户补偿的原则。

（3）承认农户承包经营土地的完全转让权，包括为农业用途和非农业用途转让承包土地的权利；农户在非农用地市场转让土地经营权，在符合土地利用规划和土地用途管制的前提下，可以自愿选择各种合约形式和开发方式。

（4）在丈量全部土地、划清土地权属的基础上，全盘考虑新的税制，降低企业税，开征包括土地在内的资源税。

注　释

① 例如，国务院发展研究中心预测，我国的城市化指数将在2020年达到60%。

② 限于篇幅，本次发表删除了原稿中的第三节和第四节（即全部案例研究），以及关于政策选择的一部分说明。感兴趣的读者可以在由北京大学出版社出版的拙作《产权与制度变迁（增订本）》中查看全文。

③ 为了节约篇幅，下文分别把这两部法律简称为《农村土地承包法》和《土地管理法》。

④ “承包方有权依法自主决定土地承包经营权是否流转和流转的形式”（第34条），“国家保护承包方依法、自愿、有偿进行土地承包经营权流转”（第10条）。

⑤ 本条款还有一个例外条款，我们在下文引用并分析。

⑥ 全民讨论中有人指出，全国各地情况不同，有些地方镇的建制较大，今后还要发展，实际上是小城市。因此删去了有关镇的规定。就是说，建制较大的镇的土地，将来也属于国有，而不再是农民集体所有。

⑦ “建设单位使用国有土地，应当以出让等有偿使用方式取得”（第54条）；必须“缴纳土地使用权出让金等土地有偿使用费和其他费用后，方可使用土地”（第55条）。

⑧ 这里所说“旧作”，主要是指作者发表在2001年《21世纪经济报道》评论版连载的专栏文章“农民收入是一连串事件”，后被收入《收入是一连串事件》一书中（香港花千树出版公司2003年版，发展出版社2004年版）。

⑨ 《中共中央关于完善社会主义市场经济体制若干问题的决定》，人民出版社，2003年10月，第17页。

参考文献

Alston, L. J. , G. D. Libecap and R. Schneider, "The Departments and Impact of Property Rights: Land Titles on the Brazilian Frontier", *Journal of Law, Economics and organization*, 1996, 12, pp. 25—61.

Bazel, Y. , *Economic Analysis of Property Rights*, Cambridge University Press, 1989.

Cheung, Steven N. S. , "The Fable of the Bees: An Economic Investigation", *Journal of Law and Economics*, 1973, XVI, pp. 11—33.

Coase, T. H. , "The Nature of the Firm", *Economica*, 1937, 4, pp. 386—405.

Coase, T. H. , "The Problem of Social Cost", *Journal of Law and Economics*, 1960, 3, pp. 1—44.

David, J. Bledsoe and Roy L. Prosterman, "The Joint Stock Share System in China's Nanhai County", RDI Report 2000#103.

Eggertsson, I. , *Economic Behavior and Institutions*, Cambridge: Cambridge University Press, 1990.

Libecap, G. D. , "Distributional Issues in Contracting for Property Rights", *Journal of Institutional and Theoretical Economics*, 1989, 145, pp. 6—24.

Libecap, G. D. , *Contracting for Property Rights*. New York: Cambridge University Press, 1989b.

North, D. C. , "Institutions and Credible Commitment", *Journal of Institutional and Theoretical Economics*, 1990, 149, pp. 11—23.

张五常,《经济解释》(三卷本),花千树出版社,2002年。

周其仁,《产权与制度变迁——中国改革的经验研究》,社会科学文献出版社,2002年。

周其仁,《收入是一连串事件》,中国发展出版社,2004年。

(原载《经济学季刊》第4卷第1期)

图书在版编目（CIP）数据

中国经济学.2004/北京天则经济研究所编.
—上海：上海人民出版社，2006
ISBN 7-208-06130-0

Ⅰ.中... Ⅱ.北... Ⅲ.经济学-中国-2004-文集 Ⅳ.F120.2-53

中国版本图书馆 CIP 数据核字(2006)第 013656 号

责任编辑　钱　敏
封面装帧　王晓阳

中国经济学——2004
北京天则经济研究所 编

出　　版　世纪出版集团　上海人民出版社
(200001　上海福建中路 193 号　www.ewen.cc)

出　　品　上海世纪出版股份有限公司高等教育图书公司
(上海福建中路 193 号 24 层　021-63914988)

发　　行　世纪出版集团发行中心
印　　刷　上海商务联西印刷有限公司
开　　本　850×1168 毫米　1/32
印　　张　14.25
插　　页　5
字　　数　324,000
版　　次　2006 年 5 月第 1 版
印　　次　2006 年 5 月第 1 次
ISBN 7-208-06130-0/F·1396
定　　价　32.00 元